Cultures and Styling in Folk Dance

Related High/Scope Products

Teaching Folk Dance: Successful Steps
  ❋ Accompanying teaching videos
  ❋ Accompanying set of over 200 dance notation cards

Rhythmically Moving 1–9 (cassettes, CDs)

Guides to Rhythmically Moving 1, 2, 3, and 4

Changing Directions 1–6 (cassettes, CDs)

Beginning Folk Dances Illustrated 1–5 (videos)

Teaching Movement & Dance: A Sequential Approach to Rhythmic Movement, Fourth Edition (in press)

Foundations in Elementary Education: Movement

Foundations in Elementary Education: Music
  ❋ Accompanying music recordings (cassette, CD)

Round the Circle: Key Experiences in Movement for Children

Movement Plus Music: Activities for Children Ages 3 to 7, Second Edition

Movement Plus Rhymes, Songs, & Singing Games, Second Edition
  ❋ Accompanying music recordings (cassette, CD)

Movement in Steady Beat

Available from
High/Scope Press
600 North River Street, Ypsilanti, Michigan 48198-2898
ORDERS: phone (800)40-PRESS, fax (800)442-4FAX
e-mail: press@highscope.org
web site: www.highscope.org

Cultures and Styling in Folk Dance

Sanna H. Longden and Phyllis S. Weikart

a division of High/Scope Educational Research Foundation

Published by
HIGH/SCOPE PRESS
A division of the High/Scope Educational Research Foundation
600 North River Street
Ypsilanti, Michigan 48198-2898
(734)485-2000, FAX (734)485-0704
e-mail: press@highscope.org

Copyright ©1998 by High/Scope Educational Research Foundation. All rights reserved. Except as permitted under the Copyright Act of 1976, no part of this book may be reproduced or distributed in any form or by any means, electronic or mechanical, including photocopy, recording, or any information storage-and-retrieval system, without prior written permission from the publisher. High/Scope is a registered trademark and service mark of the High/Scope Educational Research Foundation.

Marge Senninger, *High/Scope Press Editor*
Linda Eckel, *Cover design, text design, and production*

Library of Congress Cataloging-in-Publication Data
Longden, Sanna Hans.
    Cultures and styling in folk dance / Sanna H. Longden, Phyllis S. Weikart
        p. cm.
    A companion vol. to: Teaching folk dance / Phyllis S. Weikart.
    Includes bibliographical references (p.) and index.
    ISBN 1-57379-016-8
    1. Folk dancing—Study and teaching.   I. Weikart, Phyllis S.
    Teaching folk dance.   II. Title.
    GV1753.5.L65   1998
    796.31'071—DC21   97-52345
                                                                                  CIP

Printed in the United States of America
10 9 8 7 6 5 4 3 2 1

Contents

Preface ix

1 Folk Dance Cultures 3
Folk Dances Come From Peoples 5
How Are Folk Dances Different From One Another? 6
Why Are Folk Dances Similar to One Another? 8
Gender Roles in Folk Dance 8
Village Dances, Folk Ballet, and International Folk Dancing 11
What Are the Sources for the Dances in These Books? 13

2 Folk Dance Teaching 17
The Folk Process 19
Folk Dance Etiquette 19
"Segregated" Dances 23
Music for Folk Dances 23
Modifying Ethnic Folk Dances 24
General Dance Styling 25
Ethnic Styling Encourages Success in Dance 28

3 African Dances 29
West African Dance 31
    Formation 31
    Steps and movements 32
    Hands and arms 32
    Modification and teaching tips 32
    Music 32
    Clothing and costumes 34
South African Dance 35
    Formation 35
    Steps and movements 35
    Hands and arms 35
    Modification and teaching tips 36
    Music 36
    Clothing and costumes 36
Resources Used for Chapter 3 37

4 Andean Dances 39
Formation 42
Steps and movements 43
Hands and arms 43
Modification and teaching tips 43
Music 43
Clothing and costumes 43
Resources Used for Chapter 4 44

5 Armenian Dances 45
Formation 49
Steps and movements 50
Hands and arms 50
Modification and teaching tips 52
Music 52
Clothing and costumes 52
Resources Used for Chapter 5 54

6 Assyrian Dances 55
Formation 59
Steps and movements 59
Hands and arms 59
Modification and teaching tips 59
Music 60
Clothing and costumes 60
Resources Used for Chapter 6 61

7 Bulgarian Dances 63
Formation 68
Steps and movements 68
Arms and hands 69
Modification and teaching tips 70
Music 70
Clothing and costumes 70
Resources Used for Chapter 7 73

8 Czech and Slovak Dances 75
Formation 80
Steps and movements 80
Hands and arms 81
Modification and teaching tips 82
Music 83
Clothing and costumes 83
Resources Used for Chapter 8 85

9 Danish Dances 87
Formation 89
Steps and movements 89

        Hands and arms 90
        Modification and teaching tips 90
        Music 92
        Clothing and costumes 93
   Resources Used for Chapter 9 94

10 English Dances 95
        Formation 101
        Steps and movements 101
        Hands and arms 103
        Modification and teaching tips 104
        Music 104
        Clothing and costumes 104
   Resources Used for Chapter 10 106

11 French Dances 107
        Formation 110
        Steps and movements 110
        Hands and arms 112
        Modification and teaching tips 112
        Music 112
        Clothing and costumes 113
   Resources Used for Chapter 11 115

12 French-Canadian Dances 117
        Formation 119
        Steps and movements 120
        Hands and arms 121
        Modification and teaching tips 121
        Music 123
        Clothing and costumes 124
   Resources Used for Chapter 12 125

13 German Dances 127
        Formation 132
        Steps and movements 132
        Hands and arms 134
        Modification and teaching tips 135
        Music 136
        Clothing and costumes 137
   Resources Used for Chapter 13 138

14 Greek Dances 139
   Living Greek Dances 143
   Movements and Styling—Introducing Freestyle
     Dancing 145
        Formation 145

        Steps and movements 148
        Hands and arms 148
        Modification and teaching tips 150
        Music 150
        Clothing and costumes 150
   Five Common Dances 152
     Hasapikos 152
     Vari (Varys) Hasapikos 152
     Syrtos 153
     Kalamatianos 154
     Tsamikos 154
   Resources Used for Chapter 14 155

15 Hungarian Dances 157
        Formation 162
        Steps and movements 165
        Hands and arms 166
        Modification and teaching tips 169
        Music 171
        Clothing and costumes 172
   Resources Used for Chapter 15 173

16 Irish Dances 175
        Formation 179
        Steps and movements 179
        Hands and arms 180
        Modification and teaching tips 180
        Music 180
        Clothing and costumes 181
   Resources Used for Chapter 16 183

17 Israeli and Jewish Dances 185
   Israeli Dance Background 188
   Israeli Dance Styling 190
     Arabic Influence and Styling 191
        Formation 191
        Steps and movements 192
        Hands and arms 192
        Modification and teaching tips 193
        Music 193
        Clothing and costumes 193
     Chassidic (Hassidic) Influence and Styling 194
        Formation 195
        Steps and movements 195
        Hands and arms 195
        Modification and teaching tips 195

　　　　Music 195
　　　　　Clothing and costumes 197
　　　European Influence and Styling 197
　　　Yemenite Influence and Styling 199
　　　　Formation 199
　　　　Steps and movements 200
　　　　Hands and arms 200
　　　　Modification and teaching tips 201
　　　　Music 202
　　　　Clothing and costumes 202
　　　The Homeland (or Sabra) Influence and Styling 202
　　　　Formation 202
　　　　Steps and movements 204
　　　　Hands and arms 204
　　　　Modification and teaching tips 204
　　　　Music 204
　　　　Clothing and costumes 204
　　Resources Used for Chapter 17 206

18 Italian Dances 207
　　　Formation 211
　　　Steps and movements 211
　　　Hands and arms 213
　　　Modification and teaching tips 213
　　　Music 213
　　　Clothing and costumes 214
　　Resources Used for Chapter 18 215

19 Japanese Dances 217
　　　Formation 222
　　　Steps and movements 222
　　　Hands and arms 223
　　　Modification and teaching tips 225
　　　Music 225
　　　Clothing and costumes 225
　　Resources Used for Chapter 19 226

20 Mexican Dances 227
　　　Formation 232
　　　Steps and movements 232
　　　Hands and arms 233
　　　Modification and teaching tips 234
　　　Music 234
　　　Clothing and costumes 235
　　Resources Used for Chapter 20 236

21 Philippine Dances 237
　　　Formation 242
　　　Steps and movements 242
　　　Hands and arms 242
　　　Modification and teaching tips 242
　　　Music 242
　　　Clothing and costumes 243
　　Resources Used for Chapter 21 244

22 Portuguese and Brazilian Dances 245
　　　Formation 248
　　　Steps and movements 248
　　　Hands and arms 248
　　　Modification and teaching tips 251
　　　Music 251
　　　Clothing and costumes 252
　　Resources Used for Chapter 22 254

23 Romanian Dances 255
　　The Hora 258
　　　Alunelul 260
　　　Other easy horas in *TFD* 262
　　The Brîul 263
　　Other Fast Dances 264
　　Slow Dances 264
　　　Modification and teaching tips 265
　　　Music 265
　　　Clothing and costumes 266
　　Resources Used for Chapter 23 268

24 Russian Dances 271
　　Katia, or *Our Katia* 277
　　Kohanochka 277
　　Korobushka 278
　　Troika 280
　　　Modification and teaching tips 281
　　　Music 281
　　　Clothing and costumes 281
　　Resources Used for Chapter 24 286

25 Scottish Dances 287
　　　Formation 292
　　　Steps and movements 292
　　　Hands and arms 292
　　　Modification and teaching tips 293

Music 293
Clothing and costumes 293
Resources Used for Chapter 25 296

26 Swedish Dances 297
Formation 303
Steps and movements 303
Hands and arms 304
Modification and teaching tips 304
Music 304
Clothing and costumes 305
Resources Used for Chapter 26 308

27 Turkish Dances 309
Formation 313
Steps and movements 314
Hands and arms 314
Modification and teaching tips 317
Music 317
Clothing and costumes 318
Resources Used for Chapter 27 319

28 Dances From the United States 321
Alley Cat 323
Amos Moses 324
Bossa Nova 326
Good Old Days 326
Hot Pretzels II 326
Jessie Polka 326
The Little Shoemaker 328
Twelfth Street Rag 328
Resources Used for Chapter 28 329

29 Dances From the Former Yugoslav Republics: Slovenia, Croatia, Serbia, and Macedonia 331
General Dance Background 335
Dances of the Slovenian People 336
Formation 336
Steps and movements 337
Hands and arms 337
Modification and teaching tips 337
Music 337

Clothing and costumes 339
Dances of the Croatian People 339
Formation 340
Steps and movements 341
Hands and arms 343
Modification and teaching tips 343
Music 344
Clothing and costumes 346
Dances of the Serbian People 347
Formation 350
Steps and movements 351
Hands and arms 353
Modification and teaching tips 353
Music 354
Clothing and costumes 355
Dances of the Macedonian People 357
The Lesnoto 359
Formation 360
Steps and movements 360
Hands and arms 361
Modification and teaching tips 361
Music 362
Clothing and costumes 363
Resources Used for Chapter 29 365

30 Dances by Phyllis S. Weikart 369

General Resources 373
General Information 373
Clothing and Costumes 378
Music 378
Videos 379
Miscellaneous 380

Dances Discussed in This Book 383

Index 389

Preface

Cultures and Styling in Folk Dance does not attempt to describe *all* the world's cultures. It is meant to be used as a companion to Phyllis S. Weikart's *Teaching Folk Dance: Successful Steps,* which explains how to teach the more than 200 dances on her nine *Rhythmically Moving* recordings (*RM1–RM9*) and six *Changing Directions* recordings (*CD1–CD6*). *Cultures and Styling* also contains information about some additional dances—ones not included on those recordings. Descriptions of these additional dances may be found in *Teaching Movement & Dance: Intermediate Folk Dance,* an earlier dance book by Phyllis S. Weikart.[1] Of course, the information contained here on folk dance cultures and styling can also be used with dances from other teaching sources. Readers wanting more detailed information on specific styling or cultures should consult the resource lists given throughout and at the end of this book.

Each chapter treats a different cultural background and lists the dances from *Teaching Folk Dance: Successful Steps* (identified hereafter as *TFD*) or *Teaching Movement & Dance: Intermediate Folk Dance* (identified hereafter as *TM&D*) that pertain to that background. The following information is given for each dance listed: a guide to pronouncing the name; the English meaning of the name, if known; the book by Phyllis S. Weikart (*TFD* or *TM&D*) in which the dance description can be found; and the recording (from *RM1–RM9* or *CD1–CD6*) on which the dance music can be found, if applicable. Following the dance lists are chapter subsections on **formation, steps and movements, hands and arms, modification and teaching tips, music,** and **clothing and costumes.** Not every dance or culture will have this complete array of information, however.

Most of the dances presented in *TFD* and *TM&D* are part of the general repertoire of recreational, or international, dance groups in the United States and in many other countries, including France, Holland, Japan, and Taiwan. Some are authentic dances being done today within their respective cultures; the majority have been choreographed by well-known ethnic dance teachers using carefully documented folk sources (the choreographer's name, when known, is given in this book); other dances presented in *TFD* and *TM&D* are choreographies by Phyllis S. Weikart, intended for use in the classroom or in a beginner's group because they employ movements that will prepare inexperienced students for actual folk patterns—these very useful dances are listed in Chapter 30 of *Cultures and Styling.*

---

[1] The lists of dances preceding the chapters of *Cultures and Styling* are not specifically keyed to Phyllis S. Weikart's other dance book, *Teaching Movement & Dance: A Sequential Approach to Rhythmic Movement* (4th edition in press). However, users of *A Sequential Approach* will also find all of its dances (which are absorbed in *Teaching Folk Dance*) discussed in *Cultures and Styling.*

The main source of information for this book has been the more than 80 (combined) years of folk dancing experienced by the two authors. Other sources were publications on folk dance, myriad ethnic dance notes, and numerous conversations with ethnic dance experts. Many people supplied support, suggestions, and critiques.

For providing information on specific cultures, we thank Nader Azarnia (Assyria), the late Vyts Beliajus (Portugal/Brazil), Tom Bozigian (Armenia and Assyria), Penny Brichta (Israel), Andor Czompo (Hungary), Sharlene Garfield (Israel), Jeannette Geslison (Denmark), Joe Graziosi (Greece), Bob Hruska (Slovakia), Peter Jasim (Assyria), Danka Kornosova (Slovakia), Sandra Lamb (Scotland), Roo Lester (Denmark and Sweden), Yves Moreau (Bulgaria, France, and French Canada), Robert Pollack (Israel), Barbara Seaver (Israel and Hungary), Kent Smith (Scotland), Haruno Yamakami (Japan), and Reuel Zielke (Scotland).

Special thanks go to the following people for their scrutiny of many specific-culture chapters as well chapters on teaching and folk dance in general: Sunni Bloland (Romania and others), Dick Crum (Yugoslavia, Bulgaria, and others), Cathy Engel (folk dance teaching), Karin Gottier (Czechoslovakia, Germany, France, Japan, and others), Ron Houston (Israel, Mexico, and others), Michael Kuharski (Bulgaria, Yugoslavia, and others), and Olga Kulbitsky (folk dance teaching).

Sanna also thanks the children and teachers she has taught and learned from in her travels around North America. She especially expresses gratitude and deep affection to Mars Longden, her partner in dance and in life, for his years of every kind of loving support on this project. Phyllis would like to thank her husband, Dave, and their four daughters, Cindy, Cathy, Jenny, and Gretchen, who have danced for all their years together; she is also grateful to the many adults who have attended workshops and summer institutes in Education Through Movement when folk dance is included; and she is grateful to the many teenagers encountered in 35 years of summer institutes, who have taught her so much about the need to modify dances in order to create successful experiences.

Sanna and Phyllis are also deeply grateful to Marge Senninger, the gifted and patient editor who speared every inconsistency with her eagle eye and penetrating pencil, who danced around her desk to verify the movement patterns, and who with helpful humor has steadfastly kept this complex project on track.

Cultures and Styling in Folk Dance

Folk Dance Cultures

Chapter 1: Folk Dance Cultures

*P*hyllis S. Weikart's two books titled *Teaching Folk Dance: Successful Steps (TFD)* and *Teaching Movement and Dance: Intermediate Folk Dance (TM&D)* provide a comprehensive introduction to the steps and patterns of many of the world's folk dances. As a supporting book, *Cultures and Styling* sheds additional, valuable light on these dances.

Folk dances are more than combinations of certain movements done to specific melodies. In their original settings they are one of the more important and enjoyable ways that human cultures celebrate their festivities and mark their major events. In addition, every culture has its own traditional way of dancing. The music and the elements of style—those choreographic features such as handholds, arm movements, body language, posture, even vocal sounds—make each people's dance unique. The stylistic elements of folk dance can be compared to the accent marks, ways of pronunciation, and intonations that differentiate various human languages.

In this book, so you and your students might further understand and enjoy the peoples of our world as you move to their music, we provide cultural background as well as many stylistic elements for the dances described in *TFD* and *TM&D*. Reading about and talking with people certainly teaches us much about them. However, when we sing their songs and dance in their boots, sandals, clogs, or moccasins, we can respect, appreciate, and enjoy them even more.

Folk Dances Come From Peoples

Folk dances reflect a people's culture, not necessarily its national boundaries. World political events in the post–Berlin Wall era illustrate how fiercely people feel about their own special groups, no matter where their nations begin and end. All of us know how sensitive we must be to these issues as ethnic peoples struggle to replant their cultural roots and as immigrants from many different places become our neighbors. In our increasingly multinational classrooms and communities, we are no longer talking about "others"—we are talking about "us."

Regional identification of folk dances is also helpful for many cultures and countries. Regardless of whether its boundaries have changed over the years, almost every nation is home to various groups of peoples, each with its own characteristic dance form. For example, the dances of France clearly show the strong influence of geography as well as culture. People dance line dances in Brittany on the western edge of France, where the culture has Celtic ties (most French dances in *TFD* and *TM&D* are dances of Brittany); they do the Teutonic-flavored couple dance called the *shottish* (what others call the schottische) in Alsace, the part of France closest to Germany; the French who live on the slopes of the Pyrenees Mountains, closest to Spain, dance the lively *jota;* and those in the central regions of Berry and Auvergne form the long double columns of the *bourrée*. (The importance of having an up-to-date world map at hand while reading this book—and while teaching folk dance—might properly be stressed at this point.)

Another interesting aspect to consider when discussing folk dancing is the immigrant experience. People who have settled in a new country do not always do the same dances or retain the same dance movements as those who have remained in the homeland. Often, the expatriates—those who live abroad for one reason or another—value their original cultures and try not to lose the old ways in the new country. They may remember or recreate their favorite traditional music and dances while their relatives back home begin to prefer rock-and-roll or Western ballroom dances. However, even the remembered ethnic dances change as people are assimilated into the new host society and as their young people add movements, music, and instrumentation from the popular culture. A number of dances in Phyllis S. Weikart's books have entered the folk dance repertoire through the expatriate communities.

Performing at the Folkmoot USA festival in Waynesville, North Carolina, young dancers from Peru execute a dance that combines both traditional and contemporary style.

How Are Folk Dances Different From One Another?

People's cultural history can be seen in their clothing, footwear, geography, religion, material resources, and social customs, all of which affect the stylistic features of their dances.

For example, Israeli youngsters dancing *Kuma Echa* in the freedom of shorts and sandals give an entirely different character to their movements than do the Japanese elders when they are dancing *Tanko Bushi* in constricting kimonos, *tabi* (divided toe socks), and high wooden *getas* (clog-type shoes). Bulgarian women dancing *Neda Voda Nalivala* while garbed in kerchiefs, massive bodices, bulky blouses, cumbersome shawls, long wool aprons, weighty wool skirts, thick wool hose, and dangling coin-like necklaces certainly move more heavily and closer to the ground than do Sicilian women step-hopping through the tarantella, dressed in light blouses, silk skirts, and short vests.

In this discussion of cultural clothing, we should explain our use of the term "costume." Costumes are what people wear for Halloween and what performers wear on the stage. Generally, it is more respectful to describe what people wear in their everyday or ceremonial lives as ethnic clothing, native outfits, modes of dress, etc. When planning students' dress for a staged dance program, however, the "ethnic language police" will allow you to say "costume."

On the stage, costumes often emphasize dance movements, just as, in the native setting, some dance movements are meant to draw attention to what dancers are wearing—the men's shoe tassels in the Greek *Karagouna,* or the women's coin ornaments in the Croatian *Ajde Noga Za Nogama* and *Sukačko Kolo,* for example. And some movements are meant to display the body under the traditional clothing, as in the Hungarian women's *Lakodalmi Tánc* and the Turkish *Kendime*.

Members of the Brigham Young University International Folk Dance Ensemble perform an elegant Ukrainian dance with movements that display their beautiful shawls.
Photo by Mark Philbrick

Folk Dance Cultures

The high-heeled boots and shoes of Norteño Mexican men and women allow for sharp, staccato stamps in *Santa Rita*. Contrast this with the soft, flat traditional footwear of the Greek people that make possible the smooth, sinuous movements of the *Tsamikos* and the soft leaps of the *Hasapikos*. African and Caribbean dancers with their strong bare feet gripping the ground as they do movements like those in *Bele Kawe* look very different from Irish dancers on their toes, in their soft shoes, doing a jig similar to the *Irish Lilt*.

The role of religion in society has also had a great deal to do with dance differences. In Islamic societies such as those of the Ottoman Empire, for example, men and women traditionally danced separately, as seen in the Macedonian *Makedonsko Bavno Oro* and the Armenian *Toi Nergis*. The Eastern Orthodox, Roman Catholic, Jewish, and Protestant religions also greatly affected certain cultures' social mores and therefore their dances. Other examples of interesting folk dance contrasts can be cited: Balkan peoples of southeastern Europe danced to their own singing on isolated, grassy plateaus, as in the Bulgarian *Pravo Horo*, while, in the same historic period, central and western European couples were gliding to formal orchestras in well-appointed ballrooms, and dance masters were teaching formal-figured partner patterns like the English *Hole in the Wall*.

Why Are Folk Dances Similar to One Another?

In spite of all these differences, however, folk dances have many similarities, because most humans have basically the same emotions and urges. And in almost every culture, people dance for similar reasons. The details may be different, but traditionally most ethnic communities danced during courtship; at weddings, harvest festivals, and religious events; and whenever they got together for fun. Dancing can be an expression of joy, sorrow, or thanksgiving—or simply an expression of the universal urge to move to music.

Not long ago, dancing was a natural part of the lives of most nationality groups, and in many cultures this is still true—have you ever been to a Polish or Armenian wedding, an Irish pub, an Israeli festival, or a Greek picnic? The *horas* of Romania similar to *Hora pe Gheaţa*; the *kolos* of Croatia similar to *Kriči Kriči Tiček*; the line dances like *Lé Laridé* from Brittany, *Legnala Dana* from Macedonia, and *Eleno Mome* from Bulgaria—all are typical of dances still being done by these peoples. Through the dances, not only is ethnic tradition maintained, but also a sense of community is created and continued—a true reason for dancing by any folk.

Gender Roles in Folk Dance

One important similarity among nationalities, which sadly has been lost in our modern society in this country, is that some of the most admired members of the community were the best dancers—and these were often men. It was a mark of

*A Norwegian dancer, attempting to dislodge the hat from a branch, tries his skill at the high kick, or **hallingkast**, during Scandia camp in Mendocina, California.*

Photo by Roo Lester

virility or leadership if one was skilled enough to lead the lines in Serbia, to kick the hat from the branch in Norway, to do the highest leaps and sharpest squats in the Ukraine, to strut and stamp with the most fire in Spain, to perform the

Folk Dance Cultures 9

The International Dancers of Chicago are noisy and masculine in the Bulgarian Šop choreography.

Members of the Brigham Young University International Folk Dance Ensemble perform an Austrian dance in their gender roles.

Photo by Mark Philbrick

most intricate and precise footwork in Ireland, or to compete with the greatest strength and endurance in Senegal. It was macho to dance—and in some cultures it still is.

Today, although urbanization has overridden many of the traditional ways (unlike shepherds and blacksmiths, computer programmers have not yet developed their own work dances), it is still the best dancers who are the most admired at a Mexican fiesta, a Scottish games day, or a Hungarian dance house.

Even in traditional U.S. cultures, people tried to emulate the patriots who could execute the most graceful minuet, the mountaineers who could create the most complex clogging sequences, and the cowboys who could swing through every square without a hitch after a hard day on the range. In the old West, because men loved to dance so much, they would take the women's parts when there weren't enough female partners. Perhaps the interest in country/western dancing has brought back some of this enthusiasm.

In the carefully nonsexist North American society, it seems anachronistic to emphasize the separate roles of men and women when teaching folk dance. But these roles were an important feature of some ethnic dance cultures—a feature that explains the formation of their dances as much as footwear, clothing, and societal mores do. Through folk dance, boys in gender-segregated lines can experience how it is to feel proud, confident, strong, and masculine; girls in all-female circles can feel graceful, poised, and feminine. Dancing in their gender roles, however, will not prevent boys from becoming sensitive, caring parents—or girls from becoming successful business executives. The confidence and poise achieved in such gender roles will carry over to many of life's other activities.

Village Dances, Folk Ballet, and International Folk Dancing

The terms "folk dance," "traditional dance," and "ethnic dance" are often used interchangeably, as are the labels of "ethnic folk dancing" and "international folk dancing." Whatever the terms used, it is a good idea to be aware of some definite categories, each of which has an important place in the folk dance world. These categories do not include dances that are considered cultural art forms, such as the flamenco and the exquisite dances of India, which are also referred to as ethnic dance by some contemporary dance scholars.

The ***authentic folk dances,*** sometimes called ***village dances,*** are the ones that people have enjoyed in traditional contexts and settings, whether in the original homeland or in expatriate communities. Because they are living dances, most of the patterns are improvised, and variations have evolved. It does not matter if the music sounds raw, untutored, or dissonant to outsiders or if the movements look ungainly, for there is no audience to engage—the dancers have only themselves to please.

When there is an audience and authentic ethnic dances are arranged for the stage, folk dance may move into the realm of *folk ballet.* Sometimes these are called folklore performances, or sometimes, according to ethnochoreological researchers, "fakelore." To excite an audience, knees are raised higher; heads, turned in unison; circles, extended into spirals; and patterns, performed with perfect precision. The music is played the same way for every performance—something unheard of in the village! A clear sign of folk ballet is that the performers are special—they are rigorously trained, often have similar physical characteristics, and are uniformly excellent dancers—which is also unheard of

An example of a folk ballet group with excellent dancers is the Brigham Young University International Folk Dance Ensemble, shown here wearing Ukrainian costume, with their heads turned in unison.

Photo by Mark Philbrick

in the village. As Nick Jordanoff, former long-time director of the Duquesne University Tamburitzans, once said, "Guys in the village don't do twenty pirouettes—they drink too much."

Through exciting performances of national ethnic ensembles such as the

12   *Cultures and Styling in Folk Dance*

Ballet Folklorico of Mexico and the Moiseyev, which showcased dance cultures of the former Soviet Union, people learn more about these cultures and even about their own roots. Such companies raised the self-esteem of the peoples involved and also enhanced the folk dance movement with their introduction of teachers, dances, and performers from cultures that had been little-known in the West. Now, thanks to artists who have come through national folk ensembles, North Americans have been exposed to Moldovan, Albanian, Transylvanian, Ukranian, and Moravian dances, and so many more.

Many researchers, however, feel that by raising traditional folk dance to such an art form, much has been lost in terms of authenticity and true folklore. These are interesting and important issues that those involved with folk dance might want to consider, but they should not detract from the enjoyment of the dance.

Both folk ballet choreographies and village dances are the bases for the third folk category: *recreational folk dancing,* sometimes called *international folk dancing.* Groups of people who are interested in other cultures, who like to move to interesting music, or who enjoy a social or aerobic experience meet regularly in communities throughout the U.S. and Canada and in numerous other countries, such as Germany, Sweden, Australia, and Japan. During a typical evening the leader or leaders teach or review a few dances and then play recordings of dances that are in the general repertoire. Some groups are lucky enough to have live music. Participants often switch from Poland to Greece to Scotland to Bulgaria to Brittany to Israel to Croatia to Mexico in the same hour. There are also clubs and classes devoted solely to one dance culture, such as Hungarian, Scandinavian, New England, Israeli, Cajun, or Scottish.

We encourage teachers to seek out such groups in their communities. There are folk dance directories (see General Resources on p. 373) that list useful North American and international contacts. It is also possible to find folk dance groups sponsored by universities and park districts. Although the teaching in these groups is fairly casual and most of the dances taught may not be appropriate to teach schoolchildren, by participating you will gain confidence in your own ability, meet some interesting and helpful people, and have an enjoyable experience.

What Are the Sources for the Dances in These Books?

Like numerous dances done in the international folk dance community, many of the dances in *TFD* and *TM&D* are based on traditional steps and movements but would not be classified as authentic. Instead, they are dances choreographed by teachers who may or may not be members of the particular ethnic groups attached to the dances. The teachers may be former members of national folk ensembles, recreational dancers who developed a special interest, anthropologists

Students in an after-school folk dance class show great enjoyment as they work on the movements of an Armenian dance.

Photo by Zoltan Horvath

who love to dance, researchers who are interested in a particular ethnic culture, etc. These teachers/choreographers are mentioned in the appropriate chapters of this book, and we send our gratitude and appreciation to them all. The dances were chosen for *TFD* and *TM&D* because people of all ages and levels have enjoyed them for decades in recreational, or international, folk groups.

Some of the dances in *TFD* and *TM&D*—particularly those from Greece and from Balkan cultures—are forms of authentic, or village, dances still enjoyed by various cultures at social events and occasions in their homelands and in expatriot communities. Generally, however, although the village dances are usually simple with repetitive step patterns, they can be difficult to translate into classroom and international, or recreational, group settings. Although they may look

14   Cultures and Styling in Folk Dance

This line of recreational folk dancers is doing a belt-hold dance from southeastern Europe.
Photo by John Nemerovski

easy on paper, such dances are often more successfully used with experienced or mature students.

True traditional folk dances were meant to be just a small part of a larger event such as a wedding or festival, one that also included singing, socializing, eating, and other activities. Therefore, when such dances are featured in a school lesson plan, it is important to include background information about the reasons why people do them and about who these people are and where they come from. This is true for all dances of all cultures, of course, but particularly true for those of people who are still dancing spontaneously for their own enjoyment.

However, whether the dances you teach are those from an active village repertoire, choreographies from folk ballet ensembles, or patterns that have been created based on traditional movements, they can be an important part of many educational programs, and they can be called folk dances. As Louis Armstrong once said, "If we ain't the folk, who is?" We hope you will enjoy teaching these dances and dancing them!

Chapter 2: Folk Dance Teaching

The introductory chapters of Phyllis S. Weikart's books *TFD* and *TM&D* discuss many of the basic guidelines for presenting movement activities and beginning folk dances to students. This chapter builds on that information, offering further helpful insights into teaching folk dance.

The Folk Process

You may find that some dances are described one way in a book and another way at a workshop or at a folk dance party. In the case of living traditional dances—such as the Greek *Tsamikos*, the Israeli *Hora*, the Bulgarian *Dajčovo Horo*, the Serbian *U Šest*—there are many variations, and more are created every time people get on the dance floor. In this natural way, authentic dances may be changed. This is called the folk process.

The folk process may also operate on the choreographed dances, although not as actively. Sometimes a pattern is changed inadvertently because a dance leader forgets or misunderstands a step; sometimes a dance is changed on purpose because a teacher wants to make it easier for students. Occasionally you may find that more than one dance is done to the same melody because different choreographers used the same music to create their own patterns, as in *Erev Shel Shoshanim* or the *Romanian Hora*. It also sometimes happens that dances with the same name and the same music are done differently in various cities and in various dance groups.

Teachers should guard against becoming deliberate agents in the folk process. As discussed below, if you need to change a dance for classroom convenience and students' initial success, be sure that the students know the original pattern, as it is described in your dance notes, before you send them out into the wider folk dance community.

If you are not sure whether the "real" dance is the one in the written description, the one you've been taught, or the one you've seen done, teach the pattern with which you are most comfortable. But tell your students, if they are likely to be dancing outside the classroom or in other groups, "There are other ways to do this dance. This is the way I learned it [indicating, if relevant, from whom or when]. If you see it done differently in other folk dance classes, try to do it their way. A good dancer must be flexible!"

Folk Dance Etiquette

Doing the pattern the way the group you are dancing with does it, even though you learned it differently, is part of folk dance etiquette. As in every activity, there are do's and don'ts of folk dancing. Awareness of these will make your own sessions go more smoothly and will help you and your students be especially welcome when venturing out into the wider world of folk dance.

In that "wider world," outside the school setting, most recreational folk dance groups are for adults, although there are also some very friendly family-oriented groups. This doesn't mean that skilled and considerate elementary-aged youngsters aren't welcomed in adult groups, but it isn't likely they would find many people there in their own age group. Teachers who lead after-school folk dance activities or organize student exhibition groups are doing a tremendous

One example of an organized student dance group is the Eyestone Folk Dancers from Eyestone Elementary School in Wellington, Colorado. Here (top photo) they demonstrate an Israeli dance during a school festival and (bottom photo) perform for residents at a local nursing home.

Photos by Catherine Engel

service by giving young students as many opportunities as possible to develop their love of dance.

For anyone who would like to dance outside the classroom, here are some etiquette suggestions:

❈ Don't get in a line or circle of a dance you've never seen, unless it is being taught or the leader invites everyone to join in. Listen to what the leader says as he or she announces the dance: "This is easy to follow, why don't you all join us?" or "If you don't know this dance, please try it behind the line."

When you dance behind the line, it is easier to see footwork and you are not in danger of interfering with your neighbors. Some people feel embarrassed, conspicuous, or left out if they cannot be part of the main group during every dance; they don't like to be recognized as greenhorns. However, some experienced dancers may not be very tolerant of people who get in the dance and then proceed to have difficulty with their own and others' feet. If you pick up the pattern before the music ends, then do join the others (read on to find out how to do this).

❈ In a recreational group, it is usually best to join a line at the end, either as it is forming or when you have learned the steps. If the end is not in sight, it is acceptable to join in the middle. Before you move in between two people, however, it is courteous to dance behind them and ask "May I join in?" Usually they'll open up and let you in, appreciating your consideration. If they don't, it may be because they have been looking forward all evening to holding each other's hand. If they are polite, one may say, "Not here, but join us on the other side." This is also true for joining closed circles.

Do not take it personally if once in a while someone prefers that you don't join in at a particular spot. However, if it happens often, or if lines seem to end as soon as you join, you should honestly ask yourself why. Do you always get in dances you really don't know? Do you dance only for yourself and not with the whole group? Are you careless in your personal hygiene? Is your behavior somehow inappropriate?

❈ Be aware of where the leader is, and don't join next to him or her unless you're very sure of the dance. Most, but not all, line dances move to the right; some move to the left; and occasionally there's a leader at both ends. Watch the leader for cues and for changes in steps. Generally, you shouldn't lead a line until you are completely confident about a dance. However, if the teacher indicates that he or she is sure you can do it, try it—you may be more than ready.

❋ In longways sets, join at the bottom as they are forming. If you've had some experience, it is all right to get in many of these progressive dances even if you don't know them. The patterns for American dances are usually "called" by the leader; the steps for English or Scottish dances should be "reminded" once or twice by the leader, although in many international groups, the leader prompts the dancers all the way through. Avoid starting in the active position, however, if you're not sure of the pattern. As famed teacher Olga Kulbitsky said, "If you don't know what you're doing, don't be the first one to do it."

❋ Do try the easy couple dances with a partner, even if you don't know a particular dance well. With a partner, you have only one person rather than many to worry about, and it's a good way to learn. Watch the others once or twice, then join in on the outside of the group, especially if the dance moves quickly. Being on the outside enables you to get out of the way if you get confused.

Girls and women should not be shy about asking boys and men to partner them; neither should they be embarrassed about dancing with other females. One of the facts of dance life is that many groups do not have as many men as women; another fact is that men are sometimes less willing to take a chance on a dance they don't know. It is not only acceptable but often appreciated if a woman asks a man to dance. In situations where there are too few women partners, it is also perfectly acceptable for two men to be partners.

It is also appreciated if boys and men do not hang back from choosing a woman to dance with when couple dances are announced—the only way to learn them is to do them. A man not sure of the pattern can tell his partner. She'll probably say "Me either" or pleasantly guide him through it. It's worth the risk—any male who is comfortable on the dance floor has his social life assured.

❋ Ethnic communities may have their own internal etiquette rules regarding joining a dance. If you are a guest at another culture's festivity, watch the dance scene before jumping in enthusiastically, or ask someone first, as a mark of respect.

Most of these etiquette suggestions arise from common sense and consideration, but unfortunately, both of these are in shorter supply than they used to be. It would be a tremendous service if teachers could give some attention to the art of conducting oneself on the dance floor as well the fundamentals of asking and being a partner. Recreational folk dance leaders should definitely stress these concepts. They are as important as knowing the steps of the dance.

"Segregated" Dances

Many of the dances that have been taught to recreational folk groups, especially those dances from eastern Europe and the Balkans, were traditionally done only by men or only by women. For a variety of reasons, the dances came to us as mixed-gender lines or circles. However, there are a few that have been taught as "segregated" dances and have remained that way in most recreational groups for a long time. In this series, such dances include the Hungarian men's dance *Mátrai Verbunkos,* the Slovakian women's dance *Horehronsky Czárdás,* the Hungarian women's dance *Lákodálmi Tánc,* and the Romanian women's dance *Dragaicuţa.*

Times are changing in many ways having to do with gender differences, however, and this has had its repercussions in the international folk dance community. Once, there were leaders who wouldn't allow women to dance if they weren't wearing skirts, but by the end of the 1960s, that became a losing battle. (Interestingly, today in the contra dance community, there is a trend toward men wearing skirts, which some find cooler than trousers.) Some recreational groups now do these segregated dances in mixed lines, because the original teachers found it more convenient to present them like that or because group leaders do not know or do not care about the traditions. More than once, men have stamped out of a folk dance hall in a huff when teachers or dancers have asked them not to join the women's circle. One solution we have found is to suggest two circles or lines, one that is segregated and one that is mixed genders.

However, it is not unfriendly or elitist for teachers to try to preserve a few of the men's and women's dances. There is something special about a circle of women or girls moving softly and smoothly together, and about a line of men or boys stamping strongly and proudly. These movements feel like more than just dance patterns. They evoke an authentic village ambience as well as the special camaraderie that arises among those of the same gender. This camaraderie can be experienced even today, in North American urban classrooms, when boys and girls are seen to move more freely if put into separate groups to learn dances.

In these busy times, such feelings are not easy to come by among peoples of such varying backgrounds. It is not a bad thing to keep just a few of the dances to their men-only and women-only traditions.

Music for Folk Dances

Ethnic music is one of the main things people love about folk dance. Steps and patterns are important, but a dance with clever choreography seldom lasts long if the music isn't appealing; there are, however, many dances in the general repertoire with humdrum, even annoying or silly choreography, that have been popular for generations because their music is irresistible.

The music for all of the dances described in *Teaching Folk Dance: Successful Steps (TFD)* can be found on the nine *Rhythmically Moving* and six *Changing Directions* recordings produced by Phyllis S. Weikart with the excellent folk music duo Gemini. (These recordings are referred to in this book as *RM1–9* and *CD1–6*.) Also, although many of the original recordings of this ethnic dance music are out of print, some may still be available from several record dealers and distributors throughout the country (see General Resources on p. 373).

When teachers and students become comfortably familiar with their favorite dances, you might wish to try various versions of the music, if available. This is particularly true of the living dances of Greece (for example, *Hasapikos, Syrtos,* and *Tsamikos*), and the generic dances of Bulgaria (such as *Jambolsko Pajduško Horo,* and *Pravo Horo*), as well as the Croatian *Drmeš*, the Macedonian *Lesnoto Oro,* the Serbian *U Šest,* and the French-Canadian *La Bastringue.* Separate recordings of many of the other listed dances also exist.

Music educators particularly might enjoy hearing the various versions. All of this music is interesting, much of it is very beautiful, and some is extremely exciting. If you'd like musical transcriptions for some dances, see the guides to the *Rhythmically Moving* recording series as well as other music sources listed in the General Resources list on pp. 378–379.

Please be aware, however, that much of the music for folk dancing is not appropriate for classroom instruments. Those music teacher texts from earlier generations that reduce dances from such varied cultures as Hungarian, Spanish, Ibo, and Inca to simple piano pieces came from a more Eurocentric, less culturally sophisticated society. If "multicultural education" means nothing else, it should mean teaching respect for all cultures.

Modifying Ethnic Folk Dances

Occasionally you may feel that a particular folk dance is not appropriate for the specific group you are teaching unless you modify it in some manner. Before changing the ethnic material, however, consider these ideas: (1) Can you find other dances that may be appropriate without having to be simplified? (2) Can you prepare your students with easier dances and movement exercises to lead up to the difficulties presented in the dance you'd like to teach? (3) Is it possible that the students may surprise you and be able to achieve this dance?

If the answer to each of these questions is no, then follow the suggestions in *TFD* and *TM&D* for modifying and for adding style. Select the dances carefully. If you think it might take more than two or three class periods for the students to enjoy a dance with its ethnic styling, the dance may not be appropriate for this particular group.

You might try letting the students modify the dances for themselves. Show them a dance as it should be done, and ask what parts are difficult for them. Using their own suggestions for simplifying will make them more interested in learning the dance and being comfortable with it, and perhaps they will be ready sooner to add the ethnic parts. They may give you some good ideas, too!

The students will probably modify the patterns in the way that is most natural for them. For example, at first they may omit the front and back crossing movements in a grapevine pattern and just travel forward, or they might eliminate big hops in favor of small bounces. This is the way a young child or older adult might follow along at the village festival, leaving out the more complex movements but still retaining the flavor and spirit of the dance. With these simplified movements, younger brother and grandmother can join the line or circle without interfering with others' pleasure.

In all modifications, it is important to treat with respect the ethnic underpinnings of the dances. The simplified versions should reflect, at the very least, the spirit of the peoples from which they come—for example, the heartiness of the Danes, the self-containment of the Japanese, the exuberance of the Mexicans. If the modified dances can also include some characteristic styling details, all the better—for instance, the pinkie-hold in the *Armenian Misirlou* or the basket-hold in the Croatian *Kriči Kriči Tiček*. The ethnic "soul" of a folk dance should not be trivialized.

There is also a practical reason for keeping the simplifications as pure as possible. Before a group of students finally leaves you, they should know that their modified dances can be done in other ways—ways that are more ethnic. It will be much easier for them to graduate to the standardized choreographies if, early on, the dances have been modified in a natural manner, as described in *TFD* and *TM&D*. One of the beauties of this approach is that anyone who knows even a few of the standardized choreographies common to most group repertoires will be welcomed into the community of folk dancers anywhere in the world. It is a joy to join a circle of strangers and immediately become accepted through the dance. You will give your students this opportunity if they go out into the wider world of folk dance doing the dances the way most others do them.

Modification is appropriate for the beginning dances in *TFD*. By the time your students are ready for the intermediate ones in *TM&D*, it should not be necessary to simplify many of them for their enjoyment and success. During your presentation of the more difficult dances, you will often omit some movements at first—by, for example, leaving out a hop or stamp—but usually these movements are added by the time the music is played or at least by the next time the dance is experienced. This is the *teaching process,* which is different from modification.

General Dance Styling

Along with styling details for specific ethnic dances, here are some general suggestions that will help students progress from shuffling along in a series of steps to actually dancing. When they begin to enjoy and be successful with the basic movements, you might casually include some of these points with each day's instruction, until they become instinctive.

These young folk dance students learn that excellent dance styling includes keeping shoulders back and "earlobes upright."

Photo by Zoltan Horvath

✤ Keep ribs up, shoulders back, tummies tucked, and "earlobes upright," as master folk dance teacher Richard Crum says.

✤ Make sure feet are "clean"—step, don't schlep.

✤ Keep steps small and underneath your body, for balance and poise.

✤ Let motions flow from one to another.

✤ Pay attention to movements of head, arms, hands, even faces.

✤ Keep movements appropriate—don't "overdance."

❊ Move with conviction and confidence.

❊ Dance *with* your partner, next to your neighbors, within the circle.

❊ Show your enjoyment of the dance.

These young students realize that good dancers do not hesitate to show their enjoyment of moving to music with their friends.
Photo by Zoltan Horvath

These suggestions lead from *styling* to *style*—which is how each person expresses himself or herself through dance. As another master folk dance teacher, Yves Moreau, has said: "'Stylings' can be taught, style can't be."

Ethnic Styling Encourages Success in Dance

The dance books *TFD* and *TM&D* have one major goal—to give all people success in dance. We hope the ethnic styling information in this book will help you make folk dancing so interesting, exciting, and successful for your students—and for you—that you will be responsible for a whole new generation of dancers.

The dances mentioned in this book as examples of various cultures and styling are selected from those described in *TFD* and *TM&D*. There are also many other folk dances you may find useful and fun. To enhance students' enjoyment, plan field trips to ethnic festivals and culture museums. Bring in folk costumes, traditional instruments, and ethnic dance videos. Invite folk artists for presentations, or ask local folk dance teachers to lead a party. Let the students see that many people, both men and women, do these dances with gusto and pleasure. We also encourage you yourself to go to folk dance groups and workshops, as well as ethnic events and performances, whenever possible.

We believe that after your students feel successful with the basic patterns, learning the ethnic styling will pleasurably increase their knowledge of the world's cultures while enhancing their enjoyment of the movements and music and insuring their competence in dance.

African Dances

Chapter 3 African Dances

African Dances in Phyllis S. Weikart's Books

Bele Kawe [BAY-luh-KAH-wee] (A dance in the Creole style of the Caribbean Islands) *TFD, RM3*

Jambo [JAHM-bo] (Hello; a dance similar to some from Ghana, West Africa) *TFD, RM7*

Pata Pata II [PAH-tah PAH-tah] (A dance from South Africa known simply as *Pata Pata* around the world; see Chapter 30 for Phyllis Weikart's choreography, which she names *Pata Pata I*) *TFD, RM6*

Tant' Hessie [tahnt hess-SEE-yah] (Aunt Hester; a dance from South Africa, about Aunt Hester's white horse) *TFD, RM7*

*E*arlier we made the point that folk dances come from peoples and not from geographical entities, so it may seem strange for this chapter to use the name of an entire continent as a dance category. "African" is even a further misnomer, since the top third of the continent in question is made up of Arab peoples, whose dances are generally described by their culture's name (e.g., Egyptian) or as North African.

However, although "African" dances are as varied as the many different African peoples, one historic fact justifies binding much of the folklore of the diverse cultures south of the Sahara Desert under a single label. In the sixteenth, seventeenth, and eighteenth centuries, native black peoples, most of whom were from West Africa, were sent as slaves to America, Brazil, and the West Indies. As a result, tribal and ethnic differences were fused into a common culture as the enslaved peoples all endured similar experiences and supported one another in their trials. In terms of dance, it is possible to differentiate specific movements or themes as those of the Yoruba or Ibo or Akan tribe, for example, but it is also accepted to refer to an entire group of dances as West African, East African, or sometimes just African.

There are also European and Asian communities in the African countries; this chapter includes one European-style dance from South Africa.

The four dances listed on the previous page are not from a single culture. *Bele Kawe* and *Jambo* are adapted forms of West African dance movements. *Pata Pata II* is a novelty dance popularized by black South Africans, and *Tant' Hessie* is an arranged traditional dance of white South Africans. We will describe the West African and South African styles separately here.

West African Dance

Bele Kawe is a choreographed example of the urban "Highlife" dances that are done at parties and nightclubs in West African cities, the Caribbean islands, and everywhere else in the world that West Africans have migrated.

Jambo is a choreographed form of a more primitive greeting dance. Generally, most African dances are improvisations, with perhaps a basic movement and a specific underlying rhythmic tempo. Behind almost every movement, there is a meaning, perhaps a story or a true-life experience. Participants seldom touch one another, but they may compete in creativity and endurance—the drums can go on a long time.

FORMATION. *Bele Kawe* has been arranged as a big drum dance from the Creole culture in the Caribbean island chain near Grenada. Dances like this one are traditionally done by only one, two, or three people at a time rather than by a whole group. Sometimes such dances were originally done by men alone or by women alone; *Bele Kawe* is one that African women liked to do, but it should not be limited to one gender—all students enjoy this dance.

Jambo, from Ghana, is a greeting dance that has dancers facing one another. Probably it was also done traditionally in more free form.

For classroom and recreational dancing, choreographers have arranged these dances, and others like them, in fixed, repetitive forms for entire mixed groups, so everyone can enjoy them at once.

STEPS AND MOVEMENTS. The basic feel of this style is strong, fluid, and earthy. African-based dances play one part of the body against another, and there is much movement of the torso. Legs are bent, feet are flat with splayed toes gripping the ground. Dancers use the whole body as they crouch and reach, pulse, and shimmy. For schoolchildren, it is enough that they use their knees to "sit in" or "get down," spread their legs and feet, and try to use their heads and midsections as well as their limbs.

HANDS AND ARMS. Since in African dances every part of the body has a role, even when hand and arm movements are not described for a given dance, these parts usually move with the same energy and deliberation as the legs and feet. Fingers are also part of the dance, sometimes with all spread, sometimes with one pointing, sometimes with all planted firmly on thighs or back.

MODIFICATION AND TEACHING TIPS. Follow the general modification suggestions in Chapter 2 of this book and the suggestions in the specific dance descriptions in *TFD*. You might begin by encouraging students to move spontaneously to the music of these dances, then add the structure of steps. For many people repetitive patterns are easier and safer to do than freestyle and creative movements; these are dances that can help students, and also teachers, to unlock their bodies.

MUSIC. Present-day interest in "world music" has made traditional West African instruments and rhythms somewhat familiar and accessible to schools. Although both *Bele Kawe* and *Jambo* are choreographed to specific songs, they can each be danced to any music that has the right rhythms. In the music room, bongos, bass drums, gourds, shakers, and other hand percussion instruments are appropriate for beating the basic rhythms. Double gongs and agogo bells also help keep the beat. Recorders, flutes, wooden pipes, and barred instruments can provide melodies.

For even more authenticity as well as economy and fun, search a plumbers' equipment house, an office supply store, an automobile service station, or your own pantry shelves for materials for creating some wonderful instruments. A terrific band can be organized with "found" items, such as cardboard boxes, wastebaskets, mailing tubes, tail pipes, large nails and other iron pieces, plastic cups, glasses, bottles, tin cans, and sections of bamboo. Packing tape can be wound around oatmeal boxes to make squeeze drums or around frames such as tennis racket holders to make some interesting percussion instruments.

These U.S. schoolchildren are enjoying a West African Highlife-type dance—a kind done at parties and night clubs in West African cities, the Caribbean islands, and other places where West Africans have migrated.

African Dances 33

A special headdress is worn by a young woman from Côte d'Ivoire, the Republic of the Ivory Coast, performing at the Folkmoot USA festival in Waynesville, North Carolina.

CLOTHING AND COSTUMES. When demonstrating the more primitive dances, students can wear brightly patterned shirts or blouses, denim or white pants, ruffled skirts, and no shoes. Girls might braid and bead their hair, and both girls and boys can wear colored head kerchiefs, tied in back, or research special headdresses. Boys might roll up or cut off their pants at the knees; for added authenticity, they might wear no shirts at all. Both boys and girls can wear beautiful African cloths tied or wound in creative ways.

It can be very effective in a school or community program to have students design African-style masks for costumes or decorations. However, in the native setting masks have specific symbolism in religious rituals. Using them merely as props may be trivializing their significance, like tacking up crude crucifixes as background for dances from a Christian culture. Rather than avoid using masks, however, have students find out what each mask represents as well as what it looks like, and add this dimension to the program.

To demonstrate urban dances, usually the ones with the Highlife beat as in *Bele Kawe,* students might wear the kind of clothing once described as Sunday-go-to-meetin'. This would be a nice shirt and slacks, perhaps a pretty dress, and appropriate shoes.

34　　　　　　　　　　　　　　　　　　　　　*Cultures and Styling in Folk Dance*

South African Dance

Pata Pata is a song recorded in 1967 by the well-known South African Zulu singer Miriam Makeba. The recording was an instant international hit, and the dance appeared in the folk dance repertoire shortly thereafter, where it is still popular, especially with young people. It may not be exactly the same as the "dance we do down Johannesburg way," as the song says.

Tant' Hessie, originally a Dutch folk game *(volkspel)*, was a recreational dance done by Afrikaners, who are South Africans of primarily Dutch descent. It was introduced to the North American folk dance community in the 1950s by a dance teacher named Huig Hofman.

FORMATION. *Pata Pata II* is usually performed with individuals scattered around the floor, all facing the same direction. When a teacher is giving instruction, however, it might be better to have students learn in a circular formation, so the teacher does not have to turn her back or mirror the movements. After the students become comfortable with the pattern, they can try some personal variations, such as facing in other directions or changing levels.

Tant' Hessie is meant to be a partner dance, typical of some dances in central Europe. It was probably arranged as a mixer for recreational reasons.

STEPS AND MOVEMENTS. *Pata Pata II* has a pan-African feeling in its relaxed movements and touch-step pattern. Dancers should stay loose and enjoy moving with the music. Although the pattern may seem simple, remembering 16 different movements requires good concentration. Students will have better success if the pattern is taught by rehearsing four beats at a time, then adding the next four.

Tant' Hessie is an amusing combination of European heritage and South African environment. The walking, or step-bend, movements are proud, little strutting steps. Communication is an important ingredient of the pattern, which in fact has been described as acting out a familiar theme: In Part IA (the A section of the music), partners find each other as they move toward and away, smiling in greeting, nodding when their shoulders are adjacent. In Part II (the B section of the music), they lose each other, going their separate ways as they pass back to back. In Part IB (the A section of the music), they find each other again, opening their arms wide and shouting "Hey!" just before the buzz turn.

HANDS AND ARMS. In *Pata Pata II*, as in all indigenous African dances, arms are an important part of the pattern. Relax arms and shoulders and follow the directions given for the arm movements, adding others if it feels good.

In *Tant' Hessie,* during the strutting walk of Parts IA and II, arms hang naturally at the sides and move with the motions of the body. Do not fold them up in front for the do-si-do, as U.S. western square dancers used to do (and as many of us still do whenever we hear the call "do-si-do!"). For the buzz turn in Part IB, there are alternate holds described, with the choice of hold depending on the group. For the double arm-hold, partners hold each other just above each elbow. A variation of this is the modified ballroom position—the man's right arm is around the woman's waist, and her left hand is on his right shoulder, as usual, but their other arms are joined by each person gripping the other's elbow.

MODIFICATION AND TEACHING TIPS. *Pata Pata II* could be modified by omitting the turn on the last three counts and then adding it later—the natural teaching process. The pattern could also be honed down to just the first eight beats, but the rest should be added as soon as possible.

For *Tant' Hessie,* follow the simplification suggestions given in *TFD*. If you find it best to teach it first in the alternate formation of a circle without partners, do pair up students as soon as possible, because the fun of this dance is to communicate with another person through movement. The mixing part, which can be added later, gives a little more interest to the dance, especially when students are ready for partners of the other persuasion.

MUSIC. The pattern of *Pata Pata II* could be done to any strong, regular, African-sounding beat, but the popularity of the dance is tied to that wonderful song. When students feel comfortable with the steps, they will be ready for the original recording by Miriam Makeba, which is still available.

The music for *Tant' Hessie* has a flavor that hints of its central European origins, especially in the original recording with its oompah-sounding brass. The South African flavor is in the music's bouncing drum beat. The melody comes from a song about Aunt Hester's white horse, and dancers are encouraged to sing "tra-la-la" in Part II and "oompah oompah oompah-pah" in Part IB.

CLOTHING AND COSTUMES. *Pata Pata II* comes from a relaxed urban scene. When performing this dance for a program, students might wear the Sunday-go-to-meetin' outfits mentioned earlier or simply their usual t-shirts, jeans, and athletic shoes.

Tant' Hessie, which is traditional but fairly modern, can be performed in simple street clothes—plain-colored or white collared shirts and blouses with perhaps darker trousers and skirts, and flat dress shoes. To dress this up a bit, add colored sashes or vests.

Resources Used for Chapter 3

Amoaku, Komla. 1995, October. Sessions at National Symposium on Multicultural Music, University of Tennessee–Knoxville by this music educator from Accra, Ghana.

Berger, Renato. 1984. *African Dance—Africa, Brazil, Caribbean, U.S.A.* Amsterdam: Heinrichshofen's Verlag Locarno.

Boyer-White, René. 1995. Sessions at American Orff-Schulwerk Association national conference, Dallas, TX. Boyer-White is a professor of Music Education at the University of Cincinnati College Conservatory of Music and president of the National Black Music Caucus of Music Educators National Conference (MENC)

Emery, Lynne Fauley. 1988. *Black Dance from 1619 to Today.* Pennington, NJ: Princeton Book Co. This is a scholarly, readable book with numerous quotes from original sources, and an excellent bibliography.

Gottier, Karin. 1992, 1994. Comments and conversation with this expert in many types of the world's dances.

Huet, Michel. 1978. *The Dance, Art, and Ritual of Africa.* New York: Pantheon Books.

May, Jan. 1994, February. "Heartbeat of the Village: An Introduction to the Music and Culture of Ghana." Presentation and dance descriptions for workshop with Chicago chapter of American Orff-Schulwerk Association, Berwyn, IL.

Morgan, Clyde. 1994. Sessions at American Orff-Schulwerk Association national conference, Philadelphia, PA. Clyde Morgan is a professor of African Dance at SUNY College, Brockport, NY.

Mynatt, Constance, and Bernard Kaiman. 1975. *Folk Dancing for Students and Teachers.* Dubuque, IA: Wm. C. Brown Co. This book contains a description of *Tant' Hessie* that is more complete than usual.

Strahlendorf, Mary Joyce. 1969. *African Heritage Dances.* Freeport, NY: Educational Activities, Inc. This is the original music recording for *Bele Kawe* with background facts on the cover.

Tyrrell, Barbara. 1976. *Tribal Peoples of Southern Africa.* Cape Town: Books of Africa. This is a gorgeous book on African attire.

Andean Dances

Chapter 4: Andean Dances

Andean Dance in Phyllis S. Weikart's Books

Carnavalito [car-nah-vah-LEE-toe] (Little Carnival) *TFD, RM5*

North Americans and Europeans are becoming increasingly better acquainted with the cultures of the peoples who live in the Andes Mountain region of South America. It is possible now to see, on the street corners of our large cities, groups of musicians from Bolivia, Ecuador, Peru, Chile, Colombia, and Argentina playing their upbeat rhythms on some fascinating instruments. We can also buy clothing, bags, and wall hangings made from their colorful weavings.

The Andean region has great contrasts: eternal snow and tropical rain forests, wild rivers and dry deserts, volcanos and glaciers, enormous reptiles and 163 varieties of tiny hummingbirds, rich aristocrats and primitive people who still shrink human heads.

The Andean highlands are one of the highest inhabited regions in the world, with altitudes up to 17,000 feet, way beyond what most of the world considers comfortable. Over centuries of living in this thin air, the Indians have developed a physique especially adapted to the lack of oxygen. Their lungs and heart are larger than normal, and their pulse is slower. Their small hands and feet and their short arms and legs make it easier for the heart to pump blood to these areas; as a result, they can walk barefoot in the snow with no ill effect. In an altitude at which most of us could barely sit up, Andean men can work in the mines all day, then play a fast game of soccer.

Although the Andean dance discussed in this chapter is identified as Bolivian, the peoples of the highlands have similar cultures, no matter what country they live in. Bolivia became a nation in 1825, naming itself for the Venezuelan freedom fighter Simón Bolívar. However, the Inca culture began in the highlands more than seven centuries earlier. Today more than half the people in Bolivia are Indians, mostly from the Quechua and Aymara groups, and a third of the population is Mestizo, a combination of Indian and Spanish. There are still signs of the ancient Inca culture in their lives. For example, on Lake Titicaca—at 12,000 feet, the highest navigable body of water in the world—Bolivians are still using boats made of reeds as they have for thousands of years. The indigenous peoples of the Andes dress as they did centuries ago and practice their distinctive textile-weaving techniques that are many millennia old. The dance festivals and other pastimes also have not changed very much over the years.

Andean dances are represented here by a single dance, one of the few Latin American dances in the general folk dance repertoire. There have been a handful of others taught in the past, but they are the typical flirting-partner dances of the Latin lands and not as useful for schoolchildren as this energetic snake dance. It is described as Bolivian but could be from other Andean countries as well.

There are many dances known as *Carnavalito* in the Spanish-speaking countries. They all incorporate the movements and patterns done during

Andean culture is becoming increasingly familiar to people around the world. Here, Andean musicians play their upbeat rhythms for passersby on a street in Munich, Germany.

Carnaval, the traditional pre-Lenten celebration (called Mardi Gras in the U.S.), as well as during other festivities. In Bolivia, where they are sometimes also done in a quadrille form, *Carnavalito* dances are the most popular folk dances, along with the *Takirari* and the *Cueca.*

In Bolivia, Peru, and other Andean countries, during the Carnaval parade, usually held the Sunday before Ash Wednesday, dancers snake down the street wearing devil masks and costumes to represent Satan and Lucifer. The parade ends with an intricately figured dance (a *Carnavalito*) followed by an allegorical play featuring the seven cardinal sins, Lucifer, and Archangel Michael.

The *Carnavalito* discussed here is not an example of the complicated and freestyle figured dance, but a simple, upbeat line dance choreographed from some basic steps. It comes from the town of Guadalquivir, which is another name given to this pattern, and was introduced to North American folk dancers by Laura Zanzi di Chavarria of Uruguay in the mid-1970s.

FORMATION. *Carnavalito* is done in a long line or broken circle, with the main leader at the right. However, because the line also travels to the left, it is important to have a strong leader at the other end, too. It can also be danced in shorter lines weaving in and out. In this formation, many people can be leaders.

STEPS AND MOVEMENTS. The dance is vigorous and joyous, since it is traditionally done by excited, volatile people during a particularly unrestrained holiday. The step-hops in Part II are high and happy. It may be a good idea for students to practice dancing fast around corners to avoid some inevitable pileups. Encourage dancers to make appropriate noises, such as short yelps and cheers.

HANDS AND ARMS. This is a good dance to illustrate hand-holding etiquette and techniques, for children immediately see its crack-the-whip possibilities. In addition, the strong arm-swing in Part II adds to the level of excitement, to say nothing of the aerobic energy. Discuss the importance of firm (not crushing!) hand-holds and relaxed arms and shoulders for greater flexibility. Practice hanging on while changing direction.

MODIFICATION AND TEACHING TIPS. If students are not comfortable with the schottische step in Part I, it would be appropriate to do *Carnavalito* with just large skips and arm-swings in lines and snakes and spirals. Also, you could omit the change of direction if it creates chaos. Keeping lines shorter will also prevent some horseplay and give more people the privilege of being leaders. As soon as possible, add the schottische steps and the reverse direction.

MUSIC. Because of our increasing familiarity with music of the Andean people, it is now possible to buy from music education catalogs some of the simple instruments they use. However, school instruments lend themselves well to this music. The original *charangos* (guitar-like instruments made of armadillo shell), *bombos* (small drums), and *quenas* (wood or bone flutes) can be replaced by recorders, shakers, and drums. A nice *sicu*, or panpipe, would be perfect!

CLOTHING AND COSTUMES. Traditionally, women wear a wide, brightly colored, striped skirt with many petticoats; a long-sleeved overblouse; a fringed wool cape or shawl fastened with big pins; and shiny hoop earrings. On their head is a kerchief tied under the chin and on top of that, a hat shaped liked a derby or bowler in a natural-wool color. They carry their baby on their back in a blanket or in a large scarf knotted in front. Men wear calf-length cuffed pants along with a poncho or sleeveless vest over a shirt with a sash or belt. On their head is the popular bright-colored, helmet-shaped cap with earflaps. Feet are bare or in sandals called *ojotas*. For school programs, wide skirts, shawls, and "babies" for girls, and rolled pants with vests or ponchos for boys, would look quite authentic, especially if these include using a great variety of colors. The hats would be a wonderful added touch.

Resources Used for Chapter 4

Houston, Ron (ed.). 1992. "Carnavalito." *Folk Dance Problem Solver,* 11–12. Austin, TX: Society of Folk Dance Historians.

Johnson, William Weber. 1965. *The Andean Republics.* New York: Time, Inc.

Lipner, Ronnie, and Stu Lipner. 1957. "The Argentine Gaucho Folk Dances." *Viltis* (December): 11–13.

Muñoz, Oscar. 1989. "Music for Children from Latin America." Paper presented at American Orff-Schulwerk Association national conference, Atlanta, GA.

Posada, José. 1981. *Balaio.* Salzburg: Fidula Publishing Co.

Zanzi de Chavarria, Laura. 1975. Notes from Maine Folk Dance Camp, Bridgton, ME.

Armenian Dances

Chapter 5 Armenian Dances

Armenian Dances in Phyllis S. Weikart's Books

Armenian Misirlou, also *Sirdes* — [MEE-zeer-loo, *also* SEAR-dess] (title refers to popular Greek "Misirlou," a girl's name) *TFD, RM9*

Hooshig Mooshig — [HOO-shig MOO-shig] *TM&D*

Soude Soude — [SOO-deh SOO-deh] *TM&D*

Sweet Girl — *TFD, RM7*

Toi Nergis, also *Hoy Nergiz* — [toy nehr-GEEZ] (Dear Narcissus) *TFD, RM4*

The Armenians are members of one of the world's oldest and most distinct ethnic groups. Their land, which they have inhabited since the seventh century B.C.E.,[2] is south of the Caucasus Mountains, between the Black and Caspian seas, bordering on Turkey, Iran, Georgia, and Azerbaijan (see p. 48). In 301 C.E. they became the first people to adopt Christianity as a state religion, and still today the Armenian Orthodox Church is a focal point of social and religious life.

Although Armenia's ancient territory has narrowed considerably, it has always been located at one of the strategic junctures of Europe and Asia. This location has exposed Armenia to the migration and commerce of many peoples, and their influences can be seen in its rich culture. The location also placed Armenia in the path of marauding armies and empires, a fact that has had a grave effect on the country's history.

Like so many others in the region, the Armenians spent hundreds of years under the domination of the Ottoman Empire, beginning in the late 1400s. In the nineteenth century other subjugated minorities gradually liberated themselves from the Turks, and the Armenians also began to engage in revolutionary activities. The most dreadful period of their history, known by all Armenians as the Genocide, occurred at the beginning of the twentieth century and culminated in the year 1915. During these few terrible years 1,500,000 Armenians and 750,000 neighboring Assyrians were reportedly massacred or brutally deported by the Ottoman Turks, leaving a deep scar on both cultures. Armenians divide their history into before and after 1915, when most of western Armenia was destroyed and the survivors were uprooted from their ancestral homeland to be scattered around the world, a situation known as a diaspora, or dispersion. Another wave of immigration occurred in the 1970s, when the eastern Armenians fled the wars in Lebanon and Iran.

After World War I, when many national boundaries were redrawn, Armenia was officially proclaimed an independent state, but it was not able to remain so for long. In December 1920 it was taken over by the U.S.S.R. and became the smallest of the Soviet republics until the dissolution of that empire in December 1991. Today Armenia is struggling with economic problems, but it is again an independent nation.

Those few who escaped the Genocide were dispersed to many parts of the globe, including the United States, where there are now thriving Armenian communities in such cities as New York; Boston; Philadelphia; Detroit; Racine, Wisconsin; Fresno, California; and Los Angeles, home to the second-largest Armenian community in the world. In these new settings, preserving their traditional music and dance is one way that Armenians are able to maintain their ethnic identity. The Armenian dances that are done today in North America

---

[2] The abbreviation B.C.E. stands for "Before the Common Era," a terminology that respects the many cultures represented in this book. The authors will use B.C.E. and C.E. instead of the specifically Christian B.C. and A.D.

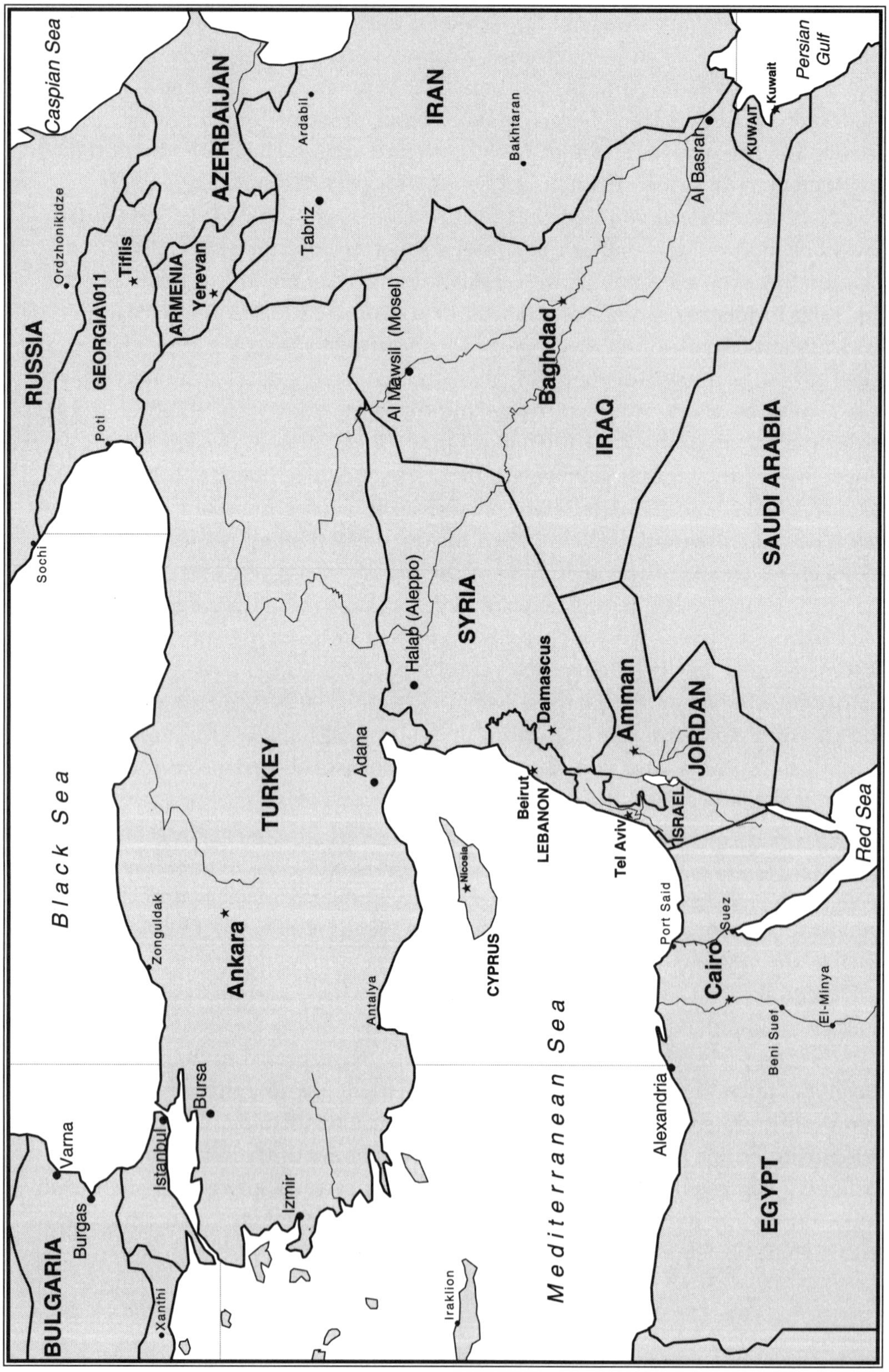
Caspian Sea
RUSSIA
Ordzhonikidze
GEORGIA
Tiflis
AZERBAIJAN
ARMENIA
Yerevan
Ardabil
IRAN
Tabriz
Bakhtaran
Al Basrah
KUWAIT
Kuwait
Persian Gulf
Poti
Sochi
Al Mawsil (Mosel)
Baghdad
IRAQ
SAUDI ARABIA
Halab (Aleppo)
SYRIA
Damascus
Amman
JORDAN
Beirut
LEBANON
Tel Aviv
ISRAEL
Red Sea
Black Sea
TURKEY
Adana
Ankara
Zonguldak
CYPRUS
Nicosia
Port Said
Suez
Cairo
Beni Suef
El-Minya
Alexandria
EGYPT
Mediterranean Sea
Antalya
Bursa
Istanbul
Varna
Burgas
Izmir
BULGARIA
Xanthi
Iraklion

were retained from original immigrants or created in these new-world centers of Armenian culture.

The dances listed on p. 46 are actually Armenian-American arrangements of traditional dances. The original immigrants who arrived before 1922, from both Anatolian (western) and Caucasian (eastern) Armenia, still do dances brought from their own regions. *Hooshig Mooshig,* an example of these that is also known as *Shavalee From Erzeroom,* was learned from Armenians living on the U.S. East Coast by Gary and Susan Lind-Sinanian, directors of the Armenian Cultural Museum in Boston, and Ron Wixman, an ethnic dance expert who danced with the Armenian community in New York City.

However, many new dances have also been created in this country. The new dances are based on traditional movements and rhythms but have their own style and energy, reflecting the greater freedom of expression in the United States. Some examples are *Soude Soude, Sweet Girl, Armenian Misirlou,* and *Toi Nergis.* The first three examples originated in dance creation contests held by the Fresno community and were introduced to U.S. folk dancers by Tom Bozigian (there is also a slightly different Armenian *Misirlou* being danced in the Milwaukee Armenian-American community).

The fourth example, *Toi Nergis,* also known as *Hoy Nergiz,* originated in the Soviet Armenian immigrant community in the New York area. It was presented first by Vyts Beliajus as *Hoy Nergiz* and later by the Lind-Sinanians as *Toi Nergis.* The story of *Toi Nergis* is of a girl, Narcissus, who asks her mother to find her a husband and finally settles—happily, we hope—for a musician.

FORMATION. The dances listed here are open- or broken-circle dances, with the leader on the right end. In a small space with many dancers crowded in, the lines snake and spiral. *Toi Nergis* is described in *TFD* in the traditional formation with separate lines of men and women, although the folk process has begun to change it to a mixed open circle. However, since it is one of the few dances in Phyllis S. Weikart's books described in the original gender-segregated style, it might be interesting to retain the separate lines. The students will probably prefer it that way!

Men and women in Armenia (and in other western Asian and Balkan cultures) danced separately for a number of reasons. One was that the Moslem religion of the ruling Ottoman Turks imposed this restriction. Another, some people have said, was that dancing in separate lines behind their women enabled Armenian men to protect the women from marauding Turks. In addition, separate lines—and in all of these cultures, separate dances—gave each gender the opportunity to look over the other for possible marriage partners. Physical differences are also an important reason for the evolution of separate dances, with the men's dances calling for movements that are stronger, faster, and more pronounced and the women's dances calling for movements that are soft, graceful, and demure.

Also, some dances had motions imitating some facet of work, nature, or daily life that was clearly the domain of women or of men.

STEPS AND MOVEMENTS. Armenian styling involves smooth, strong movements, with a flexible knee and a flat foot, reflecting the soft footwear. Dancers stay close to one another, moving in unison with the whole group. As dancers travel forward, there is a characteristic body sway from side to side, but not much bounce. In fact, the dancer should try to move as though carrying a water glass on the head, although traditionally young women modestly kept their eyes down.

Another body movement to be aware of, and another example of the folk process at work, occurs in *Sweet Girl,* a dance also known as *Siroon Aghchig.* For at least two decades, folk dancers have been bending forward on the clap (see beat 9 in the dance notes in *TFD*). However, Tom Bozigian, the Armenian dancer and teacher who choreographed and presented the dance in 1959, says there is *no bend* in this dance. He gives a speech about this at all his workshops and, as people do the dance, he shouts at the appropriate spot—just in case they forget—"Don't bend!" It is true that in most cultures there can be several interpretations or variations of traditional steps, but when the choreographer himself makes the correction, it is better not to argue. So, don't bend in *Sweet Girl!* There is bending, however, in other Armenian dances.

A characteristic Armenian dance step is the two-step, found in this series in *Soude Soude* and *Sweet Girl.*

The traditional dances tended to be more dramatic than today's more sedate ones. Interestingly, some of the choreographed Armenian dances done by the famous Soviet Moiseyev Folk Ballet, as well as those from other peoples, have been adopted back into the youth performing groups of the villages and émigré communities—a reverse form of the folk process (and one that most ethnic researchers deplore). Thus, many of the more complex Armenian dances done in recreational groups (not those we are discussing here) have strong folk ballet movements—straight legs, pointed toes, poised heads, and other staged gestures of display.

HANDS AND ARMS. In Armenian dances, arms and hands are equal partners with legs and feet. Arms are often in the W-position, with hands at shoulder height and little fingers interlocked—the "pinkie-hold" that is the most visible and important part of Armenian dance styling. This hold has evolved so as to allow the dancer to have the most freedom of arm movement possible while in contact with adjoining dancers. In some regions, for wedding festivities, the little fingers are dyed red with henna, and their joining symbolizes unity of the families. The shoulder-hold, or T-position, and the back basket-hold are also common positions.

These young dancers use the "pinkie-hold" in an Armenian dance, interlocking their little fingers by hooking the right pinkie under and the left pinkie over.
Photo by Zoltan Horvath

When interlocking little fingers, the dancers hook the right pinkie under and the left pinkie over. Forearms should be close to those of one's neighbors to avoid pulling or yanking on sensitive fingers, and wrists are a bit forward of the elbows. Often, when traveling forward, each dancer's left arm (still in pinkie-hold) is bent behind his or her own back.

In the shoulder-hold, generally the right arm goes behind and the left arm goes in front (see Chapter 15, p. 167, for an illustration). The hand of each arm should firmly grasp the adjoining dancer's deltoid muscle (at the top of the shoulder) with the elbow straight, not rigid, while the dancer maintains an erect body posture. Dancers should not hang heavily on one another but should hold their own arms up lightly to move with the body's movement. It is sensible to have people dance next to others who are approximately their size.

In *Toi Nergis,* men-only lines use the T-position; those at either end hold arms out to the side, palms down. In *Hooshig Mooshig* and in the women's lines in *Toi Nergis,* arms sway from side to side in relation to the footwork, like gentle windshield wipers. In other Armenian dances, especially the traditional ones,

Armenian Dances

women's hands and arms move in graceful, rounded ways, as in Oriental dances. Men's hands and arms are also graceful, but often move in stronger, straighter fashion.

MODIFICATION AND TEACHING TIPS. Armenian dances should probably not be attempted until students are comfortable being joined with arms in the W-position, so they can easily progress to the pinkie-hold. This is one of the main characteristics of Armenian dance and should not be modified. It helps to practice the hold with the little fingers joined for a while, talking through the steps of the dance without moving the feet, especially when pinkies must be unjoined and rejoined, as in *Sweet Girl*.

The only difficult step pattern of the dances here is the two-step in *Soude Soude* and *Sweet Girl*, which can be simplified at first to walking. However, the two-step should be soon added to the pattern. If a group is not developmentally ready for the two-step, probably these dances should be saved until they are.

As in almost all dance teaching, make sure students are successful with step patterns before adding hands and arms. This is especially true for the pinkie-hold, which can be quite distracting for adults as well as for young dancers.

MUSIC. Traditionally, the most common village instruments were the large drum called *davoul/tahul* and the primitive oboe, or *zourna*. Other village instruments were shepherds' flutes, tambourines, and lute-like stringed instruments. Some dances were not accompanied by musicians at all but done to traditional dance songs, called *bari-yerker*. In the cities, ensembles were larger and emphasized the less "peasant," more urban music of Europe and the Eastern cultures.

Today in the U.S., open circles snake around the floor to the sounds of clarinets, accordions, percussion, and electronic stringed instruments. However, there is a charming recorded version of *Hooshig Mooshig* played only on a somewhat tinny piano during a party, indicating that a piano can be appropriate for the classroom.

CLOTHING AND COSTUMES. The folk costume most associated with Armenians is a stage version of the traditional clothing worn by people who live in the Armenian Caucasus. For women, it is a dress with a flared skirt and long, narrow sleeves, sometimes with a jacket, and a headpiece that looks like a tiara with a long white veil down the sides and back. For men, this costume is a dark fitted suit and soft leather boots. For school programs, try short vests, sashes, and trousers and long skirts trimmed with rickrack. Soft footwear is appropriate—perhaps ballet shoes or the cloth "Chinese" shoes. Lead dancers

The traditional flowing dress, tiara, and long veil are seen on these dancers from Eastern Armenia performing at the Folkmoot USA festival in Waynesville, North Carolina.

can wield handkerchiefs. Girls can pin gauzy scarves to the back of their heads, and boys might wear hats shaped like those lamb's wool Russian ones. For quick changes over basic costumes, the short vests and sashes would give an Armenian flavor.

Armenian Dances

Resources Used for Chapter 5

Bozigian, Tom. 1972–94. Workshops, with accompanying syllabuses, in Chicago; Evanston, IL; Mukwonago, WI; Capon Bridge, WV.

Bozigian, Tom (producer). 1975, 1977, 1979. *Tom Bozigian Introduces Dances of the Armenian People* (GT 3001); *Tom Bozigian Presents Songs & Dances of the Armenian People, Vol. 2* (GT 4001); *Tom Bozigian Presents Songs & Dances of the Armenian People, Vol. 3* (GT 5001). There are notes accompanying these three record albums of this well-known Armenian dance teacher.

Bozigian, Tom. 1993–94. Conversations and comments on Armenian and Assyrian dances at Regional Camp, Mukwonago, WI, June 1993; at Buffalo Gap Camp, Capon Bridge, WV, May 1994; in letter and phone conversations, October 1994.

Lind-Sinanian, Gary. 1986, August. Armenian dance workshops, Stockton Folk Dance Camp, University of the Pacific, Stockton, CA.

Lind-Sinanian, Gary, and Susan Lind-Sinanian. 1982. "History of the Armenian Dance." *Viltis* (January–February): 5–13. The Lind-Sinanians are Directors of the Middle East Folk Arts Cooperative, 4 Belmont St., Newton, MA, 02158.

van Geel, Tineke. 1993, 1996. *Hayastan Armenian Dances* and *Armenia, General Information*. Booklets from Chicago workshops on "Dances of Armenia."

Assyrian Dances

Chapter 6 Assyrian Dances

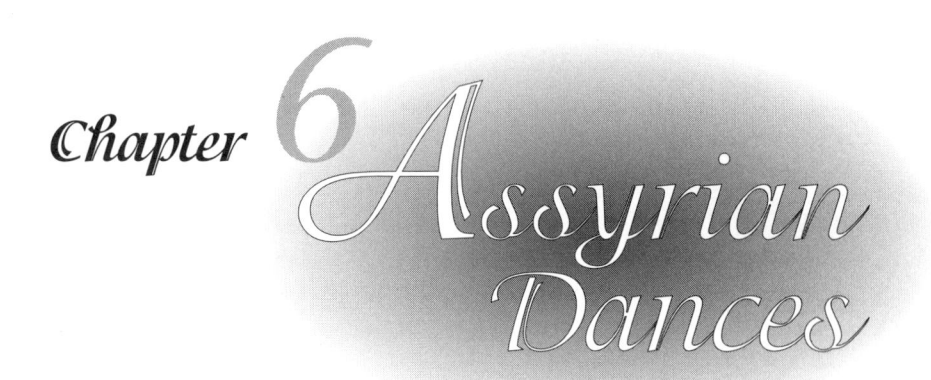

Assyrian Dance in Phyllis S. Weikart's Books

Sheikani, or *Sheikhani*   [shay-<u>CH</u>AH-nee] (Little Sheik, a boy's name meaning "come, be happy") *TFD, CH4*

The Assyrian people live in many different countries, but there is today no geographical place called Assyria. They are members of what is called a diasporic nation, meaning that they were forced to leave their land and disperse around the world. However, unlike other diasporic nations, such as the West Africans, the Armenians, or the Jewish people, the Assyrians no longer have a homeland they can return to.

The Assyrians—who should not be confused with Syrians, a different culture entirely—are an ancient Semitic people from the region around Mesopotamia, which is now modern Iraq. (Other Semitic cultures are the Arabs, Jews, and Ethiopians.) Two cataclysmic events were the cause of their permanent scattering throughout the world. In 1250 C.E., the brutal Mongol Tamerlane, following the example of his great-grandfather, Genghis Khan, swept through Asia to the borders of Europe, destroying everything in his path. Among the casualties were the Assyrian people, who were forced to retreat to the Hakkary Mountains of eastern Turkey, where they stayed for 700 years, until 1914.

Then came the dreadful period of the Genocide, when, like their Armenian neighbors, they were decimated by the Ottoman Turks. More than three quarters of a million Assyrians and a million and a half Armenians were reportedly killed. Those Assyrians who survived left the mountains and went down into southeastern Turkey, present-day Iraq. After 50 years there, they began their great migration. Today there are still Assyrians in Iraq, Iran, and Syria, but many have also emigrated to other continents. There are, for example, large communities in New Zealand and São Paolo, Brazil. In the United States the greatest number of Assyrians live in the Chicago and Detroit areas.

In many parts of the world, religion is closely connected to ethnicity; often the story of a culture's history is not complete without some mention of its ecclesiastical history. It is important for an understanding of the Assyrians' background to know that they are Christians who have lived for centuries as minorities in Moslem countries. Some are members of the Holy Apostolic Catholic Church of the East, the oldest Christian church in the world, founded in 33 C.E. and maintaining an unbroken apostolic succession to this day. Others belong to the Syrian Orthodox Church or are Roman Catholics. Some, who follow the liturgy in the Assyrian language, are called Chaldeans (not related to the ancient Chaldeans) and are members of a uniate church of Rome called the Chaldean Church of Babylon.

Because of their common Christian heritage as well as their geography and history, Assyrians and Armenians are sometimes linked together in people's minds. Indeed, they have often intermarried, and during the Genocide, until the enemy turned its attention to them also, the Assyrians did their best to hide and help the Armenians. The difference between the two peoples is that the Armenians are descended from an Indo-European race and are not a Semitic people.

Chicago has a sizeable Assyrian community. Here, some members of that community, wearing early-twentieth-century mountain clothing, are shown participating in the Soccer World Cup festivities.

Photo courtesy of Isho Balou

The Assyrian émigré communities are tightly knit, and dancing is one of the main threads that binds them together and helps them hold on to their culture, no matter how far from home they have traveled. In the United States, for example, each year during the Labor Day weekend there is a convention attended by about 6,000 people who dance for hours each night and some days. Three or four state-level conventions take place on other long weekends each year, and most Assyrian communities have at least one general dance party a month.

The one Assyrian dance in *TFD*, because it is not a choreographed number, but an authentic dance being done today by all Assyrians as well as by folk dance groups, is important enough to rate a chapter of its own. *Sheikhani* (in the phonetic spelling on p. 56, the underlining in "CHAH" indicates that the first two letters are pronounced with a soft gutteral) is sometimes called the Assyrian national dance; it is certainly the most popular, done more than half the time at every party. The description in *TFD* is the basic version, introduced to North American folk dancers by Dennis Boxell, a respected folk dance researcher, as well as by native dancers.

Other popular Assyrian dances are the *khigga*, which is similar to the pan-Balkan hora; the *balatee, goobareh,* and *toulama;* and 73 other identified patterns. These are all true traditional dances that were brought from the mountains before 1914. The Assyrians share some dances with the Armenians, and there are variants with similar names. Most Assyrian dances are ritualized war marches. This can be seen in *Sheikhani* as it moves dancers inexorably forward in strict formation.

Because it is a living dance, *Sheikhani* has innumerable variations. For example, in the Assyrian-American community in Cleveland, those from Iraq do it differently than those from Iran. A new style *Sheikhani* developed by Assyrians from Syria has a syncopated beat. As in other cultures, the younger immigrants have added more energetic movements, ones with hops and twists. All of these variations are rhythmically equivalent even if their steps are not identical, so people can and do dance different styles within the same line without disrupting their neighbors. Although there are no dances just for them, children are welcomed at the dance parties. They absorb their dance heritage by imitating their elders or just bouncing around in the middle of the group.

FORMATION. Almost all Assyrian dances are done in open circles or short lines, moving to either the right or the left. There are no couple dances. The lead position is an important and respected one. It is usually taken by a talented man—or now, in modern expatriate communities, by a woman—who flourishes a kerchief and embroiders the pattern with intricate movements. Everyone else, as is true in most western Asian and Balkan line dances, carries on with the basic step.

Sheikhani is best done in lines of about three to eight people, but it is also danced in a large open circle with the leader on the right.

STEPS AND MOVEMENTS. In *Sheikhani,* dancers are shoulder to shoulder, so their steps are necessarily quite tight, with up-and-down bouncy movements. On the traveling part there is a characteristic side-to-side rocking movement with the shoulders.

HANDS AND ARMS. To begin the dance, the dancers' arms are held straight down at the sides, with adjacent dancers' fingers interlocked and shoulders close, in the Arabic Kurdish style. On beat 6, as dancers each pivot to start the forward traveling step, the left arm bends behind to tuck its hand into the small of the back while holding the neighbor's right hand (this is illustrated on p. 192 of Chapter 17). On the last beat, dancers' hands are brought down into the original position as everyone faces center again.

MODIFICATION AND TEACHING TIPS. The footwork for *Sheikhani* should not be modified. Be sure students are at ease with the reverse two-step before introducing this dance. The pattern is short but a little tricky because it is asymmetrical, so it requires a lot of practice before adding the hand-holds.

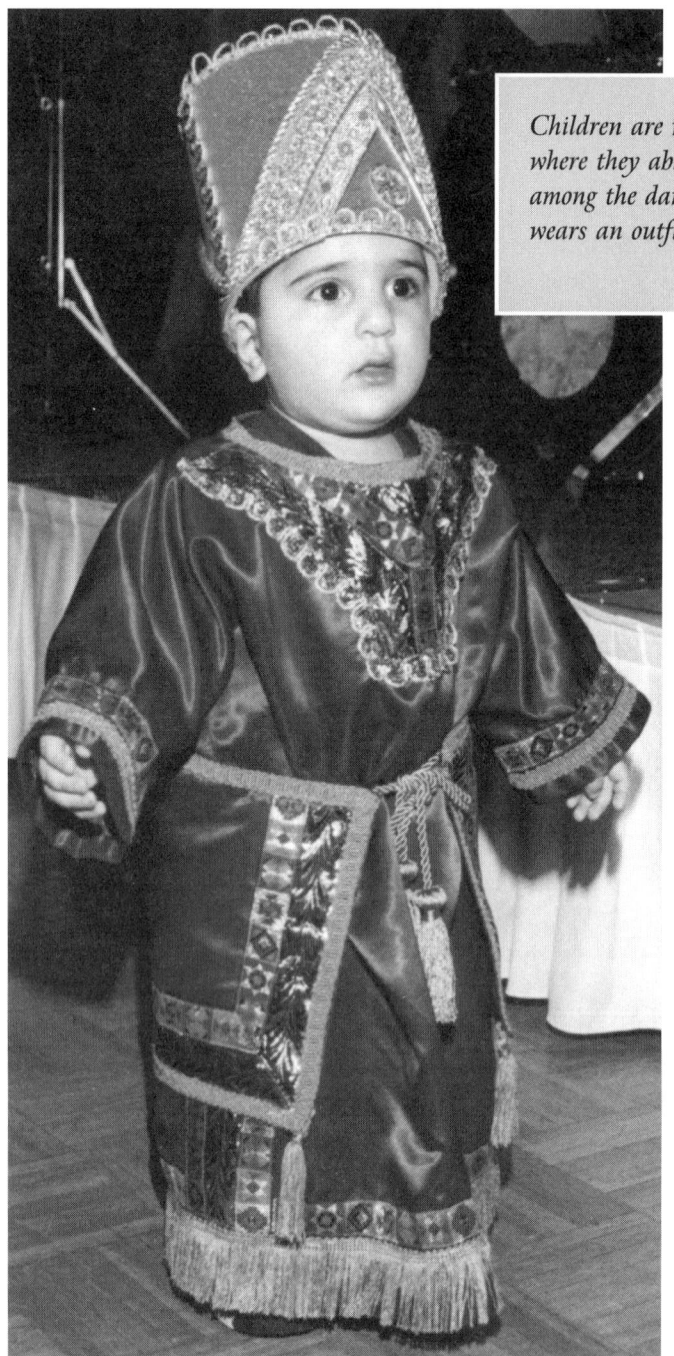

Children are welcomed at Assyrian dance parties, where they absorb their heritage as they wander among the dancers. This child at a dance party wears an outfit based on ancient Assyrian fashion.
Photo courtesy of Isho Balou

The hand-holds and arm-holds are as important to dances of this culture as the footwork is. If occasional twisted fingers cause anguish, it is possible for inexperienced dancers to omit interlocking fingers and to just grasp hands. Dancers should not stretch out their arms, however, and they should learn to bend left elbows to place hands in back when moving forward. Practicing holding fingers lightly will help them to swivel comfortably when changing direction.

MUSIC. Traditional instruments include the *ood,* similar to the lute; the *zurna,* a double-reed instrument; and hand drums called *dumbeg davul;* as well as the strong voices of the singing dancers. Today the music for the dances is played with plenty of percussion, electronic keyboards, and even accordions. The dancers sing, whistle, and enjoy themselves vocally.

CLOTHING AND COSTUMES. For school purposes, appropriate dress might be modified Turkish-style trousers (loose-fitting sweat pants, for example), long white shirts or tunics, sashes, scarves for the girls, and soft shoes for everybody. The basic Armenian costume would also be acceptable.

Resources Used for Chapter 6

Azarnia, Nader. 1990, 1993–94. Conversations on Assyrian dance. Nader is a folk dancer of Persian descent, born in Teheran.

Boxell, Dennis. 1977. Notes on Assyrian dances from University of Chicago 15th International Folk Dance Festival, Chicago, IL. Boxell is one of the earliest American ethnic dance researchers.

Bozigian, Tom. 1993–94. Conversations and comments on Assyrian dance. Bozigian is an Armenian dance teacher, choreographer, and performer.

Jasim, Peter. 1993–97. Conversations on Assyrian dance. Jasim is an Assyrian musician and folk dancer who was born in Baghdad and is one of the dance leaders in the Chicago Assyrian community.

Van Buren, Adina. 1993, November. "The Assyrians, An Ethnic Culture." Paper about the author's ancestry, submitted in an ethnic dance course, University of Illinois–Chicago.

Bulgarian Dances

Chapter 7
Bulgarian Dances

Bulgarian Dances in Phyllis S. Weikart's Books

(*Note:* Dance names are transliterated from the Cyrillic alphabet, so spelling variations might exist in other sources. Also, some English-language pronunciation keys do not correspond exactly to Bulgarian pronunciation; the phonetic spellings here are approximations.)

Baldâzka	[bal-DUHZ-kah] (Sister-in-law) *TM&D*
Bičak	[bee-CHACK] (Knife) *TM&D*
Bregovsko Horo	[BREH-goff-skoh hoh-ROH] (Horo from Bregovo) *TM&D*
Dajčovo Horo	[DYE-chaw-voh hoh-ROH] (A dajčovo-type of horo) *TFD, CD6*
Delčevsko Horo	[dell-CHEFF-skoh hoh-ROH] (Horo from Delčevo) *TM&D*
Dobrolŭshko, or *Dobroluško Horo,*	[doh-broh-LOOSH-skoh] *TM&D*
Eleno Mome	[eh-LEH-noh MOH-meh] (Dear Helen) *TFD, CD6*
Jambolsko Pajduško Horo	[YAHM-bowl-skoh pie-DOOSH-koh hoh-ROH] (Pajduško from the town of Yambol)
TM&D	
Kjustendilska Ruchenitsa, or *Râčenitsa*	[cue-sten-DILL-skah rah-che-NEET-tsa] (Râčenitsa from the town of Kjustendil) *TM&D (Note:* "Krustenkilska" spelling in *TM&D* is a typographical error.)
Kulsko Horo	[KOOL-skoh hoh-ROH] (Horo from the village of Kula) *TFD, CD5*
Lilka	[LEEL-kah] *TM&D*
Neda Voda Nalivala	[NEH-dah voh-DAH nah-LEE-vah-lah] (Neda was pouring water) *TM&D*
Novo Zagorsko Horo	[NOH-voh zah-GORE-skoh hoh-ROH] (Dance from the town of Nova Zagora) *TM&D*
Osmica	[ohs-MEE-tsah] (The eight) *TM&D*
Pasarelska	[pah-sah-RELL-skah] (From the town of Pasarel) *TFD, CD5*
Plevensko Dajčovo Horo	[PLEH-ven-skoh DIE-choh-voh hoh-ROH] (Dajčovo from the town of Pleven) *TM&D*
Porunceasca	[poh-roon-CHEEAHS-kah] *TM&D*
Pravo Horo	[PRAH-voh hoh-ROH] (Straight dance, one direction) *TFD, RM8*
Shopsko, or *Šopsko, Za Pojas*	[SHOHP-skoh zah POH-yahss] (Belt dance in Šop style) *TM&D*
Sitno Zhensko, or *Žensko*	[SEET-noh ZHEN-skoh] (Women's sitno, a dance with small steps) *TM&D*
Trŭgnála, or *Trâgnala, Rumjana*	[TRUG-nah-lah room-JAH-nah] *TFD, CD2*
Za Pojas	[zah POH-yahss] (By the belt) *TM&D*

Bulgaria is a small nation, rich in fine arts and folklore. A mountainous land about half as big as Kansas in the U.S., it is bounded by Romania, Yugoslavia, Macedonia, Greece, and Turkey and has a long, beautiful coastline on the Black Sea. Bulgaria is one of a group of countries sometimes known as the Balkan states (*Balkan* is a Turkish word meaning chain of wooded mountains). This southeasttern European region has been the center of quite a bit of turbulence in world history, situated as it is on both sides of the cultural chasm between Occidental and Oriental civilizations. (See Chapters 23 and 29 for more on this area.) Bulgaria is on the eastern side of the region. (See the map on p. 66.)

The first people in the area came from the Proto-Bulgarian, Slavic, and Thracian tribes. The Proto-Bulgarians were a tribe of warlike horsemen from central Asia who conquered and absorbed the inhabitants of the area that is still Bulgaria today.

The peoples of Bulgaria have a strong song and dance tradition dating back to before the start of their state in the seventh century. Like the history of many cultures in that part of the world, theirs is dominated by five dark centuries of Ottoman Turkish rule beginning in 1396. Instead of destroying their Slavic traditions, however, the Ottoman oppression forced Bulgarians to be more conscious of their heritage and to make efforts to preserve it. This was done secretly in the monasteries' underground "houses of culture" as well as quietly in homes and mountain hideouts.

With the help of its neighbors Russia and Romania, Bulgaria finally vanquished the Ottoman Empire in 1878 and became the Principality of Bulgaria shortly thereafter. Like others in that region, the Bulgarians next struggled through the Balkan Wars of 1912 and 1913, then through World War I and all the turmoil that led to World War II. After its monarchy was overthrown in 1944, Bulgaria became the part of the Soviet Bloc known as the Bulgarian People's Republic. In 1989 the people began to demand more voice in their government, and some volatile political years coupled with worsening economic conditions followed. In recent times it has once again become an independent nation. The President of the Republic of Bulgaria elected in 1992 is the country's first democratically chosen head of state since World War II.

After the defeat of the Ottoman Empire in the late nineteenth century, several scholars began to study the culture and traditions, including the songs and dances, that were preserved and honored through Bulgaria's many centuries of repression. Others have continued this work, and the Bulgarian government itself supported music and dance research and performance. There were government-sponsored folklore festivals, including the world-famous Koprivshtitsa Festival, a gathering of authentic Bulgarian folk song and dance groups that was held every five years and drew enthusiasts from every continent; recently the festival has had to find new funding. In their regular lives, although most Bulgarian communities no longer hold the traditional Sunday village-square get-togethers called *horos*, they still spontaneously sing and dance at weddings, fairs, and other celebrations.

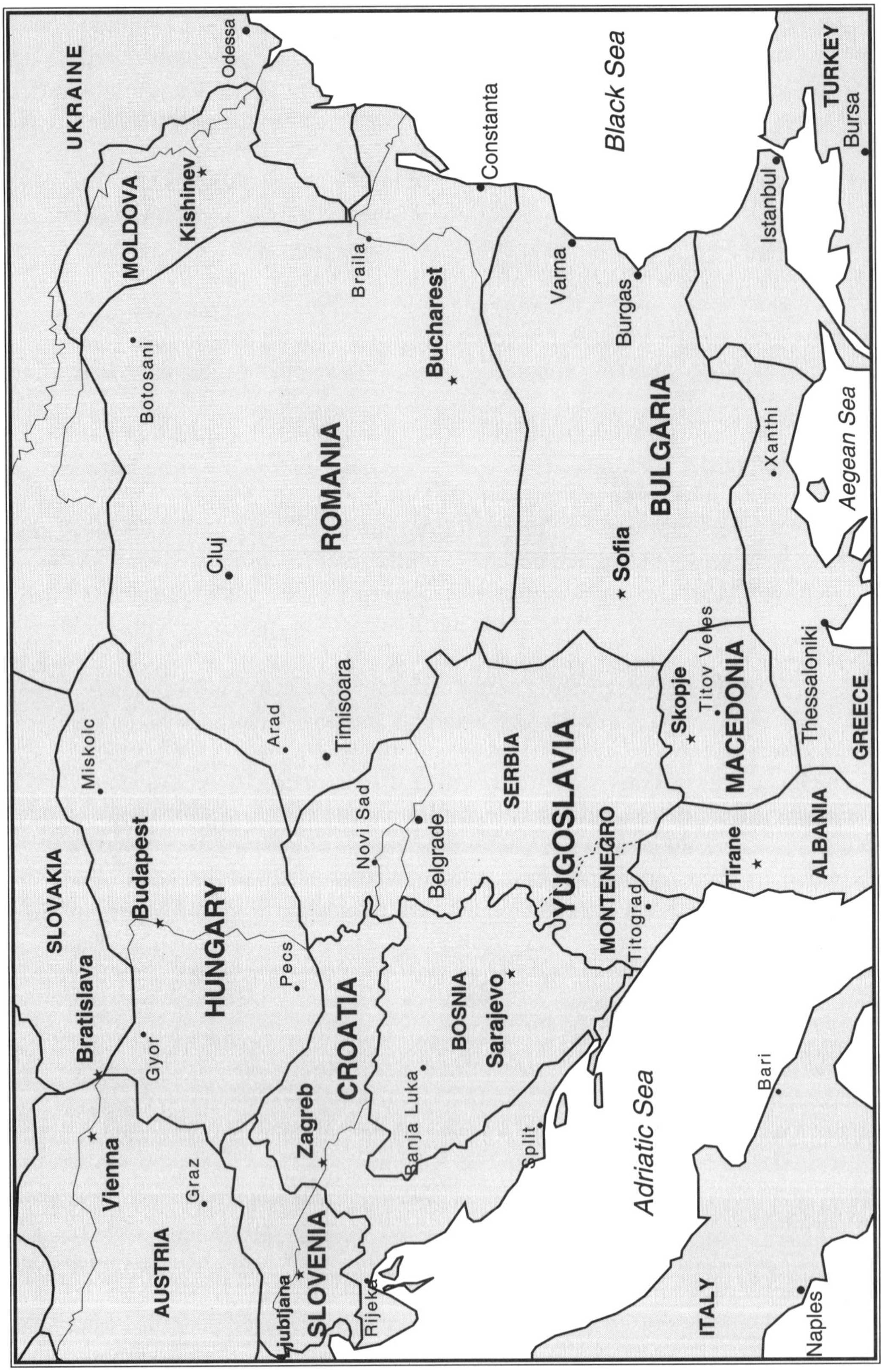
UKRAINE
Odessa
MOLDOVA
Kishinev
Constanta
Black Sea
TURKEY
Bursa
Istanbul
Braila
Varna
Burgas
Bucharest
Botosani
ROMANIA
BULGARIA
Xanthi
Aegean Sea
Cluj
Sofia
Titov Veles
Skopje
MACEDONIA
Thessaloniki
GREECE
Arad
Timisoara
Miskolc
SERBIA
YUGOSLAVIA
Novi Sad
Belgrade
MONTENEGRO
Titograd
Tirane
ALBANIA
SLOVAKIA
Budapest
HUNGARY
Pecs
Bratislava
Gyor
CROATIA
BOSNIA
Sarajevo
Banja Luka
Zagreb
Vienna
Graz
AUSTRIA
SLOVENIA
Ljubljana
Rijeka
Split
Adriatic Sea
Bari
ITALY
Naples

As a result of the respect for and continuation of Bulgarian folklore, there is a great deal known and notated about the traditional dances—much more than we will discuss here. Since the late 1950s, a number of North American ethno-choreographers have brought back from Bulgaria an exciting array of stage choreography and village dances for recreational folk dance groups in the U.S. and abroad. In recent years, former members of professional dance ensembles have traveled to North America, Europe, and Japan teaching more Bulgarian dances. These dances are among the most popular in the general repertoire, and to achieve the complex ones is the goal of many active folk dancers. Any reader with these aspirations should consult the end-of-chapter and end-of-book resource lists for detailed information and should try to regularly attend folk dance groups. The information in this chapter serves as general notes for classroom use or for those who'd like to sample Bulgarian folk dance.

There are definite regional differences in Bulgarian dances. For example, dances of the Šop area are usually fast and vigorous and performed higher off the ground than most dances of Thrace, which are slower and done with a lower, heavier step. Dances of the Pirin region, home of the Bulgarian Macedonians,

These members of the Brigham Young University International Folk Dance Ensemble enthusiastically perform a choreography from Bulgaria's Šop region.
Photo by Mark Philbrick

have the same subtle movements and rhythms as the Macedonian-style dances found in northern Greece (Greek Macedonia) and in the independent nation of Macedonia (formerly in Yugoslavia). The Romanian-influenced Vlach and Turkish-influenced Dobrudžan dances are exuberant and exciting, with many stamping patterns and accompanying arm movements.

The dances listed in this chapter cover all the regions just mentioned, but to enjoy them and be successful it is not absolutely necessary for students to achieve all the subtle regional styling differences. They should, however, understand the general movements of Bulgarian dance.

The *horo,* or chain dance, might be called Bulgaria's national dance. As mentioned earlier, traditionally, and up to very recently in rural areas, people gathered in their village squares every Sunday and holiday to gossip, eat, drink, and do horos. There are many variations in music, rhythm, formation, and pattern, which is what makes Bulgarian dance so interesting.

Men's styling and women's styling, which are influenced by societal mores as well as by clothing, differ in these dances. For example, women were expected to be modest and reserved yet strong and earthy, and this is reflected in their movements. Men worked hard and vigorously—and danced the same way. Traditionally, women wore long wool skirts, bodices, aprons, stockings, and headcoverings; obviously, in this clothing, they couldn't do the high leg-lifts of the men. Men wore wide sashes and Turkish-style (itchy) wool trousers that wound around their waists and thighs; this might be why many of their dances are done in a slightly squat position.

FORMATION. Horos are closed or open circles, with leaders primarily to the right. Men and women often dance mixed together. Nowadays anyone can dance next to anyone, but traditionally the best male dancer usually led, with his cronies alongside of him, the women next, and the older men at the end. In some villages, the married men led the line, followed by the married women, the single women, and then the bachelors.

There are also separate dances for women and men. The women's dances often started with a spontaneous song to which the women slowly began to move with grace and dignity, watched of course by the men. Then a man would signal the band, perhaps tucking some money into the leader's hatband or shirt, and he and the others would strut into the center in a competitive display of masculine strength and agility. There are almost no couple dances other than the popular *râčenitsa,* which is sometimes an open circle or line dance, sometimes a couple dance, sometimes even a trio dance. When two or three people dance together, they face, but do not touch, and communicate through the dance.

STEPS AND MOVEMENTS. In most Bulgarian dances, knees are slightly bent, steps are small and close to ground, and the upper body is proud and erect. Some dances have a heavy, semisitting feeling, especially for the men, although no such dances are represented in this series. In leg-lifts, men may lift their thighs parallel to the ground with relaxed ankle; women do not lift very high (remember those heavy skirts!).

ARMS AND HANDS. Horos can be done with arms in the W-position, in a belt-hold, in a front basket-hold, or in the V- or T-positions (see *TFD Glossary*). When using the belt-hold each dancer grasps the belt of the person next in line (many folk dancers have an extra belt hanging over their midriffs for this reason). For flexibility, it is best to hold the belt in the center, above the person's navel and close to the hand of the dancer holding this person's belt from the other side; holding a belt at the side is often awkward. Dancers should be cautioned to carry their own weight and not yank on one another's belts.

Generally arms and shoulders are relaxed, so they can feel the rhythm, although there are some dances that require strong, deliberate arm movements.

These dancers learning to use the belt-hold in a Bulgarian dance are attempting to hold the belt near the center, close to the hand of the person holding the belt from the other side.

Photo by Zoltan Horvath

Bulgarian Dances

69

MODIFICATION AND TEACHING TIPS. By the time students are ready for these dances, it should not be necessary to do any serious modification for them. Certainly, you should practice the rhythms first and should teach the dances in small segments. It is also a good idea to be comfortable doing one or two parts with the music before attempting the longer choreographies. But don't omit difficult steps, such as hop-step-step, because they're hard to learn. Rehearse them a lot with learner SAY & DO (from *TFD*) until students can do them, or wait until they are more experienced dancers. We recommend that teachers not try teaching Bulgarian dances in depth until they feel confident about their own ability to do them.

MUSIC. Bulgarian music is known for its assymetric meters, called by the Turkish term *aksak*. (*TFD*, on p. 78, uses the term "uncommon" rather than "assymetric" to describe such meters because, to many Western music-listeners, they are uncommon.) These meters are shown in the basic Bulgarian dance types represented here: the *pajduško* in 5/8 or 5/16 meter (for example, *Jambolsko Pajduško Horo*); the *râčenitsa* in 7/8 or 7/16 meter (*Kjustendilska Ruchenitsa, Pasarelska*), and the *dajčovo* in 9/8 or 9/16 meter (*Plevensko Dajčovo Horo, Lilka*). There is also the *gankino*, or *kopanica*, in 11/8 or 11/16 and, actually, the *pravo* in a 2/4 symmetric meter. Some dances combine meters; an example is *Bičak*, which is 14/16, a combination of 9/16 and 5/16. Other dances in this chapter may have the same meters but not the same labels as these just mentioned.

These meters are played by traditional instruments, such as the *kaval*, a reed pipe; the *gâdulka*, a bowed fiddle; the *gajda*, or bagpipe; the *tambura*, a fretted lute; the *tâpan*, a large two-headed drum; the *duduk*, a seven-holed whistle; and other whistle flutes. The *zurna*, a primitive oboe, and the ocarina are also used in some regions. These aren't just museum pieces, however. There are some excellent Bulgarian folk music ensembles, made up of non-Bulgarians as well as natives, playing these instruments in North America. Obviously it's difficult to duplicate these in the classroom, but various drums and recorders might be used to try out the exciting rhythms. Modern instruments that are popular for folk music are the accordion, clarinet, saxophone, and trumpet.

As in other neighboring cultures, the singing voice is an important instrument in Bulgaria. Southeastern European voice production, which may be unfamiliar to Western ears, has in recent years been brought to global attention through the recordings called *Le Mystère des Voix Bulgares*. These are, in reality, recordings of The Bulgarian State Radio and Television Female Vocal Choir from Sofia, Bulgaria. If teachers would like to learn more, they can find Balkan singing groups in many cities of North America, generally sponsored by the local folk dancers.

CLOTHING AND COSTUMES. Like people in many other countries, the various peoples who inhabit Bulgaria wear their traditional dress on festive occasions. For school programs, a generic women's costume could be a long-

A U.S. amateur ensemble wears generic costumes from two western Bulgarian regions.
Photos courtesy of the International Dancers of Chicago

A Bulgarian dancer wears the traditional head covering for married and adult women—a tied scarf with a rose tucked into it.
Photo courtesy of Penn State International Dancers

sleeved white blouse tucked into a calf-length skirt, with an apron showing a geometric or striped design. The blouse could also be worn under a long tunic, with a sash or wide belt, and knee socks in white, black, or red. Married and adult women cover their hair with a head scarf tied behind the head and often a flower tucked on the sides, but young girls wear a wreath of flowers or looped ribbons in their braids. A white handkerchief hung at the front of their belts also adds a real touch.

Boys can wear black pants; some kind of swirly pseudo-embroidery down the front would be really effective. White pants are also acceptable—but it will probably be difficult to get them to wear the traditional baggy ones! White long-sleeved shirts, black vests, striped or colored waistbands with belts over them, and white socks over the pants will also give a Bulgarian look. Black fur-like "Russian" hats would be extremely impressive.

For shoes, traditionally both men and women wear the typical soft, flat leather sandals called *cârvuli* (folk dancers use the Serbian name *opanki*). Regular black shoes or soft "Chinese" shoes will work fine. For belt dances, dancers should all wear a strong, thin leather belt over their sashes.

Resources Used for Chapter 7

"Bulgarian Folk Instruments." 1970. *Viltis* (October–November): 8–10. This is an article adapted from one by Ivan Kaculev, who at the time was a member of the Bulgarian Academy of Sciences.

"Bulgarian National Costume." 1970. *Viltis* (October–November): 11. This is an article adapted from one by Maria Veleva, who at the time was curator of the Ethnographical Museum in Sofia.

Cartier, Michel. 1981. "Bulgaria." *Viltis* (September–November): 6–15. This is one of a series of articles by a French-Canadian expert on Bulgaria.

Crum, Dick. 1986–95. Notes and discussions from many dance workshops given by this Balkan dance and folklore expert.

Eastern Europe Phrasebook. 1992. Victoria, Australia: Lonely Planet Publications. This is a handy book for a brief overview of the history and pronunciation of Bulgarian, Czech, Hungarian, Polish, Romanian, and Slovak.

Ilieva, Anna. 1977. *Bulgarian Dance Folklore*. Pittsburgh: Duquesne University Tamburitzans Institute of Folk Arts.

Jordanoff, Nicholas. 1991. Notes, lectures, discussions, conversations about Bulgarian dance during a course on Balkan dance and cultures at Duquesne University, Pittsburgh, PA, given in July 1991 by this former artistic director of the Duquesne University Tamburitzans.

Katzarova-Kukudova, Raina, and Kiril Djenev. 1976. *Bulgarian Folk Dances*. Cambridge, MA: Slavica Publishers.

Kavardjikova, Nina. 1995–97. Workshops and conversations with this Bulgarian professional dancer and teacher.

Kuharski, Michael. 1993–95. Conversations and workshops with this Balkan dance expert and leader of the Narodno ensemble from Madison, WI.

Kuteva, Maria. 1970. "Bulgarian Folk Song." *Viltis* (October–November): 7–8. This is an article by a member of the Bulgarian State Folk Song and Dance Company.

Moreau, Yves. 1969–95. Notes from many Bulgarian dance workshops given by this French-Canadian folklorist and Bulgarian folklore expert.

Moreau, Yves. 1981. "Folk Dances of Bulgaria." In *Syllabus of Mexico 27th International Folklore Festival*, December 1990–January 1991, abridged for presentation at Symposium on Bulgarian History and Culture, Carleton University, Ottawa.

Moreau, Yves. 1989–96. Comments and conversations.

Moreau, Yves (producer). 1997. *Bulgarian Folk Dances Introduced by Yves Moreau*. Vol. 1 and 2. Folklora Balkana FB–003 V. On these videotapes, popular ethnic dance teacher M. Moreau presents many of the dances that are described in *TM&D*. This is his video series showing him demonstrating many of the dances he has taught since 1967. (Contact Yves Moreau, PO Box 158, St-Lambert, Québec, J4P 3N8; <ymoreau@odyssee.net>.)

Sotirov, Ventzislav. 1991–95. Workshops and discussions with this former member of the Bulgarian National Folk Dance Ensemble.

Czech & Slovak Dances

Chapter 8 Czech & Slovak Dances

Czech & Slovak Dances in Phyllis S. Weikart's Books

Doudlebska Polka   [dood-LEB-skah] (Czech dance; Doudleby is a village in Bohemia) *TFD, RM2*

Horehronsky Czárdás   [hoar-eh-HRON-ski CHAR-dash] (Dance from the Hron Valley) *TFD, CD6*

The title of this chapter represents a sign of our times. When Phyllis S. Weikart first wrote her dance books, there was a European country called Czechoslovakia. It had been created in 1918, as part of the reapportionment of the Austro-Hungarian Empire after World War I. The main cultures in this hybrid land were the Bohemians, Moravians, Silesians, and Slovaks.

The country's subsequent history is complex and symbolic of the twentieth century turmoil in the eastern part of Europe. Two statesmen, Tomaš Masaryk and the priest Father Beneš, led their nation as a democratic government until 1938–39, when the country was occupied by Germany and Hungary, who partitioned the nation into several pieces. The country was liberated by the American and Soviet armies in 1945, and its eastern part was ceded to the Soviet Ukraine. In 1948 what was left of Czechoslovakia became part of the Eastern Bloc.

With the crumbling of the Berlin Wall in 1989 and the disintegration of the Soviet Union in 1991, the peoples of the Eastern Bloc countries began to strive again toward democracy and autonomy. In 1993 Czechoslovakia divided into two nations—the Slovak Republic, known as Slovakia, and the Czech Republic, which has not yet chosen a name. (See p. 78.)

Dances from the former Czechoslovakia should be described as Slovak or Czech, and even more specifically with the Czech dances, as Bohemian or Moravian. The noted Czech scholar and dance teacher František Bonuš has been mainly responsible for introducing folk dancers to dances of these cultures, although he is not the source for the two discussed in this chapter.

The peoples from this region have enjoyed dancing since far back in history, and they particularly enjoy couple dances. In the mid-1800s they were among the most enthusiastic practitioners of the polka, mazurka, waltz, schottische, and various figure dances. The *Doudlebska Polka* and *Horehronsky Czárdás* are good examples of the variety in this area and have been long-time staples of the folk dance repertoire.

Polka dances are particularly popular in central Europe. Although its name is connected to Poland, the polka is said to have originated in Bohemia in the 1840s. The legend is that a young peasant woman named Anna Slezak, upon getting a letter with good news from her boyfriend, jumped up and in her joy began to dance a simple, spirited rhythm. This dance, the polka, created a world dance mania, immediately becoming wildly popular all over Europe and North America. It was elaborated by dancing masters, choreographed for stage productions, and enjoyed in its more basic form by regular people. The polka does have variations among cultures, however. Polka styles in Russia, Germany, and Poland, for example, are all somewhat different, and they changed a little more when the polka got to the U.S. and Mexico.

Doudlebska Polka is a variant of a dance form that comes from both sides of the Czech/German language border. Going by the name *Stern Polka* and by still other names in Austria and Germany, all these variants have some kind of polka part, walking part, and clapping part. (*Stern* means star and refers to the

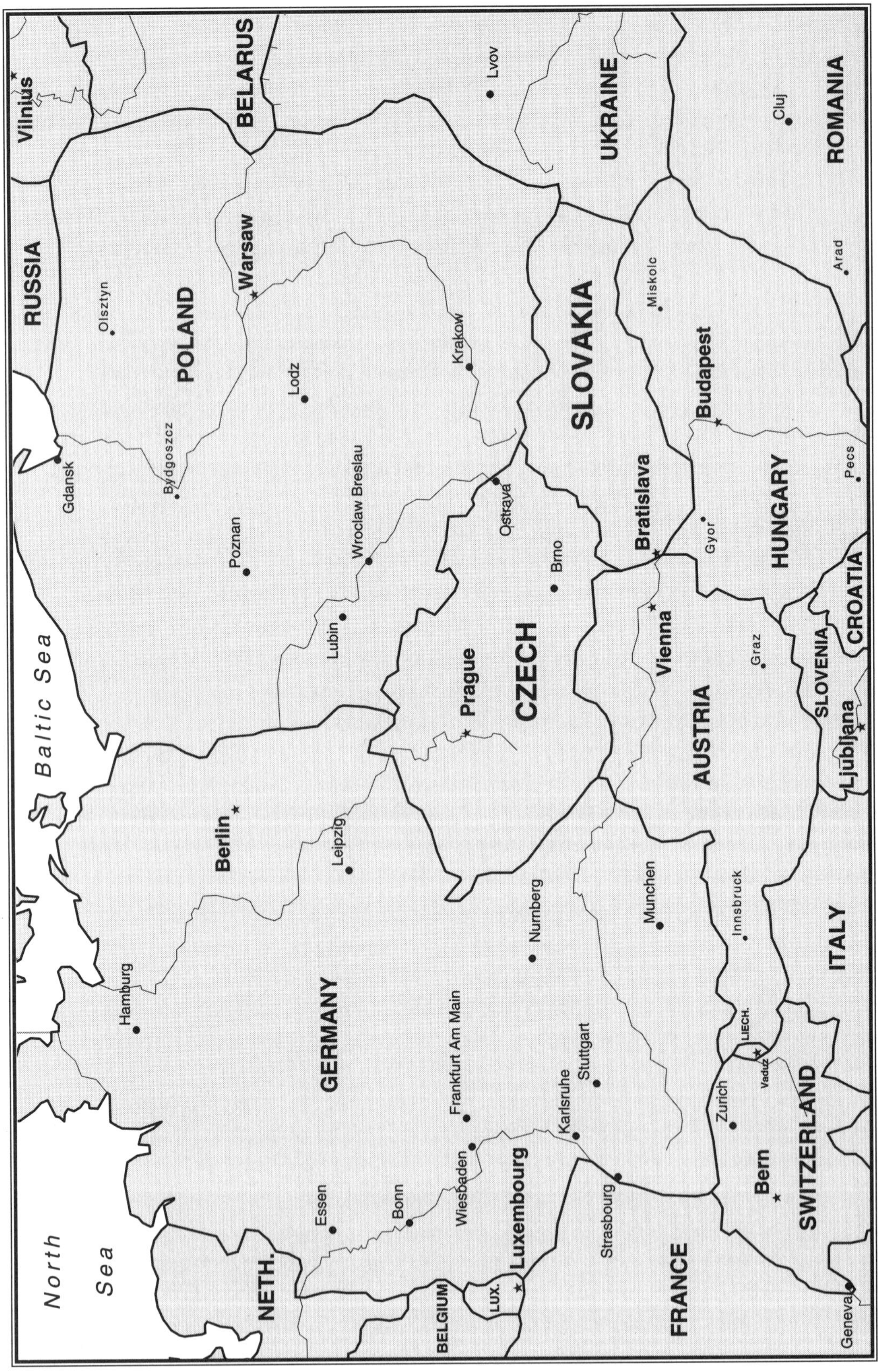
North Sea
Baltic Sea
RUSSIA
Vilnius
BELARUS
POLAND
Olsztyn
Warsaw
Gdansk
Bydgoszcz
Lodz
Poznan
Wroclaw Breslau
Lubin
Krakow
Lvov
UKRAINE
ROMANIA
Cluj
Arad
SLOVAKIA
Miskolc
Budapest
HUNGARY
Gyor
Pecs
Bratislava
Ostrava
Brno
CZECH
Prague
Vienna
AUSTRIA
Graz
CROATIA
SLOVENIA
Ljubljana
GERMANY
Berlin
Hamburg
Leipzig
Nurnberg
Munchen
Innsbruck
Frankfurt Am Main
Stuttgart
Karlsruhe
Wiesbaden
Essen
Bonn
Strasbourg
Luxembourg
LUX.
NETH.
BELGIUM
FRANCE
SWITZERLAND
Bern
Zurich
Geneva
LIECH.
Vaduz
ITALY

promenade circle in Part II of the dance.) The dance was known as the *Czech Polka* in Scandinavia and West Germany. In fact, at an international dance festival in Szeged, Hungary, in July 1989, one of the authors saw the West Germans performing this dance as theirs.

Doudlebska Polka was learned in Czechoslovakia by Jeannette Novak, a U.S. resident and folk dancer of Czech heritage who worked in Prague after World War II. When she returned to the United States, she taught it to her dance group and others. It was a big hit, made even more so when pioneer folk dance leaders Michael and Mary Ann Herman recorded and taught it. The story is told in a lovely letter from the 88-year-old Mrs. Novak in the 1995 *Folk Dance Problem Solver* (see Houston, 1993, 1995, in the resource list at the end of this chapter).

Since Slovakia shares a border and a history with Hungary, *Horehronsky Czárdás* has many of the characteristics of Hungarian dance, including a Hungarian name. (*Czárdás*, or *cárdás*, is the Slovak spelling; the Hungarian spelling is *csárdás*.) The czárdás is again today a living dance in Slovakia as a result of a revival of interest in traditional arts. The music for *Horehronsky Czárdás* is from

The peoples from the former Czechoslovak region have enjoyed dancing—particularly couple dances—since far back in history. This couple from the Slovak Republic show obvious enjoyment as they perform at the Folkmoot USA festival in Waynesville, North Carolina.

Czech and Slovak Dances

Young couples in Bratislava, Slovakia, enthusiastically dance a freestyle czárdás as musicians sing and play.
Photo by Robert Hruska

the upper Hron Valley. There is at least one other dance with a similar name but with steps that are somewhat more Slovakian. This version was introduced to U.S. folk dancers in 1967 by noted ballet dance expert Anatol Joukowsky.

FORMATION. Typical of dances from this area, the two dances are both circle formations. *Doudlebska Polka* is a hearty couple pattern, done as a mixer in North American recreational groups, and occasionally in Europe. The notes in *TFD* say merely "partners," meaning two people of any gender; in its traditional setting, of course, "partners" means male and female.

Horehronsky Czárdás is traditionally performed as a women's dance, of which there are many in the Slovak and Hungarian cultures. However, most recreational folk dance groups have begun to allow men to sneak into the circle (see the discussion in Chapter 2 on this issue). We prefer to keep this lovely dance for girls only and to teach the boys a dance for men (see the Hungarian *Mátrai Verbunk* in Chapter 15).

STEPS AND MOVEMENTS. Doudlebska-type dances are done much more sedately in Europe than in U.S. international dance groups, where there can be plenty of horseplay. Sometimes men fling women into the center and physically prevent them from escaping (in the past, this has gotten so out of hand that the dance had to be banned from some school programs). Women may "cheat" by polkaing flirtatiously within the circle and nabbing partners by choice instead of by chance. Extra women may join their sisters for the circling in Part III, to make sure they get a partner for the next round. Extra men may join during the promenade circle in Part II. These boisterous embellishments to the original dance are an example of the folk process and can be fun as long as the horseplay is kept within bounds. How teachers choose to present *Doudlebska Polka*—ethnically or rowdily—depends on the point of the lesson. It might be instructive to point out how the dance was changed in the United States.

Horehronsky Czárdás is a more subtle dance. The tempo and the intensity build to a satisfying finish. The most important point to remember is that dancers try to move with one another as much as possible. If men or boys are in the circle, they should keep their stamps quiet and their steps fluid, so this lovely pattern can truly remain a women's dance.

HANDS AND ARMS. In *Doudlebska Polka* hands and arms are strong and firm. Originally the polka part was done in shoulder-waist position (woman's hands on his shoulders, man's hands on her waist or mid-back), which may be more comfortable for classroom situations than the ballroom hold more commonly

These babičky (old women) wearing Slovak folk costume will take part in a women's dance.
Photo courtesy of Elizabeth Hanley

With hands in shoulder-waist position, young Czech dancers (the Czech men are hatless) enjoy a polka with dancers from others cultures during a festival week.

Photo by Mars Longden

done in folk dance groups. The clapping part, which is almost always done by folk dancers as described in *TFD*, is a good chance for improvisation. Traditionally, men also slapped thighs, crossed hands, and added other clapping embellishments. Traditionally, also, women put hands on hips while doing the clockwise polka around the circle.

In *Horehronsky Czárdás* hands and arms do not have a life of their own but follow naturally the movements of the body. Adjacent dancers' hands are joined down at the sides in the V-position. On the diagonal step, there is a tendency to raise arms as dancers move toward the center. This should not be done too abruptly or dramatically, as sometimes happens in folk dance groups.

MODIFICATION AND TEACHING TIPS. It would be difficult to modify either of these dances without losing the qualities that make them special. The difficult part of *Doudlebska* is the polka itself, which is not just a step but a partner dance that is meant to be a mixer. This means that students must be mature enough to dance with any partner who appears and at the same time not let the boisterousness get out of hand. However, it is possible to use this delightful music as a creative three-part polka for the littlest learners—a skipping part, a marching part, and a clapping part.

Horehronsky Czárdás has five patterns in this choreography. It would be natural to omit the most difficult part, but that would mean omitting the open *rida* step at the end, the moment toward which the whole dance has been building and one of the more authentic steps in this pattern. It is characteristic for the czárdás to have a slow part and a fast part. Probably this dance should be saved until students can achieve and appreciate it.

MUSIC. Certainly any three-part polka music or even just a strong polka beat would work for *Doudlebska*. However, it is meant to be danced to the music of the same name, and the special Bohemian quality of the several recordings is important to keep it from being just another polka. Traditional Bohemian bands play on violins, clarinets, double basses, horns, and trumpets.

The specific recordings for *Horehronsky Czárdás* should be used. The beautiful melody is one of the reasons for its continuing popularity. Slovak dances were done traditionally to sung music. Original instruments included violins and the hammer dulcimer called *cymbalom*. Gypsy musicians had great influence on Slovakian music and dance and, through their talents and their travels, are responsible for making the czárdás so popular in this region.

CLOTHING AND COSTUMES. There is, of course, a difference between the Bohemian and the Slovak clothing, but for school purposes, a

Czech and Slovak clothing varies. Vonnie Brown, Slovak dance expert, wears an outfit from the Čataj region of Slovakia; her partner is in Zemplín attire.

Czech and Slovak Dances

This photo shows the clothing worn by some Czech men as they perform at a dance festival in Szeged, Hungary.
Photo by Mars Longden

generic costume is acceptable for the girls for both dances; the boys should not be doing this czárdás in a program.

Girls could wear white blouses with full sleeves and perhaps lace trim, full skirts with wide petticoats underneath, lace-trimmed aprons, and possibly sashes or bodices. Traditionally, girls wore their hair in a long braid interwoven with ribbons. Black, red, or white knee socks or tights, and flat black shoes would work well.

For the polka, boys' shirts should be white, with cuffed, full sleeves, if possible, and perhaps some trim. Bohemian men wore yellow knee-length breeches, white stockings, and dark shoes or boots. Maybe khaki pants tucked into boots or into white knee socks would give a similar effect. Wearing a dark vest and a colored neck scarf or tie under the collar would be an authentic touch.

Resources Used for Chapter 8

Beliajus, Vytautus Finadar (Vyts). 1960. "The Story of Czechoslovakia." *Viltis* (March): 4–6.

Bonuš, František. 1983–93. Notes from dance workshops.

Brown, Vonnie R. 1993. "Slovak Folk Dances" (Parts 1 and 2). *Viltis* (September–October): 5–11 and (November–December): 7–10. Brown is a Slovak dance expert.

Brown, Vonnie R. 1994. "Slovak Folk Dances" (Part 3). *Viltis* (January–February): 12–15.

Eastern Europe Phrasebook. 1992. Victoria, Australia: Lonely Planet Publications. This is a handy book for a brief overview of the history and pronunciation of Bulgarian, Czech, Hungarian, Polish, Romanian, and Slovak.

Gottier, Karin. 1991–97. Letters and conversations, dance notes, and articles. Gottier is an expert in central European dance and costumes and director of the German Folklore Center in Middletown, CT.

Houston, Ron (ed.). 1993. "Doudlebska Polka." *Folk Dance Problem Solver,* 11–13. Austin, TX: Society of Folk Dance Historians. This article provides much background on *Doudlebska Polka.*

Houston, Ron (ed.). 1995. "Doudlebská Polka—Additional Information." *Folk Dance Problem Solver,* 7–9. Society of Folk Dance Historians. This article includes a letter from Jeannette Novak, collector of the dance.

Hruska, Robert. 1994–97. Conversations with this folk dancer of Slovak background.

Kornosova, Donka. 1997. Conversations with this Slovak speaker.

Lubinova, Mila. 1949. *Dances of Czechoslovakia.* London: Max Parrish & Co. This book is one of the Handbooks of European National Dances series produced by the Royal Academy of Dancing and the Ling Physical Education Association.

Danish Dances

Chapter 9: Danish Dances

Danish Dances in Phyllis S. Weikart's Books

Danish Masquerade — (sometimes spelled "Maskerade" or "Maskarade"; sometimes simply called *Masquerade*, or *Swedish Masquerade* or *Svensk Masquerade*) TFD, CD4

Danish Sextur, or *Familie Sekstur* — [fah-MEEL-yeh SEKS-toor] (six turns) TFD, RM5

Seven Jumps — TFD, RM2

Denmark is the smallest of the Scandinavian countries. Part of it extends like a hand off the "wrist" of Germany, and the rest floats in large pieces in several cold, stormy seas. (See p. 300.) In spite of this chilly geography, the Danish people are known for their special warmth, friendliness, and playfulness (Hans Christian Andersen and Victor Borge are good examples). This pleasant personality is reflected in their sociable dances, often called *familie* dances.

Danish dances are very much alive. Although some known by U.S. folk dancers were formally introduced by the late well-known Scandinavian folklorist Gordon E. Tracie, others have found their way into the general repertoire because someone enjoyed them at a Scandia get-together and showed them to their friends. The dances listed here were presented to the international dance community by folk dance leader Michael Herman and the late, well-known recreation specialist Jane Farwell, as well as by Gordon Tracie. *Danish Sextur* and *Danish Masquerade* are examples of two characteristic forms, the figured circle dance and the couple dance, and both are mainly simple social dances. *Seven Jumps* is a dance game, now done mostly by children, but originally danced only by men.

FORMATION. *Danish Sextur* is a circle dance performed by six couples—sometimes by more. *Danish Masquerade* is done by couples scattered around the floor but progressing in the same direction. Some dance notes wax poetic about how *Masquerade* symbolizes the peasants mimicking the aristocracy, which makes a good story but probably is not true. *Seven Jumps* is usually done in a single circle formation but can also be performed as a partner dance.

STEPS AND MOVEMENTS. *Danish Sextur* is a hearty dance. Steps are precise and brisk, making it possible to get from one figure to the next on time. They are also slightly heavy, with an emphasis on stepping down *into* the floor rather than lightly skimming over it. As will be described in discussing clothing and costumes, Danish women traditionally wore long, heavy skirts and aprons, which gave their dancing a weighted feeling.

Danish Masquerade has three clearly differentiated parts, each emphasizing a specific movement. The first part is a rather stiff and pompous march in which the dancers pretend to be members of the snooty aristocracy. Next is the super-graceful *tyrolervals,* mimicking the ladies and gentlemen in their fancy waltzes. Finally, the peasants do their own noisy *hopsa,* a step-hop polka. Part of the fun of this dance is the abrupt switch from the happy hopsa in the third part to the regal march, as dancers begin to repeat the entire dance.

Danish Masquerade is generally done as a partner dance, but some Danes do it as a mixer. The opening march progresses in one direction, and continuous cutting-in is encouraged until the waltz begins.

In *Seven Jumps,* the step-hop of Part I should be strong and sturdy. The nonweightbearing leg swings forward and across the hopping leg. Sometimes people omit the jumps and instead do eight step-hops in each direction.

HANDS AND ARMS. In *Danish Sextur,* hands of adjacent dancers are joined in the W-position. On the buzz turn, children are usually most comfortable using the shoulder-waist position, with the boy (or the taller partner) being the "waist person." "Shoulder-waist" is, however, a misnomer. In most dances that use this position, the waist person's hands actually should be not on the partner's waist, but above it, toward the mid-back. The hands are placed firmly—not clutching—with arms rounded and fingertips close. When the partner presses back a bit against those supporting hands, she can easily feel the subtle signals that guide her around the floor. This is how one person leads another in many dances. In *Danish Sextur,* this firm hand-and-arm position will enable the leading person to guide his partner into a smooth buzz turn in Part ID, then a flowing transition to open up into the next step of Part II.

The "shoulder person" is not a passive tool, however. Her hands are placed on the partner's shoulders with just the right amount of pressure—enough to make friendly contact and offer efficient resistance in the buzz turn, but not enough to restrict movement. Her arms are also rounded (there is a good illustration of rounded arms in Chapter 15, p. 168).

The three parts in *Danish Masquerade* each have a different hand and arm position, as described in the dance notes in *TFD*. In the first, arms are extended a bit and are a little stiff, in keeping with the military feeling of the march. The woman's free hand is on her hip, fingers forward. The man's free hand holds his lapel, shirt pocket, or vest armhole.

In the waltz part, the joined hands move forward and backward at shoulder level but do not swing; the free hands sweep backward and forward with the body's movement, exhibiting an exaggerated grace. The woman may do some ostentatious skirt-work.

In the hopsa part, inside hands are again joined at shoulder level, and outside hands are on hips, fingers forward. In keeping with the more peasant feel of this part, hands and arms are strong and solid in contrast to the gracefulness of the waltz.

When enjoying *Seven Jumps* in the circle formation, dancers join hands in the V-position for Part I. When dancing as couples, face and join both hands. For the cumulative figures, of course, hands are not held.

MODIFICATION AND TEACHING TIPS. *Danish Sextur* can be simplified quite a bit without losing its point—six couples having fun with alternating figures. The notes for *Danish Sextur* in *TFD* have suggestions for simplifying Parts II and III. In Part ID, you probably will also need to simplify the buzz turn: For this turn, just substitute walking 16 steps around. In addition, it might be better not to teach all the parts immediately, so dancers can concentrate on the tricky give-and-take of Parts II and III. Add additional parts when your students are ready.

The "shoulder-waist" position is misnamed. As these dancers show, the leading person actually holds his partner firmly at mid-back, not at the waist, while the following partner places her hands with friendly weight on his shoulders. All arms should be rounded.

Photo by Zoltan Horvath

The insert below shows a modified version of *Danish Sextur* for any number of couples that teachers might also find useful and enjoyable. Called *Familie Sextur,* or *Danish Family Circle,* it was introduced by both Jane Farwell (mentioned on p. 89) and Gordon Tracie, who taught the version he saw in Sweden. This is the version usually done at folk dance groups and events.

The *Danish Masquerade* partner dance should probably not be modified. Instead, save this dance for when your students are mature enough to appreciate its satire and to be comfortable waltzing with a partner—or at least *next* to one. However, it's wonderful music for practicing changes in tempo and rhythm and could be used that way for any class that is ready to move in 3/4 meter.

MUSIC. Danish music, which uses instruments familiar to western European and North American ears, emphasizes strings. As indicated on p. 88, *Danish Sextur* is recorded on *RM5; Danish Masquerade,* on *CD4;* and *Seven Jumps,* on *RM2.* It is also possible to reproduce the music for these dances in the classroom with piano, percussion, and other instruments.

A Modified Version of
Familie Sextur *

FORMATION: Partners in a single circle, facing toward center to begin. Hands are joined in W-position.

ACTION:

MEASURES 1–8: **Figure 1—Buzz steps first time through, buzz swing thereafter.** All take 16 buzz steps to the left (circle moves CW), starting on right foot. (The buzz step is like the buzz turn but done individually, without a partner.)

MEASURES 9–16: **Figure 2—Walk in and out.** All walk 4 steps into the center, starting on right foot, then 4 steps backward, going out from the center; repeat in and out.

MEASURES 17–23: **Figure 3—Grand right and left.** Partners do grand right and left to 7th person, counting own partner as "1." Take 2 steps per hand-clasp. Stop with "7" (the 7th partner), and use the last measure to get ready for the buzz swing.

When dance begins again with Figure 1, partners should buzz swing together.

*Notes by Sanna Longden based on those of the late Jane Farwell in *Folk Dances for Fun* (Delaware, OH: Cooperative Recreations Service, Inc., 1960), pp. 20–21.

The long skirt, long apron, and sleeveless bodice are traditional Danish dress for women. Men wear knickers, white shirts, vests, and sometimes a top hat, sometimes a tasseled red stocking cap.

CLOTHING AND COSTUMES. Girls could wear a long skirt with a long apron over it, a sleeveless bodice over a long-sleeved blouse, and a bonnet. Suggested colors are green, red, and yellow, favorites of Danish women.

Boys can wear knickers in yellow, white, or black, with knee socks. Put up the collars on their white shirts, and knot a colorful handkerchief underneath. Add a vest, maybe a jacket over that (cold country!)—both with silver buttons, of course—and on their heads, a tasseled red stocking hat or a black top hat. Both men and women wear low black shoes with silver buckles.

Danish Dances

Danish dancers pose in regional clothing. The man sports the commonly seen red stocking cap.

Resources Used for Chapter 9

Duggan, Anne Schley, Jeanette Schlottman, and Abbie Rutledge. 1948. *Folk Dances of Scandinavia* (Folk Dance Library Series). New York: Ronald Press. This book has basic dances and background information.

Farwell, Jane. 1960. *Folk Dances for Fun*. Delaware, OH: Cooperative Recreation Service, Inc. Jane Farwell was one of the people who popularized *Danish Family Circle*, (another name for *Familie Sekstur*), which she describes on pp. 20–21 of her book.

Foreningen til Folkedansens Fremme. 1991. *Håndbog over trin og udtryk i dansk folkedans* (Handbook of Steps and Expressions in Danish Folk Dances). Copenhagen: Author.

Geslison, Jeannette, 1996–97. Conversations with this native of Denmark, who is also a teacher of folk dance at Brigham Young University, Provo, UT.

Gottier, Karin. 1993–94. Comments and conversations with this expert on European dance.

Gudmand-Høyer, Kamma. 1995. "Danish Folk Costumes." *Viltis* (September–October): 6–8.

Harris, Jane A., Anne M. Pittman, and Marlys S. Waller. 1994. *Dance Awhile*, 7th ed. New York: Macmillan International. This book has descriptions of *Familie Sekstur* (with counting in Danish) and *Danish Masquerade*.

Houston, Ron (ed.). 1993. "Sekstur and Sextur Dances." *Folk Dance Problem Solver*, 49–53. Austin, TX: Society of Folk Dance Historians.

Houston, Ron (ed.). 1993. "(Svensk) Maskerade." *Folk Dance Problem Solver*, 36–37. Austin, TX: Society of Folk Dance Historians.

English Dances

Chapter 10 English Dances

English Dances in Phyllis S. Weikart's Books

Cumberland Square	(sometimes called *Cumberland Square Eight*) TFD, RM3
Hole in the Wall	TFD, RM4
Sellenger's Round	TFD, RM7

The prehistoric megaliths of Stonehenge in southern England indicate that the area known as the British Isles was inhabited by a developed culture long before it became part of the Roman Empire in the first century B.C.E. After the Roman occupiers departed, Britain's earliest invaders—the Celts—and its post-Roman invaders—the Germanic tribes of Angles, Saxons, and Jutes—inhabited England as a collection of uncouth warring kingdoms. Then, in 1066, the Battle of Hastings brought William the Duke of Normandy from France to reign as King of England. With him came a semblance of order and manners that initiated many of the political and cultural traditions still existing in England today.

The country of England is actually one of four political subdivisions of the United Kingdom of Great Britain and Northern Ireland; the others are Northern Ireland, Scotland, and Wales. (See the map on p. 98.) Scotland came under the British Crown in 1603 with the accession of James I, son of Mary Stuart and cousin of Elizabeth I; it united with England and Wales as Great Britain in 1707. Ireland, which had been conquered in the early 17th century, became part of the United Kingdom of Great Britain and Ireland in 1801. Great Britain also gradually extended its rule to the Far East, Africa, India, and the Americas through colonial and economic expansion. This far-flung empire began to weaken during the industrial revolution and World War I, and many colonies gained independence following World War II. Today, the United Kingdom continues to hold a number of small territories in the Caribbean, the North and South Atlantic, and the South Pacific.

England was known as a great dancing nation for much of its history. Morris dances and sword dances are recorded as far back as at least 1400 C.E., and there is evidence of other ritual dances much earlier than that, perhaps thousands of years earlier. The Medieval processionals and Renaissance country dances, two of which are described here, were an important part of every community's activities.

During Tudor times, both aristocracy and country folk enjoyed round dances on the green. Henry the VIII and his daughter Elizabeth I loved to dance and encouraged it. There is a legend that Queen Elizabeth made a certain gentleman the Lord Chancellor because he danced so beautifully and wore green bows on his shoes.

In the Puritan years of the mid-seventeenth century, public dancing was discouraged, but people continued to dance in their homes. When the Stuarts were restored to the throne in 1660, dancing began to be very fashionable. Dancing masters were hired to give instruction to ladies and gentlemen in the long ballrooms of their large houses. Described by the term "longways," these dances "for as many as will" were developed with many intricate figures, and they eventually spread to other countries. Early U.S. settlers brought them to New England, where they took firm root and flourished, and today we know their evolved forms as the popular contra, or barn, dances.

By the end of the eighteenth century, the industrial revolution had created a growing middle class, and this had an effect on the development of English

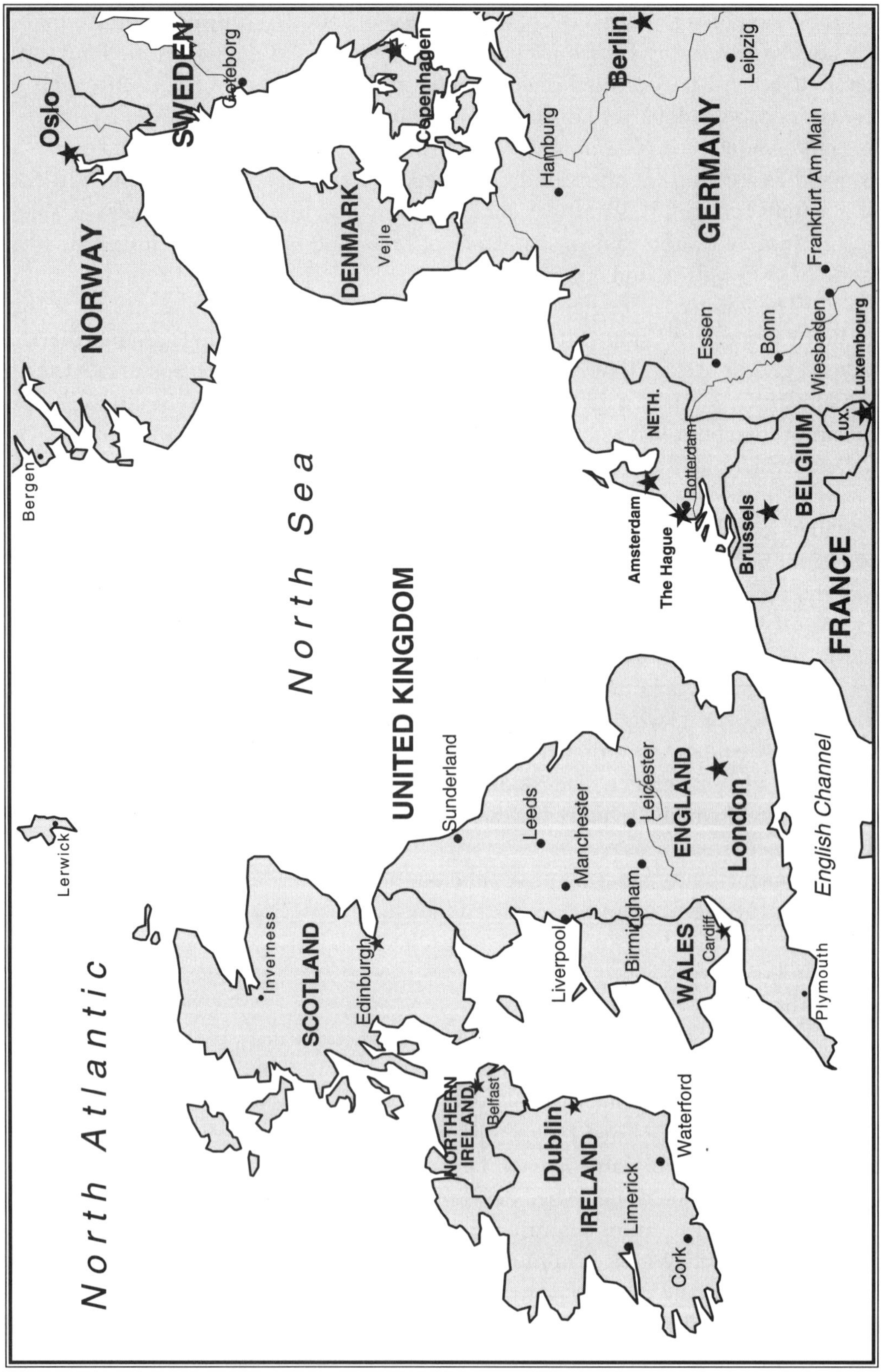
North Atlantic
North Sea
NORWAY
Oslo
Bergen
SWEDEN
Goteborg
DENMARK
Vejle
Copenhagen
GERMANY
Berlin
Hamburg
Leipzig
Frankfurt Am Main
Essen
Bonn
Wiesbaden
Luxembourg
LUX.
NETH.
Amsterdam
The Hague
Rotterdam
BELGIUM
Brussels
FRANCE
UNITED KINGDOM
Lerwick
SCOTLAND
Inverness
Edinburgh
Sunderland
Leeds
Manchester
Liverpool
Birmingham
Leicester
ENGLAND
London
WALES
Cardiff
Plymouth
English Channel
NORTHERN IRELAND
Belfast
IRELAND
Dublin
Waterford
Limerick
Cork

English Morris dances and sword dances, which we still see today, are recorded at least as far back as 600 years ago. Here, the International Dancers of Chicago triumphantly show their successfully woven "nut," or "star," at the completion of the **North Skelton Sword Dance.**

dances. Country dancing became a popular activity at large commercial resorts, such as Bath, but the intricate figures were simplified and standardized so a crowd of vacationers could enjoy this recreational activity without first having to be carefully coached.

However, along with courtly dances like the minuet, country dances rapidly declined in popularity at the beginning of the nineteenth century, when the exciting waltz glided across from the Continent to the English ballrooms. After discovering the possibilities of dancing in close embrace with a partner, no one wanted to merely touch fingertips any more. Next the exuberant polka bounced onto the scene from Bohemia in the 1840s and created a European dance mania. At that point, country dancing all but disappeared for almost 75 years.

English Dances 99

Country dancing revived in the early twentieth century under the strong guidance of an English lawyer and musician named Cecil Sharp. After coming across some Morris dancers in 1899, he was inspired to look into the archaic dances of his nation, and his research uncovered thousands of manuscripts from past centuries. As founder and president of the English Folk Dance Society, he was responsible for starting a new wave of appreciation for English country dances in both England and the United States, based on his reconstruction and interpretation of the dances in these manuscripts as well as in other sources. The English Country Dance and Song Society and the Country Dance and Song Society of America, along with other fine instructors and researchers, have continued his work. One measure of the extent of the English country dancing revival in this country is the present count of Morris dance teams—they now number about 200 in the U.S.

Although teachers using this book may be more familiar with English country dances than with dances from some other cultures, we have included a large amount of dance background in this chapter. Because students enjoy the familiar movements and music, many educators teach a lot of these friendly dances along with their easier "cousins," the traditional American dances. Knowing some of the historical background and styling details of such dances should make them even more interesting and exciting to students.

English country dancing, like U.S. barn dancing, is a very social form of dance. While there are specific styling points, the way that dancers relate to one another as the patterns progress is equally important. It is what makes this form of dance especially fun.

Country dances are also useful for lessons in socialization. Sibyl Clark reported in *English Folk Dancing for Schools* (1956), "I know of one headmistress of a mixed school who started country dancing because the boys and girls behaved so badly out of school when they met. After a month of mixed dancing, she had no more complaints on this score."

The three dances described here represent two types of English country dances, the **traditional** and the **historical**. Traditional dances are those that have been handed down informally. People learn them while dancing at community events and teach them to others. Generally, the patterns are easily learned and have standard figures that recur within and throughout the dances. Through the years the dances have of course changed (the folk process at work), so for a given tune, there might be varying dance patterns, and these might have either the same or different dance names. These traditional dances are particularly good for introducing students to figure dancing.

Cumberland Square is a well-known traditional English square dance, named for a county in northwest England, on the border of Scotland. It was introduced to U.S. folk dancers by May Gadd, an English transplant who was our foremost authority on English country dancing from her arrival in the U.S. in 1927 until she died at the age of 89 in 1979.

Hole in the Wall and *Sellenger's Round* are among the best known of the historical dances. These interesting and more complex patterns come from a collection of 104 dances and tunes first published in 1650 (dated 1651) by John Playford, an English bookseller and musician. His work, *The English Dancing Master,* went through 17 editions, the last dated 1728. Many of the English country dances done today come from this collection, thanks to Cecil Sharp's research, and are referred to as Playford dances. *Hole in the Wall* appeared first in the 1721 edition, and *Sellenger's Round* is from the earlier, fourth edition dated 1670.

FORMATION. The three dances discussed here represent three different traditional formations: a square for four couples, a longways "for as many as will," and a round dance for any number of couples. The round dance is the most archaic, which makes it historically interesting, since today most country dances are not done in circles.

STEPS AND MOVEMENTS. Most modern English country dance notes begin by saying that this type of dancing should be "completely natural." This means, of course, natural to people of European and North American cultures—teachers in Tangier, Tokyo, or Tehran might interpret this instruction differently. A relaxed, musical movement to the beat, the rhythm, and the phrasing is what to strive for. Dancers should not come to a full stop at the end of each phrase but should hold themselves in readiness to smoothly move into the next pattern.

The point of these dances is group movement and flowing motion. Emphasis should be on dancing with a partner—on how the dominant person guides and the following partner responds, how each pattern flows into the next, how each couple fits into the set, and how each set relates to the others around them.

As in so many other cultures, the movements are affected by what the dancers are wearing. The traditional dances like *Cumberland Square* have been enjoyed through many centuries of fashion changes, so the instruction to move naturally would be appropriate whether dancers were wearing bustles or blue jeans. The Playford dances, however, were originally done by people in fairly constricting clothing. In their tight bodices, heavy petticoats, and elaborate hairdos, aristocratic ladies curtsied by bending from the knees and not the waist. Gentlemen were also somewhat bound by girdles and waistcoats, but they could bow from the waist and extend an elegant, silk-hosed leg. The peasants, in their traditional dances, were more relaxed in dress and movement, but for all historical dances, we say to move with grace and dignity (sometimes we say, "It looks like Grace has gone home!").

A specific figure in these dances is the cast-off. This is executed in *Hole in the Wall* at the beginning of the movement pattern, when the #1 couples turn away from their partners to walk behind the #2 couples, and then this is repeated

English Dances

Following the instruction to "move naturally," the Goodman Theatre of Chicago players get into the spirit of a traditional English dance.

by the #2 couples; the movement pattern also ends with a cast-off by the #1 couples. The cast-off occurs in many historical dances and usually needs a lot of practice, because there is a tendency for beginners to take a shortcut down the center of the set rather than turn away from their partners to the outside. An added traditional touch is the preparatory dip toward the partner on the inside foot while turning away—when done well, this is a lovely motion.

Sellenger's Round has the characteristic *doubling, siding,* and *arming* figures of the Playford dances. These are described in Playford's first edition and in many later manuals on English country dance. An interesting note about siding is that some modern dance historians believe that Cecil Sharp misinterpreted this figure. Although most people are still doing it the way Sharp described it, which is the way it is described by Playford, you may find a few people doing the following alternate figure when the cue is for "siding": Toward partner's right shoulder, FWD, FWD, FWD, TOUCH; BWD, BWD, BWD, TOUCH; repeat to other shoulder. This alternate is actually easier to teach and might have been the traditional way.

Another interesting point about movement in historical dances is the bow to the Presences before the dance begins. Many of the sixteenth- and seventeenth-century melodies have an 8-beat or 12-beat introduction. For half of this music, the dancers give a deep reverence or bow toward the top of the room, where the royalty or high-ranking aristocrats would be sitting, smiling benignly on the assemblage. In the other half of the introductory music, partners bow to each other. If the music has a similar *coda* at the end, dancers finish by bowing again to partners and then to the Presences. This acknowledgment of the Presences is not only fun (you can put nondancing students or visiting administrators on the throne), but it sets up an authentic ambience that encourages historic role-playing and better teamwork.

HANDS AND ARMS. In all figure dances, hands and arms are as important as footwork, because it is with hands and arms as well as with the face that dancers communicate. Look at your partner at all times—sometimes we say "eyeball to eyeball"—and smile. Really reach and really grasp, as though you're happy to be dancing with this other person. Keep the active hands and arms up and ready for the next movement. Inactive arms can hang loosely down at the side.

In *Cumberland Square* or other traditional dances, when couples slide across the set, they join hands with arms out to the sides. The stars are made by each person joining hands with the person diagonally opposite, traditionally girl with girl and boy with boy (same-gender partners are okay unless dancing in role or on television).

To form a back basket, girls join hands in the center of the set, and boys join hands above the girls' hands. Then boys raise their joined hands and bring them down behind the girls' backs; girls then bring their joined hands up and over and down behind the boys' backs. To do a buzz turn in this position, point the right foot toward the center and pivot on it (as on a scooter) as the circle revolves clockwise (CW); it helps the spin if dancers lean back a bit on the joined arms.

When walking or skipping clockwise, which is sometimes cued as "circle left," dancers in the set form a circle by all joining hands, with elbows slightly bent. To give weight, each individual in the circle leans back a bit, so the circle moves smoothly. Promenade in any comfortable promenade hold; children probably prefer the skater's, or cross-hand, hold, but some instructions say arm in arm, and some suggest the varsovienne position (see the Glossary in *TFD*).

After the initial cast-off in *Hole in the Wall*, partners' inside hands are joined, with the dominant partner actually leading the other up or down the set. When the #1 man and #2 woman (or their respective partners) change places by passing right shoulders, they should turn toward each other—never turn backs—as they go by, and they should smile!

In *Sellenger's Round*, all dancers join hands, with elbows slightly bent, when slipping CW and slipping CCW (often called circling left and circling right) and when moving in and out of the center. On the elbow turns, or arming, each person should give weight by slightly leaning away from the partner, so there is a tension and balance between partners as they go around.

English Dances

MODIFICATION AND TEACHING TIPS. These dances should not need much modification. By the time your students are ready to dance in groups of couples, they will probably have mastered most of these movements. In *Cumberland Square,* the basket with the buzz step is the hardest figure; perhaps you could teach the whole dance without that figure, possibly repeating the stars, until they are successful. Then practice the basket without the buzz, and the buzz without the basket. Without a lot of practice, even adults have trouble combining the two movements.

Hole in the Wall is the most sophisticated of these three dances, but it is too beautiful to modify. The cast-off and progression (movement of couples up and down the set) are often confusing to beginners and need much rehearsal, particularly in *Hole in the Wall,* because this dance ends with couple #1 casting off and then starts over immediately with the same couple casting off again. It would help if students first had experience with the easier American progressive dances (see the *Progressive Circle Dance* and *Soldier's Joy* in *TFD* as well as the Hendrickson publications listed at the end of this chapter) or with some easier English dances (see Martha Riley's publication in the same list).

Because it has no progression, *Sellenger's Round* is usually one of the English country dances people are first taught. When students can do a two-step, they can be taught the setting step and then will probably enjoy this entire dance.

MUSIC. One characteristic of English country dances is the many beautiful dance melodies. Most traditional dances can be danced to a variety of traditional tunes. For example, *Cumberland Square* (which is a dance but not a musical selection) is often danced to such tunes as *My Love Is But a Lassie Yet* or other 32-bar reels or jigs. These can be played on classroom instruments with great success.

The historical dances usually are connected with specific tunes of the same name. *Hole in the Wall* is a lovely baroque triple hornpipe from a suite by Henry Purcell and lends itself wonderfully to recorder playing. *Sellenger's Round* is a simple and spritely seventeenth-century jig. The *Rhythmically Moving* series includes recordings for all three of these dances, and there are other good recordings available, including some using period instruments.

CLOTHING AND COSTUMES. For period costuming, children may be more comfortable in peasant dress. For the girls, this means long skirts with tucked-up ruffles around the hips, laced-up bodices, and bonnets or mob caps; for the boys, this means smocks, knickers, and wool caps. All wear heavy shoes.

If they'd like to be more aristocratic, the girls might add lace at neck and wrists, pile up their hair, paste on beauty spots, widen their skirts, put on graceful shoes and a haughty but pleasant expression. The boys should also have lace at the wrists, along with fancy waistcoats, long jackets, hats with feathers, buckles on their heeled shoes, and a dignified but charming demeanor.

Wearing one version of period costuming, actors in a Goodman Theatre of Chicago production enthusiastically perform an early-nineteenth-century English dance.

The International Dancers of Chicago used this simple modern English country dance costume when quick change was required.

English Dances

Resources Used for Chapter 10

Arbeau, Thoinot. 1589, reprint 1967. *Orchesography.* New York: Dover. This is the classic reference for anyone interested in historical dances.

Clark, Sibyl. 1956. *English Folk Dancing for Schools.* London: Cecil Sharp House. Today's children are not the same as those Clark wrote about, but this book has useful information about the dances.

Country Dance and Song Society. *Country Dance & Song Society News.* This is *the* source for English and Anglo-American traditional dance, music, and song. (Contact CDSS, 17 New South Street, Northampton, MA 01060; 413/584-9913; <office@cdss.org>; <http://www.cdss.org/>.)

Duggan, Anne Schley, Jeanette Schlottmann, and Abbie Rutledge. 1948. *Folk Dances of the British Isles* (Folk Dance Library Series). New York: Ronald Press. Written for an earlier generation, this includes some dances of England with history, step patterns, and costumes.

Greenleaf, Sarah. 1976. "The English Country Dance." *Viltis* (January–February): 14–15.

Hendrickson, Charles Cyril. 1989. *Early American Dance and Music: A Colonial Dancing Experience, Country Dancing for Elementary School Children.* Sandy Hook, CT: The Hendrickson Group.

Hendrickson, Charles Cyril, with Frances Cibel Hendrickson. 1989. *Early American Dance and Music: John Griffiths, Dancing Master, 29 Country Dances, 1788.* Sandy Hook, CT: The Hendrickson Group.

Hyde, Dale. 1983. "English Playford Dances." Notes for this recording on *Hit & Misse* album by Passamezzo Players. Dancecraft LP 123324.

Keller, Kate Van Winkle, and Genevieve Shimer. 1994. *The Playford Ball,* 2nd ed. New York: Dover Press. This book contains 103 early English country dances with background by two of the experts in the field.

Kerlee, Paul. 1993. *Welcome in the Spring: Morris and Sword Dances for Children.* Danbury, CT: World Music Press. This is an excellent resource with dance descriptions, musical transcriptions, and Orff arrangements, plus recordings for practice and performance.

Riley, Martha Chrisman. 1988. *English Country Dances for Children,* Vols. 1–3. Delphi, IN: Riverside Productions. These give good information on background and teaching, with dances increasing in difficulty. Comes with cassettes, six dances on each. A 1995 videotape of children doing the dances is also available. (Contact the author at P.O. Box 26, Delphi, IN 46923.)

Senior, Tom. 1994–97. Conversations and instructions from this Chicago English country dance teacher, as well as his notes in the syllabus of the Regional June Camp held 8–10 June 1997 in Mukwonago, WI.

Sharp, Cecil J. 1984. *Country Dance Tunes,* revised edition. North Hampton, MA: Country Dance and Song Society.

Sharp, Cecil J., 1985. *The Country Dance Book, Parts 1 & 2.* North Hampton, MA: Country Dance and Song Society.

Sharp, Cecil J., and George Butterworth. 1985. *The Country Dance Book, Parts 3 & 4.* North Hampton, MA: Country Dance and Song Society.

Sharp, Cecil J., and Maud Karpeles. 1985. *The Country Dance Book, Parts 5 & 6.* North Hampton, MA: Country Dance and Song Society.

French Dances

Chapter 11 French Dances

French Dances in Phyllis S. Weikart's Books

An Dro [ahn DROH] (a line dance from Britanny) *TM&D*

Bannielou Lambaol, or *La Ridée* [bah-NYEH-loo lahm-BAH-ohl; lah rree-DAY] (Banners of Lampaul; a line dance from Brittany) *TFD, RM8*

Gavotte d'Honneur [gah-VOHTT dunn-HEHRR] (a type of gavotte, from Brittany) *TM&D*

Le Laridé [luh la-rree-DAY] (The laridé; a line dance from Brittany, usually referred to as just *Laridé*; also may be known as *Laridé de la Côte* [duh lah COAT]—the laridé of the coast) *TFD, CD6*

Branle Normand [branl nor-MAHN] (a branle from Normandy) *TFD, RM6*

The dances of France include an interesting variety of styles and formations. France's geographical differences are clearly reflected in its dances—the Germanic couple dances from Alsace, the Spanish-like dances from the Pyrenees, the longways figure dances from central France, the line dances from Celtic Brittany. (See p. 130 for France and bordering countries.) It is common for French dances to be described with regional labels: "This is a French dance from the Auvergne." "That is a French dance from Upper Berry." "Here is a French dance from Brittany." (You may not find some of these regional names on a modern map, however. Names like "Berry" and "Auvergne" are those of provinces that existed before 1790; some atlases show both the modern and the historical provinces.)

It is probably not necessary to get too specific when first introducing elementary students to these dances. But if you are making curriculum connections, it would be interesting to use a map of this exciting country to show why some of the music of Brittany sounds so Irish and why some of the dances of Provence feel so Italian.

Although most French dances are done in couples, all of the dances discussed in this chapter are line dances, and most are from the westernmost province of Bretagne (Brittany). These are among the most ancient dances we know, direct descendants of the simple *branles* of the Middle Ages. Details of these branles and other dances of the fifteenth and sixteenth centuries have been preserved in the classic and delightful book *Orchesography*, which was written by an elderly churchman named Thoinot Arbeau and first published in 1589 (see the Chapter 10 and end-of-book resource lists).

Many of these line dances are also being done today at community dance parties called *festou noz* (literally, night feasts). This is a result of the recent revival of traditional Breton culture, particularly that of Lower Brittany, which is closely connected to the Celtic peoples.

Typical forms of Breton dances include the *ridée*, or *laridé*, and the *gavotte*. Because these are still living dances, other patterns with the same or similar names also exist.

Except for *Bannielou Lambaol,* the other Breton dances were introduced to North American folk dancers by Yves Moreau, a well-known ethnic dance expert who learned them in Brittany when he was director of a cultural exchange group from Montreal. Germain Hébert, a noted French dance researcher, first presented the children's game *Bannielou Lambaol* in the mid-1960s. (For everything you wanted to know about this dance, plus a transcription of the music, see Ron Houston's 1991 *Problem Solver.*) *Branle Normand,* named for France's northernmost province of Normandy, is characteristic of the archaic branles that are simple rounds, open or closed, and related to Balkan and Scandinavian chain dances. It was reconstructed by Madame Jeanne Messager of Caen and taught to Madelynne Green, a popular folk dance teacher, who presented it to U.S. folk dancers at camps and workshops in the early to mid 1960s.

The names of *An Dro* and *Bannielou Lambaol* are Celtic, a language related more to Irish and Scottish Gaelic than to French. Students will understand this when they see the geographical proximity of Brittany to the British Isles and connect the sound of the names.

Gavotte d'Honneur is a more complicated pattern than the ridées, although related to them. In Europe there are many different kinds of gavottes, ranging from circles and lines to partner gavottes and figure dances. *A gavotte d'honneur* was traditionally a competition dance. In fact, in Brittany even today, a champion dancer is as admired as a sports hero!

FORMATION. One of the main styling points to remember about the ridées and gavottes of Brittany is that they are open circles with the leader on the left and that they almost always progress clockwise, which is not the case in the majority of round dances in the folk dance repertoire. (You may come across articles that attribute movement that is clockwise—or sun-wise, as the Europeans say—to pre-Christian sun-worship ceremonies; it's an intriguing concept, but not everyone agrees with it.) This is also true of most branles, although *Branle Normand* is a closed circle and moves counterclockwise.

STEPS AND MOVEMENTS. *Bannielou Lambaol* can be described as a work dance, because some of its movements are supposed to mimic washing clothes in a stream. According to fakelore (as opposed to authentic folklore), the horizontal push and pull of the arms shows the clothes being scrubbed, and the little lift on the side step to the left is said to symbolize stepping over a stone in the water. Whether or not this is true, the stone story might be a good way to teach this unusual movement. (Imagery is always a good way to make a point when teaching a dance movement. In *Orchesography,* Arbeau (1589) described a movement as "scraping the foot backwards along the ground as if one were treading down spittle or killing a spider" (p. 181).

These side steps and arm movements, however, are characteristic of ridées in general and appear, with slight variations, in *An Dro* and *Le Laridé*. Because the dances originated on the wild Breton coast, some notes describe such actions as showing waves rising and falling—a lovely thought but probably an overly romantic one, since these movements are also done by people who live on waterless mountain plateaus. Generally, there is a bouncy, somewhat jaunty feeling to the movements. The rhythm of the music drives the pattern and may take a little time to feel correctly. The smooth coordination of leg and arm movements is part of the challenge and the fun of ridées.

Gavottes have vigorous movements, but feet should stay close to the ground. In Part I of *Gavotte d'Honneur,* the body is in a slight sitting-in position with knees a bit bent. Feet are apart with the inside toes pointing toward the center, and the movement is quite springy. Part II has heel clicks, the left heel against the right foot, on beats 1, 2, and 8. These additional rhythmic sounds are made by the wooden shoes, or *sabots,* that people from France as well as from other parts of central Europe used to wear.

*Members of a **folklorique** group from southern France, wearing the traditional **sabots** on their feet, acknowledge the crowd at the Folkmoot USA festival in Waynesville, North Carolina.*

French Dances 111

HANDS AND ARMS. As suggested already, arms are as important as legs in the ridées. The forward circling and pushing-pulling of the arms is described in the notes for the specific dances in *TFD* and *TM&D*. On the arm swing in *Le Laridé*, it is important not to lock the elbows, but to keep them relaxed and slightly bent. Arms should not flop back and forth, but should keep accurate timing; this may require concentration, because the rhythm of arms and legs is not always the same.

In *An Dro, Bannielou Lambaol,* and *Le Laridé,* as well as in other Breton round dances, dancers are linked by their little fingers. Bodies should be kept close, almost shoulder to shoulder, so no one gets yanked apart from the others. In *Gavotte d'Honneur* and *Branle Normand*, adjacent dancers hold hands firmly in the W-position; even the leader and end person keep their free hand up at shoulder level.

MODIFICATION AND TEACHING TIPS. These dances probably should not be modified. It is better to teach *Branle Normand* with the step-hop, so when students can do that, they can do the whole dance. The hop of each step-hop can be left out initially if, by so doing, the pattern can more easily be established. In fact, the original French directions call for "4 *pas marchés*" (four walking steps). The coordination required in *Bannielou Lambaol* is the interest as well as the challenge of that dance and cannot be separated from the steps. Once students master it, they are physically ready for *An Dro* and *Le Laridé*.

However, these ridées are rather sophisticated dances in spite of their seemingly simple patterns. The wholistic beauty of movement, song, camaraderie, and appreciation of culture is what makes these dances so attractive and is thus important to convey along with the patterns.

The gavotte can stand on its own as a dance without having to evoke the ambience, but it needs a good deal of dance experience to master. By the time your students can do this energetic dance, they should be excellent dancers.

MUSIC. Many Breton dances are accompanied by singing, either with or without a traditional band. The *Rhythmically Moving* recordings have good versions of *Bannielou Lambaol (RM8)* and *Branle Normand (RM6)*. The melody for *Branle Normand*, which is *Mon Pere Avait un Petit Bois*, comes from a collection printed in Caen, Normandy, in 1615. *Le Laridé* is recorded on *CD6*. Also, *An Dro* and *Le Laridé* can be done to songs on the recordings of an exciting Breton folk musician named Alan Stivell (do *Le Laridé* to the song *Tri Martolod* and *An Dro* to several, including *Pachpi Kozh*). These two dances and *Gavotte d'Honneur* can actually be done to any song in the ridée or gavotte rhythm, although there is a recording called *Gavotte d'Honneur* that most people use.

Traditional instruments include the *biniou*, a type of bagpipe; the *bombarde*, a rustic oboe or reed instrument; the Celtic, or Irish, harp; and the *vielle*, or hurdy-gurdy. The button accordion and various percussion instruments are more recent

Some of the traditional instruments are carried by these musicians leading a festival parade in France. They play (from left to right) the hurdy gurdy, the button accordion, and the bagpipe.

additions. The tunes are usually simple and catchy and can be produced on classroom instruments, even those without the characteristic reedy sound. At the least, everyone should sing "la la la" along with the extremely singable melodies.

CLOTHING AND COSTUMES. The piece of clothing that identifies a French costume as Breton is the woman's stiff lace headdress, which can come in many varieties of height and elaborateness. Norman women also wear high, intricately devised bonnets. So, to distinguish clothing of these regions from the pan-European peasant costume that may be efficient for school programs, you may want to provide these lace confections for the girls—or let them construct them and compete for the fanciest. The Breton man also has nice headgear—a black felt hat with a ribbon around the crown and down the back. The Norman man may wear a black fedora or a cap similar to the Greek fisherman's headgear.

French Dances

The International Dancers of Chicago perform a dance from central France. The men wear blue tunics, red ties, and gaiters, while the women are in simple generic outfits for quick changes on the street.

Otherwise, use the usual long skirt, puffed-sleeve blouse, bodice, and low black shoes for the girls. The boys can top their long pants and white shirt with a short jacket instead of a vest or with a blue tunic with a red tie, for more authenticity. They can also wear the sabots mentioned earlier or other wooden shoes.

Resources Used for Chapter 11

Gottier, Karin. 1991–97. Comments and conversations on northern and central European dance; also a course at Duquesne University, Pittsburgh, PA, July 1991.

Houston, Ron (ed.). 1989. "(Le)Laridé." *Folk Dance Problem Solver,* 30–31. Austin, TX: X-Press.

Houston, Ron (ed.). 1991. "An Dro." *Folk Dance Problem Solver,* 4. Austin, TX: Society of Folk Dance Historians.

Houston, Ron (ed.). 1991. "Ridée." *Folk Dance Problem Solver,* 40–41. Austin, TX: Society of Folk Dance Historians.

Houston, Ron (ed.). 1992. "Gavotte d'Honneur." *Folk Dance Problem Solver,* 22. Austin, TX: Society of Folk Dance Historians.

Houston, Ron (ed.). 1992. "Ridée— Additional Information." *Folk Dance Problem Solver,* 43. Austin, TX: Society of Folk Dance Historians.

Moreau, Yves. 1980–. *Dances of Brittany (Bretagne).* This is the author's syllabus used at camps and workshops.

Moreau, Yves. 1991–96. Comments and conversations.

Sainsard, Andrée, and Françoise Pierre. 1973. *Costumes folkloriques provinces françaises [French Provincial Folk Costumes].* Paris: Fleurus.

Tennevin, Nicollette, and Marie Texier. 1951. *Dances of France: Provence and Alsace.* London: Max Parrish & Co. This is one of the Handbook of European National Dances series produced by the Royal Academy of Dancing and the Ling Physical Educational Association. The books include information on culture, music, and costumes and dance descriptions with color plates. The series is an excellent source for background but may be dated as to what's going on today.

French-Canadian Dances

Chapter 12 French-Canadian Dances

French-Canadian Dances in Phyllis S. Weikart's Books

La Bastringue   [lah bah-STRAYNG] *TFD, CD2*

Les Saluts   [lay sah-LEU] *TFD, RM1*

Because the center of French-Canadian culture is the Province of Québec, the culture is referred to as Québecois. French-Canadian dances are hearty and humorous, like the people from which they come. Other major cultures in Canada have dances similar in formation but with a decidedly more English or Scottish flavor. (This is a good spot to remind ourselves that Canada is as much a part of America as is the U.S.—and as are Mexico, Panama, and Brazil. To be correct and respectful of other cultures, we should be careful to identify people as North, Central, or South Americans and to not say "America" when we mean the United States.)

Besides the *gigue,* or jig, which is a specialized type of step-clog dance, other typical Québecois dances are quadrilles, round dances, reels, cotillions, and dancing games. Originating in the British Isles and France, these various dances also are similar to traditional U.S. dances and playparty games, with some small differences. No French-Canadian quadrilles appear in *TFD* or *TM&D,* but two of the round dances *are* included in these books, and therefore we describe them here.

Generally in French-Canadian dances the most important thing is not every small detail of the pattern, but the communication and enjoyment of the people as they move through the pattern.

Both round dances in Phyllis S. Weikart's books were introduced to recreational folk dancers by Yves Moreau, a researcher, teacher, and performer of Bulgarian dances who also teaches the folk dances of his native Québec and of Brittany. *La Bastringue* is one of the most popular folk dances in the recreational repertoire. It is choreographed to an amusing French-Canadian party song that tells of an old man who asks a young woman to dance—and then admits his feet are too sore (see the insert on p. 120 for the text of the song).

Les Saluts is actually a small part of the long quadrille *Le Saratoga*—still done today on Orleans Island in the St. Lawrence River near Québec City. The pattern in *TFD* was arranged by Richard Turcotte of Québec as a modification for younger children of a traditional dance. It is extremely useful for teaching children to walk to the beat, change direction, position themselves, coordinate arm movements, and listen to the music.

FORMATION. Most Québecois dances require partners, although the formations vary from closed circles to longways lines to quadrilles and other kinds of set dances.

La Bastringue is a couple mixer, done in a closed circle of couples with everyone facing toward the center. The woman begins on the left side of the man, which is uncommon, so original partners—presumably the two who chose each other—can dance together once before moving on to dance with others. In its traditional form, this dance should be done with a partner of the opposite gender, so it is probably more appropriate for students who are mature enough to enjoy mixing and who are comfortable with the ballroom swing. A modified version is also described on p. 121.

La Bastringue

Mademoiselle, voulez-vous danser	Miss, will you dance
La bastringue, la bastringue?	La bastringue, la bastringue?
Mademoiselle, voulez-vous danser?	Miss, will you dance?
La bastringue va commencer.	La bastringue is starting.
Oui, Monsieur, je veux bien danser	Yes, Sir, I like very much to dance
La bastringue, la bastringue.	La bastringue, la bastringue.
Oui, Monsieur, je veus bien danser	Yes, sir, I like very much to dance
La bastringue, si vous voulez.	La bastringue, if you wish.
Mademoiselle, il faut arrêter	Miss, it is necessary to stop
La bastringue, la bastringue.	La bastringue, la bastringue.
Mademoiselle, il faut arrêter;	Miss, it is necessary to stop;
Vous allez vous fatiguer!	You will get tired!
Non, Monsieur, j'aime trop danser	No, sir, I love too much to dance
La bastringue, la bastringue.	La bastringue, la bastringue.
Non, Monsieur, j'aime trop danser.	No, sir, I love too much to dance.
Je suis prête a r'commencer!	I am ready to start again!
Mademoiselle, je n'peux plus danser	Miss, I cannot dance any more
La bastringue, la bastringue.	La bastringue, la bastringue
Mademoiselle, je n'peux plus danser,	Miss, I cannot dance any more,
Car j'en ai des cors aux pieds!	Because I have corns on my feet!

Les Saluts can be done several ways. In its original partner formation, the two partners begin in separate circles, and when the circles join, they dance next to, rather than actually with, each other. It is best to save this version for older children and adults. Because it also can be done in a very simplified form, however, *Les Saluts* is appropriate for even the youngest children. A simplified form is described in *TFD*, but the patterns for the traditional version of the dance are described in the insert on p. 122.

STEPS AND MOVEMENTS. French-Canadian dances are particularly comfortable for students in the "Lower 48" (another way to describe the continental U.S.), because the movements are very much like those of U.S. traditional dances—not so "foreign." In the two dances listed here, dancers generally need only to move strongly and confidently on the well-defined beats.

However, there is a styling comment to make about *La Bastringue.* Because it feels so familiar and is so popular in the U.S., most people dance it as though it originated in the mountains of Appalachia—a good example of the folk process in action. When done by French colonists, however, it was a more sedate dance. In Part I, for example, the original Québecois-style IN, IN, IN, TOUCH has evolved in U.S. folk dance groups into a broader and noisier IN, IN, IN, KICK accompanied by loud shouts of enthusiasm.

In addition, originally there wasn't any clogging done during the dance, but because of the exuberance of the music, clogging is hard to resist. It is true that French-Canadians are famous for a particularly vigorous form of clog dancing, but they usually don't do it in *La Bastringue.* (The foot tapping that can be heard in some of the recordings is not clogging, but only the musicians keeping the beat.) However, after conscientiously telling your students all of this, let them enjoy the dance in their own rip-roaring style.

HANDS AND ARMS. In *La Bastringue,* the man raises his left arm and turns his partner under it once or twice before the buzz turn. It works well to turn the woman clockwise (away from the center of the circle) to make a smooth transition into the swing. However, some men just naturally turn their partners the other way; as usual, the woman takes cues from her partner.

In the final promenade—the eight CCW two-steps—the natural position is for the man to keep his right arm around the woman's waist and for the woman to keep her left hand on his right shoulder as they open up facing forward from the swing. Note that the woman's hand is comfortably on her partner's closest shoulder and not clutching behind his neck, as tends to happen with less experienced dancers. Sometimes, for the promenade, people use the skater's hold (both hands held and crossed), which is acceptable but a bit more awkward to get into.

When dancing the traditional version of *Les Saluts* (see p. 122), those in the back circle must be sure to place themselves to the left of their partner and *between* two people as their joined hands are raised before forming the front basket. And if those in the front circle would bend their knees a bit (not their backs) so the back circle's arms can go over their head, there will be less bumping.

MODIFICATION AND TEACHING TIPS. *La Bastringue* is a wonderful dance just as it is, but it is possible make a small modification, so students who are not ready for or not comfortable with the ballroom swing can enjoy it. Change the underarm turn and buzz turn in social dance position to a right-elbow swing, or use the social dance position and walk around smoothly (eight counts for each). Do the promenade in a skater's hold (both hands held and crossed). As in all transitions, students should plan ahead; in this case, it means switching from holding right elbows to holding crossed hands on counts 6, 7, and 8. It is

Les Saluts

This dance has many teaching possibilities. The following pattern was described as traditional by Richard Turcotte and presented in the U.S. by Yves Moreau, an expert in French-Canadian and Bulgarian dance.

RECORD: *Rhythmically Moving 1*

FORMATION: Inner circle of W with joined hands and outer circle of M with joined hands. M stands behind partner, a bit to her left. Keep circles small—four to eight couples. See below for modified versions of the dance.

MEASURES 1–4: W walk 8 steps to R, while M walk 8 to L, ending behind partner again.

MEASURES 5–8: Repeat in opposite direction. As M return to partners' left, they bring joined hands over W's heads and down in front of them in front basket.

MEASURES 9–12: In basket position, everyone circles to L, 8 steps.

MEASURES 13–16: Still in basket, everyone circles to R, 8 steps.

MEASURES 17–18: Still in basket, all walk to center, 4 steps.

MEASURES 19–20: Walk backward 4 steps while releasing basket and joining hands down at sides again.

MEASURES 21–22: All walk in to center 4 steps again and take a low bow, holding it as long as the chord continues (*fermata*).

MEASURES 23–24: When chord ends, M take 4 steps backward and rejoin hands; W reform the inner circle with joined hands.

Notes by Yves Moreau

MODIFIED VERSION: See *Les Saluts* notes in *TFD* for the modification that the original notes offered for children 6 to 8 years old.

Very young children can walk anywhere in the room through measure 16, then walk toward the center or the teacher for the bows. Other versions between this very basic one and the most complex above are also possible.

also possible to change the two-step to a walking step; however, too much modification will dilute the spirit of this dance, so it is best to teach it to students who are comfortable with opposite-sex partners and can relate to one another in an adult manner.

Les Saluts may be modified in stages, so every age group can enjoy the humorous music. The youngest children can merely walk around the room in scatter formation or in their own spaces or "nests" for Part I and then do some

Dancers from Québec do a buzz turn on stage at Folkmoot USA in Waynesville, North Carolina.

nonlocomotor movements, perhaps straightening up and bending, for Part II. At the next developmental stage, they can circle with or without hands, as described in *TFD* and as done in Québec. After that, they could try the concentric circles. When students are ready for the basket formation, it is certainly not necessary that they have opposite-sex partners; it is more important for the taller partner to be in the back circle.

MUSIC. The characteristic instrument for *La Bastringue* is the fiddle. Wooden spoons are also traditionally played for dancing. *CD2* is a good recording for this dance, and there are several others produced in Québec, including one by the late Jean Carignan, one of the most famous French-Canadian musicians. In the music classroom, the catchy tune can be played on barred instruments along with a strong, steady percussion. It is also possible to vary the music and enjoy doing *La Bastringue* to other 32 bar reels or reel medleys with strong beats, preferably ones in the French-Canadian style, to keep the authentic feel. *Les Saluts* also uses a fiddle but can be similarly adapted

French-Canadian Dances

*This is an example of the costumes a folk ballet group might wear for French-Canadian dance. Here the Brigham Young University International Folk Dance Ensemble performs their **Dance Québecois** suite, using the traditional wooden spoons.*

Photo by Mark Philbrick

to the classroom, with thought given to reproducing the *fermata.* These surprise notes might be re-created in other ways after students become familiar with the recorded ones.

CLOTHING AND COSTUMES.

The generic western European folk costume is appropriate in a program that includes Québecois dances. Girls could wear a white or dark blouse, a fitted bodice or shawl, a calf-length full skirt with bottom ruffles, and a striped apron. Boys might wear long dark pants or knickers with knee socks, a white shirt with vest, a bright kerchief around the neck, and a sash.

Resources Used for Chapter 12

Bennett, Karen. 1996. "Costume Corner: French Canada." *Ontario Folk Dancer,* 15 April 1996, 29.

Legault, Normand, Adélard Thomassin, and Richard Turcotte (producers). 1979. *La Bastringue et autres danseries.* Laridaine ML 7902. This is a double record album produced in Québec. Notes and descriptions are in French.

Moreau, Yves. 1970–75. Conversations on many subjects and cultures, many occasions.

Moreau, Yves. 1984. *Dances of French Canada (Québec).* This is the author's syllabus used at his camps and workshops.

German Dances

Chapter 13: German Dances

German Dances in Phyllis S. Weikart's Books

Bekendorfer Quadrille	[BECK-en-door-fur quad-RILL] (Quadrille from Bekendorf) *TFD, RM4*
D'Hammerschmiedsg'selln	[DHAH-mehr-shmeeds-g-ZEHL-n] (The journeyman blacksmith or the blacksmith's apprentice) *TFD, RM7*
Man in the Hay	*TFD, RM3*
Sauerländer Quadrille, or Sauerländer Quadrille #5	[ZOWER-lender quad-RILL] *TFD, CD3*
Zigeunerpolka	[tsee-GOY-nehr-poka] (Gypsy polka) *TFD, RM2*

*O*ver the past three centuries, the area we call Germany has produced some of the world's greatest composers, writers, and other artists, but the German Empire as a unified political entity only came into existence in 1871, after the Franco-Prussian War.

People the Romans described as *Germani* (tribes of Germans, Cimbri, Franks, Goths, and Vandals) actually inhabited the area of Germany as early as 1000 B.C.E. In the first century C.E., these Germanic tribes stopped the spread of the Roman Empire, and over several centuries, they gradually weakened it. This process culminated in the 800 C.E. crowning of Charlemagne, the first Germanic ruler to become Emperor of the Romans. Although the term Holy Roman Empire continued to be used to include Germany for many centuries thereafter, Germanic peoples ruled from Charlemagne's time on. From then until its political unification in the late nineteenth century, Germany was composed of many separate entities—monarchies, duchies, ecclesiastical states, and free cities. These included Teutonic, Slavic, Romanian, and Scandinavian peoples, as well as many others. In recent times, the results of two world wars once again changed the nation's political and geographical boundaries, and this story is not yet ended, as the two post–World War II Germanies—East and West—have cautiously reunited.

Thus the German culture, like the cultures of all large European nations, can be viewed as a collection of peoples—Silesians, Swabians, Bavarians, and many others. The fact that Germany borders on nine other countries (Denmark, the Netherlands, Belgium, Luxembourg, France, Switzerland, Austria, the Czech Republic, and Poland) also accounts for regional variations in cultural expression. (See p. 130.) Yet Germany's various peoples share at least one thing—an intense enthusiasm for dance and music. There's an old German proverb that speaks for all of them: "He who doesn't love wine, women, and song/remains a fool his whole life long."

Written records about German dance go back to Tacitus, the first-century Roman historian. At that time the *Reigen,* the ritual round dance related to all European chain dances, appeared in early Christian festivals, and it can be seen even today. In the Middle Ages, other types of dances developed, including dances of death—which is not surprising considering the area's history of wars, plagues, and violence. However, most dances in Germany, as well as in other countries, celebrate life.

In Bavaria, the Oktoberfest is celebrated at the end of harvest, usually in late September and early October. Although it started as an agricultural fair and a horse race to honor the royal wedding of Crown Prince Ludwig, Oktoberfest is now somewhat like Thanksgiving, and an occasion for festivals all over Germany. Oktoberfest celebrations have also become popular in the U.S. There is usually lots of German food and beer and often a band with oompah-type music that encourages people to get up and polka.

Bekendorfer Quadrille, Man in the Hay, and *Sauerländer Quadrille* are all quadrilles, which means they are danced by four couples, and *D'Hammerschmiedsg'selln* is done by four people. The three quadrilles are typical of dances descended from

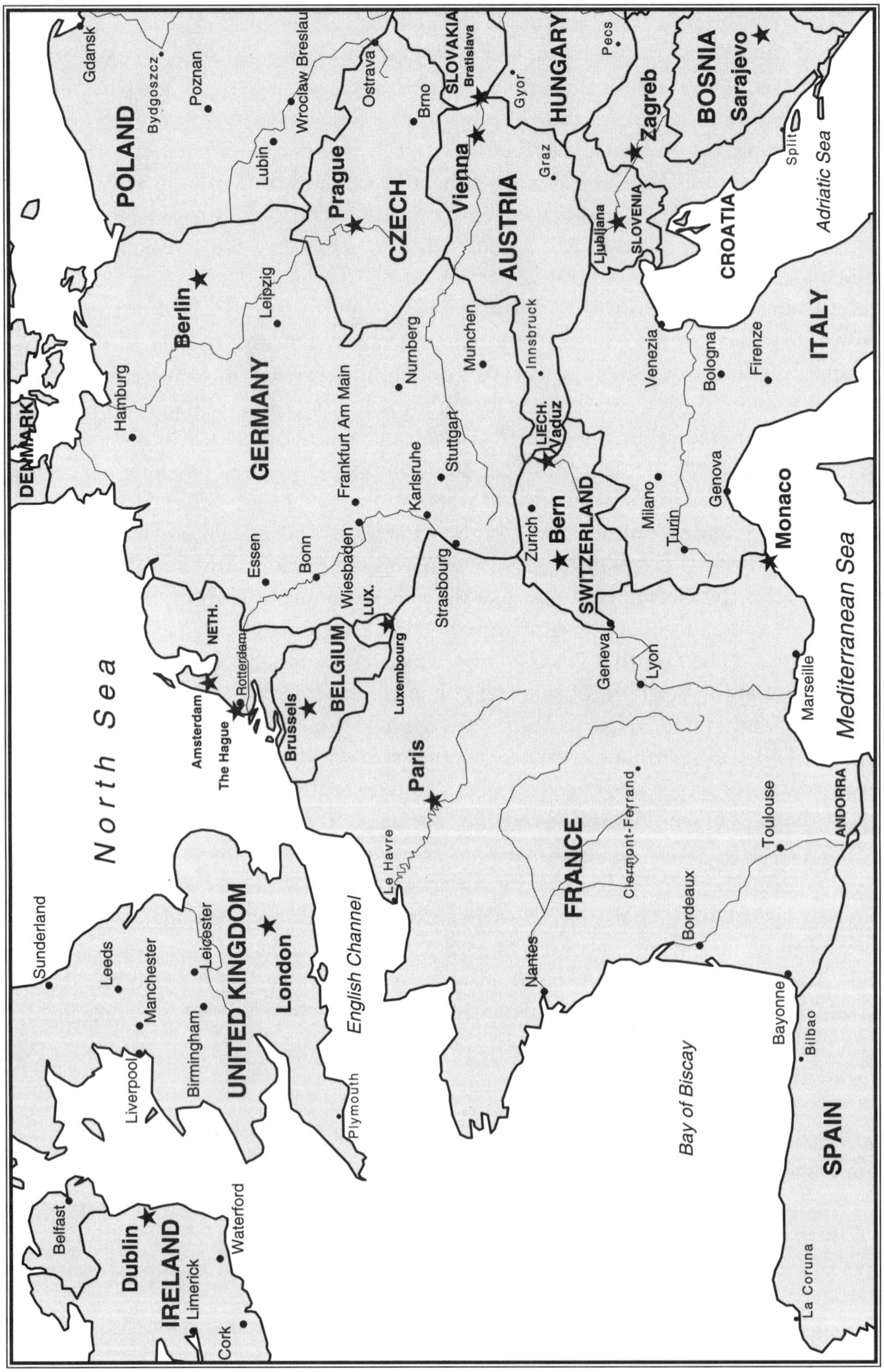
North Sea
English Channel
Bay of Biscay
Mediterranean Sea
Adriatic Sea
IRELAND
Dublin
Belfast
Limerick
Cork
Waterford
UNITED KINGDOM
London
Sunderland
Leeds
Manchester
Liverpool
Birmingham
Leicester
Plymouth
FRANCE
Paris
Le Havre
Nantes
Bordeaux
Clermont-Ferrand
Toulouse
Lyon
Marseille
Strasbourg
SPAIN
La Coruna
Bilbao
Bayonne
ANDORRA
BELGIUM
Brussels
NETH.
Amsterdam
The Hague
Rotterdam
LUX.
Luxembourg
GERMANY
Berlin
Hamburg
Essen
Bonn
Wiesbaden
Frankfurt Am Main
Karlsruhe
Stuttgart
Nurnberg
Munchen
Leipzig
DENMARK
POLAND
Gdansk
Bydgoszcz
Poznan
Lubin
Wroclaw Breslau
CZECH
Prague
Brno
Ostrava
SLOVAKIA
Bratislava
AUSTRIA
Vienna
Graz
Innsbruck
HUNGARY
Gyor
Pecs
SWITZERLAND
Bern
Zurich
Geneva
LIECH.
Vaduz
ITALY
Milano
Turin
Genova
Venezia
Bologna
Firenze
Monaco
SLOVENIA
Ljubljana
CROATIA
Zagreb
Split
BOSNIA
Sarajevo

the aristocratic eighteenth-century French quadrilles and the more down-home nineteenth-century German social dances. *Bekendorfer Quadrille* and *Man in the Hay* were collected by Anna Helms-Blasche from Heinrich Nord, a musician in Bückeburg who played for all the dances; she published the two dances in 1918. *Sauerländer Quadrille* was arranged in its present form by Otto Ilmbrecht and published in 1931.

D'Hammerschmiedsg'selln (known familiarly as *D'H*, for obvious reasons) comes from the Alpine area. Introduced to American folk dancers by the noted researcher of German dancers Huig Hofman, *D'Hammerschmiedsg'selln* was originally a work dance, like the fourteenth- and fifteenth-century guild dances, in which men celebrated their livelihoods. The coopers (barrelmakers) had hoop dances, the drapers (cloth dealers) had flag dances, the cutlers (people who made and repaired cutting instruments) had sword dances. In more modern times, occupational dances such as the shepherd's dance and the shoemaker's dance came to be. Although the dance is named for the blacksmith, the special clapping sequence of *D'Hammerschmiedsg'selln* is named for the *Zimmermann Klatsch* (carpenter's clap). These tradesmen still wear a striking guild uniform and, at their guild parties, play games with complex clapping patterns.

Zigeunerpolka is representative of the many polka dances that swept central Europe in the nineteenth century and are still popular. The *Zigeunerpolka* pattern in *TFD* is meant to be an enjoyable, getting-started dance and was choreographed by Phyllis S. Weikart for

Dancers from former West Germany, wearing stage versions of native clothing, share the bride in a wedding polka during a festival in Szeged, Hungary. The bride, who is from the U.S., wears an authentic bride's outfit from the Kalotoszegi region of Hungary.

German Dances   131

her book, but there are a number of other dances by the same name that have been collected not only in Germany but also in Czechoslovakia, Switzerland, and the Netherlands. In the current general folk dance repertoire, *Zigeunerpolka* is an easy mixer originally collected by Erna Schutzenberger in 1930 and spread across North America by several recreational specialists and ethnic dance teachers. So you and your students might enjoy that one also, it is described on the opposite page.

FORMATION. The three quadrilles are in the form of square dances. The #1, #2, #3, and #4 couples in German squares are traditionally placed differently than they are in U.S. western squares. Specifically, a German square has its #1 couple *facing* the music instead of having backs to the music, as in a U.S. western square. The placement of couples #2, #3, and #4 is also different, with the U.S. square placing #2, #3, and #4 consecutively counterclockwise from couple #1, and the traditional German square placing them #3, #2, and #4 counterclockwise from #1 (that is, #1 faces #2, and #3 faces #4). The formation designated for *Sauerländer Quadrille* in TFD, however, shows a clockwise #1, #2, #3, #4 arrangement of couples. This means, for example, that in Part I of the *TFD* description, #1 lady peek-a-boos with #3 man. In a description using the traditional German square, #1 lady would peek-a-boo with #2 man.

Traditionally, *D'Hammerschmiedsg'selln* was done only by men—women were not blacksmiths. Because of the folk process (in this case, changes by a folk dance leader), recreational dancers usually pair up in any gender combination. In the classroom, however, you have the luxury of legitimately encouraging the use of same-gender partners, as well as the use of all-boy or all-girl sets. It's important to remember that the two individuals who are partners are placed opposite each other (instead of next to each other), so their clapping hands meet in the center of each small set. When the dance is performed by two mixed-gender couples, sometimes the two men clap with each other, as do the two women.

Also in this dance, Part IIC can be done either by repeating the same circle of four, as in the *TFD* notes, or by joining everyone in a large circle to finish the dance in a friendly fashion. This works best in a smaller group, of course. Some adult groups do this final figure by waltzing in pairs around the room, as was begun in the nineteenth century. If the dance is done in mixed couples, each man either waltzes with his lady or takes the other man's partner. When the dance is done by men only, they finish by finding a woman to waltz with—the blacksmiths did not twirl around the floor with each other.

STEPS AND MOVEMENTS. Generally, German dances should be done in a solid, hearty, energetic manner with crisp, springy steps. The rhythms for the dances listed here are steady and strong, and so is the footwork. In German folk dance, according to Karin Gottier, a renowned teacher of European dances, "There is no room for wild abandon or limp passivity."

Man in the Hay is a vigorous dance full of slide steps and skips and ending with the always exciting buzz step basket-turn, which is sometimes done so vigor-

Another Version of
*Zigeunerpolka**

This is one form of the pattern taught in North America in the late 1950s and early 1960s by German dance experts Gretel and Paul Dunsing, recreation specialist Jane Farwell, and pioneer folk dance leader Mary Ann Herman. Many folk dance groups and schools still enjoy this version.

FORMATION: Circle of couples in ballroom dance position, ready to progress CCW (counterclockwise).

Part I: Polka

MEASURES 1–8: Couples polka CCW around circle. The traditional turning polka is generally done, with each pair rotating CW as they progress CCW around the dance space. For newer dancers, this polka may be done in an open ballroom position. Finish the figure with partners facing, men (or leaders) with backs to the center of the circle.

Part II: Bowing or Salutations

MEASURES 9–10: Bow or curtsy to partner (slowly—one measure down, one up).

MEASURES 11–12: Bow or curtsy diagonally to the right (righthand neighbor's partner).

MEASURES 13–14: Bow or curtsy diagonally to the left (lefthand neighbor's partner). *Some notes say bow to the left first, then to the right—it doesn't matter.*

MEASURES 15–16: Bow or curtsy again to partner.

Part III: Clapping

MEASURES 17–24: Clap own hands once, clap both hands with present partner. Continue this pattern (clap own hands, clap next person's, clap own hands, clap next person's, etc.) while walking around the circle to the right (men go CW, women go CCW). Clap with eight people in all, original polka partner being No. 1, taking one step per clap (16 steps in all). Begin the dance again with the eighth person, the new polka partner. *Some notes say walk around circle to the left (men CCW, women CW)—it doesn't matter.*

To slow down the action, dancers can clap with *seven* people instead of eight, using the last measure of Part III to get ready to polka with the new partner.

*Notes by Sanna Longden, based on many years' observation and adapted from notes in *Folk Dancing for Students and Teachers* by Constance Mynatt and Bernard Kaiman (Dubuque: Wm. C. Brown Co., 1975), p. 72; Olga Kulbitsky's original notes for Folkraft record 1486; and Ron Houston's *Folk Dance Problem Solver* (Austin, TX: Society of Folk Dance Historians, 1997), p. 57.

ously that the woman's feet fly up in the air (you may not want to mention this to your students). *Bekendorfer Quadrille* takes the step-hop into the schottische step in the *TFD* folk dancers' version, although the original notes for the traditional dance describe sliding and "bleking" steps.

D'Hammerschmiedsg'selln uses a big uneven step-hop that is similar to the "stalking" step in the Bavarian *Schuhplattler*. When students get proficient at the clapping part in this dance, it's fun to give a sharp knee-bend on count 1. For an added challenge, see if they can pivot a full turn to the right on each "me, me, me" clap. Some German-American groups have both couples doing the clapping sequence simultaneously, instead of alternately, but with one pair hunkering down and clapping below the other pair's hands.

The movement in *Sauerländer Quadrille* is more subtle than the movement of other dances. The basic Neheimer step, named for its home village of Neheim-Hüsten in Westphalia, requires a flexible ankle and lots of practice: The TOE, TOE, HEEL, TOE pattern is particularly difficult to do in rubber-soled athletic shoes. Dancers hold themselves straight and tall, and there is a steady bouncing feeling all through the figures. One of the playful points of this dance occurs when the dancers give no hint of which couple's turn is next. This surprise element can be achieved if all four couples stay steadily facing center, not waving their feet around, until each pair abruptly begins their figure right on the music. And they should always end each figure facing center again as the feet close on the last count.

Zigeunerpolka, as choreographed in *TFD,* has no special ethnic styling; students should just use their bodies in whatever ways seem natural to them. In the dance described on p. 133, do an exuberant German/Bohemian polka step (covering a lot of ground) instead of the more precise Polish polka (which goes up and down more), and exaggerate the bows.

When teaching German dances, it is appropriate and traditional to also include some social niceties, such as acknowledging partners with a slight bow, friendly smile, or nod of the head. It is also appropriate to teach boys to be the dominant partner in male-female pairs.

HANDS AND ARMS. In partner figures as well as in group patterns like circles, adjacent dancers join hands at chest height in the W-position and give some tension to aid in the movement. In right- and left-hand stars, called mills, each person grasps the wrist of the person ahead of him or her, leaning a bit away from center. The free hand is on the hip, with fingers forward and thumb back.

In the typical arm-swings that begin *Man in the Hay,* partners' hands are joined in the V-position, with arms held close to the sides. The swings are vigorous, with small staccato movements, and traditionally, elbows were fairly straight. When the women, and then the men, join hands to skip in a circle in Parts IB and IC, they also use the V-position. To coordinate the arms in the basket figure, in four swift movements (1) women join both hands across the circle, (2) men join both hands across the women's hands, (3) men raise arms up and over, placing them at the small of the women's backs, (4) women raise arms up and over, and hold tight across the men's shoulders.

The dancers' arms in *Sauerländer Quadrille* should hang naturally at the sides or be clasped behind the back, unless they have another job to do. For *Bekendorfer Quadrille* and the *Zigeunerpolka* mixer, there is nothing fancy to worry about, but make sure students keep their hands up and ready for clapping. The free hand is always on the hip when not otherwise occupied.

On an outdoor stage at a dance festival in Szeged, Hungary, dancers from former West Germany perform **Sauerländer Quadrille** *with hands clasped behind the back.*

MODIFICATION AND TEACHING TIPS. The quadrilles can be successfully modified by omitting a figure or two until the basic steps are achieved. *D'H* can be used for uneven step-hop practice. If step-hops are difficult for the students, however, they can step on the macrobeat (beat 1 of each measure). If the clapping sequence confuses at first, have the students rehearse alone with their partners awhile before they join another couple; the interweaving of the two pairs of hands should not be abandoned. Part I (simplified) is an excellent place to begin teaching the clapping sequence ("me, me, me, you, you, you"); if some students never progress beyond this point, they can still participate fully without losing the "soul" of the dance.

Zigeunerpolka novelty dance doesn't require rights and lefts, so it can be taught in its entirety as a pre-folk dance to second-graders, and to all ages as

German Dances

> "These boys practice the clapping sequence—*"me, me, me, you, you, you"*—in **D'Hammer-schmieds'gselln**.
> Photo by Zoltan Horvath

entertaining choreography. Save the exciting *Zigeunerpolka* mixer for when students can do a polka step and enjoy mixing.

These are all figure dances and meant to be done with partners, which is one essential German styling element. Therefore, though it may be appropriate to teach specific steps without partners, it is definitely not good German dance etiquette to leave dancers without partners when this teaching is finished. And, of course, be sure to retain the vigorous and jolly German feeling.

MUSIC. Unfortunately, most classrooms cannot come up with tubas, cornets, sousaphones, euphoniums, and other wonderful brasses, or even an accordion or two, for these hearty melodies. However, classroom instruments that are traditionally German are the triangle and the barred instrument called the glockenspiel. A piano and a bass drum might complete the ensemble. These dances do need a strong, steady beat.

CLOTHING AND COSTUMES. Not every region in Germany includes in its dress the lederhosen (leather shorts-and-suspender outfit) for men and the dirndl (colorful sleeveless dress with lacy blouse) for women; these are specific to the Bavarian region in southern Germany and lower Austria. If any students have these, however, they immediately evoke Germany/Austria for all audiences. It is interesting to note that the dirndl is really not native dress, but folklore fashion based on Alpine indigenous styles (similar to the U.S. western fashion known as the "rhinestone cowboy" look).

Otherwise, dress the girls in full, plain-colored skirts with white or flowered aprons; dark, sleeveless bodices; white blouses with puffed sleeves and lacy collars; white kneesocks or pantyhose; and low black shoes. The boys should draw up their pants to knicker length and tuck them into long white or colored knee socks worn with black shoes. Add suspenders and dark vests or jackets, perhaps ones with big, shiny buttons.

*Members of a Munich **Verein** (club), in the 1950s, demonstrate the **Schuhplattler**, a well-known dance from southern Germany. Some of its figures are typical of other German dances. Pictured are Morry Gelman, a researcher and teacher of German and Austrian dances, and his wife, Nancy.*

German Dances

Resources Used for Chapter 13

Burchenal, Elizabeth. 1934. *Folk-Dances of Germany.* New York: G. Schirmer. This is a classic book; the photographs as well as the text give good information.

Dunsing, Gretel, and Paul Dunsing. 1976–77. *A Collection of the Descriptions of Folk Dances, Second Collection of Dance Descriptions,* and *Third Collection of Dance Descriptions.* These are put together by the authors, who specialized in German folk dances and taught them in many workshops in the U.S. and abroad during the 1960s and 1970s.

Farwell, Jane. 1981. "Man in the Hay." *Folklore Village Christmas Festival Syllabus.* Dodgeville, WI: Folklore Village Farm. This beloved recreational leader was particularly fond of German dances. Her dance descriptions, which include the lyrics for *Man in the Hay* in German and English, are available through Folklore Village Farm, 3210 Co. Hwy. BB, Dodgeville, WI 53533; 608/924-4000.

Fyfe, Agnes. 1951. *Dances of Germany.* London: Max Parrish. This is one of the Handbook of European National Dances series produced by the Royal Academy of Dancing and the Ling Physical Educational Association. It includes information on culture, music, and costumes, as well as several dance descriptions with color plates.

Gelman, Morry. 1997. Workshop during National Folk Organization annual conference, Murfreesboro, TN, 8–11 July 1997.

Gottier, Karin. 1991, July. "Some Thoughts on Folk Dance in the Classroom." Paper from ethnic dance seminar at Duquesne University, Pittsburgh, PA, July 1991.

Gottier, Karin. 1991–97. Comments, criticisms, and conversations.

Houston, Ron (ed.). 1993. "Man in the Hay." *Folk Dance Problem Solver,* 33–35. Austin, TX: Society of Folk Dance Historians. This description includes the words in German and English.

Greek Dances

Chapter 14 Greek Dances

Greek Dances in Phyllis S. Weikart's Books

(*Note:* Many of these names are generic; there may be other patterns or choreographies with the same names. Also, because these names are transliterated from the Greek alphabet, there are likely to be spelling variations in other sources. The use of accent marks on Greek dance names may likewise vary from source to source, and there is a tendency among choreographers to drop them altogether. We are dropping them here, also, as do some of our experts.)

Ais Giorgis	[eye yor-GHEE] (St. George) *TFD, RM7*	
Argos Hasapikos	[ARE-gohs hah-SAH-pee-kohs] (A butcher's dance from Argos) *TFD, CD5*	
Chiotikos	[he-YO-tea-kohs] (Dance from the Isle of Chios) *TFD, RM9*	
Dirlada, sometimes *Dirlanda*	[dear-LAH-dah] *TFD, RM5*	
Fissouni	[fee-SOU-nee] (The wind; a dance from Epiros) *TM&D*	
Hasapikos	[hah-SAH-pee-kohs] (A butcher's dance; a dance type common to many regions) *TFD, RM4*	
Hasaposervikos	[hah-sah-poe-SEHR-vee-kohs] (A variant of *Hasapikos*—the "fast hasapikos," named for the Serbs) *TM&D*	
Iatros	[yah-TROHS] (The doctor; a dance from Epiros) *TM&D*	
Ikariotikos	[ee-kah-ree-OH-tee-kohs] (Dance from the Isle of Ikaria) *TFD, CD4*	
Kalamatianos	[kah-lah-mah-tee-ah-NOHS] (Dance from the town of Kalamata) *TFD, CD4*	
Kamara	[kah-mah-RAH] (Dance from the Isle of Skiathos) *TM&D*	
Karagouna	[kah-rah-GOO-nah] (Dance of the Karagounides—plainsmen and farmers of Thessaly) *TFD, CD3*	
Karagouna	(9-part) [see above] *TM&D*	
Koftos	[koff-TOHS] (A cut; a dance from Epiros) *TM&D*	
Kritikos Syrtos	[KREE-tee-Kohs seer-TOHS] (A dance from Crete) *TFD, CD5*	
Lakhana	[lah-kah-NAH] (A dance of the Pontic Greeks) *TM&D*	
Laziko	[lah-zee-KOH] (A dance of the Pontic Greeks) *TM&D*	
Lefkaditikos	[leff-kah-DEE-tee-kohs] (A dance from the Isle of Lefkas) *TM&D*	
Lemonaki	[leh-moe-NAH-kee] (Little lemon tree; a Greek Macedonian dance) *TFD, CD3*	
Len Irthe Mais	[len EAR-they MAH-ees] (May is here; a harvest dance from Thracian Greece) *TM&D*	
Makedonikos Horos	[mah-keh-DOE-nee-kohs hoe-ROHS] (A Greek Macedonian dance) *TFD, RM9*	
Makrinitsa	[mahk-ree-NEET-sah] (A Greek Macedonian dance) *TM&D*	
Misirlou-Kritikos	[MEE-zeer-loo kree-tee-KOHS] (Well-known *Misirlou,* based on a Kritikos syrtos) *TFD, RM8*	

Nizamikos	[nee-ZAH-mee-kohs]	(from the Turkish word *nizam*, a regular army; a Greek Macedonian dance) *TM&D*
Palamakia/Koftos	[pah-lah-MAH-kee-ah koff-TOHS]	(Clap your hands; a clapping *koftos* from Epiros) *TM&D*
Pentozalis	[pen-toe-ZAH-leese]	(Five dizzying steps) *TFD, CD4*
Pogonissios	[poe-goe-NEE-see-ohs]	(A dance from Epirus) *TM&D*
Rebetic Hasapikos	[reh-BEH-tick hah-SAH-pee-kohs]	(*Hasapiko* of the Rebetic music culture) *TFD, CD6*
Silivrianos, or *Kykladitikos Syrtos*	[see-lee-vree-ah-NOHS]	(A *syrtos* from the Cycladic and Dodecanese islands) *TFD, CD5*
Soultana	[sool-TAH-nah]	(The sultan's wife) *TFD, CD2*
Syrtaki #7	[seer-TAH-kee]	(The name means little *syrto*, but the dance is actually a modern version of the hasapikos) *TFD, CD5*
Syrtos	[seer-TOHS]	(A dance of a type common to many regions; the name means to drag or pull) *TM&D*
Tai Tai	[TAH-ee TAH-ee]	(A dance from Thessaly named for the refrain of the song, which means ascending, to which it is danced) *TM&D*
Trata	[TRAH-tah]	(An island dance celebrating fishermen) *TFD, CD2*
Tsakonikos	[tsah-KOH-nee-kohs]	(A Peloponnesian dance from Tsakonia) *TFD, RM9*
Tsamikos	[TSAH-mee-kohs],	(A dance type common to many regions; probably named for the *ta tsamika*, the regalia worn by its originators) *TFD, CD2*
Vari (Varys) Hasapikos	[vah-REE hah-SAH-pee-kohs]	(The heavy, or slow, butcher's dance) *TM&D*
Zagoritikos	[zah-goe-REE-tee-kohs]	(A dance from Epirus) *TM&D*
Zervos Karpathos	[ZEHR-vohs KAHR-pah-thos]	(A dance from the Isle of Karpathos) *TM&D*
Zonaradikos	[zoe-noe-RAH-dee-kohs]	(Most popular dance of Thracian Greece; named for the *zonari*, a belt or sash) *TM&D*
Zorba	[zohr-BAH]	(Named for the title character of book and movie fame) *TM&D*

The beautiful country of Greece consists of a jagged-edged peninsula jutting into the Mediterranean Sea from the southeastern corner of Europe, plus 1,400 large and small islands; the largest of the Greek islands is Crete. The country's closest neighbors (something that is helpful to know when discussing ethnic dances) are Turkey, Bulgaria, Macedonia, and Albania. (See the map on p. 142.)

Greek people feel very strongly about their politics, their honor, and their culture, which is one of the oldest in the Western world. The Golden Age of Greece, those brilliant decades in the fifth century B.C.E., laid the groundwork for much of Western civilization's literature, architecture, mathematics, philosophy, and politics, and the Greeks are justly proud of this past greatness. Beginning in about the first century B.C.E., Greece went through centuries of dark ages, being conquered by the Roman, Byzantine, and Ottoman empires. Although most of the country was liberated by 1832, some remnants of the Ottoman Empire were not forced out of northern Greece until as late as the Balkan Wars of 1913.

After World War II, ironically, modern technology and trends did more to conquer Greek traditions than did the Ottoman Turks. The recent revival of interest in traditional Greek culture—by the urban Greeks themselves as well as by the rest of the Western world—was partly the result of two Hollywood films, *Never on Sunday* and *Zorba the Greek*. From then on, *bouzouki* music (the bouzouki is a mandolin-like instrument that leads in many Greek melodies) and *hasapikos* dances (described in this chapter) became popular, and tourists discovered the *tavernas* (these are exactly what they sound like). Expatriate Greek communities in other countries, who have always held tight to the traditions of their homeland, felt a renewed pride in being Greek and began to sponsor public festivals and events to celebrate their heritage. Thus, today we have the unique chance to join in dances that are related to those among the most ancient in the world.

The impressive list of 41 dances on pp. 140–141 represents several basic types and their variations, as well as dances specific to certain mainland regions and island groups. Geography and culture have great influence on the patterns and styling of Greek dances. The mainland regions were isolated by mountain ranges, and the islands, by water, so each area retained its own dialect and customs for an unusually long time. In fact, in ancient days individual regions or islands were separate kingdoms. Their names evoke the events of ancient history:

There are, for example, the mainland regions of Epirus, Macedonia, and Thrace to the north; Thessaly and Central Greece in the middle; and Peloponnesus in the south. The Ionian Islands are to the west; the Aegean Islands, to the east; and the Dodecanese Islands, to the southeast.

Thus, even today we find different identifiable musical and dance styles for dances of the same name. We can say, for example, "This is a *syrtos* from Epiros," or "This is a *syrtos* from the island of Skiathos." Among all the regions and islands, Greece has at least 20 distinct subcultures, each with at least 10 dances of its own—at least!

However, you'll be glad to know that a complete and detailed account of each region is not necessary for the success and enjoyment of Greek dances in the classroom or even in the folk dance group. We will concentrate here on general styling, which is useful for any dances you teach, and then discuss five dances that are done in some form in most parts of Greece and are the basis of many of the dances in this list: the *Hasapikos,* the *Vari Hasapikos,* the *Syrtos,* the *Kalamatianos,* the *Tsamikos.* If you have further interest in Greek folk dance, check the resource list at the end of this chapter for a start on this fascinating subject.

Living Greek Dances

As emphasized in this book, ethnic dances are not just a series of steps and patterns. Greek dances, in particular, cannot be reduced to words on paper. Although most of them appear to be merely a repeated, fairly simple structure with a few variations, the dances are actually quite sophisticated and subtle. There is a special mystique connected with Greek dance that is based on its roots in ancient history. The chain dances depicted on early friezes and urns, for example, are stylized illustrations of people doing movements similar to many of the dances listed in this chapter.

Greek dances are not just museum pieces, however. They continue to play an important part in the activities of the people, both in Greece and in expatriate communities around the world. Unlike the traditional dances of many other peoples, Greek traditional dances are not done only at occasional festivals or on stages; even today the Greek people naturally celebrate most events by music and dancing. So Greek traditional dances are living dances, which means that they are constantly changing, or done differently in different places, or never danced the same way twice.

An interesting example of a living dance creating a reverse folk process is *Misirlou,* the music that people all over the world instantly recognize as a Greek dance, even if they know no others. It is actually a tango, composed by a Greek musician named Roubanis and recorded in the 1940s by Xavier Cugat, among others. When a teacher in Pittsburgh was preparing a demonstration of the Cretan *Haniotikos Syrtos* for a Greek festival, she could not find the right traditional music, so she used *Misirlou*. It was such a hit that it was adopted by the expatriate Greek communities as authentic, and 20 years later it could be found in Greece as a traditional dance. Other cultures, particularly the Israelis and Armenians, have also adapted this popular dance into their own styles.

Greek dances are not just upbeat and lively, however. They also can be a deeply personal form of self-expression. The strong sense of the past that most Greeks share may lead them to dance out mournful feelings when they remember their tragic history, not only the ancient legends but also the living memories of the atrocities of World War II and the extremely bitter civil war that followed. The spirit of Greek dance also encourages a private expression of joy, often done by individuals—usually men—by themselves (such dances are not represented in this series). Zorba spoke for all Greek people when he expressed his feelings through the *Syrtaki:* "My joy was choking me—I had to find some outlet!"

This, of course, does not imply that only Greek people should do Greek dances or that we recommend serving *ouzo* in the classroom to get everyone in the mood. These are dances for all people to enjoy—and this is why so many (41) are included in *TFD* and *TM&D*. However, all but 6 of the 41 dances are intermediate level, which means that for most of them, much groundwork must be laid with your students. Greek dances are most successful with students who have a good understanding of life as well as of folk dancing.

More sophisticated students especially may appreciate one of the explanations for the tradition that Greek men break dishes while dancing in the tavernas. According to Athan Karras, a Greek dance researcher and teacher, the dishes are "a symbol

*The Balkanske Igre Ensemble of Chicago creates a little context—a **taverna**—for its Greek dance suite.*

of matter that he [the dancer] breaks in order to free himself from being enslaved by material things." Everyday life is so difficult that the act of flinging crockery against walls and floor shows that "they need to have that moment when doing their thing brings them back to . . . sanity with a harmless act of insanity" (1983, p. 17). After discussing this philosophy with students, however, it might not be a good idea to teach Greek dances in the school cafeteria!

It is particularly important to be aware of context when teaching Greek dances. We offer more cultural information in this chapter than in others, because Greek dances can lose a great deal when taken out of context. This is also true of traditional dances from other southeastern European cultures, especially the Macedonian and Bulgarian. "Out of context" here might mean a group of sweat-shirted schoolchildren dutifully plodding around in untied high-tops in a single circle on the carpet of the music room or the slippery floor of the gym to recorded sounds played on a small machine. Conversely, "in context" might mean a taverna with music and dancing. Or it might mean a community of babies to grandparents wearing party togs or traditional clothing, joyously jammed together within a snaking line of friends and family at a festive event, and moving in rhythm to the driving sounds of a native band accompanied by humorous shouting or loud singing, with food, drink, and socializing all part of the scene.

Movements and Styling— Introducing Freestyle Dancing

Although obviously we cannot always create appropriate context for a dance in the classroom, it is helpful if teachers understand the traditional situations in which Greek dances are enjoyed and then describe such scenes to their students for greater appreciation of the movements and styling discussed here. Photographs in books and, better yet, videotapes are available (see in this chapter's resource list, for example, *A Greek Folkloric Celebration* produced by Athan Karras, and Sanna Longden's video *Living Ethnic Dances for Kids & Teachers*). Videotapes, in particular, can help students to appreciate the freestyle nature of Greek dance, which we are about to describe.

FORMATION. The predominant form of Greek dances is an open circular chain with a leader who guides it to the right; this formation is also referred to as a line dance. There are actually only two or three partner dances in the Aegean cultural region (none are in *TFD* or *TM&D*); in these, partners do not touch and may be of the same gender. Until recent generations, Greek men and women did not dance in the same line, and the leader was usually a man. Nowadays everyone dances together, except in very traditional immigrant communities, where "customs are preserved like family heirlooms" (Gage, 1989, p. 200). In fact, in the U.S. urban nightclubs, often it is women who leap up at the first note of the amplified *klarino* (clarinet) and bouzouki, and often it is women who lead the dances.

But whether men or women, the important word is "lead" when discussing Greek dances. Every dance has a basic pattern, and almost every pattern can be naturally embellished with turns, extra steps, pauses, hops, and rhythmic changes, all initiated by a leader at the front of the line. This type of dancing is called **freestyle,** or **improvisational,** meaning that the leader chooses which steps to perform, as long as they are within the structure of the dance. It is similar to a musical theme and variations. Ballroom dances, for example, are freestyle patterns in that one person leads another through variations based on a rhythmic structure. Contemporary dances are also freestyle.

A few of the 41 dances on pp. 140–141 were arranged by Greek dance teachers to fit specific music and are usually not done in a freestyle form. These include *Ais Giorgis, Chiotikos, Dirlada, Soultana, Syrtaki #7, Tai Tai,* and *Trata.* The others, though presented to the folk dance community by Greek dance teachers in particular patterns and published as choreographies, are traditionally meant to be freestyle dances.

When teaching Greek dances in the classroom, it is not necessary to emphasize this freestyle aspect immediately, or perhaps ever. Indeed, many recreational folk dance groups are more comfortable doing Greek dances as though they were defined choreographies with a set leader and one or two pattern changes. Although not truly the traditional way, this is still fun and provides a good base from which to someday encourage a more freestyle way of dancing. Your students may be ready for the freestyle dances if they have had successful experiences with other forms of creative, or improvisational, dance. In fact, a few creative-movement sessions might be a good preparation for the five more common Panhellenic dances discussed in the concluding section of this chapter.

When you begin to present the freestyle format, note that in *TFD* and *TM&D,* many Greek dances have several variations, or parts. For teaching purposes, these subpatterns are listed in sequences. Use their numbers, or give them descriptive labels, and practice them in the order shown. Then, when students are comfortable with this system, destroy it. Try a follow-the-leader game in which each student chooses a variation, any variation, and the others follow that for a short time; then another student leads another variation, and so on. Break up the group into several semicircles, so three or four leaders can practice at once. If mixing girls and boys causes chaos, put them in separate lines—it may make the learning less distracting, and it is also culturally appropriate. In fact, many Greek dances are extremely masculine and could be presented with this emphasis to capture the attention of anyone who thinks dancing is just for girls.

Freestyle dances need good leaders. Good leading means knowing the appropriate variations, planning ahead well enough to change steps to the beat and rhythm, setting a dependable dance example, and having the confidence and skill to guide others to the music. Ideally, many leaders are needed, for the Greek way is to change the head of the line often during the dance, as well as to have several lines moving at one time.

Not every Greek dance requires the same type of leadership. In many of the dances, the leader calls the changes or guides people in his or her line through appropriate variations. In other dances, the leader at the head of the line does what amounts to a solo improvisation, with turns, leaps, twists, and other feats of agility and strength, while everyone else continues the basic steps. In a few of the dances, the leader does not have to think about variations or improvisations but just maintains the basic pattern and guides the line around the floor.

In the dances we emphasize here, the leader is always at the right end of the line or semicircle and guides the dance in line-of-direction (counterclockwise), coiling and uncoiling. Each line has only one leader—it is not acceptable to lead from the middle of the line. If the leader gets trapped in the center of the group, he or she can duck under arms to the outside or ask someone to break the line to allow escape.

Encourage changing leaders during these dances, not only because this is the Greek style but also because it gives many people a chance to lead. Generally, the best dancers are at the beginning of the line; they are the ones who are capable of leading and usually eager to do it. This was the accepted way in the village, when a man or youth who wanted to lead would tuck some money into the drum straps or paste a bill on the band leader's forehead, then start the dance with his special buddies lined up next to him. People who don't want to or can't lead should not seek to be among the first in line.

When ready, and without breaking the rhythm of the dance, the leader relinquishes lead position by joining the very end of the line; the second person in line then becomes the leader. Instead of joining the end of the line, the leader can break into another place in the circle or simply change places with the second or third person. The soon-to-be new leader should be given some warning of this, like a hand squeeze or a significant smile or a muttered signal, so he or she can continue the dance without a hitch. Sometimes, in the taverna, the leader is offered a glass of *retsina* as he passes some friendly spectators, at which point he may drop out of the dance.

Another technique is for the leader to hold a kerchief aloft in the free hand. With well-timed waves, the leader may use it to signal step changes, to help with a spin, or to add more movement to the dance. When relinquishing the lead, the leader passes the kerchief to the next leader. Some researchers suggest that this handing on of the dance kerchief led to the torch pass in the Olympics and the baton pass in relay races. Yes, the dance came before both of them! The kerchief itself is a relic of the days when everyone carried cloths soaked in perfume and waved them around to mask less attractive scents.

Traditionally, holding a handkerchief was more than a technique for leaders. Your students might be intrigued to know that not so long ago in Greek society, as well as in other cultures, unmarried young people were not supposed to touch—in fact, it was considered immodest if a young woman raised her eyes to a young man's face. Therefore, unless the young people were joining hands only with relatives, they held handkerchiefs between them while dancing. Today, though, the handkerchief is not mandatory for either leaders or unmarried people.

The leader is not the only important person in the dance. The second person in the open circle also has a role—maintaining the basic pattern for the rest of the circle to follow and remaining always prepared to take the lead. In addition, the number-two person provides solid physical and emotional support for the leader's self-expression through fancy footwork. And, of course, as in any line dance, everyone else must follow the steps and respond to the variations in a timely fashion, so all the dancers can enjoy themselves.

STEPS AND MOVEMENTS. Generally, the steps are clean and clear—with no shuffling or scraping of feet. Movements are smooth and appear to flow one into another. As in any other kind of dance, when the music gets faster, the steps get smaller. Dancers' bearing is erect and proud in a natural, nonrigid manner. They keep their feet directly beneath their bodies—making no big kicks or reaching-steps out to front or side, for example. For slower steps, the whole body often takes the movement—from the neck and face concentrating on the next spot, through the poised torso, and down through the leg, ankle, and ball of the foot, which leads into the careful step.

Typically, in most southeastern European countries, men's movements are larger. Men leap higher, raise their knees higher, use their bodies more vigorously. Those who wear the short-skirted *foustanella* of the Greek soldiers often choose movements that show off the costume's fringes and pleats and their own strong legs.

Women traditionally danced more sedately. It was not ladylike to lift knees and legs high, and the heavy, long, multilayered dresses made such movements impossible and invisible. Subtle sways and twists do, however, cause intriguing skirt ripples and necklace jingles.

A further point about movement styling is that the Greeks' sense of pride and honor can be seen in their dancing. The men are not only proud to be Greek, they are proud to be men. Their grace and fluidity is strong, controlled, and masculine. Although good Greek girls were taught to keep their eyes demurely downcast, even that modesty contained strength and pride and a sense of feminine togetherness. Nowadays, in North American Greek communities, young women dance almost equally with young men; shorter skirts as well as changing customs help make this possible. But there is still that sense of masculine and feminine awareness and pride.

The best way to learn how Greeks dance is to go to a public Greek church picnic or Greek restaurant where musicians entertain. Take the students! It is special to participate with people who still do traditional dances as a natural part of their lives.

HANDS AND ARMS. The most common hand-holds for Greek dances are joined hands with bent elbows (the W-position), joined hands down at sides (the V-position), and hands on shoulders (the T-hold), which used to be for men only. A few dances use the escort-hold, with the forward arm tucked into the elbow of the person ahead or with bent arms and clasped fingers. Some others, usually those from Thrace near Bulgaria, might use a belt-hold or a front basket-position, sometimes called a chain dance. These are positions common to most Balkan dances. One difference between Greek dances and others is that in the W-position, arms are held farther back toward the dancers' own shoulders, and sometimes higher.

The leader's free arm should not hang down but is either held straight out at shoulder height or, when tired, placed on the hip. The last person in line does the same with the free arm or bends it behind the

Two of the most common hand-holds for Greek dances are shown by these fifth-graders—the T-position (top photo) and the W-position (bottom photo).
Photos by Zoltan Horvath

Greek Dances   149

back with closed fist. (Some dance notes describe this closed fist as a symbol of defiance to the Ottoman oppressors; however, like many romantic tales, this is probably fakelore).

MODIFICATION AND TEACHING TIPS. The basic patterns and rhythms in these dances should not be modified. If this seems necessary, we suggest teaching a different dance entirely until students are ready. However, dances can be modified by not teaching variations right away or by limiting the number of variations presented (although heed our earlier comments about teaching tedious simple patterns out of context). Also, the whole discussion of leading can wait until the basics are solidly entrenched.

MUSIC. As might be expected, Greek music varies from region to region. There are simple melodies and intricate ones, there are duple (2/4), triple (3/4), and assymetric (e.g., 7/8, 9/16, 19/16) meters. The music's characteristic combinations of beats with different durations are said to be based on the poetic meters of the ancient dramatist Aeschylus (another romantic tale).

The music of the five common Panhellenic dances we focus on in this chapter has more even meters. It is probably best to teach these dances to recorded music rather than to music played on classroom instruments. Urban ensembles generally use a klarino and one or two bouzoukia, which are instruments shaped and plucked somewhat like the mandolin. They also use a great deal of percussion and sometimes a guitar and an accordion. Vocalists are a vital part of the ensemble. More traditional groups have a *santouri* (or hammered dulcimer) and the bagpipe called *gaida,* perhaps a flute, and a bowed *lyra,* particularly for Cretan music. Students could accompany the recorded music with drums, tambourines, finger cymbals, bells, and other wood or metal that can be struck. It would be very appropriate to dance while singing the music but not traditional to dance to a piano accompaniment.

The five common dances can be done to any music with the appropriate rhythm. The *Rhythmically Moving* and *Changing Direction* series contain a good version of each, but if these dances become a regular part of the repertoire, try some variety. None of these five dances should be associated with just one melody, any more than we would consider, for example, dancing the polka only to *The Pennsylvania Polka.* Most Greek recordings include excellent music for these basic dances.

CLOTHING AND COSTUMES. As in all countries, traditional clothing in Greece is specific to areas and islands. For more generic costumes, however, dress the girls in ankle-length skirts of plain but pretty colors, perhaps with gold hem embroidery, and maybe long aprons with embroidered flowers (perhaps made with fabric markers). Short jackets can be worn over their blouses. The headwear can be a long, embroidered scarf draped under the chin. White stockings and black flats are appropriate footwear.

> This young dancer in an elaborate red-and-gold costume with ribboned headdress is from Corfu, an island in the Ionian Sea off the northwest corner of Greece near Albania.

Greek Dances

It might be difficult to convince boys to wear those short white skirts of the Greek guards, so try the other style of baggy, dark trousers, a long-sleeved white shirt, and a short sleeveless vest. Add color with a red sash, and verve, with the internationally popular Greek fisherman's cap. Boots or dark shoes, and bright socks, are adequate footwear.

Five Common Dances

The five dances we emphasize in this chapter are common to most regions in one form or another. Like other cultures' polkas, tangos, and waltzes, these Greek dances can be done to an infinite number of melodies, as long as the rhythm and tempo are correct.

Hasapikos

The *Hasapikos* was the dance of the butchers' guild in Byzantine times, and it is still called "the butcher's dance." There is a slow and a fast version, although they were once part of the same dance. The *Hasapikos* in *TFD* is the faster version and the most accessible of these Panhellenic dances for North American schoolchildren. It is also known as *Hasaposerviko* (a similar dance in *TM&D*), *Servihasapikos,* or *Servikos*. The prefix *servi-* means Serbian, implying that this dance is like fast Serbian dances. The name *Hasapikos* also can refer to the slow version of this dance, which in *TFD* and other folk dance literature is called *Vari (Varys) Hasapikos.*

Traditionally, the fast *Hasápikos* is done by a few male cronies dancing in the shoulder-hold (T-position), but it is also enjoyed in long lines of both men and women. Usually dancers in a mixed line join in the W-position, although the first few men dancers may want to hold shoulders. The basic pattern is a hora step with a lot of optional variations. The leader initiates the variations, and everyone copies his or her steps. Movements are fast and vigorous.

Vari (Varys) Hasapikos

Vari (Varys) Hasapikos is a *rebetic,* or taverna, dance that originated in the early twentieth century. In this *Hasapikos,* movements are slow, heavy, and dramatic. Traditionally, two or three men—dancing buddies—move back and forth together with deliberate steps. Today women dance too, and usually there are more than two or three people, although lines still should be kept fairly short. Dancers are joined in the shoulder-hold. As in the fast *Hasapikos,* the first person in line leads variations for the others to follow. The variations described in *TFD* and *TM&D* are typical; leaders could use them to create others that fit the basic structure.

The *Hasapikos* is the basis of the *Syrtaki* (as illustrated by *Syrtaki #7*) and *Zorba,* two versions of a new dance that became a fad after the films *Never on*

Sunday and *Zorba the Greek* (some cynics say the dance was created to sell records). In some music, this new dance combines both the slow and the fast *Hasapikos,* almost re-creating the original form of the dance.

*The men of the International Dancers of Chicago, joined in shoulder-hold, perform a joyous **Servihasapikos**.*

Syrtos

Syrtos means dragging, pulling, drawing, and the dance is so-named because the leader draws a long line of dancers behind him or her. It is one of the oldest of the Greek dances and yet one of the most popular today. Some scholars believe that Greeks of antiquity, as seen on ancient artifacts, danced the *Syrtos* around the altar in their religious rituals.

There is a more recent and tragic story connected with this dance. During the long siege of the mountain village of Souli in 1803, soldiers of the Ottoman Empire killed all the village men and then started up the cliffs toward the women and children, who were gathered at the top. To avoid the approaching dishonor, the women threw their babies and children into the rocky ravine and then, one by one, danced the *Syrtos* over the edge to their deaths.

The dance is in duple meter (2/4), but the rhythmic pattern is one step of longer duration and two steps of shorter duration (*slow*, quick, quick). Have students practice this reverse two-step pattern to the music for quite a while before adding the actual steps. In fact, if this rhythmic pattern is as far as they get, they will be doing a perfectly adequate *Syrtos*.

Hands are joined in the W-position, the leader is on the right. In this dance, only the leader does improvisations while the others keep the basic pattern. Of course, as is done in many folk dance groups, the leader can simply repeat the basic pattern also and concentrate on coiling and uncoiling the line.

Greek Dances

If the leader does choose to do variations, they need not be fancy gymnastic feats, although this is encouraged in the Greek community. Simple turns and slaps are often just as impressive as complicated pyrotechnics. And, as the Greeks do, encourage students to change leaders during the dance.

Kalamatianos

This is one of the most popular dances of Greece and is named for a town in the southern mainland that was first liberated from the Turks. Men used to give silk kerchiefs from Kalamata to their ladies as a token of love.

The *Kalamatianos* has the same rhythm (*slow,* quick, quick) and the same footwork as the *Syrtos,* but it has 7/8, asymmetric, meter (1-2-3, 4-5, 6-7). This gives the dance a bouncier feeling. Steps should be quite small, as this dance moves more quickly than the *Syrtos.*

As in the *Syrtos,* the leader may do some improvising while the others keep the basic pattern. These improvisations are meant to be an expression of the leader's emotions but can also be a test of skill.

Tsamikos

The *Tsamikos,* also known as *The Eagle,* has been danced by military men since pre-Biblical days. During the Turkish occupation, this dance symbolized a desire to be free, like the eagle.

As in the *Syrtos* and *Kalamatianos,* in the *Tsamikos* only the leaders do personal improvisations; the others keep the pattern. The second person in line must be strong and steady if the leader plans to express himself with vigor (usually women don't do somersaults). There are basic pattern variations possible, as seen in the dance notes. The meter is triple (3/4), and the dance rhythm is *slow* (beats 1 and 2), quick (beat 3); *slow,* quick; *slow,* quick. Dancers' hands are joined in the W-position, sometimes held a little higher than usual.

This is the dance of those who wear the *tsamika,* the complete, mostly white outfit of the Greek guards called Evzones, which includes a short pleated skirt and soft shoes with pom-poms. The Evzones are an elite corps that, among other responsibilities, guards the palace in Athens. The acrobatic improvisations performed by these young men are meant to show their courage, skill, and manliness—the best dancers are therefore the best soldiers.

Today it is still possible to see these dance feats in Evzone demonstrations and folk ensemble performances. But it is even more impressive and moving to watch them being done at parties and cafes—to witness the leaps and somersaults and the more subtle improvisations of the *Tsamikos* and other Greek dances being proudly performed by older men in business suits and black shoes, and by their sons and grandsons in jeans and tennis shoes, as they continue to carry on the traditions.

Resources Used for Chapter 14

Bambra, Audrey, and Muriel Webster. 1972. *Teaching Folk Dancing.* New York: Theatre Arts Books. This book has excellent information on history, style, costume, and music of Greece, with descriptions in Labanotation for each dance.

Cowan, Jane K. 1994. *Dance and the Body Politic in Northern Greece.* Princeton, NJ: Princeton University Press. This published Ph.D. dissertation discusses traditional dance events in a northern Greek town and shows how people work out their peer relations, gender expectations, and social strata.

Gage, Nicholas. 1989. *A Place for Us.* Boston: Houghton-Mifflin. This author of *Eleni* tells of his family's coming to America from a mountain village in Greece. His description of traditional codes of behavior and how the immigrant community was affected by their new country is the story of many expatriates.

Graziosi, Joseph Kaloyanides. 1986–98. Descriptions of the dances of Greece in many workshops.

Graziosi, Joseph Kaloyanides. 1992, June. Comments and conversations.

Henry, David. 1997. Comments and e-mail conversations with this expert in Greek dance.

Hunt, Yvonne. 1996. *Traditional Dance in Greek Culture.* Athens: Centre for Asia Minor Studies. This book focuses on the role of dance in the lives of the Greek people. Dance genres and styles are presented by region, and one chapter discusses improvisation and leading. (Contact Yvonne Hunt, 1837 38th Ave. NE, Seattle, WA 98105; 206/523-2477; <bg901@scn.org>.)

Karras, Athan. 1976. "Folk Dancing Among the Greeks." *Viltis* (May): 14–15.

Karras, Athan. 1983. "Dancing in Greece." *Viltis* (December): 17.

Karras, Athan. 1985. "An Overview of Greek Folk Music and Dance." *Viltis* (September–November): 8–10.

Karras, Athan. 1991. "An Overview of Greek Folk Music and Dance." *Viltis* (May): 6–8.

Karras, Athan (producer). 1995. *Greek Dances on Video.* Los Angeles: R & R Video International. Karras teaches basic dances such as *Syrtos, Hasaposervikos, Tsamikos, Hasapikos,* and *Karsilamas.* (Available from R & R Video International, 3649 Whittier Blvd., Los Angeles, CA 90023; 213/262-5942.)

Karras, Athan (producer). 1995. *A Greek Folkloric Celebration.* This is a video featuring re-enactment of 1940s Greek picnics performed by the Greek Heritage Society of Southern California. (Available from Basil Caloyeras, Modern Greek Studies Center, Loyola Marymount University, 7107 W. 80th St., Los Angeles, CA 90045.)

Longden, Sanna (producer). 1997. *Living Ethnic Dances for Kids & Teachers.* Evanston, IL: FolkStyle Productions. This video shows sixth-graders learning a Greek dance in a classroom, Greek young people doing a similar dance at a festival, and Evzones from Athens doing the same movements. (Contact FolkStyle Productions, 1402 Elinor Place, Evanston, IL 60201; 847/328-7793; fax 847/328-5241; <SannaMars@aol.com>.)

Papantoniou, Ioanna. 1996. *Greek Regional Costumes.* Athens: The Peloponnesian Folklore Foundation. This is a costume map of Greek clothing for the period 1835–1945 with text in Greek, French, and English. (Order from folkthings, P.O. 13070, San Antonio, TX 78213-0070; 210/530-0694; <folkthings@msn.com>.

Pappas, John. 1970. *Notes on Greece.* Maine Camp, Bridgton, ME, July–August.

Petrides, Theodore. 1976. *Greek Dances and How to Do Them.* Athens: Lycabettus Press; New York: Peters International.

Petrides, Theodore, and Elfreida Petrides. 1976. "A Minor Dissertation on the Greek Dance." *Viltis* (October–November): 5–6.

Raftis, Alkis. 1987. "The Greek Dance." *Viltis* (June–August): 10–12.

Raftis, Alkis. 1991. "Dance in Greece." *Viltis* (March–April): 7–11.

Stratou, Dora. 1991. "Greek Dances." *Viltis* (March-April): 4–6.

Tasulis, Chris, Jr. 1976. "The Greek Heritage of Traditional Folk Songs and Dances." *Viltis* (May): 12–14.

Traditional Greek Clothing [CD-ROM]. This is the first optical compact disk collection of Greek clothing: 150 different outfits representing villages, islands, expatriate Greek communities, plus folk jewelry, shoes, and other accessories, from the collection of the late Dora Stratou and other researchers. Each outfit is accompanied by appropriate music. (Available from the Dora Stratou Theater of Greek Dances, Scholeiou 8, Plaka, Athens, Greece GR. 105 58; (30-1) 32-46-188.)

Travels with Karagiozis. 1996. A sound recording from the band Ziyia. This is 64 minutes of traditional regional Greek music for dancing and listening, on CD (includes song words in Greek and English) or cassette (with songbook). (Available from Lise Liepman/George Chittenden, 1108 Neilson St., Albany, CA 94706; 510/525-4342.)

Hungarian Dances

Chapter 15 Hungarian Dances

Hungarian Dances in Phyllis S. Weikart's Books

(*Note:* Spelling and accents of Hungarian dance names may vary slightly from source to source.)

Circle Csárdás, sometimes *Körcsárdás*	[KUR-char-dahsh] *TFD, CD3*
Körcsárdás I	[KUR-char-dahsh] (Circle csárdás) *TM&D*
Körcsárdás II	*TM&D*
Körtánc	[KUR-tahnts] (Circle dance) *TFD, RM3*
Lákodálmi Tánc	[LAW-koh-dawl-mee tahnts] (Wedding dance) *TFD, CD3*
Mátrai Verbunk	(called *Mátrai Verbunkos* in *TM&D*) [MAH-traw-ee VAIR-bunk] (Men's dance from the Mátra Mountains) *TM&D*
Oláhos	[OH-lah-hosh] (Fox dance) *TFD, CD6*
Palóc Táncok	[PAW-lohts TAHNTS-ohk] (Dances from the Palóc region) *TM&D*
Somogyi Csárdás	(called *Somogy Csárdás* in *TM&D*) [SHOH-moh-dyee CHAR-dahsh] (Couple dance from the Somogy region) *TM&D*
Somogyi Karikázó	(called *Somogy* in *TFD*) [KAW-ree-kah-zoh] (Circle dance for women, from the Somogy region)
Szakacsne Tánc	[SAW-kawch-neh tahnts] (Women's cooking dance) *TM&D*
Ugrós	[OO-grosh] (Leaping, or jumping, dance) *TFD, RM3*

Hungary is a beautiful country with a complex political and geographic history, a complex language, a complex people, and, yes, a complex dance heritage. Wedged into the center of eastern Europe, it also has complex boundaries: Hungary is neighbor to the present-day nations of Slovakia, Austria, Slovenia, Croatia, Yugoslavia, Romania, and a bit of Ukraine. (See p. 66.) Because of this central position, Hungary is a particularly interesting place, with spices from both Eastern and Western cultures added to its own indigenous flavoring.

The peoples of this ancient country have been traced back to Asiatic nomads from the Ural Mountains, centuries before the Common Era. These nomads were part of a group of nations called Finno-Ugric, and even today the unique Hungarian language is closer to Finnish and Estonian than to the languages of its immediate Slavic and Germanic neighbors. The founder of the Hungarian state was King Stephen (1001–1038 C.E.), who organized a state, accepted Christianity as its leading religion and was later canonized, and paved the way for Western culture. Students might be interested to know that August 20, the anniversary of his death almost a thousand years ago, is still celebrated as a national holiday and that during the festivities, there is an exhibition of St. Stephen's preserved, intact right arm.

King Stephen's new country prospered for several centuries, until the Ottoman Turks attacked in the early 1500s. Hungary was divided among the Transylvanian, Turkish, and Hapsburg empires for the next 150 years, accounting for its intriguing combination of Oriental and Occidental characteristics. In 1686, European armies finally defeated the Turks, and Hungary became a Hapsburg satellite for two more centuries, adding strong Germanic tastes to the goulash.

As half of the Austro-Hungarian dual monarchy, Hungary entered the twentieth century as a strong nation economically. At the end of World War I, however, with the defeat and breakup of the Austro-Hungarian empire, Hungary lost two thirds of its territory and population. Today, therefore, there are approximately 10 million people within its borders and 3 million ethnic Hungarians who are citizens of neighboring countries. Those of us who have lived in the U.S. all our lives cannot know how confusing and demoralizing these kinds of boundary shifts can be to a culture. Although it may not be important to know all this when teaching a Hungarian dance in the classroom, such information can lead to other discussions, such as why displaced peoples find it vital to retain their own cultures.

In the 15 years following World War I, Hungary again made great strides toward economic recovery. Then came World War II, and Hungary again was on the losing side and again suffered serious losses. After that war, the nation became the Hungarian People's Republic, part of the Soviet system. In 1956, a people's uprising called the October Revolution failed, and Hungary remained a Communist satellite until Communism collapsed in December 1991. At present, having been one of the more developed and open countries behind the former Iron Curtain, Hungary is again rapidly becoming a strong nation, both politically and economically.

These dancers performing during a festival in Budapest are from the Hungarian people called Csángó. They live outside present-day Hungary in the Gyimes region of Transylvania, in what is now Romania, and in Moldava.

Hungary, which has always been strong artistically, has been associated with dancing since its earliest beginnings, although not everyone appreciated this fact. There were writings in the thirteenth century about the "dancing Hungarians," a sarcastic and derogatory term. In 1681, a minister of the Reformed Church wrote, "We must break all violins, hang the gypsy musicians, and nail the feet of dancing Hungarians fast to the earth."

By the mid-nineteenth century, however, Hungarian dance was appreciated with enthusiasm. Hungarians themselves had begun to be interested in their own culture at the end of the 1700s. Interest spread quickly after 1840, when the national orchestra played a *csárdás* [CHAR-dahsh], and 24 aristocratic couples got up to dance. Always on the lookout for something new, other members of the nobility began to do the csárdás. This led to a craze all over Europe, resulting in artificial versions of this lively couple dance as well as romanticized ideas of other things Hungarian: An example is the music and character for the disguised countess in the opera *Die Fledermaus* by Johann Strauss, Jr.

Modern appreciation of the true folk culture was initiated in the early twentieth century by the work of Béla Bartók and Zoltán Kodály, whose studies of authentic Hungarian music encouraged the current research movement into the genuine folk arts. They recorded traditional folk music and filmed peasants dancing, discovering more than 10,000 variations of dance from 700 different villages. As in other Soviet satellite countries after World War II, the Communist government of Hungary, for its own reasons, supported folk culture research and performing groups, leading to the existence of a great deal of knowledge today about the fascinating subject of Hungarian dance. Basically, however, there is a lot to write about the dances of most eastern European people, because dance is still an integral part of their everyday lives.

The Hungarian words *ugrós, csárdás, karikázó,* and *verbunk* are names for generic dances; therefore, you may come across a variety of dance choreographies with these words in their names. The German-origin words *tánc* (meaning dance) and *táncok* (meaning dances) will also appear often.

The Hungarian dances listed here were presented to the international folk dance community in the 1960s, 1970s, and 1980s by three Hungarian dance teachers who came to live in the U.S. after the Hungarian people's uprising in 1956. The teachers, Andor Czompo, Judith Magyar, and Kálmán Magyar, arranged these dances from traditional movement motifs, for recreational and classroom use. In native Hungarian settings similar dances were done at social events wherever people gathered—in courtyards, inns, barns, fields, village streets, even cemeteries. As in all cultures where dancing is a natural part of the society's activities, the Hungarian children hung around the edges of the dancing and learned by imitation, while their grandparents sat at the side nodding their heads, clapping their hands, tapping their feet, and recalling the days of their frisky youth.

Most of the traditional Hungarian dances do not have set patterns but are improvisational, with regional styling differences. In Hungary, since the early 1970s there has been an upsurge of interest in the peasant dances and music. Called the *táncház* (dance house) movement, this upsurge is similar to the "back to our roots" movements in the U.S. and in other countries where groups meet to learn and enjoy their own traditional dances. Many of the regional dances, especially those of

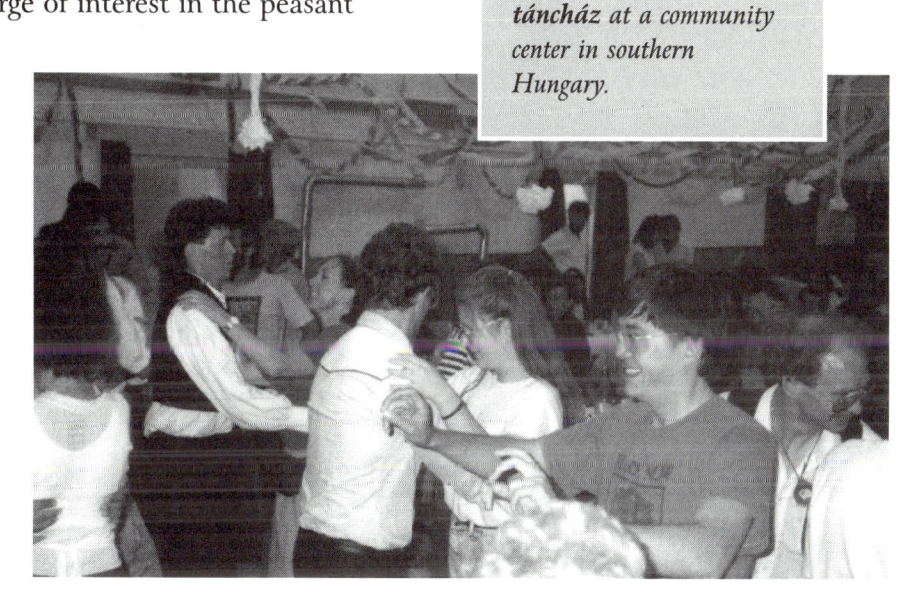

Hungarians and North Americans enjoy a **táncház** *at a community center in southern Hungary.*

Hungarian Dances

161

Hungarians who live in Transylvania, have been brought to North America by professional dancers. These groups of dances, or cycles, although considered to be more like what actual villagers did (and in some cases, still do), are quite sophisticated. Compared to dances with memorizable patterns, they require a more dedicated effort to achieve, and there are groups in the U.S. and Canada that specialize in trying to achieve them. The arranged dances remain popular among folk dancers, however, and are more appropriate for our purposes here.

FORMATION. The Hungarian dances in *TFD* and *TM&D* come in a variety of formations—mixed circles (the *Kör-* dances plus *Palóc Táncok,*); open mixed individual free formations (*Oláhos, Ugrós*); dances for couples (*Circle Csárdás, Somogyi Csárdás*); open circles of men only (*Mátrai Verbunk*); and closed or open circles of women only (*Lákodálmi Tánc, Somogyi Karikázó, Szakacsne Tánc*).

This last type, the women's circle, or round dance, is considered the oldest type and even today can be seen during wedding celebrations and other festivities. Similar to many European chain or round dances, circle dances were done to the dancers' singing, with no instrumental accompaniment—which was sometimes a welcome break for the band. The song, in fact, was more important—the movements were merely adjuncts to the singing. During Lent, for example, when dancing was forbidden, the Karikázó—not being a dance—was allowed. In modern times the movements that accompanied the singing became known as dances. Only the marriageable maidens could join in, and the young men watched from the outside, looking over the girls for future wifely qualities. At the end of the song, some of the boys were likely to pull their favorite girls

As they have for hundreds of years, Hungarian young women sing and dance in a circle around the bride—and in modern-day Hungary, around the groom also.

*The International Dancers of Chicago perform a traditional Hungarian men's **verbunk**—a dance that originated as a way to lure unwary youths into the military.*

out to do a partner dance or just to tease.

Another example of an old form of dance is *Ugrós*. The ugrós type of dance came out of the even older dance, the weapons dance of the Middle Ages, in which men performed fancy movements with axes, swords, or herdsmen's sticks. When weapons were no longer used in these dances, the dancers' hands were freed to do the clapping and snapping we see in today's similar dances.

The verbunk type of dance was originally a men's recruiting dance used to lure unwary youths into the military. The best dancers from each regiment would perform in neighboring town squares and taverns, encouraging the local youth to join the drinking, the dance, and—before they realized what they were doing—the regiment.

The csárdás, or partner, type of dance (as in *Circle Csárdás* and *Somogyi Csárdás*) is considered Hungary's national dance, although it is relatively new.

*The **csárdás** can be done as a couple dance, as a circle dance, or as both at the same time.*

It appeared in the early nineteenth century and was influenced by couple dances of the Renaissance and after. Its name comes from the word *csárdá* meaning country inn, where this type of dance was first enjoyed. Today many versions of the csárdás can be seen wherever there are Hungarian people, as well as people of some other cultures.

The mixed-circle patterns are very modern; they probably arose after World War I, when Western ideas began to seep into the old peasant ways, making the separation of unmarried men and women seem unnecessary. Many of the dances originally intended for only men or only women are also being done as mixed circles in recreational folk dance groups. As discussed in Chapter 2, however, there are good reasons for keeping such dances segregated, even though you might be tempted to combine the genders for efficient teaching.

One way to handle the gender issue is described in *TFD* in the notes for the women's dance *Somogyi Karikázó* (called *Somogy* in *TFD*): Have the boys learn it and then dance in a line behind the girls' circle. In the men's dance *Mátrai Verbunk,* folk dance groups often have a line of women doing a more feminine version, behind the men. Ironically, students in contemporary North

American classrooms might be more comfortable being separated into the archaic male-only and female-only circles, although by the time they are developmentally ready for these sophisticated dances, perhaps they will also be socially ready for mixed-circle patterns.

STEPS AND MOVEMENTS. The basic single and double csárdás steps appear not just in the couple dances but in all types of Hungarian dances (see, for example, *Ugrós,* Parts II and III; *Körcsárdás II,* Part I). Experienced Hungarian dancers bend and straighten their knees as they do this step pattern; they bend on each beat for the downbeat csárdás and straighten on the first beat for the upbeat csárdás. Beginners might prefer to just give the csárdás steps a little bouncy feeling.

The *rida* step also occurs in many dances. This, too, has a rolling feeling from bending and straightening the knees. The open rida has an "up" feeling: Take the SIDE step on the ball of the foot, then do a small knee-bend on the CROSS step (see *Körtánc,* Part II; *Körcsárdás II,* Part IV). The closed rida has a "down" feeling: Do a small knee-bend on the CROSS step, then lift a bit on the ball of the foot for the SIDE step (see *Circle Csárdás,* Part I; *Körcsárdás I,"* Part III).

The *cifra* step (*Ugrós,* Part VII; *Körcsárdás I,* Part II) is a three-movement pattern. Like the two-step in place, it has a quick, quick, *slow* rhythm. The *cifra* has a light feeling with its initial small leap to the side.

Styling points for these and other characteristic step patterns are difficult to pick up from the printed page. They are best learned first from a qualified teacher and then later can be reviewed from written notes or videotapes. If those with little Hungarian dance experience will do these steps with the appropriate feelings or "attitude," that should be more than acceptable.

For example, women's round dances are graceful, feminine, and somewhat earthy. The joined circles insure that every dancer moves as part of a small community. The girls enjoy their closeness and communicate this verbally, as well as with eloquent faces, during the dance. They are very much aware, however, of the admiring young men outside the circle and indicate this awareness in subtle and individual ways.

In their dances, the men are upright, proud, and masculine; balance and strength are very important. Since the men's dances are open, unjoined formations, the dancers have more scope for individuality and competitiveness. Even in the men's choreographed patterns, the goal (unlike that of the joined circles) is not to move exactly as everyone else does, but to exhibit one's own personality. In Hungary, Hungarian-speaking communities in eastern Europe, and Hungarian–North American communities, the best male dancers were—and still are—much admired.

When the women and men dance together as couples, it is important that the man does the leading and that the woman allows herself to be led. The partners should move together in harmony and, in the traditional spirit of improvisation, each couple does not have to dance just as the others do.

HANDS AND ARMS. The dances listed here employ a variety of armholds and hand-holds, sometimes two or three in the same dance. Some, such as the T-hold and V-hold and the front and reverse baskets, are common to other cultures and are described in the Glossary of *TFD* (see insert on p. 167).

The front basket-hold in *Lákodálmi Tánc* has a tricky transition in Part IIA. The girls must drop their crossed arms on measure 9 to make small individual circles to the right, and then reconnect the basket on measure 13. Since this is a transition also found in other eastern European dances, here is a suggestion to make it quite smooth: Each dancer should let her right hand lead her around into the turn. Then, leaving her right arm extended for her righthand neighbor to grasp and keeping her head and her focus toward the left, she joins the basket by slipping her own left arm beneath the extended right arm of her lefthand neighbor. This joining is completed as the girls do the footwork for measures 13–16 (two two-steps or a single csárdás step to right and left).

In another one of the women's dances listed in this chapter, *Szakacsne Tánc*, a type of ugrós, dancers do not join hands. This pattern is based on a freestyle dance in which the women who have prepared the festive food emerge proudly from the kitchen, happily banging their cooking utensils on pots and pans. They parade around the banquet hall to be applauded by the guests, who have just finished overindulging in the wonderful meal. It would be fun to work up to this scenario for a multicultural program. When cooking utensils are not available, women's freestyle hand

These women have come out of the kitchen after a festival banquet in Szeged, Hungary, to do their special dance, a type of **ugrós**, *for the appreciative guests.*

166   *Cultures and Styling in Folk Dance*

Front Basket Dancers stand in a circle or line and spread their own arms sideward in front of the persons on either side. Hands are joined with persons who are one beyond the dancer on each side. The underneath arm usually—but not always—corresponds to the traveling direction. (If the basket moves right the right arm is under.)

Reverse Basket Same as front basket, but hands are joined in *back* of the dancer on each side. The arm on top may correspond to the traveling direction, although comfort also dictates whose arms are where.

V-Hold Hands are joined with arms down. Generally, the left palm faces to the rear (OUT) and the right palm faces to the front (IN), with the left palm on top.

T-Hold (Shoulder) Arms are extended sideward at shoulder level to the near shoulders of the dancer on either side. Elbows are almost straight. Right arms are usually in back, and left arms in front.

positions include hands on waists with fingers forward, or one or both hands above the head with palms forward.

Men also have a variety of hand and arm positions in their open-circle dances. Some arrangements call for clapping and slapping patterns, as in *Mátrai Verbunk*. (When women do this dance behind the men's line, as mentioned earlier,

> *U.S. recreational folk dancers enjoy a **csárdás** using the high, rounded Hungarian dance hold—the shoulder–shoulder-blade position.*
>
> Photo by Zoltan Horvath

their knees are not as high, their slaps and claps are more gentle, and they use the V-hold instead of the T-hold.) *Ugrós* and its relative, *Oláhos,* also have strong masculine styling characteristics, although these recreational arrangements include women also. In such dances, participants have choices of ways to use their hands and arms. When women do these unjoined dances, they can move their hands and arms as described for *Szakacsne Tánc* in the previous paragraph.

For men some choices include holding arms somewhat to the front and sides with hands up, either close to the body or farther forward. Palms can be open, or fingers can be snapped. Or one hand can be held down at the side, and the other can be holding the hat on top or at back of the head. When hands are on hips, men usually use fists, and when clapping is called for, it should be done with strength and deliberation, in front and above the middle of the body. In men's dances partifcularly, attitude is all-important—dance with triumph and pride.

In the couple dances, the "shoulder–shoulder-blade" csárdás position mentioned in *Circle Csárdás* and *Somogyi Csárdás* is an important partner-hold in many cultures, and in most situations it should replace the shoulder-waist position.

Instead of putting his hands in back on his partner's waist, the man places them on or just below her shoulder blades, rounding his arms as though holding a basket or a large beach ball. Her hands are on his shoulders, and her arms are also rounded, resting lightly on his. His hands should be firmly on her shoulder blades, and hers, firmly on his shoulders. Then if they each pull back a bit, using hands and arms for support, the partners will create a good connection. This support and tension allows the man to successfully lead and the woman to easily respond to his kinesthetic directions without verbal cues or shoving.

When walking around clockwise and counterclockwise in this position (as in *Circle Csárdás,* Part II, beats 7–10 and 13–16, and in *Somogyi Csárdás,* Part III), partners will have right hips (moving CW) or left hips (moving CCW) together.

MODIFICATION AND TEACHING TIPS. These dances should not be modified too much, or they will lose the qualities that make them interesting, enjoyable, and Hungarian.

Two of the dances in *TFD—Körtánc* and *Ugrós—*have basic step patterns that should be achievable by upper-elementary students who have had movement and folk dance experience. In *Körtánc,* the front basket-hold could be modified to a V-hold until students are comfortable with the steps. *Ugrós,* being an individual dance, is easier, because hands are not joined; however, it seems to have a lot of parts. The natural teaching progression is to work on just a few of them, perhaps the first three, then add others when appropriate. Since most of these nine steps build on the ones that come before, they might offer a successful challenge and prepare students, especially the boys, for other Hungarian dances. Perhaps they could try out their own variations, once they get a feeling for the structure and styling. This would be a truly traditional way of dancing.

The dances in *TFD* and *TM&D* have other challenges that can be overcome, although some of these choreographies should be saved for the after-school performing troupe. A reverse, or back, basket-hold is a difficult position even for adults; the pattern could be practiced with a V-hold, then a front basket, before adding the back basket-hold. The cifra step should not be attempted until students can do the two-step and the pas de bas (quick two-step); it can be replaced naturally, and often is, with a single csárdás step in the same direction.

When teaching couple dances, unless one gender outnumbers the other, boys should be expected to dance with girls, and vice versa. Such dances were meant for people who looked forward to dancing with someone of the opposite gender. Sometimes it is tempting to modify these couple dances for use with the younger students, those young enough so boys and girls haven't yet developed hang-ups about dancing with each other. Making nine-year-olds into miniature grown-ups, however, trivializes the important function of the partner dances. It is best to save the csárdás for students who will appreciate it and understand its social possibilities. Intermediate dances such as the csárdás are not appropriate before grade 5 or 6.

*As a circle **csárdás** forms, the **cimbalom** player warms up with the other village musicians. The women are wearing versions of the Kalocsa region clothing.*

*A duo of **cimbalom** players (above) seems oblivious to a modern backdrop. A trio of violin, viola, and bass (at right) plays for a wedding celebration.*

170   *Cultures and Styling in Folk Dance*

*Young women of the Penn State International Dance Ensemble perform a **karikázó** wearing a costume in the style of the Palóc region and using their petticoats to advantage.*

MUSIC. The subject of Hungarian folk music is, naturally, a complex one. In the mid-nineteenth century, itinerant Gypsy musicians were playing composed popular pieces; now, at the end of the twentieth century, educated urban young people have revived rural peasant music. The music for the dances in this series is a combination of both, with rhythms and melodies that are hard to resist. It is difficult to just sit when Hungarian music is played.

Much of this music can be translated to classroom instruments, since many of the folk melodies are pentatonic. The sound of Hungarian music is quite unique, however, so for the true flavor, recordings may be preferable. And if you're lucky enough to have Hungarian musicians in the vicinity, do whatever is necessary to get them to your school or dance group!

The most common instrumental combination is a trio of a violin, a three-stringed viola, and a three-stringed bass. Another basic folk instrument is the *cimbalom,* or hammered dulcimer, which sounds like piano strings being played with a soft mallet. Other traditional instruments are the oboe-like *tárogató,* bagpipe *(duda),* lute-like *tambura,* zither, and hurdy-gurdy. One of the most interesting instruments is the *ütögardon,* a primitive cello that is beaten with a bow; this is often used to accompany a violin in the Gyimes region of Transylvania. These old instruments, originally usually played by rural Gypsies, have become fashionable

Hungarian Dances

among the sophisticated urban musicians of the modern táncház movement, and some exceptional ensembles have sprung up, both in Hungary and in the U.S. Much of this archaic music has been recorded.

One of the most important instruments of Hungarian music is the voice, because traditionally, people danced to the accompaniment of teasing chants and songs about male-female relationships.

CLOTHING AND COSTUMES. Each region has its own style of dress, but there are some generalizations that can be considered when planning costumes for programs.

At a minimum, girls can wear a white, puffed-sleeve blouse and a very full, knee-length skirt with at least one full, stiff petticoat underneath; in women's dances, the swaying of skirt and petticoat is used to great advantage. (Pleated skirts are popular in many areas.) A bodice or shawl can be added on top, and an apron over the skirt. In a number of regions, there is a profusion of embroidery, lace, ribbons, fringes, and flower designs, so make the girls' outfits colorful and not necessarily matching one another. Some peasant women have elaborate headresses, and some wear flowered babushkas, but the unmarried girls usually have their long hair in braids with red ribbons. For the legs, red or white kneesocks or tights are appropriate, with low black shoes in place of dance boots, or those clever little backless slippers.

Boys' attire is a little more sober, although in some areas large bright flowers bloom down the front and on cuffs and collars of white shirts. The shirts have long sleeves, full if possible. Boys might wear black vests, which traditionally were often full of colorful embroidery, and white or black pants with black shoes. If they are going to perform a men's recruiting dance, they could tuck their pants into boots and each put on a black bowler at a jaunty angle, in order to lure the locals into their regiment. And for a real male-Hungarian look, each boy should wear a bushy moustache.

Resources Used for Chapter 15

Bakonyi, Erika. 1993–94. Conversations and workshops with this dance teacher from Hungary.

Buday, George. 1950. *Dances of Hungary.* London: Max Parrish & Co. This is one of the classic books in the Handbook of European National Dances series, giving real flavor of the culture.

Czompo, Andor. 1967. "The Hungarian Gypsies." *Viltis* (March–April): 4.

Czompo, Andor. 1980–96. Conversations, criticisms, comments on many occasions.

Czompo, Andor. 1994. "Hungary" and "Hungarian Motifs." In *Dance Awhile,* 7th ed. Jane A. Harris, Anne M. Pittman, and Marlys S. Waller, eds., 309–12. New York: Macmillan International. The author of these articles has since amended the information on dance style and music in "Hungary."

Czompo, Andor, and Ann I. Czompo. 1968. *Hungarian Dances.* Cortland, NY: Quik-Print Service. Andor Czompo is one of the first to teach Hungarian dances in North America, and many of his dances are part of the basic folk dance repertoire. His wife, Ann, is a jazz and modern dancer. Their book has notes for 17 dances, plus basic steps and Hungarian dance background.

Dömotor, Tekla. 1988. *Hungarian Folk Customs.* Budapest: Corvina. This is one of the Hungarian Folk Art series, translated from Hungarian, with wonderful photos of real people celebrating.

Dreisziger, Kálmán. 1988. *The Szatmar Dance Dialect and its Environment.* Toledo, Ohio: Toledói Találkozó (Toledo Hungarian Dance Gathering). The author describes this interesting and amusing work as "an oversimplified explanation of how Hungarian folk dances fit into the general European dance picture."

Eastern Europe Phrasebook. 1992. Victoria, Australia: Lonely Planet Publications. This is a handy book for a brief overview of the Hungarian language and how to pronounce it.

Gáborján, Alice. 1988. *Hungarian Peasant Costumes.* Budapest: Corvina. This is from the Hungarian Folk Art Series, with gorgeous photographs.

Juhász, Katalin. 1990, 1992. Conversations and workshops with a dance teacher from Hungary.

Karikázó. This is a newsletter for those interested in Hungarian folk dance, edited by three Canadian Hungarians. (Write Karikázó, 55 Steeles Ave E., Willowdale, Ontario, M2M 3Y3.)

Lidster, Miriam D., and Dorothy H. Tamburini (eds.). 1965. *Folk Dance Progressions,* 60–62. Belmont, CA: Wadsworth Publishing Co.

Magyar, Kálmán. 1981. "Hungarian Folk Dancing." In *International Folk Dancing USA,* Betty Casey, ed., 156–60. Garden City, NY: Doubleday.

Manga, János. 1988. *Hungarian Folk Songs and Folk Instruments.* Budapest: Corvina. This book is one of the Hungarian Folk Art series, translated from Hungarian with antique photos—the last one, a photo of a grandmother teaching her tiny granddaughter to dance, says it all.

Martin, György. 1988. *Hungarian Folk Dances.* Budapest: Corvina. This is one of the basic books on this subject; György Martin carried on the research initiated by Bartók and Kodály and is considered the inspiration for the modern *tanchaz* movement in Hungary.

Nagy, Zoltán. 1990, 1992, 1993. Conversations and workshops with this dance teacher from Hungary.

Reisz, Alice. 1958. "Genuine and Artificial Folk Dance in Hungary." *Viltis* (June–July): 9–10.

Reisz, Alice. 1958. "Hungary—Land of the Magyars." *Viltis* (November–December): 5–10.

Seaver, Barbara (producer). 1994–96. Hungarian dancing, teaching, and review videotapes from workshops with Nagy Zoltán, Bakonyi Erika, Sára Ferenc, and others. (Available from 9133 Emerson, Des Plaines, IL 60016; 847/635-0543; <Karikáz618@aol.com>.)

Viski, Károly. 1937. *Hungarian Dances*. London: Simpkin Marshall. First published in Budapest; for serious aficionados; has great photos.

Irish Dances

Chapter 16 — Irish Dances

Irish Dance in Phyllis S. Weikart's Books

Irish Lilt   (Intermediate dance) *TFD, RM3*

It is said that in Ireland people carry tunes in their heads, and when meeting others at the crossroads, they may do a dance together. Whether or not this is still true, the Irish culture truly appreciates the aesthetic and emotional value of music and dance.

Irish dancing reflects the Irish character. The people are known to be warm, humorous, sprightly, and spontaneous, while also showing strength and endurance. The Irish have needed all these attributes, for their history is one of constant struggles for independence and unremitting religious hostilities. The white color on the flag of the Republic of Ireland represents peace between the symbolic green (Roman Catholic) and orange (Protestant) factions, but sadly, unceasing struggles and hostilities have continued to bring violence to the beautiful Emerald Isle.

The original settlers of the British Isles were Celts, who celebrated a nature-based religion with Druid priests. When St. Patrick brought Christianity to Ireland in the fifth century, the Celtic people converted but were allowed to keep some pagan elements in their music and dance. There was a peaceful period for the next 400 years as Catholicism took root in the Irish soil. The Vikings ruled briefly in the ninth century, adding a bit of their culture and customs to the mix.

During the following centuries, the Normans and English began to take over what had been Irish land, producing a series of revolts and rebellions through the 1700s. Worse troubles occurred during the mid-1800s, when a succession of potato crops failed, causing disease and starvation for thousands of peasants. The government handled this crisis by forcing almost 40 percent of the population to emigrate, most of them to North America.

Those left in Ireland struggled for survival as well as for independence from the English. After many broken treaties and bloody skirmishes, the mainly Catholic Irish Free State, Eire, was established in 1921 and officially became the Republic of Ireland in 1949, while the mainly Protestant Northern Ireland remained part of Great Britain. (See p. 98.) Now, approaching the twenty-first century, hopes are at last high for an end to the violence over the issues of Irish independence and unification.

Most other cultures also can relate to these emotional issues, and they often do every March 17, when many people in North America become temporarily and affectionately Irish to celebrate St. Patrick's Day with sad songs and happy dances.

Irish folk dances are mostly variations of jigs, hornpipes, or reels. Reels use more gliding, shuffling movements, whereas jigs and hornpipes emphasize stamping and rapping movements. The *Irish Lilt* is a type of jig. There are two broad categories of Irish dancing—the large-group, community **set dances** and the solo or small-group **step dances**. The first type, the set dances, are named in Gaelic *ceilidh*, or *ceili*, [CAY-lee] dances, after the music and dance party at which they are enjoyed. These are progressive dances done in longways, couple-facing-couple or trio-facing-trio formations; they are similar to dances of the British Isles and U.S., ancestors to the *Virginia Reel*. There are perhaps 10 standard ceili dances (such as *Walls of Limerick*, *Siege of Carrick*, and *The Bridge of Athlone*), each with a specific pattern. These patterns are usually guided by a caller, so they may be easily learned. The set dances are generally lively, noisy, and joyous, and they may happen spontaneously whenever Irish music is played.

The second type, the step dances, are traditionally competitive exhibition dances. They are usually learned at an Irish dance academy or from a special teacher and require considerable effort to achieve. The *Irish Lilt* fits into this exhibition dance category. It is a solo double-jig pattern that is achievable by experienced upper-elementary students and recreational folk dancers. In contrast to the relaxed, social, set dances, the step dances are performed in a very controlled manner with most of the action in the legs and feet. These competitive dances are usually done at a *feis,* a type of thanksgiving celebration and dance contest that goes back to the time of the Druids.

There are various explanations for the development of these two contrasting forms of Irish dance—the joyous and relaxed versus the rigid and controlled. Some believe the reason can be found in the advent of Christianity, when two types of priests developed—the humanitarian and the ascetic. Another explanation is that in the sixteenth century, dance masters were hired to refine the exuberance of the native dances to make them more acceptable at court. In addition, during that time, the jig was banned in Ireland because its stirring rhythms and originally vigorous arm movements were thought to incite riot and revolt; therefore, the arm movements were suppressed, probably leading to the more rigid stance we see today.

Religion may also be responsible for the characteristic rhythmic tapping and shuffling foot movements of Irish dance. It is believed that in their pre-Christian religious rituals with the Druids, the Celts communicated with certain spirits by

Young women compete at an Irish dance contest in Estes Park, Colorado.

178 *Cultures and Styling in Folk Dance*

stamping rhythms into the ground. An interesting connection here is that the Celts lived as far south as what is now Spain—where another group of people developed dances based on stamping rhythms with their feet.

The centuries of rigid dance traditions, however, have lately been undergoing a change. There has been a recent surge of interest in Irish arts as a result of the popularity of the Irish music and dance extravaganza "Riverdance." Originally choreographed by Michael Flatley, a Chicagoan who won the 1975 World Irish Dancing championships at age 17, "Riverdance" and Flatley's subsequent production, "Lord of the Dance," take Irish dance beyond its traditional parameters to connect with other cultures' dance and music, such as Spanish flamenco and Bulgarian bagpipes. Dance movements are more dramatic, with performers' arms strongly extended, sharply bent, or swinging, and face and body language expressing exuberance instead of inhibition. Observers report that both boys and girls are again flocking to Irish dance schools in Ireland as well as North America after seeing these productions. It may be that Michael Flatley and other talented contemporary Irish choreographers, while still recalling their roots, are causing an evolution of traditional Irish performance dance styling.

FORMATION. The *Irish Lilt* is an individual dance, usually done with all dancers facing the same direction. In classroom and recreational situations, it is also fun to have the dancers in a circle facing center. This way they can see one another, which encourages the competitive feeling of the dance. In a performance situation, dancers should face the audience.

Generally, of course, the solo jig is meant to be performed by only one or two rather than a whole stageful of people. Traditionally, each dancer adds his or her own elaborations on the pattern, so students can add their own touches to the basic footwork. Perhaps someone goes to Irish dancing school and can share some other steps.

STEPS AND MOVEMENTS. As mentioned above, the dancer's upper body is upright and vertical. The movements, which are almost solely in the legs and feet, should be neat, graceful, and agile. Steps and positions are precise and carefully placed, with feet turned out 45° at the ankle. When feet are lifted, toes should be extended and the foot arched, as in ballet dancing. Knees should be close together, but not tight. When feet are lifted in front, the knees should align with the nose; when feet are lifted behind, try to touch your own backside (but don't really do it!).

The solo dances can be in soft shoes or hard. Usually, in the soft-shoe type, dancers step not with flat feet, but on the balls of their feet, with heels off the ground.

The hard-shoe types are best done on a wood floor or some other surface that allows the characteristic percussive sounds to be heard. During jigging

A performer at the Folkmoot USA festival shows excellent solo jig form by aligning her knees with her nose.

competitions in Ireland, sometimes the judges sit *underneath* the stage to better hear the speed and precision of the fancy footwork. These hard-shoe dances are related to percussive dances of other cultures, including English and French-Canadian step dances, Spanish flamenco, North Indian kathak, South American gaucho, Appalachian clogging, and U.S. tap dancing.

HANDS AND ARMS. In a solo dance such as the *Irish Lilt,* arms hang relaxed at the sides. In a contest or performance, arms are less relaxed, with lightly clenched fists anchored at the body's "corners," where the thighs join the buttocks—a nice comfy resting spot. In competitions, dancers lose points if their hands stray from that spot.

When holding another person's hand during a couple jig or a ceili dance, the adjoining dancers' elbows are sharply bent in the W-position, while the unjoined hand is held relaxed down at the side.

MODIFICATION AND TEACHING TIPS. Solo jigs like the *Irish Lilt* are very individual. Dancers continually add new ideas and further refinements. Therefore, it is perfectly permissible to modify this choreography for teaching purposes. Perhaps at first, instead of doing the six separate patterns, students could repeat several of the easier ones. Once they are able to do these patterns, they can be encouraged to create their own steps. Be sure, however, that they keep their creativity within the structure of the jig and the specific movements of Irish dance.

MUSIC. The music listed for this dance in *TFD* is the well-known *Irish Washerwoman,* which dates from the late eighteenth century, when it appeared in a popular music comedy as *The Irish Washwoman.* It is in duple, double-jig (6/8) meter (the less common hop, or slip, jig is in 9/8). Any other double-jig tune would also be appropriate; try *O'Keefe Slide/Kerry Slide* on the *Rhythmically Moving 1* recording.

Irish dancers in hard shoes create impressive sights and percussive sounds as they parade during the World-Fest in Branson, Missouri.

When starting to teach the *Irish Lilt* or other solo jigs, it is helpful to have variable-speed audio equipment. This is useful for all dance teaching, but particularly for teaching Irish step dancing. Competitive Irish dancers have with them fiddlers and other musicians, whose tempo they control with subtle hand-motions.

Traditionally, fife and piping instruments, as well as the Celtic harp and the Irish drum (*bodhran*) were used. Instruments used today, besides violins, are flutes, pianos or piano accordions, and drums.

CLOTHING AND COSTUMES. Competitive Irish dancers have adopted a basic outfit. The girls wear a dress, usually green or deep blue, with a fitted waist, long sleeves, and a knee-length flared skirt. Over one shoulder, they have a waist-length cape pinned with a brooch, and sometimes they add a wide laced belt or sash at the waist. The garments may be embroidered with Celtic designs. Black

Irish Dances

An Irish dance team participating in the Folkmoot USA festival show the beautiful Celtic designs on their costumes.

tights and low black shoes complete the outfit. This costume can be simplified to a white blouse, a plain-colored (not necessarily green) skirt with a wide black belt or sash, and a little cape—or even a simple long white dress.

Boys wear a dark kilt or long trousers, a white shirt and green tie, a short or standard-length jacket, kneesocks, and black shoes. This outfit can be simplified to a white long-sleeved shirt, a green vest or tie, long trousers or knickers with kneesocks, and black shoes.

Resources Used for Chapter 16

Burchenal, Elizabeth. 1938. *National Dances of Ireland*. New York: G. Schirmer. The author is one of the U.S. pioneers in collecting and notating folk dances.

Duggan, Anne Schley, Jeanette Schlottmann, and Abbie Rutledge. 1948. *Folk Dances of the British Isles*. New York: Ronald Press. Notes for the *Irish Lilt* are on pp. 98–100 of this book.

Hall, Maureen. 1990. *Irish Dances*. Syllabus from dance workshop at conference of American Orff-Schulwerk Association, Denver, CO.

McCourt, Frank. 1997. "Gotta Dance." *The New Yorker,* 10 March 1997, p. 37. McCourt tells how his admiration for Flatley's "Riverdance" has changed his own attitude toward Irish dance.

O'Farrell, Una, and Sean O'Farrell. 1972. "Chart of Basic Steps for Irish Dancing." Stockton Folk Dance Camp, University of the Pacific, Stockton, CA.

Tiritelli, Margie Lenihan. 1981. "Irish Folk Dancing." In *International Folk Dancing USA,* Betty Casey, ed., 167–68. Garden City, NY: Doubleday.

Israeli & Jewish Dances

Chapter 17 Israeli & Jewish Dances

Israeli and Jewish Dances in Phyllis S. Weikart's Books

(*Note:* Though Hebrew names are not always spelled consistently in English because of discrepancies in transliteration from the Hebrew alphabet, we will try to be consistent in this book. Please note that in the dance lists of this chapter, the underlined ch in phonetic spellings is a guttural sound, like the ending sound in the Scottish word *loch*.)

Arabic-Influence Dances
See page 191.

Chassidic-Influence Dances
See page 194.

European-Influence Dances
See page 198.

Yemenite-Influence Dances
See page 199.

Homeland-Influence Dances
See page 203.

Tucked between Asia, Africa, and Europe, Israel occupies a tiny strip of land where much of the world's history, both ancient and modern, has taken place. (See p. 48.) The land was known as Canaan in biblical times, then as Judaea in the first century under the Romans, and sometime later as Palestine, before it became the State of Israel in 1948. It is also revered as the Holy Land by those who practice Judaism, Christianity, and Islam.

The Hebrews, a Semitic race who inhabited the land at least as far back as 1900 B.C.E., became known as Jews, or the Jewish people—that is, Judeans. (Other Semites—peoples descended from Noah's son Shem—are Arabs, Ethiopians, and Assyrians.) About 70 C.E., after being enslaved by the Romans, the Jewish people were sent from their homeland and dispersed all over the world, resulting in a situation referred to as the Jewish diaspora (the West Africans, Armenians, Assyrians, and Gypsies are other cultures who have experienced diaspora, an enormous displacement of their people).

No matter where on the globe the Jews moved, through centuries of persecution, they managed to retain their strong cultural and religious traditions. Because Jewish people were seldom allowed to own land and were always outsiders, they developed individual skills as merchants and traders, professions as doctors and lawyers, and artistic talents as musicians and dance masters. They were usually forced to live in specific areas, such as the enclosed *shtetl* communities of eastern Europe. Sad history has shown them that it is important to be equipped to take care of oneself no matter what life brings and that one's own home is the safest place. Therefore, Jewish family life is most important, and education of Jewish children was, and still is, the most revered accomplishment.

After centuries of dispersal and persecution, the Jewish people longed to put down roots. In the late nineteenth century a movement called Zionism arose. Its goal was to return the Jewish people to Palestine to establish a nation that would be a much-needed haven and homeland for them. The first migration to this new homeland came mainly from Europe, as did many more migrations after the devastating Second World War. Since then, millions of Jewish people have moved to Israel from at least 100 countries.

The Israeli nation's early pioneers, mostly young European Jews, were farmers trying to reclaim barren lands. During the day, they worked hard, draining, irrigating, fertilizing, and cultivating; in the evenings—in an attempt to create a community in this harsh homeland—they socialized around campfires. They danced together, sharing the dances from their respective countries—the *krakowiaks* from Poland, the *cassatschok* from Ukraine, the polkas from Lithuania, and the circle horas from southeastern Europe. The Romanian horas and *sîrbas* became particularly popular, because the values of the settlers, especially on the *kibbutz* (collective agricultural settlement), were expressed in the energetic, close-knit dance circle, where all were equal, regardless of gender, ability, or rank. This was a concept not honored in the lands from which they had come. Thus, the hora type of dance was to become the foundation of the unique Israeli dance culture.

An important point about Israeli dances is that they are not the only dances of the Jewish people. This subject is complex—Judaism itself is not easy to pigeonhole. More than a religion but not exactly a race, it is a strongly rooted culture with many branches. One large branch is that of the Ashkenazi Jews from central and eastern Europe, whose common tongue was the German-based Yiddish. In the last part of the nineteenth and first part of the twentieth century, many of these people emigrated to other continents, particularly North America. The majority of those who did not leave Europe by 1939 perished in Hitler's Holocaust, but their spirit lives through the recent revival of klezmer music.

Another branch is the Sephardic Jews, who were expelled from Spain in 1492 when they would not convert to Christianity and who settled in North Africa, South America, southern Europe, the Balkan lands, and Turkey. Known as Spanish Jews, their common language is Ladino, a combination of Spanish and Hebrew. Other branches include Oriental Jews from Persian and Arab countries; Chassidic Jews, who practice a form of Judaism begun in eighteenth-century Poland; and the Falasha of Ethiopia, a Black orthodox sect. All these branches have been planted in Israel, and now there is also an important offshoot that was born in the land itself—the *sabras,* descendants of the Israeli nation's first pioneers and well named after the soft but sturdy fruit of the prickly cactus plant.

From the earliest biblical times, all of these branches of the Jewish people have celebrated holidays and occasions by dancing. Each culture had their own dances, and the styles of these dances can be seen in the great wealth of Israeli dances. We discuss these influences and characteristics in the following sections.

Israeli Dance Background

You may have noticed that in *TFD* and *TM&D,* Israeli dances outnumber those from other peoples or geographic regions. One reason for this (besides the fact that Phyllis Weikart herself loves them) is that most Israeli dances have been choreographed especially for the *youth* of Israel. This makes them appropriate for the youth of the United States, particularly for older children who have had some earlier folk dance experience.

Because Israeli dances have been consciously created, they are unique in several ways. In most cultures, parents and grandparents pass dances on to children. Young people learn the dances by tagging along at community events and participating in family parties. The dances of many older cultures show their age with their slower, heavier movements or intricate, sophisticated steps and rhythms. Dances of modern Israel are special, however, because they were not taught over centuries by generations who shared a basic culture; instead, they were choreographed specifically for children and young adults. If the Jewish people had always remained in their original homelands, today they might be doing centuries-old native dances, as other peoples do. Their dances, moreover, might have been among the most ancient of all, considering that the Old

Testament has many references to the music and dance of the biblical Jews.

Modern Israeli dance has its roots in the German youth movement, which began at the turn of the twentieth century. Within it there were many political and philosophical groups of both Christian and Jewish young people, all rejecting what they saw as the conformist, materialistic, authoritarian values of their society and working toward creating a brave new world. Among the movement's various ideals (a return to nature, communal living, unconventional clothing styles, healthful eating habits), was an interest in a less formal type of dance that expressed feelings of community and physical freedom. Called *Jugentanz*, this dance trend had a lasting impact on the subsequent history of dance; Isadora Duncan, Martha Graham, and Emile Jaques-Dalcroze all began their work during this period.

Some of the young German Zionists recognized that their new nation must have a solid cultural base, and what cultural form is more accessible than folk dancing? So they began creating communal dances that celebrated how they were bringing new life to the desert—watering the land, communing around the campfire, harvesting the grapes, tending the flocks, and finding romance. In 1944, they organized a festival to share the new dances—such as *Mayim* (created in 1938 to commemorate their finding water after 10 years of searching) and *Kol Dodi*—as well as the traditional ones brought from other nations. When asked how a dance gathering could take place during this horrible period in Jewish history, the organizers responded, "Precisely now!" and the Hebrew word *davka* (precisely) became the password. This festival inspired the creation of many more dances that quickly spread throughout the country to fulfill the need for a form of joyous cultural expression.

Particularly important and poignant was the need for security for the orphaned children of Europe who were sent by boatloads to Palestine after Hitler's Holocaust. The basic Israeli form of dance, the hora—a closed circle with dancers connected to each other by hand, waist, or shoulder—became a symbol of the community lost by these children in the concentration camps but regained in the welcoming country of Israel.

The subsequent proliferation of Israeli dances brought enjoyment, exercise, commitment to the new homeland, and a sense of community—all of which reflect the very reasons we teach folk dance today. Unlike dances from most other cultures, Israeli dances are an increasingly popular form of recreation throughout the homeland as well as in North America, Great Britain, and many other places. In Israel, the dancing has progressed from small groups around the kibbutz campfire to sessions of sometimes more than a thousand people. Even as you read this, new dances are being choreographed by enterprising teachers and musicians, who compete to get their dances into the weekly "Top 10" and to teach at the important camps. This exciting, creative outpouring has somewhat changed the nature of communal dance in Israel but is very much in the spirit of the young country.

Israeli dancing also continues to be popular in North America; active groups exist in most major metropolitan areas. For many of the participants, it is

Israeli dancing is a joyous activity at weekly recreational groups and at yearly camps such as the one shown here—the Hagigah Israeli Dance Camp, held every October in Oconomowoc, Wisconsin.

not just a recreational activity but also a joyous way to maintain connection with the Jewish homeland and with the Israeli people, some of whom they often meet right there in the Israeli dance groups. A number of group "regulars" attend not because they are Jewish or connected to Israel, but because they are attracted to the beautiful movements and music.

Many of the newer dances are quite complex and challenging. *TFD* and *TM&D* use mostly pre-1970, "older" Israeli dances because they are symmetrical, straightforward, and set to singable melodies.

Israeli Dance Styling

The Israeli dances in Phyllis S. Weikart's books are loosely based on several recognizable influences. These were contributed by Israeli immigrants whose former cultures included strong dance traditions—the Arabic, the Yemenite, the Chassidic, the European—and by the land of Israel itself. A number of the dances combine some or all of these influences and have many steps in common with other dances. However, for purposes of discussing specific stylings, we have separated the Israeli dances into categories according to the predominant influence. (See Longden [1997] for illustrations of the specific stylings.)

Israeli dances are choreographed to traditional melodies, popular songs, or specially composed music. The music of the dances in *TFD* and *TM&D* almost always has the feel of duple (2/4, 4/4) or triple (3/4) meter. The titles, which may be biblical quotations, place descriptions, or romantic phrases, usually have nothing to do with the actual dance steps. Because more than one choreographer may have worked with the same piece of music, sometimes a given melody has more than one dance identified with it. The newer dances are choreographed to popular songs and exhibit the individual expression of American rock dances, the asymmetrical patterns of Balkan dances, and the rhythms of Latin dances.

Arabic Influence and Styling

Debka is an Arabic word meaning line dance. If a dance is called a debka, you know its movements have been influenced by the dances of Israel's Arab citizens and neighbors, both Jews and non-Jews, although some debka dances cannot be identified as such by their title (see the last seven dances listed below). These dances are strong and powerful, using movements originally done mainly by men, on flat, sandy surfaces. Students enjoy the sharp, stamping movements. Like almost all other Israeli dances, the debkas listed here are not truly traditional. They have been choreographed in the debka style, using movements similar to those in "real" Arab dances.

FORMATION. Debkas are often line dances done in columns of no more than seven or eight people, one in front of the other (*Debka Chag, Debka Druz, Debka Le Adama, Kol Dodi, Mishal, Sapari*). They can also be done in

Arabic-Influence Dances in Phyllis S. Weikart's Books

Debka Benot Hakfar	[DEB-kah beh-NOUGHT hahk-FAHR]	(Daughters of the village) *TM&D*
Debka Chag	[DEB-kah chahg]	(Festive debka) *TFD, CD1*
Debka Daluna	[dah-LOO-nah]	(Debka from Daluna) *TFD, RM9*
Debka Dayagim	[dye-ah-GEEM]	(Fisherman's debka) *TFD, CD5*
Debka Druz	[drooze]	(Debka of the Druz people) *TFD, CD2*
Debka Kurdit	[koor-DEET]	(Debka of the Kurdish people) *TFD, RM7*
Debka Le Adama	[leh ah-dah-MAH]	(Debka of the soil) *TFD, RM9*
Horat Hasor	[hoh-ROT hah-SORE]	(Hora from Hasor) *TFD, CD4*
Ken Yovdu	[ken yove-DUE]	(Thus shall they perish) *TFD, RM8*
Kol Dodi	[cool doe-DEE]	(Voice of my beloved) *TFD, CD3*
Marhaba	[mar-ha-BAH]	(Welcome) *TM&D*
Mishal	[mee-SHAHL]	(A referendum) *TFD, CD3*
Sapari	[sah-pah-REE]	(Tell it to me) *TFD, CD1*
Ya Abud	[yah ah-BOOD]	(An Arabic word or name) *TM&D*

closed or open circles (*Debka Benot Hakfar, Debka Dayagim, Marhaba*), or in short, tight lines (*Debka Daluna, Debka Kurdit, Ya Abud*).

STEPS AND MOVEMENTS. Movement is vertical, up and down as much as possible, in contrast to the more horizontal movements of other Israeli dances. Steps are sharp and precise, with movements directly beneath the body, lots of knee action, and feet turned out a bit. Posture is erect and proud.

These young dancers are learning to do an Israeli dance in the Arabic style, with lots of knee action and erect and proud posture.

Photo by Zoltan Horvath

HANDS AND ARMS. In columns, dancers face forward and join hands by bending one arm behind the back to clasp the hand of the person behind while extending the other arm to join the hand of the person in front. In circles, use the shoulder-hold (T-position), or join hands down at sides (V-position). In the short lines, dancers use a strong shoulder-hold or firm V-position and move in unison, shoulder to

Dressed in traditional desert garb, the Shalom Israel dance troupe from Ayala, Israel, performs an Arabic-influence choreography at Folkmoot USA in Waynesville, North Carolina.

shoulder, with their neighbors. When clapping, they use open hands with fingers spread.

MODIFICATION AND TEACHING TIPS. For basic simplifying concepts, read "Modifying Ethnic Folk Dances" on p. 24 of Chapter 2. One specific suggestion for modifying the Arabic-style Israeli dances that have a long series of patterns (which is at least half of those on the debka list) is to add the styling after teaching two or three parts rather than after teaching the entire dance. For example, let the students accomplish the first three parts of *Debka Kurdit* (six parts in all) or of *Ya Abud* (seven parts). Then add the shoulder-hold or the shoulder-to-shoulder position, and talk about the sharp up-and-down movements. After the students seem to be enjoying this Arabic flavoring, you can begin to add the rest of the movements.

MUSIC. Characteristic instruments are small drums, or *darabukas*; stringed instruments called *oods* and *kanoons*; reedy desert flutes; and cymbals. These can easily be duplicated in the classroom with hand drums, recorders, glockenspiels, guitars, and cymbals and triangles. Music for all of these dances is available on the *Rhythmically Moving* and *Changing Directions* series.

CLOTHING AND COSTUMES. Typical traditional desert garb for men is the calf- or ankle-length white or striped shirt (*galabiyeh*) and wrapped head

Israeli and Jewish Dances

scarf (*kafiyah*). Women wear a long dark tunic with trousers underneath that are tight at the ankle, and a head scarf or veil covering part of their face. These outfits may be modified for dance performances. For students, a long shirt would be comfortable and appropriate; for a quick change, the shirt can be worn over some other costume. For more authenticity, add a head scarf—wrapped turban-style for boys, and tied behind the head, hanging in back for girls. Arabic peoples generally do not dance without shoes or boots, but when Israeli dancers perform Arabic-influenced (and other styles) of dance, they usually dance barefoot or in sandals.

Chassidic (Hassidic) Influence and Styling

Chassidic dance first appeared in Poland in the mid-eighteenth century when a Jewish mystic, the Baal Shem Tov, came out of the Carpathian Mountains to lead a fervent and joyous new form of Jewish worship. Basic to this spiritualism was prayer accompanied by ecstatic singing and dancing; in fact, for the early Chassidic people the song and dance *was* the prayer. The swaying movements, similar to the rocking motions made while praying, also served as a sort of release from the oppressive restrictions imposed on eastern European ghetto dwellers. Most of the people who followed this form of worship perished in the Holocaust of World War II. Those few who escaped have established small Chassidic communities in Israel, the U.S., and other countries, where they still can be seen dancing during holidays and community celebrations.

Traditionally, because of strict religious beliefs about the role of women, Chassidic men did most of the dancing. The community honors the law of no touching between genders except in marriage. At weddings, the bride and groom may hold a scarf or handkerchief between them for a traditional dance. Men and women either hold scarves between them while dancing or form separate circles,

Chassidic-Influence Dances in Phyllis S. Weikart's Books

Bechatzar Harabbi	[beh-<u>cha</u>-TZAR hah-rah-BEE] (In the rabbi's garden) *TFD, RM6*
Hora Bialik	[HOH-RAH bee-ah-LEEK] (named for Haym Bialik, originator of the modern Israeli alphabet) *TFD, RM9*
Hora Chadera	[HOH-rah <u>chah</u>-deh-RAH] (Hora of the Chader [school]) *TFD, CD1*
Hora Hassidit	[HOH-rah has-sih-DEET] (Dance of the Chassidic people) *TFD, RM5*
Tzadik Katamar	[tzah-DEEK kah-tah-MAHR] (Righteousness shall flourish) *TFD, CD2*
Zemer Atik	[ZEH-mare ah-TEEK] (Ancient song; sometimes called *Nigun* [ni-GOON] *Atik*) *TFD, RM4*

with the men's circle holding shoulders and the women's circle holding hands.

For those who do not practice Chassidism, the joyous dance style lives on to some extent in the choreography of Chassidic-style Israeli dances. However, compared to dances with other influences, few Chassidic-influence dances have been created, probably because ecstatic religiosity is not typical of most present-day Israeli dancers.

FORMATION. These dances take all forms—circle, snake, occasionally partner, but especially individual, such as *Bechatzar Harabbi*—because Chassidic dancing was traditionally done as an individual expression of joy before joining with others.

STEPS AND MOVEMENTS. The characteristic movement is stepping forward to reach up to God, then stepping backward while bending with bowed head. In most modern Israeli dances, this movement has evolved into snapping fingers above the head or reaching up with the hands, then backing out of the circle without the bend and bow.

Steps are often done with knees a bit bent and wide, a slight "sitting in" that is closer to the ground than that of the hora-type dances, with possibly a little rocking or swaying from side to side. It was older European adults who did these dances traditionally, so a little role-playing ("How would your [great] grandfather do this dance?") might produce the correct feeling in students.

HANDS AND ARMS. In today's Chassidic-style choreographies, circles join with adjacent dancers' hands in the V-position, as in *Hora Bialik,* or with each dancer's left palm up at the shoulder and right palm down on the left palm of the person ahead in the circle, as in *Hora Chadera* and *Zemer Atik.* The T-position is often used in other Chassidic dances. Arms are raised and lowered, as though reaching toward heaven.

MODIFICATION AND TEACHING TIPS. Follow the modification suggestions in Chapter 2. Omit hand-holds and turns in the beginning, but add them as soon as possible, since they are the main characteristics of this type of dance.

MUSIC. Originally these dances were done to the sounds and rhythms of fervently expressed prayers; it would not be inappropriate to dance them while singing or humming the melodies. The more secular forms of Chassidic dance were accompanied by itinerant klezmer musicians playing stringed, brass, and reed instruments. Many of these talented men became important to the early jazz movement when they immigrated to the U.S. in the late nineteenth and early twentieth centuries. Klezmer music started to become fairly popular in the 1970s and is again a well-established form of folk music.

Performing at Folkmoot USA, women of the Shalom Israel dance troupe (top photo) demonstrate a typical Chassidic movement, raising their arms as though reaching toward heaven. The men of the troupe (bottom photo), in a ecstatic Chassidic-influence dance, demonstrate how the knees are a bit bent and wide.

CLOTHING AND COSTUMES. Chassidic Jews dress today as they did 200 years ago; like present-day Amish people or others in religious communities, they wear dark sober clothes, long sleeves, ankle-length coats and dresses, heavy shoes. Men are bearded and keep their heads covered to show their respect for God. Married women cover their hair, as is common in many traditional societies. Regional variations depend on the country from which the Chassidic Jews originate.

For a school program, however, the generic Israeli costume would be appropriate (see p. 204) unless there is a specific focus on Chassidic dance. In that case, dress the dancers in dark, "old-fashioned" clothes, with brimmed hats for the boys and babushkas for the girls. For quick changes over a basic blouse/skirt or shirt/pants combination, add long dark jackets or vests (borrowed from parents) and head coverings.

Typical Chassidic-style movements and dress are shown in this photo of a member of the Nitzanim Israeli Folkdance Troupe of Chicago.

Photo by Betty Sterling Hart

European Influence and Styling

Because the eastern European countries of Poland and Russia were home to the Chassidim, the eastern European influence was similar to the Chassidic influence on Israeli dance. Many eastern European Jews, however, did not follow the Chassidic rituals; like members of all the world's sects, they practiced their religion with different degrees of intensity. The European-influence dances listed here

Israeli and Jewish Dances

European-Influence Dances in Phyllis S. Weikart's Books

Bisdot Bet-Lechem	[beez-DOH bet-leh-<u>CH</u>EM] (The fields of Bethlehem) *TFD, CD4*
Cherkessiya, or *Tcherkessiya*	[chair-kuh-SEE-yuh] (Dance of the Cherkessiyan people) *TFD, RM2*
Hora	[hoh-RAH] (Circle dance) *TFD, RM4*
Romanian Hora	[hoh-RAH] (Triple hora) *TFD, RM7*
Tarantella	*TM&D*
Ve David	[veh dah-VEED] (King David) *TFD, RM3*

have the more secular influences of the countries in which Jewish people lived. Thus we have the grapevine step from Romania, Bulgaria, and other Balkan countries (as in the *Romanian Hora*); the prancing steps of the Cherkessiyan horsemen from the Caucasus Mountains (*Cherkessiya*); the mazurkas and polkas of Poland (*Bisdot Bet-Lechem*); the flirting and buzz turn of southern Europe (*Tarantella*); and even the social mixers of England (*Ve David,* based on the *Circassian Circle*).

There is no one type of styling that is characteristic of this group of dances. The various countries' influences can be seen mainly in the steps and arm positions, which are different for each dance, as described in the dance notes. Separate costume styles are not appropriate for the different dances, however, for in spite of the variety of national backgrounds they display, these are all true Israeli dances. Costume the students in the generic Israeli outfits (see p. 204), and enjoy.

For its generic Israeli costume, the Penn State International Dance Ensemble pins blue sashes onto white shirts and blouses.

198 *Cultures and Styling in Folk Dance*

Yemenite Influence and Styling

The Yemenite Jews, for whom this dance style is named, came from the land of Yemen at the tip of the Arabian peninsula, near Africa and India. Being isolated from the rest of the Jewish culture, they retained many religious and societal customs from biblical times. Because they were among the only Jews to have lived in one land for a long time, they were able to develop a definite dance culture. The "oriental" feeling of their soft, flowing movements and of their conspicuous use of hands and arms, as well as the staccato Arabic movements, have inspired many Israeli choreographers to add a strong Yemenite flavor to their dances.

FORMATION. Traditionally, Yemenite men and women danced separately. Modern Israeli Yemenite-type dances range from couple (*Dodi Li*), line (*Hineh Ma Tov*), and joined circle (*Ma Na'avu, Tzlil Zugim*) dances to unjoined circle (*Dror Yikra, Haschachar*) and individual (*Sapri Tama*) dances. In the contemporary Israeli dance movement, many of the dances that originally used joined-circle and line formations are now being done without joining hands, this is possibly an influence of the "do-your-own-thing" disco and rock dances.

Yemenite-Influence Dances in Phyllis S. Weikart's Books

Ahavat Hadassah	[ah-hah-VAHT hah-DAH-sah] (The love of Hadassah)	*TFD, CD2*
Al Gemali	[ahl geh-mah-LEE]	*TFD, CD4*
At Va'ani	[aht vah-ah-NEE] (You and me)	*TFD, CD1*
Betof Utzlil	[bay-TOFF oots-LEEL] (With drum and ring of bells)	*TFD, CD5*
Dodi Li	[doe-dee LEE] (My beloved is mine)	*TFD, CD3*
Dror Yikra	[drawer yee-KRAH] (Call for freedom)	*TFD, CD3*
Haschachar	[hah-shah-CHAR] (The dawn)	*TFD, CD1*
Hineh Ma Tov	[hee-NAY mah-TOVE] (How good it is)	*TFD, CD4*
Im Ninalu	[eem nee-nah-LOO] (If they were locked out)	*TM&D*
Ki Hivshiloo	[key heev-SHE-loo] (For the vines have blossomed)	*TFD, CD2*
Le'Or Chiyuchech	[ley-ORE chee-you-CHECH] (By the light of your smile)	*TFD, RM8*
Likrat Shabat	[lee-KRAHT shah-BAHT] (Welcome, Sabbath)	*TFD, CD1*
Ma Na'vu, or Ma Na'avu	[mah nah-ah-VOO] (How wonderful the sound of the approaching Messiah)	*TFD, RM6*
Mit Yitneini Ohf	[meet yeet-NAY-nee off] (Would that I were a bird)	*TM&D*
Sapri Tama	[sah-PREE tu-MAH] (Tell me, my innocent one)	*TFD, RM7*
Tzlil Zugim	[tsleel zoo-GEEM] (The sound of bells and cymbals)	*TFD, CD1*

Israeli and Jewish Dances

STEPS AND MOVEMENTS. Movements in Yemenite-inspired dances are fluid and flexible, often with sideward sways or in-and-out rocking motions. The most characteristic movement is the "Yemenite step": SIDE, SIDE, CROSS, REST (see *TFD* for teaching suggestions).

For good Yemenite-step styling, dancers should keep their feet parallel and their chest facing the center or their partner as much as possible, instead of turning from side to side. The flowing motion can be achieved by slightly bending the knee on the first SIDE, slightly stepping up on the ball of the foot for the second SIDE, and stepping on a flat but flexible foot to CROSS (please notice the "slightly"). Try to avoid stepping BACK on count 2, and don't turn your torso from side to side.

HANDS AND ARMS. Hands and arms are graceful but strong and are as important to these dances as the feet. Clapping and snapping is done firmly, at shoulder height or higher. Hands are usually held crossed at the wrist, with the fingers snapping or in a picturesque position with thumbs and middle fingers touching. Dancers usually join in the V-position.

These recreational folk dancers doing a Yemenite-style dance concentrate on snapping their hands firmly, at shoulder height, with wrists crossed. The snap is done with thumbs and middle fingers.

Photo by Zoltan Horvath

200   *Cultures and Styling in Folk Dance*

A couple from the Nitzanim Israeli Folkdance Troupe of Chicago, with heads well covered, demonstrate a Yemenite love dance.

Photo by Betty Sterling Hart

MODIFICATION AND TEACHING TIPS. Students should have some solid dance experience before being introduced to Yemenite-style dances. Practice the Yemenite step a lot, particularly the transition from CROSS, REST to SIDE. If you need to simplify for a while, try SWAY, SWAY, SWAY, REST to retain the feeling of the step.

Israeli and Jewish Dances

MUSIC. Traditionally and even today, Yemenite Jews use no musical instruments, as a way of commemorating the destruction of the Temple. Their dances are accompanied by voice and percussion. Instrumentation of modern Israeli Yemenite-type dances is similar to that used with the Arabic-style Israeli dances; both dance types come from desert peoples. These dances are well represented on the *Rhythmically Moving* and *Changing Directions* recordings.

CLOTHING AND COSTUMES. For Yemenite-style dances in a school program, it is appropriate for students to wear the same costume as for the Arabic-style Israeli dances. If you'd like to differentiate between the two, replace the girl's head scarf with a black hood, and add gold coins or embroidery around the neck and to the hood. Because Yemenite Jews are quite religious, it is important that the heads of both boys and girls be well covered.

The Homeland (or Sabra) Influence and Styling

The experience of working on the land itself—helping the desert to flower and protecting it from its enemies—has had a profound influence on Israel's dances. Notice how many dance titles listed here celebrate the fields, the campfire, the vines, the wine pressers, water, or victory. All of the other styles we've discussed so far are also incorporated in these characteristic Israeli dances, and this gives these dances a special style of their own. We might find the shoulder-hold, the Yemenite step, the grapevine pattern, or the debka hop and jump in any of these choreographies, because these elements are the folk material from which the majority of Israeli dances were constructed.

Most Israeli dances, particularly the hora-type ones, are characterized by feelings of freedom and exuberance. The people who did them were literally free—because they were removed from the horror of Hitler, because they were young and not limited by aging bodies, because they danced in desert spaces instead of in cramped shtetl houses, and because they danced in shorts and bare feet rather than cumbersome traditional clothing.

FORMATION. The original hora dances were closed circles. Today in many Israeli recreational dance groups, these circles are becoming unjoined, and people are moving individually around the perimeter without touching. Please see our comment on the folk process (p. 19) to help you teach such dances.

Unlike the dances of many other, older cultures, these dances include a number of couple dances and mixers. In a great departure from the Chassidic style, not only do the men and women dance together with great pleasure, but also, in many of the dances, their steps are identical. This is a sign of the more equal roles of modern Israeli women and men.

Homeland-Influence Dances in Phyllis S. Weikart's Books

Ana Halach Dodech	[ahna hah-LA<u>CH</u> doe-DEH<u>CH</u>]	(Where did your beloved go?) *TFD, CD1*
Bat Arad	[baht ah-RAHD]	(Daughter of Arad) *TFD, CD1*
Bat Hareem	[baht hah-REEM]	(Daughter of the hills) *TM&D*
Bat Tsurim	[baht tsoo-REEM]	(Daughter of the rocks) *TFD, CD4*
Eretz Zavat Chalav	[air-RETZ zah-VAHT <u>ch</u>ah-LAHV]	(Land flowing with milk and honey) *TFD, CD1*
Erev Ba	[AIR-rev BAH]	(Evening comes) *TFD, CD1*
Hadarim	[hah-dah-REEM]	(Splendor) *TFD, CD4*
Harmonica	[har-MOAN-nee-kah]	(Accordion) *TFD, CD3*
Haroa Haktana	[hah-row-ah hahk-tah-NAH]	(Little shepherdess) *TFD, CD2*
Hashual	[hah-shoe-AHL]	(The fox) *TFD, RM6*
Haya Ze Basadeh	[hi-yuh zeh bah-suh-DEH]	(Once in a field) *TFD, RM2*
Hora Agadati	[HOH-rah ah-gah-DOT-tee]	(Named for Baruch Agadati, Romanian ballet dancer) *TFD, RM8*
Hora Chemed	[<u>CH</u>EH-med]	(Hora of delight) *TFD, CD5*
Hora Eilat	[ay-LAHT]	(Hora from Eilat) *TFD, CD6*
Hora Medurah	[meh-dyour-RAH]	(Hora of the campfire) *TFD, RM3*
Hora Nirkoda	[near-KOH-dah]	(Let us dance) *TFD, CD1*
Hora Or	[hoh-rah OR]	(Hora of light) *TFD, CD6*
Kalu Raglayim	[kah-LOO rah-glah-YEEM]	(The feet are light) *TFD, CD6*
Kuma Echa	[koo-muh e<u>ch</u>-AH]	(Arise, my brothers) *TFD, RM7*
Lamnatseach	[lahm-not-say-A<u>CH</u>]	(To the victor) *TFD, CD3*
Lech Lamidbar	[le<u>ch</u> lah-meed-BAR]	(Go to the desert) *TFD, CD1*
Machar	[muh-<u>CH</u>AR]	(Tomorrow) *TFD, RM5*
Mayim	[my-YEEM]	(Water) *TFD, RM5*
Mechol Hagat	[meh-<u>CH</u>OLE huh-GOT]	(Dance of the winepressers) *TFD, RM4*
Niguno Shel Yossi	[nih-GOO-no shell yoh-SEE]	(Yossi's tune) *TFD, RM6*
Rav B'rachot	[rahv brah-<u>CH</u>OTE]	(Many blessings) *TFD, CD4*
Ronee Bat Tsion	[roan-ee baht tsee-OWN]	(Rejoice, Daughter of Zion) *TFD, CD4*
Sham Hareh Golan	[shahm hah RAY go-LAHN]	(See the mountains of Golan) *TFD, RM9*
Sharm-el-Sheikh	[sharm-el-SHAKE]	(About the battle of Sharm-el-Sheikh in 1967) *TFD, CD3*
Shibolet Basadeh	[shih-bo-LET bah-sah-DEH]	(A sheaf in the field) *TFD, RM5*
Shiru Hashir	[sheer-ROO hah-SHEER]	(Sing the song) *TFD, CD1*
Sulam Ya'akov	[sue-LAHM yah-KOF]	(Jacob's ladder) *TFD, CD2*
Te Ve Orez	[tay veh or-RETZ]	(Tea and rice) *TFD, RM1*
Uri Zion	[you-REETS zee-OWN]	(Arise, Zion) *TFD, CD2*
U'va'u Ha'ovdim	[you-vah-OO hah-ohv-DEEM]	(The lost ones will come back) *TFD, CD5*
Yibanei Humigdash	[yib-bah-NAY hah-mig-DAHSH]	(And the temple will be rebuilt) *TFD, CD2*

Israeli and Jewish Dances

STEPS AND MOVEMENTS. In keeping with the general feeling of exuberance and space in these dances, jumps are usually done with legs apart and fairly straight (*Haroa Haktana, Ronee Bat Tsion*). Many dances have a sway, a definite move from one foot to the other (*Hora Eilat, Machar*). Often, in a grapevine pattern there is a slightly syncopated leap on the first or fourth beat (*Harmonica, Mayim*).

HANDS AND ARMS. In the circles, dancers join hands with their arms comfortably down at the side in the V-position; arms move in and out with the movement of the body (*Lech Lamidbar*). They might use the shoulder-hold, with the hands resting firmly on each neighbor's closest shoulder—not clutching around the neighbor's neck or hanging on his or her upper arm (*Harmonica*).

In the Israeli swing, each dancer puts the right arm around the partner's waist, and the left arm is outflung, with the elbow straight (not rigid) and the hand open; usually patterns require repeating with the other arm (*Ana Halach Dodech, Kalu Raglayim*). Claps and snaps are visible and accented, sometimes above the head or at shoulder level, first on one side and then on the other, using the whole arm (*Eretz Zavat Chalav, Hora Nirkoda*).

MODIFICATION AND TEACHING TIPS. These Israeli dances can be authentic even when they are taught to young students without putting emphasis on style, for the basic dance style actually arose from the openness and energy of youngsters. Leave out the hand-holds at first, especially in dances in which the arms may change from the V-position to the T-position. Follow the modification suggestions in Chapter 2.

MUSIC. A characteristic instrument for these dances is the accordion, which was brought from Europe by the early Israeli pioneers. Other instruments, especially percussion and flute, are also appropriate.

CLOTHING AND COSTUMES. The basic Israeli dance costume can be used for sabra-style dances or for all Israeli dances in a program. The girls' outfit consists of a knee-length, full-skirted dress with wide, loose sleeves that are usually trimmed with colored braid. Boys wear loose-sleeved shirts hanging outside their trousers; shirts may be trimmed to match the girls' clothing. The colors of the Israeli flag—blue and white—are often emphasized. Dancers are barefoot or in sandals, and they use no head covering (unless they are boys from religious families, in which case they wear the little skullcap called *yarmulke* in Yiddish or *kipah* in Hebrew).

For school programs, white or blue t-shirts and shorts are also appropriate. For a quick change into Israeli dance after another ethnic dance, simply add blue-and-white sashes over basic blouses/shirts and skirts/pants, or sleeveless tunics decorated with embroidery-like designs around the necks (these can even be made from crepe paper).

The International Dancers of Chicago do dances from many cultures and must change costumes quickly. For their Israeli dance suite, the women add a beaded blue tunic to their basic whites, and the men put on a blue-trimmed shirt with a blue-and-white sash.

*For their **sabra**-style dances celebrating the homeland, the Nitzanim Israeli Folkdance Troupe designed this blue-and-white dress and matching shirt.*

Photo by Betty Sterling Hart

Israeli and Jewish Dances

Resources Used for Chapter 17

Alpert, Michael. 1990–97. Workshops, notes, conversations on Jewish and klezmer dance and music by one of the world's greatest Yiddish music experts.

Avni, Shimona. 1996. "The early development of Israeli folk dancing." *Quo* (January): 4–5. In this reprint of a 1978 article, the author tells the exciting story of the 1944 Israeli dance festival and the story of the next one, in 1947, to which 25,000 people came.

Berk, Fred. 1972. *Ha-Rikud, The Jewish Dance.* New York: Union of American Hebrew Congregations.

Berk, Fred. 1975. *The Chassidic Dance.* New York: Union of American Hebrew Congregations.

Brichta, Penny J. 1978–98. Conversations and workshops in Israeli dance with this well-known Chicago-area Israeli dance teacher.

Donaghey, Robert. 1969. *Thesaurus of Israeli Dance.* Brooklyn, NY: Copen Press.

Eden, Ya'akov. 1973–92. Lectures and conversations on Israeli dance.

Garfield, Sharlene. 1973–98. Conversations on Jewish and Israeli background.

Gottier, Karin. 1993. Conversations and comments from an expert on central European dance, particularly on the subject of the early twentieth-century youth movement.

Ha-Levy, Moshe (Moshiko). 1974–90. Israeli dance workshop notes, records.

Ingber, Judith Brin. 1992. "Voices of Sepharad." *Nirkoda* (Spring): 3–4. This is an article in the newsletter of the Israeli Dance Institute, New York City.

Jagoda, Flory. 1993. *The Flory Jagoda Songbook: Memories of Sarajevo.* Cedarhurst, NY: Tara Publications. This book, by the best-known exponent of Sephardic music, is a beautiful book about the author's Bosnian Jewish background, with her songs (including *Ocho Kandelikas*).

Kadman, Gurit. 1968. *The New Israeli Folkdances.* New York: Israeli Dance Institute. This is a pamphlet written by one of the "mothers" of Israeli folk dancing.

Kaufman, Haim. 1997. "On the Origins of Israeli Dance." *Quo* (November): 2.

Longden, Sanna. 1997. *Living Ethnic Dances for Kids and Teachers.* Evanston, IL: FolkStyle Productions. This video shows Arabic, Yemenite, and European styling in Israeli dance. (Contact FolkStyle Productions, 1402 Elinor Place, Evanston, IL 60201; 847/328-5241; <SannaMars@aol.com>.)

Mosse, George L. 1971. *Germans and Jews.* New York: American Jewish Congress. Information about the youth movement.

Nirkoda: The Newsletter of the Israeli Dance Institute. This publication has good articles about historic and contemporary Israeli dance. Haim Kaufman, a contributing editor, is also coordinator of an ongoing dance session in New York City called Rikuday Dor Rishon (Dances of the First Generation), dedicated to the early dances of Israel, and of an annual Labor Day workshop in the New York area, "Shorashim—The Roots of Israeli Dance." (Contact Haim Kaufman at 212/620-0535; <rdrdance@juno.com>).

Perlman, Itzhak. 1995. *In the Fiddler's House.* Angel Records 2435-55555-4. This is the acclaimed recording of klezmer music by one of the world's greatest classical violinists and many of the world's best klezmer musicians. Listening to it (and reading the enclosed notes) gives much information about the Yiddish-speaking Jewish culture.

Italian Dances

Chapter 18 Italian Dances

Sicilian Dance in Phyllis S. Weikart's Books

Sicilian Tarantella, or *Tarantella Siciliana* [see-chee-LEEA-nah] *TFD, RM6*

The mainland of Italy is a beautiful peninsula that extends like a booted leg off the torso of Europe into the Mediterranean Sea; two islands, Sicily and Sardinia, are also part of Italy. The source of some of the world's greatest art and music, the country has a stormy political history, having been conquered at different times by a number of other cultures, dominated by city-states in the Middle Ages, and later ruled by powerful regional families. Even in the late twentieth century, political storms are not uncommon in Italy.

Italy has been a united nation only since 1870, when Victor Emmanuel II, ruler of one of the family dynasties, became King of Italy after several decades of struggle led by the patriot Giuseppe Garibaldi and others. The message "Viva Verdi" became a rallying cry for the unity movement, but this was not congratulations to the composer Giuseppe Verdi for another successful opera; in this case, "Verdi" was an acronym for *V*ittorio *E*manuele *Re d'I*talia (Victor Emmanuel King of Italy). In June 1946 the monarchy ended, and Italy became a republic.

This chapter is actually concerned not with dances of Italy in general, but mainly with one dance of Sicily that is described in *TFD*. In addition to being one of the 20 regions of Italy, Sicily is the home of a people having a unique history and culture—another example of why it is important to refer to peoples, and not just countries, when teaching folk dance.

Sicily, the largest island in the Mediterranean, resembles on the map a big rock being nudged by the toe of Italy. (See p. 210.) As large as Switzerland, it has 4.5 million people, who live mostly along its three coasts. Politically, it is referred to as a semiautonomous region of Italy, which means that it has its own government. Sicily has a long and turbulent history. The Greeks settled there in the eighth century B.C.E. (it is possible to still see monuments to the Hellenic culture that are 25 centuries old). Not long after, the Phoenicians colonized the area that became Sicily's capital, Palermo, which grew to be a rich and important city in the Middle Ages. Other civilizations came, took, and then were conquered by the next invaders, while the Sicilians tried to endure. Today the island is underdeveloped and very poor, and many of its people have had to leave their homeland in order to survive. Much of the Italian population in North America is of Sicilian origin.

Despite their chaotic history, Sicilians are a sturdy and exuberant people with a strong, joyous culture. Their cuisine is specific to the island, and their language is a distinctive dialect. The intricately painted and cheerily colored wooden carts and figures of Sicily are known worldwide, and Sicilian songs are recognizable for their dramatic pathos. Unfortunately, some of these traits are being diluted as the young Sicilians, like young people everywhere, take on Western ways and the world's cultures become homogenized.

In the U.S., whenever a tarantella is played, almost everyone thinks, "Italy!" The tarantella, however, is a traditional dance of southern Italy, not of the entire country. Other geographic regions have their own characteristic dances: *La Furlana,* for example, is characteristic of northern Italy, and the *Saltarello,* of central Italy. To be even more specific, each region of southern Italy does the tarantella with its own special movements and music, so when a tarantella is discussed, it is usually identified as being from Naples, from Calabria, or from Sicily (*Tarantella Siciliana*).

Dance researchers have debated for decades about the origin of the tarantella. Legend says (and elementary students will enjoy hearing) that it derives from the wild turnings and movements of people bitten by the tarantula spider, as prescribed by early physicians to rid them of poison. Taranto, a town in southern Italy, gave its name to the spider, to the dance, and also to a therapeutic dance frenzy called "tarantism," originating during dance manias of the Middle Ages and, according to some scholars, still occurring in recent years. There are also

A young Sicilian folklore group, Sicilia Antica, proudly poses in its home town, Agrigento, before coming to the U.S. as performers at Folkmoot USA in Waynesville, North Carolina.

other legends and explanations, none of which may be true. Whatever its origin, however, the tarantella has developed into a lively courtship dance that is still done at weddings and festivals wherever southern Italian people live.

When danced in the traditional setting, tarantella movements are improvised and have no set patterns. There are many characteristic figures, and dancers choose from these as the spirit moves them or as they remember from their elders. Convenient choreographies have been created by dance teachers to fit specific recordings and for ease in teaching students and beginning folk dancers, who are generally more comfortable with memorizable patterns than with improvisation.

FORMATION. The *Sicilian Tarantella* in *TFD* was arranged by renowned teacher Elba Farabegoli Gurzau for two couples, although tarantellas also may be danced by one couple or by groups of couples. The two-couple sets can be anywhere in the dance space or lined up in longways columns. If there are partners of the opposite gender, boys should be beside boys, and girls beside girls, and each dancer is diagonally across from his or her own partner.

STEPS AND MOVEMENTS. Tarantella movements are joyous and fast. Sicilian tarantellas are danced up on the feet, with bodies reaching high, rather than lower down toward the ground, as in tarantellas of other regions.

Italian Dances

The International Dancers of Chicago dance lightly and snap their fingers high in the tarantella.

Tarantella movements were originally based on courtship rituals and flirtatious gestures, but these have been somewhat modified for classroom comfort. To keep the original intent of the tarantella, so it is not just an exercise in fancy steps, dancers should at least show awareness of their partners and set-mates. In the case of schoolchildren, this can be as simple as looking at each other and smiling. People closer to courtship age can do what comes naturally.

As an example of a detail that can be added to emphasize the personal-connection feeling of the tarantella, in Part IIA, each dancer runs diagonally in toward the opposite person until the two dancers' right shoulders are close. As they clap, they lean backward a bit and smile at each other. On the repeat, they run toward each other with left shoulders and do the same.

HANDS AND ARMS. Hand and arm movements are definite, obvious, almost theatrical. They are part of the fun of the tarantella. People who have a little showoff in them will instinctively have the right style.

When the dance directions say "clap hands overhead," that means firmly up high and not limply at shoulder level. Snap fingers up high also, with a dramatic flick of the wrist. The free hand can be on the hip or waist, or held high—especially in the right- and left-hand stars. Stars should be held high too. When in doubt, hold hands high!

For added interest, after dancers are comfortable with the steps and patterns, the women/girls might carry tambourines. (Traditionally in Sicily the musicians use tambourines, but the dancers do not; however, in this tarantella tambourines are an accepted part of the dance.) Using tambourines requires an extra measure of dexterity and coordination, but they're worth the effort. They are held high and shaken in one hand or hit with the free hand, in time with the music. They must be changed quickly from one hand to the other when necessary. If the men/boys want to try them also, this should be encouraged.

MODIFICATION AND TEACHING TIPS. The *Sicilian Tarantella* should not need much modification. The movement skills required for this choreography are fairly basic—the most difficult skill to teach may be the finger snapping. However, the dance should probably be saved for older students and adults because of the many pattern parts and the challenge of getting four people to dance together. If modification seems indicated, simply omit a section of the pattern, so there is less to remember: For example, in Part IB, omit the do-si-do and repeat the elbow turn of Part III.

For older students and adults who really enjoy this kind of dance, it is also possible to add more pattern parts. There are many other traditional figures that can be done, such as shoulder and elbow turns, women twirling while men catch at their skirts, and polka steps. See, for example, in the end-of-chapter and end-of-book resource lists, Gurzau (1981), Casey (1981), or the Folk Dance Federation of California's *Let's Dance,* Volume C.

MUSIC. Like most tarantellas, the *Sicilian Tarantella* is in duple meter (6/8), like a jig. A tambourine, clapping, or finger-snapping accent usually occurs on the main beat, once or twice in a measure. There are generally two steps for each measure of music.

These days, tarantella music is generally played by accordion (one of the most popular folk instruments in all of Europe) plus large tambourines and perhaps a reed instrument. There are other, more traditional instruments that give a picture

For their generic Italian costume, the International Dancers dress in the colors of the Italian flag, with a bit of basic black.

of everyday village life: the *quartara,* which is a water-carrying container that sounds like the double-bass; the *marranzana,* the Sicilian version of a jaw-harp (sometimes called a Jew's harp), which is played by the mouth applied to a vibrating steel tongue; a cane whistle and a triangle type of instrument; the *sonagliera,* which is a collar of harness bells worn by mules; and the *tamburo,* which is a drum with tin plates.

CLOTHING AND COSTUMES.

Girls can wear a bright, solid-colored full skirt, possibly with a band of braid or decorative ribbon along the bottom. Add a small apron of contrasting color and a white blouse under a dark or red bodice or vest. A head scarf can be worn knotted in the back, and lots of jewelry (coral, gold) at the ears, neck, and wrists adds richness. White stockings and black leather flats are appropriate footwear.

The boys wear dark knee-breeches and long red or green waist-sashes with the ends falling free. Long-sleeved white shirts, red bows at the neck, and dark or colored vests are traditional. On their legs and feet, boys can wear white hose and low dark shoes, just as the girls do.

The tambourines can also be decked out in ribbons—green, white, and red for the flag of Italy, with an added bright yellow.

Resources Used for Chapter 18

Armentrout, Deanna. 1990, October. "Sicily, Not Just Another Spicy Meatball." Paper written for folk dance course at Northwestern University, Evanston, IL.

DiPietropaolo, Celest. 1990–94. Dance notes from workshops by expert in Italian traditional dances.

Grieco, Rose. 1979. "Tarantella, Past and Present." *Viltis,* (December): 6–10.

Gurzau, Elba Farabegoli. 1981. *Folk Dances, Costumes and Customs of Italy.* Philadelphia: Italian Folk Art Federation of America. This has excellent descriptions, written clearly, with dance background and costumes plus music, by one of the first folklorists to present Italian dances to the international dance community. It is particularly aimed at teachers "who so often have to prepare nationality programs."

Japanese Dances

Chapter 19 Japanese Dances

Japanese Dance in Phyllis S. Weikart's Books

Tanko Bushi [tahn-koh BOO-shee] (Coal miner's dance) *TFD, RM9*

The Japanese culture combines traditional and modern characteristics in an intriguing mix. On the one hand, it has a special reverence for beauty, nature, and ritual. The careful procedure of the tea ceremony, the art of flower arranging, the discipline of martial arts, the strokes of brush painting, even the customs of greeting and eating, all show a love of harmony and order. On the other hand, the Japanese people also love baseball, McDonald's, and rock music and have developed one of the world's leading industrial nations.

One reason for their love of order may be that the Japanese don't have much space in which to spread out. Their country is an archipelago, a group of islands, lying between the Pacific Ocean and the Sea of Japan and occupying a smaller area than the state of Montana. (See p. 220.) The country is 80 percent mountainous, with most people living in the other 20 percent, along the coasts. There are almost 28 million people in the Tokyo metropolitan area, probably the most populous in the world, and Japan's other large cities each house more than a million people. On the streets, crowds are dense, and in the apartment buildings, people live very close to their neighbors. In other societies, this lack of solitude can cause rudeness, even violence. However, because of their deeply felt traditions, the Japanese are self-contained, courteous, and respectful of the balance between an individual and society.

Japan's traditions and history are significantly affected by its geographical nearness to China. Buddhism and other aspects of Chinese civilization came to Japan in the sixth century C.E., laying the foundation for its writing system, excellent arts, education, and government, and combining with Shinto, the Japanese cult of ancestor worship. Even the official name for Japan, *Nippon*, came from the Chinese about that same period. It means Land of the Rising Sun, the place in the east where the Chinese saw the sun come up. There were also influences from Korea and, later, from Europe, but all have taken root and flourished through connection with the special Japanese culture.

The culture also developed *shoguns,* or military governors, who controlled Japan for the emperor until the mid-nineteenth century, and *samurai*, who were the warrior aristocracy during the same period. After several centuries of self-imposed isolation to avoid European influence and invasion, Japan's modern era began when U.S. Commodore Matthew Perry forced a trade treaty in 1854, thus pushing Japan reluctantly into commercial relations with the U.S. and Europe. About that same time, the feudal shogun rule ended, when the government centralized around the emperor, and Japan's strong interest in Western industry and technology began.

As the nineteenth turned into the twentieth century, Japan got involved in wars with China and Russia, then fought in World War I as a British ally. In the 1930s, after militarily expanding its territory to Korea, Manchuria, Mongolia, and a number of Pacific islands, Japan became part of the Axis powers, attacked the U.S. at Pearl Harbor, and the rest, as we say, is history.

Since Japan's defeat in 1945, its national systems have undergone a thorough remodeling. This has included disbanding the country's military forces, with the goal of expanding Japan's technology rather than its territory and becoming a peaceful nation.

The Japanese people's love of order and tradition appears in both their classical and their folk dances. The classical dances are connected with the famous Noh theater, an ancient and carefully preserved art form. These dances were originally done by royalty, samurai, scholars, and nobility.

The folk dances, of which *Tanko Bushi* is an example, are associated with O-Bon, the annual Buddhist Festival of Souls, or Feast of the Dead, which is a joyous reunion with departed loved ones. This Japanese holiday officially occurs in mid-August, although people in the city of Tokyo celebrate it in July, and those in Hawaii celebrate it on many weekends throughout the summer. The festival begins when people place bonfires and lanterns on graves and altars to help their ancestors' spirits find the path back home. Living and dead are reunited and celebrate for three days with songs and favorite foods. At the end of the festival, the living people light farewell fires, and with lanterns, they accompany the departed souls to the mountains or sea, to say goodbye until next year. Sometimes the spirits are sent off in tiny wooden boats filled with food.

Much of this celebration includes dances referred to as Bon-odori, or Bon dances. Musicians, including at least one *o-daiko* (also spelled "taiko") drummer, play on raised stands in the center of the circling dances. Dancing goes on until at least midnight, and everyone is invited to join. Those who do not know the dances just shuffle along with the others, picking up the movements by observation. In addition to a core of traditional dances, there are some new ones arranged by dance masters, and most of the dances have regional variations. Streets and temple courtyards (more recently, parks and parking lots) where dancers gather are well lit with many lanterns, so the spirits of the ancestors can easily find their way to the dance circles.

Bon-odori is enjoyed not only at the Feast of the Dead but also at other celebrations. As in most cultures, the young people in Japan traditionally use the dancing as an opportunity to meet one another. Although there are no actual Japanese couple dances, as the song says, "Dance well with elegance, girls; boys, choose the best one for a bride."

Tanko Bushi is one of many Japanese coal-mining songs, each one identified by its place name. This *Tanko Bushi,* officially known as *Kita-Kyushu Tanko Bushi* because it came from Kyushu, the southernmost Japanese island, is believed to date back many centuries. In 1915, a Kyushu elementary teacher arranged the song to use for teaching music in the classroom. It became nationally popular after being recorded during World War II, and American soldiers brought the song and the dance back to the U.S. after the war. *Tanko Bushi* was introduced to North American folk dancers in the mid- to late 1950s by several dance leaders, including Hiroyuki Ikema, a leader of the Japanese Folk Dance Federation who still makes annual trips to the U.S. for dance workshops. Professor Ikema, a faculty member of the Japan Women's College of Physical Education in Tokyo, has been responsible for bringing many ethnic dance instructors to Japan to give workshops for hundreds of enthusiastic participants.

Tanko Bushi was sung originally by women sorting coal. As with any song that has been around a long time, there are various versions. The most popular says that the full moon has risen from behind the hill, and because the coal mine's chimney is so tall, the moon will be taken ill from the smoke. Another version is, as might be expected, a sad love song.

FORMATION. Most Bon dances are done in a circle of individuals. In recreational groups, *Tanko Bushi* can proceed in either a counterclockwise or a clockwise direction, although a great many Japanese dances move sunwise.

STEPS AND MOVEMENTS. Like folk dances of other Pacific Rim cultures, those of Japan tell simple stories, with hand and body movements illustrating the narrative or symbolizing the action. Footwork is much less important than hand motions. The first four hand-movements of *Tanko Bushi* describe the action of a coal miner as he digs, throws the bag over his shoulder, looks up at the moon, and pushes the heavy coal car. The three-clap sequence on beats 12–14, together with the five-clap interlude, is a traditional ending as well as beginning. The step pattern is quite simple, logically following the story told by the hand movements.

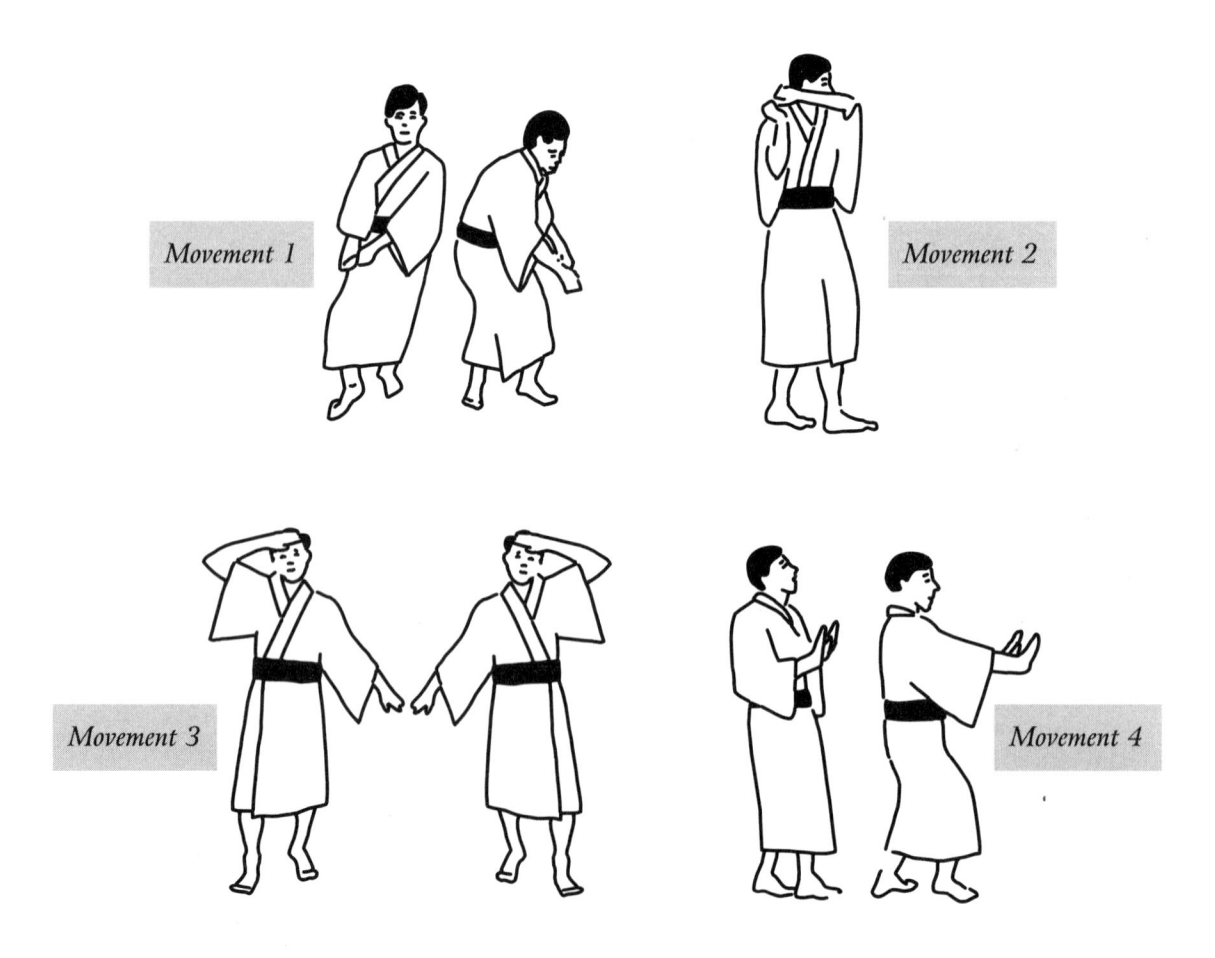

Movement 1

Movement 2

Movement 3

Movement 4

Japanese women, generally shy and modest, dance with subtle, self-contained motions. They move smoothly and gracefully, with their necks slightly bent down. (The sight of the exposed nape of the neck and a glimpse of an ankle emerging from the skirt's edge were considered quite a thrill in the old days.) They move a bit pigeon-toed, with knees bent and somewhat close together. Men dance more vigorously and somewhat bow-legged, but they use smaller movements than men dancers in most Western cultures do.

As always, in addition to cultural mores and characteristics, the dancer's clothing and footwear determine dance movements. Students should think about how to move when wearing long-skirted, tightly sashed garments with flowing sleeves, and with floppy or clunky footwear (all of this is described under "Clothing and costumes").

HANDS AND ARMS. Generally, hand motions are smooth and continuous, with one motion flowing into the next. They are executed with the same attention to detail and beauty that is the basis of all Japanese culture. The *Tanko Bushi* arms and hand movements, depicting the rugged occupation of coal mining, should be done with strong and well-controlled action.

Rhythmic hand-clapping occurs in almost every Bon dance as well as in other aspects of Japanese society, such as at the end of meetings and at sports events. The *Tanko Bushi* choreography ends with a clap pattern; like other dances, it may also begin with one, during the introduction. When clapping, start with palms together in front of the chest. Fingers are generally closed, with the thumb tucked in tight.

Often accompanying the clapping is a fifth movement called "opening a mountain" (see beats 11 & 12): With arms in front and palms down, open and bring them down and out on each side, drawing a picture of the holy Mt. Fuji. This movement is completed by swiftly bringing the arms up to finish clapping.

Movement 5

*A member of the Brigham Young University International Folk Dance Ensemble, dressed in **kimono**, **obi**, and **tabi**, demonstrates Japanese dance technique.*

Photo by Mark Philbrick

The other arm and hand motions should not be sloppy or casual; they should pantomime the action as precisely as possible (holding a shovel, shielding eyes, etc.), again keeping fingers together and thumbs tucked in.

MODIFICATION AND TEACHING TIPS. *Tanko Bushi* and other Japanese folk dances should not be modified much, if at all. As usual, use the SAY & DO method to teach the foot pattern, then layer on the hand movements. Once students are comfortable with the foot pattern and have coordinated the foot with the hand movements, if you cue the hand movements occasionally, it may lead to students' greater success with this dance.

MUSIC. At first, Western ears may find Japanese dance music unfamiliar, especially if it is played by a native ensemble. In *Tanko Bushi* and other rustic Bon dances, however, there is a strong, steady drum beat to focus on. Other Japanese folk dances may have quite complex rhythmic patterns.

Traditional instruments include the *shamisen,* a three-stringed type of guitar; the *kokyu,* a three-stringed violin; the *koto,* a flat, stringed instrument plucked like an autoharp; the *shakuhachi,* an end-blown flute; and the drums. An important instrument is the voice, since the stories of the Bon dances are traditionally told in song as well as movement.

CLOTHING AND COSTUMES. Japanese people began wearing Western clothes in the mid-nineteenth century, but many—both men and women—still wear ceremonial robes, or *kimonos,* for special occasions. The lighter summer kimono is called the *yukata,* and many wear it for dancing during the O-Bon festival. As might be expected, for robing oneself, there is a traditional ritual, which ends with donning the *obi,* a wide decorative sash. As also might be expected, kimonos can be works of art.

The characteristic footwear for dancing is the *zori,* the straw or leather sandal that is held on by a thong between the first two toes, and the toed socks called *tabi.* Sometimes people may also wear the wooden sandals, *geta,* for the heavier clogging dances.

For school demonstrations, it would be effective and respectful for students, both boys and girls, to wear some kind of cotton kimonos and sashes, rather than the generic European peasant costume of blouse and skirt, or shirt and trousers. The inexpensive rubber flip-flops worn by children all over North America are similar to zoris. For a further traditional touch, boys could wear a sweat band, thin towel, or cloth band around their head. This *hachimaki,* or band of resolution, is donned by Japanese men when making mental, physical, or spiritual effort, especially in combat. The girls might carry a parasol or fan and pin a hibiscus-type flower in their hair.

Japanese Dances

Resources Used for Chapter 19

Courdy, Jean-Claude. 1984. *The Japanese: Everyday Life in the Empire of the Rising Sun.* New York: Harper & Row.

David, Joe. 1978. "Life and Customs in Japan." *Viltis,* (December): 5–10.

Francis, Cmdr. William J. 1970. "Folk Dance Lessons in Japan." *Viltis* (June–September): 15–16.

Gottier, Karin. 1991. "Some Thoughts on Folk Dance in the Classroom." Paper from ethnic dance seminar at Duquesne University, Pittsburgh, PA, July 1991. This author is an expert on European dance but also teaches Japanese dances.

Herman, Michael, and Mary Ann Herman. 1958. *Maine Folk Dance Camp Syllabus.* New York: Folk Dance House. The Hermans were U.S. folk dance pioneers and founders of Folk Dance House in New York City and Maine Folk Dance Camp in Bridgton, ME. Their Maine Camp Syllabuses, including an excellent description of *Tanko Bushi,* were the source of many early folk dances.

Houston, Ron (ed.). 1994. "Tanko Bushi." *Folk Dance Problem Solver,* 56. Austin, TX: Society of Folk Dance Historians.

Houston, Ron (ed.). 1995. "Tanko Bushi—Additional Information." *Folk Dance Problem Solver,* 57. Austin, TX: Society of Folk Dance Historians.

Ikema, Hiroyuki. 1981. *Folk Dance of Japan.* Tokyo: Masashi Yoshida Recreation Association of Japan. Much of this information has also appeared in the May 1981 issue and other issues of the folklore magazine *Viltis.* Ikema-san, a physical education professor, is one of the "movers and shakers" of Japanese folk dance activities. He travels to North America for workshops and is responsible for bringing many international folk dance teachers to Japan.

Nippon Steel Corporation. 1982. *Nippon: The Land and Its People.* Fukoka: Gakuseisha Publishing Co., Ltd.

Yamakami, Haruno. 1994–98. Conversations on Bon-odori, Japanese language translation, and life in contemporary Japan.

Mexican Dances

Chapter 20 Mexican Dances

Mexican Dances in Phyllis S. Weikart's Books

Azul Cielo   [ah-SOOL see-EH-low] (Blue sky) *TFD, CD5*

Corrido   [coe-REE-doe] (An epic poem or ballad) *TFD, RM5*

La Raspa   [lah RAH-spah] (The rasp) *TFD, RM3*

Mexican Mixer   *TFD, RM3*

Polka Alegre   [ah-LAY-greh] (Happy polka) *TM&D*

Santa Rita   [SAHN-tah REE-tah] (Saint Rita) *TFD, CD5*

North America's colorful neighbor, Mexico, is a many-layered land. What much of the world understands as Mexican—its people, music, dances, clothing, and food—is really a small representation of a fascinating combination of ancient and modern cultures, all of which have left their influences on modern Mexico and on what we know as Mexican dances.

Some of the ancient cultures have been traced back as far as 10,000 B.C.E. Mexico's pre-Columbian cultures (i.e., those preceding Columbus's arrival in the New World) included the Olmec, Toltec, Zapotec, Tarascan, Mayan, and Mexica (later known as Aztec) Indians, all of whom created great empires and complex civilizations. Earlier than many peoples, the Aztec, for example, developed such things as padded armor, stucco floors, pictographic writing, and steam baths. With philosophies pre-dating those of Renaissance Europe, they produced music and poetry and were among the first to arrive at the concept of zero in mathematics. The Aztecs controlled most of Mexico and parts of Central America when Hernán Cortés conquered them for Spain in 1521. He overcame these powerful people, the story goes, because the Aztec emperor Montezuma believed him to be a former god returned to rule.

Like all conquerors, the Spanish *conquistadors* imposed their culture—language, religion, daily activities, even dance rhythms—on the indigenous peoples. A new race emerged called *Mestizo,* a combination of the pre-Columbian Indians and the Spaniards, who were themselves a hybrid of Celts, Arabs, Jews, Moors, Iberians, and other groups. Added into this were the Creoles, children of the immigrant Spaniards; the Mulattos, a mingling of African and Spanish/European blood; the Zambos, a blending of Mestizo and Mulatto; and, later, the Chicanos, a combination of North American and Mexican. Many pre-Columbian groups, such as the Huicholes of Nayarit, the Zapotecs of Oaxaca, the Totonacs of Veracruz, and the Otomis of Hidalgo, maintain identities.

After 300 years of dissatisfaction with Spanish rule, the Mexicans rebelled for the first time in 1810, gaining formal independence as the United States of Mexico in 1821. Napoleon added Mexico to his empire for a short time, importing as governing ruler a member of the Hapsburg dynasty, Maximilian, who liked the Mexicans and tried to help them during his rule from 1864 to 1867. A Mexican army's victory on May 5, 1862, over an invading French force at the town of Puebla near Veracruz is celebrated as the holiday of El Cinco de Mayo (the Fifth of May), a symbol for Mexican cultural pride.

Though Maximilian's reign was brief, his French and German court added its flavor to the rich melting pot that is Mexico and had a lasting influence on the culture, particularly on the development of modern Mexican folk dances. The combination of ballroom patterns with Mexican music and Mestizo personality has given the world some exciting dances, a few of which are described here.

Even up to the present day, Mexico continues to have armed conflicts and political struggles, including their bloodiest civil war, beginning in 1910 and known as the Great Revolution. The national dance of Mexico, *Jarabe Tapatío,* known also as *Mexican Hat Dance,* celebrates the unity of the republic after that war.

Dance and music have been a natural part of the lives of all Mexican cultures, whether the pre-Hispanic, the colonial, or the more contemporary mixtures. In fact, the Aztecs had special houses of song and dance for students aged 12 and up (who were punished if they skipped class!), and pre-Cortésian music has become an interesting subject of research. Modern Mexican-American young people love new dances such as the *quebradito.*

Because of Mexico's variety of peoples and regions (sometimes described as the "many Mexicos"), there are numerous types of Mexican folkloric dances, and even more varieties exist because of individual interpretations by Mexican dance teachers. In fact, the respected teacher Alura Flores Barnes de Angeles has said that in 60 years, she has never taught *Jarabe Tapatío* exactly the same way twice: "I teach part of a living folk process, which, like the butterfly, changes to become more beautiful."

Few Mexican dances taught to educators and folk dancers are strictly traditional. In almost every culture, the "real" dances are quite simple, with perhaps one or two repeated figures. These simple patterns can seem tedious when taken out of context for use in the classroom or recreational group; in the context of the fiesta, the resting, eating, drinking, flirting, singing, and celebrating would all be part of the dance. Therefore, traveling ethnic dance teachers often try to make their offerings more interesting and memorable for students by adding extra figures or teaching choreographies that have been created for performance. Although such "arranged" dances might not be purely traditional, they usually have typical steps and music, are easier to teach and learn, and are accessible to people who might not otherwise have an opportunity to experience Mexican culture through its music and dances.

The dances listed in this chapter either are arranged forms of traditional *norteño* (northern Mexico) dances or are made in the U.S.A. Our discussion here will be limited to these two types.

Azul Cielo, for example, is a choreographed Mexican *chotis,* or schottische. The Mexicans learned schottische-type dances, as well as waltzes, polkas, mazurkas, and other European ballroom dances, during the brief reign of the Emperor Maximilian of Austria, when he ruled Mexico for the French government. Señora de Angeles (known affectionately by all as Alura) was the first native Mexican teacher to bring dances to the North American recreational dance community, and she introduced *Azul Cielo* to U.S. folk dancers in the mid-1960s.

The dance called *Corrido* has an amusing history. Choreographed by one of Alura's students, Avis Landis from the U.S., it is a *pasodoble*-type dance that the record company mislabeled as a Mexican epic poem, or ballad, called a *corrido.*

*Members of the Brigham Young University International Folk Dance Ensemble perform the complicated and exciting courtship dance **El Jarabe Tapatío**, or Mexican Hat Dance.*
Photo by Mark Philbrick

Señora de Angeles insisted that it should be called *Eso Sí, Cómo No,* the title of the song to which it is choreographed (which means "Sure, why not?") and that it should be labeled a Mexican-influenced U.S. dance. However, it is solidly entrenched in the international repertoire as *Corrido,* and whatever its parentage, is an enduring and enjoyable dance.

La Raspa also needs some explanation. First, it is *not* the so-called *Mexican Hat Dance.* That dance is *El Jarabe Tapatío,* a complicated and exciting courtship dance that ends with the male partner demonstrating his devotion by placing his precious sombrero on the ground for his girlfriend to dance upon. This is not what *La Raspa* is about. Perhaps the confusion arises because many recordings

Mexican Dances

of *La Raspa* incorporate a melody from *Jarabe Tapatío* or because these are probably the two most recognized dances of Mexico.

La Raspa is sometimes called the *Mexican Shuffle*. Its name literally means the rasp, or coarse file, used for scraping or grating—a reference to the shuffling sounds made by dancers' feet. Other patterns can be done to this music, such as mixers, trios, and individuals in a circle. In the Jalisco region, it is done in a longways formation. The version in *TFD* seems to be the most universal—certainly it is the easiest and most useful for young children. The original dance is probably a Mexican adaptation of a dance of central European origin, as it is similar to dances seen all over Europe, from Lithuania to Italy to Denmark. Although this version may not be truly Mexican, so many peoples have danced it for so many decades that it is truly "folk."

The *Mexican Mixer* was choreographed by Nelda Drury of San Antonio, a well-known teacher of Mexican dance and an early student of Alura. Although it is based on the polka rhythms in Mexico that were popular during the reign of Maximilian, traditionally Mexicans did not dance mixers. *Mexican Mixer* is closer to dances from the southwestern U.S., and we call it a Tex-Mex dance.

Polka Alegre and *Santa Rita* are also *polkas norteñas*. They are more traditional than several other dances mentioned here, although also arranged in specific patterns for recreational dancing; other versions exist in Mexico. These choreographies were introduced to North American folk dancers by Alura.

FORMATION. The six dances described in Phyllis S. Weikart's books are couple dances, as are most nineteenth- and twentieth-century European-based northern Mexican folk dances. Dances from other regions of Mexico have a wider variety of formations because of their Spanish, Meso-American, or African backgrounds.

STEPS AND MOVEMENTS. In northern Mexican dances, partners definitely enjoy their separate gender roles, even when the steps for men and women are the same. This is true in dances of all cultures to some degree but more true of dances from Latin and certain other cultures. For example, when partners move toward and away during Part I of *Polka Alegre,* they bend toward each other and keep eye contact as much as possible. During the "crazy walks" in Part IVA of *Santa Rita*, adult partners are actually cheek to cheek. This strong male-female identification may make it difficult to find appropriate Mexican dances for certain grade levels. *La Raspa* and *Mexican Mixer* are the most useful, because they were created specifically for young people and recreational situations, and it doesn't matter who is the boy and who is the girl.

In *La Raspa,* the bleking step, with the heel touching the floor, is a motion found in many similar dances. The Mexican adaptation instructs dancers to slide their feet forward and backward on the floor to imitate the cutting action of the rasp.

The basic step in *Polka Alegre* is a strenuous traveling pas de bas (quick two-step). For good styling, keep the knees high during the sharp leaps.

The dance *Santa Rita* is much happier than the fifteenth-century nun for whom it was named. It has not one, but two, polka steps: The Mexican polka that begins the dance is actually a two-step, as described, with a scuff on each first beat, and no hop. The free-style polka in Part IIA is the European HOP, FORWARD/ CLOSE, FORWARD. The "broken ankle" step in Part IB requires careful practice: On beat 3, bend the right ankle and place weight on the outside edge of the shoe; then step firmly over it with the left foot. Partners may support each other by pressing together the palms of their joined hands.

HANDS AND ARMS. When their hands are not otherwise occupied, women do "skirt work." Their hands hold the full skirts at the sides or front and move them gracefully back and forth. Men hold their wrists behind their backs, or they hook their thumbs into their belts in front.

The fancy "skirt work" so typical of some Mexican folk dances is demonstrated by women of the Brigham Young International Folk Dance Ensemble during a suite of Mexican dances from the Jalisco region.
Photo by Mark Philbrick

Mexican Dances

While dancing Mexican polka steps, dancers bend their joined hands and upper bodies toward the floor on the first polka step, then up toward the ceiling on the second, and so on. Joined hands also point toward the floor on those satisfying multiple stamps that end phrases (for example, in *Santa Rita,* Part IA, beats 15–16).

When holding both hands with a partner's for heel-toe steps (in *Polka Alegre,* Part III, and in *Azul Cielo,* Part IIB and sometimes Part IIA), extend joined hands to the side at about shoulder height.

Quick claps in *La Raspa* (Part I, beat 4) add much to the enjoyment of the dance. When planning to clap, therefore, have dancers place hands on their own waist rather than hold hands with partners.

MODIFICATION AND TEACHING TIPS. Some of the more difficult steps can be simplified without losing the Mexican flavor. For example, in *Polka Alegre,* the basic step can be naturally modified to a step-touch, a step-stamp, or a walking step. The heel-toe in Part III could be a sashay down to the bottom of the set and up again. *La Raspa* and *Mexican Mixer* do not need simplification. The three ballroom dances should be saved for experienced dancers, because a certain amount of sophistication is required for partners to be comfortable with the closed dance-position used in these dances. Perhaps some figures could be omitted at first, as has been done in *TFD* with *Corrido,* which is actually a more complex dance for adults.

MUSIC. In the Mexican cultures, music has always been extremely important from earliest times. In the pre-Agricultural era dating back thousands of years B.C.E., voices provided melody, and hands and feet provided rhythm. Later, reed pipes accompanied the singing. When Cortés arrived, the indigenous peoples were using instruments familiar to contemporary music educators: ocarinas, native marimbas, drums, gourds full of rattling stones, and a scored femur scraped with a stick, which we know as the *guiro.*

The sixteenth-century Spanish conquerors brought the European violin, trumpet, and harp—and, most important, the guitar; the nineteenth-century French-German court contributed brass instruments and the accordion. Mexico's musical styles vary from region to region. The one most familiar to North Americans is the sound of the *mariachi* musicians, which originated in Jalisco and is now known all over the world.

It is the music—melodies, rhythms, and instrumentation—that makes the six dances in this series so exciting. *La Raspa* and *Mexican Mixer* could be played on classroom instruments, but the others, unless there are some terrific trumpet or accordion players in class, would be more successful done to good recordings. *Mexican Mixer* can be done to a variety of Mexican polka recordings.

A member of the International Dancers of Chicago is caught in a spirited moment in a northern Mexican dance. For costume, he wears a western-type outfit with jeans, a decorated shirt, and a neck kerchief.

Photo by Gustav Freedman

CLOTHING AND COSTUMES.

Like dance and music, Mexican dress varies from region to region, colorfully combining the native and Spanish cultures. Women's clothing for norteño dances, as well for dances from the Jalisco region, have the added influence of mid-nineteenth-century European court dress—it is not a coincidence that the flouncy skirts look more like French can-can costumes than like simple Mestizo dresses.

For a school program, the girls might wear a full, colorful, ruffled skirt with petticoat underneath, and a square-necked, short-sleeved, white blouse with bright flowers or designs embroidered on the neckline. Other typical versions of Mexican blouses exist; perhaps the girls may have their own. Legs should be bare or with flesh-colored hose, and on their feet, if possible, girls should wear the black "character," or dancing, shoes with one-inch heel. An added touch might be a *rebozo*, or stole, draped on arms and shoulders, and perhaps a large, bright flower behind one ear.

A Mexican man's attire typical of several regions is the horseman's outfit of short black jacket, white shirt with a colorful bow at the neck, and long black trousers. A simple western-type outfit with jeans, a decorated shirt, and a kerchief would also work for a school program. Like the women's shoes, men's shoes or boots have raised heels to tap out the rhythms. Added touches could be a belt with a big silver buckle; silver buttons or cord on the jacket and sides of the trousers; a colorful *serape*, or shawl, over one shoulder; and, of course, the sombrero.

Mexican Dances

Resources Used for Chapter 20

Angeles, Alura Flores Barnes de. 1971–90. Dance notes from Festival Folklórico Internacional camps.

Dickens, Guillermina. c. 1953. *Dances of Mexico.* London: Max Parrish. One of a series of useful books produced by the Royal Academy of Dance and the Ling Physical Education Association, this one offers three choreographed versions of traditional dances and much background information.

Doran, Dolores Ann. 1979. "Pre-Cortésian Music." *Viltis* (May): 10–13.

Drury, Nelda Guerrera. 1972–79. Dance notes from many workshops.

Drury, Nelda Guerrera. 1994. "The Dance in Mexico." In *Dance Awhile,* 7th ed. Jane A. Harris, Anne M. Pittman, and Marlys S. Waller, eds., 357–58. New York: Macmillan International.

Garcia, Leopoldo (Polo). 1990–98. Conversations and workshops on Mexican dance, Chicago, IL.

Glass, Henry ("Buzz"). 1979. "Dance—A Mexican Mosaic." *Viltis* (May): 5–9.

Houston, Ron (ed.). 1993. "Biography of Alura Flores Barnes de Angeles." *Folk Dance Problem Solver,* 38–39. Austin, TX: Society of Folk Dance Historians.

Houston, Ron (ed.). 1993–95. Comments, conversations, critiques.

Miller, Robert Ryal. 1985. *Mexico: A History.* Norman, OK: University of Oklahoma Press.

Muñoz, Oscar. 1989. *Music for Children from Latin America.* Presentation at American Orff-Schulwerk Association national conference in Atlanta, GA.

Pill, Albert S. 1963. "Regional Mexican Dances." *Viltis* (March–April): 4–6.

Trujillo, Lawrence Alan. 1975. "The 'Masculine' Mexican Folk Dance." *Viltis* (May): 9–13.

Wakefield, Eleanor. 1966. *Folk Dancing in America,* 163–74. New York: J. Lowell Pratt & Co.

Philippine Dances

Chapter 21: Philippine Dances

Philippine Dance in Phyllis S. Weikart's Books

Apat-Apat   [AH-paht AH-paht] (Four-by-four) *TFD, RM4*

Dancing has been a natural part of the lives of the Filipino people throughout the history of this lovely archipelago. Lying off the southeast coast of Asia near China, Taiwan, Malaysia, and Vietnam, the country is made up of more than 7,000 islands and islets. Its terrain ranges from high mountain regions to tropical lowlands. The diverse topography of the Philippines, along with the diverse peoples who settled there, has given rise to a multifaceted dance culture.

A variety of Asian peoples were living in the islands in the fourteenth century, when Mohammedans from Arabia and India began to move into the southern area, adding Islamic influences. Ferdinand Magellan, that remarkably busy Portuguese adventurer, "discovered" the Philippines in 1521, opening the way for western European ideas and Christian missionaries. The Spanish controlled the region from the mid-sixteenth century until 1898, when the U.S. took over the Philippines after defeating Spain in the Spanish-American War. During World War II, Japan occupied the islands, and in 1946 they gained independence as the Republic of the Philippines, although the U.S. maintained air and naval bases there until 1992. The nation's postwar history includes a Communist-led rebellion in the 1950s, a presidential declaration of martial law in the 1970s, a politically motivated assassination in the 1980s, and most recently, a hopeful reassertion of democracy.

All of these shifting cultures and political changes, as well as the geography of the scattered islands, have had an impact on the cultural development of the Philippines and can be seen in the variety of its dances.

Since earliest times, the Filipinos have used dancing to celebrate almost every occasion—religious ceremonies, courtships and weddings, parties of all kinds, and formal inauguration festivities. There are war dances, comic dances, occupational dances, planting and harvest dances. The primitive tribes had dance rituals for moon- and star-worship and even for giving a hearty sendoff to head-hunting expeditions.

Most of the dances done today are an interesting combination of primitive, Oriental, Spanish, and central European movements. The vigorous, stamping movements of tribal dancers and the flexed elbows and stiff fingers of the restrained, serious, inner-directed Asian dancer blended into the softer, more rounded, flamboyant, joyous Hispanic manner. This was all joined with nineteenth-century European ballroom dance patterns to become what we see today as the strong but graceful and gracious Philippine movement style.

Filipino dancers often use objects to emphasize movements or to act out a situation. In one dance, women balance oil lamps on their heads and hands. In another, depicting a war between the Filipino Mohammedans (Moros) and the Christians, men wear and carry coconut half-shells that they strike and click as a rhythmic accompaniment. Other war dances use spears, shields, the machete called a *bolo*, and the sword called a *kris* (don't try this in the classroom). In the old courtship dance *Cariñosa*, partners each carry a comb, a powder puff that they apply gently to each other, and a handkerchief that they use for hide-and-seek. Some dances have fans and handkerchiefs for emphasis, and some use bamboo castanets, ankle bells, or wooden shoes on the hands for rhythm. And as all North American educators know, the dance of the *Tinikling* bird uses bamboo poles to show rhythm and agility.

The single dance in this series, *Apat-Apat,* is arranged to the song *Pagtanim,* which celebrates the planting of rice, an important food in Philippine culture. There is also a dance game to a similar song, *Magtanim,* in which dancers holding baskets of grass or rice stalks pantomime the movements of planting and rubbing sore muscles.

Apat-Apat was first taught to North American folk dancers in 1961 by Francisca Aquino. A physical education instructor at the state university in Manila, she was sent to the provinces in 1927 by the university president to study indigenous music and dance. Her work was one of the main reasons for the national revival of interest in traditional dances, and she became known as the mother of Philippine folk dance. *Apat-Apat,* a simple mixer, was popular for many years in recreational groups and is enjoyable for upper-elementary students.

The gracious and graceful movement style of Philippine dance is evident in these dancers, who strike a pose before going on stage at Folkmoot USA in Waynesville, North Carolina.

Philippine Dances

FORMATION. In the double circle, girls are on the outside, to the right of the boys, if the dance is done in mixed-gender pairs. In this dance, however, it is easy for boys to be partners with boys, and girls with girls; partners can even omit the joined hands at the beginning, thus shortening the touching time.

STEPS AND MOVEMENTS. Like most Philippine dances, *Apat-Apat* has little or no body-contact. The Filipinos are modest but coy, with (as someone said) "love expressed at arm's length." Except for dances from the higher, cooler regions, most dances use smooth, nonvigorous movements because of the tropical climate. The walking steps should be small but clear, with no shuffling. The women's narrow wraparound skirt, called a *patadyong,* makes small steps necessary.

Most dances begin and end with the *saludo,* a three-step turn-in-place and bow. Although the saludo is not required for this dance, it would be a nice traditional touch during the introductory beats. Also, in the spirit of Philippine dance, dancers might carry an appropriate object, such as a stalk of rice.

Try to anticipate the half-turns and quarter-turns, perhaps taking more than one beat to accomplish them instead of whipping around briskly. This will enable one step to flow into the next, as in a dance from tropical islands rather than a series of military maneuvers. And—the hardest thing of all—when meeting each new partner, smile.

HANDS AND ARMS. When the dance begins, partners' inside hands are joined at shoulder height (W-position), with their free hands hanging naturally. When meeting at the end of the pattern, partners join right hands, again at shoulder height, with their forearms touching. This makes it possible for each pair to move around as a compact unit.

MODIFICATION AND TEACHING TIPS. It probably is not a good idea to simplify *Apat-Apat.* If the small challenges in the dance are omitted, it will not be very interesting. Although the walking steps are easy, the direction changes will be difficult for younger students, and the mixing may be uncomfortable for some older ones. However, these challenges can be met and mastered and will lead to an enjoyable multicultural experience.

MUSIC. Traditional Philippine instruments range from metal sticks and nose flutes, to gamelan orchestras, to mandolins and castanets. When connecting with a multicultural curriculum, it is always best to use music that is as traditional as possible. However, when using this dance for pure movement education in the classroom, barred, string, and rhythm instruments are appropriate. For an even more ethnic experience, dancers and musicians can sing the song, as is done in the Philippines, and perhaps also do the game version, *Magtanim.*

A musician from the Philippines performing at Folkmoot USA prepares to play the gong chimes, a type of gamelan.

CLOTHING AND COSTUMES. Much variation exists in the regional dress of the Filipino people, but several popular styles are commonly seen and would be appropriate for school or community programs. The easiest for girls is a short-sleeved white blouse with wide puffed shoulders, if possible, and a sarong-type skirt in a bright pattern. The skirt is generally narrow, with the hem falling between knee and ankle; a strip of the same material can be draped over one shoulder.

Boys wear a long- or short-sleeved white shirt, sometimes one decorated with white embroidery, hanging outside long white or black trousers. In some regions, they also wear a sarong-type skirt with the shirt hanging over it.

Both girls and boys can be barefoot and bareheaded (although people in some areas wear a large, pointed straw hat). This should complete a lovely, simple outfit.

Philippine Dances

Resources Used for Chapter 21

Aquino, Francisca Reyes. 1981. "Philippine Folk Dancing." In *International Folk Dancing USA,* Betty Casey, ed., 219–21. Garden City, NY: Doubleday.

Balase, Esther. 1994. Conversations with this Philippine dance teacher, Chicago, IL.

Fajardo, Libertad. V. 1981. "Visayan Dances of the Philippines." In *International Folk Dancing USA,* Betty Casey, ed., 221. Garden City, NY: Doubleday.

Miller, Carl S. 1972. *Sing, Children, Sing.* New York: UNICEF and Chappell & Co., Inc. See "Magtanim" on pp. 56–67, which is the traditional song to which *Apat Apat* is done. The description in this book is of a children's game that mimics planting rice and the back pains that result.

Montross, Bea. 1978, 1981. Workshops with this expert in Philippine dance.

Timbancaya, Ester, and Miriam D. Lidster. 1965. "Philippine Dance." In *Folk Dance Progressions,* Miriam D. Lidster and Dorothy H. Tamburini, eds., 29–35. Belmont, CA: Wadsworth.

Tolentino, Francisco Reyes. 1946. *Philippine National Dances.* Morristown, NJ: Silver Burdett.

Portuguese & Brazilian Dances

Chapter 22: Portuguese & Brazilian Dances

Portuguese and Brazilian Dance in Phyllis S. Weikart's Books

Fado Blanquita   [FAH-doh blahn-KEE-tah] (Little white fate) *TFD, RM7*

*A*lthough based solely on one interesting dance, this chapter should be titled "Dances of Portugal/Brazil/Mexico/Spain/ California." The dance discussed here has been described by a variety of experts as being from all those places—and the experts are probably *all* correct. We have tried in this book to emphasize cultures and not countries, and here is a dance that beautifully illustrates our point. Because it is usually labeled with the Portuguese/Brazilian name *fado,* we will categorize the dance in that culture (with some "maybes" and "howevers") and thus have an interesting illustration of how peoples and dances disregard national boundaries.

Portugal shares the Iberian Peninsula with Spain, in the southwestern corner of Europe. Although the two countries' cultures are similar in many respects, Portugal has not been an official part of Spain since 1143, when it became an independent state. Today it is one of the poorest countries on the Continent, but for 200 years, between the late fourteenth and late sixteenth centuries, it was one of the most powerful nations on earth. Most of us have learned from our own school days how, at that time, the Portuguese explorers Ferdinand Magellan and Vasco da Gama, with the encouragement of Prince Henry the Navigator, changed much of the world's subsequent history with their seafaring and commercial adventures.

Brazil's history was certainly changed when Portugal claimed it as a colony in 1500. Although an independent nation since 1822, it remains the only Portuguese-speaking country in the Americas, and its cultural connections to Portugal are still very strong.

Fado Blanquita is a cheery social dance that has the combined characteristics of several similar cultures. Even its name is an amalgamation of Portuguese and Spanish, although this could be either a clear example of border crossing or a careless linguistic mistake made by a long-ago choreographer.

The Portuguese word *fado* describes a mournful ballad, somewhat like a blues song or a cowboy lament, mostly heard in Portugal and Brazil. The word itself means fate. *Blanquita,* however, is a Spanish adjective that literally means little white. (The same adjective in Portuguese is *branquenha,* and both words should probably end in "o" when modifying the word *fado.*)

Whatever the story is, this dance has for many decades been firmly rooted in the international repertoire with the bilingual name of *Fado Blanquita.* In spite of its ambiguous history, it is made up of traditional movement patterns and set to a folk tune, so there is much that can be learned of this culture through the dance.

There are several versions of *Fado Blanquita/o,* variously labeled Portuguese, Brazilian, Spanish, Moorish, or combinations thereof. There is also a similar Mexican dance called *Caballito Blanco,* and another interpretation described as a "California form devised in Brazil." Vyts Beliajus, a pioneer ethnic dance researcher and teacher, learned a *Fado for Fours* from a Spanish gypsy in 1935.

The Northern California folk dancers were taught another pattern by a professional South American dancer in the late 1940s, and even the famous Russian ballerina Anna Pavlova is said to have presented an interpretation of this dance to U.S. audiences.

To compound matters further, none of those versions are the pattern that is described in *TFD* and other manuals for those who teach children and beginners. This easiest version of *Fado Blanquita* has been modified somewhere in the dance's busy past, so inexperienced dancers and those who aren't ready for more-adult partner dances also can enjoy moving to patterns and music of the Portuguese/Brazilian (Spanish/Mexican/??) people.

FORMATION. The pattern we deal with here begins with partners in a single circle. With male-female partners, put the girl on the boy's right side. With same-gender partners, it is useful to label them "A" and "B," or "Green" and "Purple," and so on, to avoid initial confusion when learning which are partners and which are corners. Other versions of this dance have partners facing each other around the circle or in longways lines.

STEPS AND MOVEMENTS. Aside from being an enjoyable way to experience these cultures, *Fado Blanquita* is useful for practicing the schottische pattern. All steps should be as smooth as possible, and flirting can be a natural part of the dance for groups to whom this comes naturally. Movements, feelings, and attitudes that appear in dances from Latin cultures are appropriate here.

HANDS AND ARMS. Generally, hand and arm movements are important in Portuguese/Brazilian dances. In the more traditional forms of this dance, because the dancers are using finger cymbals, partners usually do not hold hands except during the schottische figure, if then. Dancers do beautiful, graceful arm curves reminiscent of Spanish dances, with careful placing of hands and wrists.

These movements, however, are not relevant to this classroom version. Here dancers' hands are joined in the V-position for the beginning circle figure and the swaying vamp. In some classroom versions, partners perform this vamp while facing and holding right hands. For more traditional vamp styling, partners could face each other, with girls holding their skirts out and boys clasping their hands behind their backs. This is also an appropriate position for Part III, the jump-kicks, which are not done while holding hands.

During the schottische in Part II, hands are joined with arms extended (but not stiff) and elbows a bit bent. Other choreographies have partners hook elbows. In more traditional styling, partners move around each other with their right shoulders adjacent and with the right arm down and curved toward the body as the left arm is curved overhead.

On the last part, on beats 17 to 32, as dancers move toward and away from center, arms can be slowly raised and lowered.

Members of Grupo Folclorico de Faro (the city of Faro is at the southern tip of Portugal) rehearse a vigorous partner dance before embarking for the Folkmoot USA festival in Waynesville, North Carolina.

Two Brazilian girls tease the boy between them during their performance at Folkmoot USA.

250   *Cultures and Styling in Folk Dance*

With their hands high and skirts twirling, Portuguese dancers spin at the Folkmoot USA festival.

MODIFICATION AND TEACHING TIPS. As already mentioned, this *is* the modified form of *Fado Blanquita*. Probably it should be saved for upper-elementary or older students who have had enough experience to accomplish the schottische step. If they are comfortable with that, the rest of the dance pattern should not be a problem.

MUSIC. The many patterns of *Fado Blanquita* have all been arranged to the same piece of music, which seems to be the unifying element in this dance's history. The music is characterized by a duple meter, syncopated rhythm, and two-part structure. Guitars should always accompany a fado, with violins and mandolins also evoking the traditional sound. The string bass and the ubiquitous

Portuguese and Brazilian Dances

accordion have been modern additions. Finger cymbals are also part of the tradition, and some dance notes give patterns for those also. The clicking of the finger cymbals can be duplicated by finger snapping or similar-sounding instruments.

CLOTHING AND COSTUMES. As is true of many cultures, there is no single national outfit that represents Portuguese/Brazilian dress, but instead there are many regional variations. Generally, women's clothing is very colorful and men's clothing is not, although there are of course exceptions.

For school programs, girls can wear colorful full skirts with bands of color and/or bright flower motifs. Their white blouses are short- or long-sleeved, also with colorful flower designs. Add aprons—yes, with colorful flower designs or not—and perhaps shawls around shoulders and tucked into waistbands. Women usually wear headgear—in some regions, a black felt, brimmed hat; in some regions, a colorful scarf tied

A Brazilian man wearing a red neckerchief prepares to gallop on stage with his partner at Folkmoot USA.

252   Cultures and Styling in Folk Dance

A couple from the southern tip of Portugal rests between performances. The woman wears both hat and scarf, the man, a brimmed, bowler-type hat.

Portuguese and Brazilian Dances

at the back of the head or not tied at all, with the ends draped down; and in some regions, both hat and scarf. To complete the ensemble, girls can wear white hose or knee socks, and black low shoes.

Men often wear short black jackets or vests, long-sleeved white shirts, and long black trousers. Color can be added by a red sash or a small string tie or neckerchief. Men also wear headgear, varying from a stocking cap to a black, brimmed, bowler-type hat similar to the women's hat. On their legs, boys may wear white or black socks; add black dress shoes, or black boots with the tops covered by the trouser legs.

Resources Used for Chapter 22

Beliajus, Vyts. 1935–65. Dance notes.

Beliajus, Vyts. 1994, March. Conversations about the history of this dance.

Folk Dance Federation of California Research Committee. 1946. *Folk Dances from Near and Far,* Vol. II. Berkeley, CA: Folk Dance Federation of California, Inc. See the *Fado Blanquita* dance notes on p. 26.

Folk Dance Federation of California Research Committee. 1951. *Folk Dances from Near and Far,* Vol. VI. Millbrae, CA: Folk Dance Federation of California, Inc. See the *Caballito Blanco* dance notes on pp. 9–10.

Houston, Ron. 1994. Conversations and much research material from Society of Folk Dance Historians. (See the "General Resources" list for the Society's address.)

Sousa, Eliziania Arnaud de. 1994. Conversations about the Portuguese language.

Romanian Dances

Chapter 23: Romanian Dances

Romanian Dances in Phyllis S. Weikart's Books

(Note: The spellings and diacritical marks we have used in this list may vary slightly from those found in other sources.)

Alunelul	[ah-loo-NEH-loo] (The little hazelnut, or hazel tree) *TFD, RM6*
Bătuta	[buh-TOO-tah] (Stamping) *TM&D*
Boereasca	[BOY-eh-rahs-keh] (Landlord's *[boyar's]* dance) *TM&D*
Brîul Pe Opt	(*Brîul Pe Opte* in *TM&D*) [brew peh OHPT] (8-count belt dance) *TM&D*
Ciuleandra	[choo-LYAN-drah] (A kind of burr that twirls in the wind) *TM&D*
Ciocărlanul	[cho-kur-LAH-noo] (The lark) *TFD, RM8*
Drăgaicuţa	[drah-guy-KOOH-tsah] (Girls' ritual dance) *TFD, CD3*
Floricica	[flor-uh-CHEEKA] (Little flower) *TM&D*
Frunza	[FROON-zah] (The leaf) *TFD, RM6*
Hora de la Rişipiţi	[day la ree-shee-PEE-tsee] (Hora from Rişipiţi) *TFD, CD5*
Hora Nuţii	[NOO-tsee] (Nuţii's hora; *Nuţii* is the diminutive of the girl's name *Elenuţa*) *TM&D*
Hora Pe Gheaţa	[pay GYAH-tsah] (Dance on the ice) *TFD, RM4*
Hora Spoitorilor	[spoy-TOH-ree-lor] (Housepainter's hora) *TM&D*
Mîndrele	[MUN-dreh-leh] (Sweet girl) *TFD, CD5*
Paiduşca	[pie-DUSH-kah] (Generic name referring to 5/8 meter) *TM&D*
Pomoleţul	(*Pomuleţul* in *TM&D*) [poh-moh-LEH-tsoo] (The little tree) *TM&D*
Rustemul	[roo-STEH-moo] (Named for a bolt used in yoking oxen) *TFD, CD5*
Trei Păzeşte Bătrinesc	[tray puh-ZESH-the bah-trih-NESK] (Three times be careful—the old ones) *TFD, CD6*
Trei Păzeşte de la Bistret	[bee-STRET] (A version of *trei păzeşte* from Bistret) *TM&D*
Vulpiţa	[vool-PEW-tsah] (The little fox) *TFD, CD6*

Romania is a small nation of great beauty located in the southeastern European region known as the Balkan Peninsula. Making up a country about the size of Oregon, the nation's six regions are separated by high mountains and fertile flatlands, while the Danube River flows along the western and southern borders of the country to its delta on the Black Sea. (See the map on p. 66.)

This attractive terrain was claimed by a long and varied list of invaders, including the Ottoman Turks in the fifteenth and sixteenth centuries. The Russians took over briefly in the early nineteenth century, but finally, late in that century, Romania's states united, and in 1881 Romania became a kingdom. After World War I, having been on the winning side, Romania expanded its boundaries when it gained the Transylvania region (in northeastern Romania) and other territories.

An historical "aside" on Transylvania that might interest your students concerns its most famous, albeit fictional, citizen, Count Dracula. Bram Stoker, the English author, based his vampire character on a real person called Prince Vlad the Impaler, a vicious brute who lived in the mid-fifteenth century. Vlad's legendary castle was actually not in the Transylvanian mountains, but on the plain of Walachia in another region of Romania, where it still stands today.

After some difficult decades during the worldwide economic depression, Romania was occupied by the Germans during World War II, until 1944, when the Soviets marched in. Romania's monarchy ended in 1947, when the country officially became Communist. The early years under Communism were harsh ones, but worse years were to come. In the early 1960s, Nicolae Ceaușescu, who was not a foreign invader but a modern-day Romanian leader, headed a 24-year regime that was so relentlessly repressive that his own people, long abused by repressive regimes, finally revolted and executed him in 1989. In the last decade of the twentieth century, life began to improve for Romania, with its new constitution leading toward representational government and its up-turned economic conditions.

As might be expected, those repressive centuries have left their mark in many ways. But surprisingly, although many cultures have invaded their territory over the centuries, the Romanian people still retain characteristics similar to those of their early Roman conquerors. They consider themselves a Latin people, and indeed, their Latin-based Romance language is close to that spoken in the second century C.E., when this land was a Roman province. Even the name *Romania* itself has remained unchanged for almost two millennia. (You may find the British spelling "Rumania" and the French spelling "Roumania" in older books, but "Romania" is the spelling now generally accepted in the homeland.) And in spite of their dark history, the Romanians' bright side comes out in their colorful embroideries, their lively music, and their exciting dances. An old saying goes, "A Romanian is endowed with seven lives," and it seems to be true.

Most of the dances listed here are choreographed versions of some basic Romanian dances. These versions are taught by U.S. Romanian dance experts as well as by former members of professional Romanian folk dance ensembles. The variations, whether carefully arranged for the stage or kept in village repertoires, are extremely numerous. More than 6,000 dances and their variants are claimed to have been collected by researchers, and more are still being created by professional choreographers. Each locality has its own group of dances based on the basic forms. As seen in the dance titles, the dance themes are common objects and activities, such as occupations, people, plants, animals, birds, place names, dance skills, and even farm implements.

Since the late 1940s, folk dancing has been a well-organized national activity in Romania and in other eastern European countries. Many young people had opportunities to learn about their own culture as well as others as they traveled with state performing troupes, and talented professional artists had opportunities for teaching and choreography. It is through some of these professional artists that the global folk dance community has been exposed to the exciting and lyrical Romanian dances.

In North America, Romanian dances have been a popular and enduring part of the international folk dance repertoire since the early 1970s. Dances listed in this chapter, such as *Ciuleandra, Hora Pe Gheața,* and *Rustemul* continue to be regularly requested by recreational groups.

The Hora

The hora, or circle dance, is the oldest and most common of the basic dance types and is generally considered the national dance of Romania. Its history goes back into antiquity, to the chain dances of the Greeks. In recent decades, the hora became a symbol of unity and solidarity and was used to open all official events. *Hora Mare* (big, or large, hora) is the name of the most common walking dance and its variants that are enjoyed at all festivities by Romanian people. Many of the Romanian dances in *TFD* and *TM&D* are choreographed versions of *Hora Mare.*

The term *hora* also refers to the traditional gathering of folks on Sundays after church or on holidays to socialize and dance. The gathering took place on the village square or, in winter, in the culture house. Dancing was an integral part of community life. In the old days, being allowed to take part in the hora gathering was a rite of passage for girls at about 13 or 14 and for boys at 18—it meant they were adults. This event is still an occasion for young people to socialize. John Omorean, a professional Romanian dancer, described the scene when he was growing up in the 1960s in the Romanian community of southern Ontario: He would join the hora dancing in a place across from a girl he admired, and then each time a new circle was formed he would work his way closer and closer to her side. Nowadays hora gatherings still take place in many areas, but ballroom and other modern social dances have been added to the traditional repertoire.

Traditionally, the Romanian horas moved counterclockwise in either an open or a closed circle, depending on how much space was available for the dance. In recent years, for staging purposes, many new ones have been arranged in open circles, short lines, and other formations. Horas often use crossing footwork in a grapevine or modified grapevine pattern. The fast horas are performed with light footwork and much stamping; the slow ones are usually based on walking patterns with smooth, majestic styling. An important characteristic is the vocalizing, which consists of dancers singing and shouting verses and commands.

A great sense of community is created through the hora. Romanians truly dance *together* as they move in harmony with one another, aware of everyone in the circle. In some dances, the music may start slowly, then accelerate to a

Helping to expose the global community to Romanian folk dance, these young Romanian folk dancers traveled all the way to the International Folkfest in Carbon County, Utah.

Romanian Dances 259

very fast tempo, and then slow back down again, going on for a long time. To urge the dancers on, the leader may shout rhythmical encouragement, such as "If you dance and do not shout, you deserve a crooked mouth." Try shouting some verses in the classroom—well, maybe not.

Alunelul

One of the most popular and enduring Romanian horas is *Alunelul*. Because it is usually the first Romanian dance taught to schoolchildren, and sometimes the only one, we have singled it out to describe in depth. Before the 1970s it was one of the few Romanian dances that most North Americans knew. Its background and subsequent travels are an illustration of the evolution of one dance.

Originally a true folk dance from the region of Oltenia, the version in *TFD*, with the count-down pattern, was standardized for schoolchildren, using motifs found in traditional dances. It became popular everywhere from urban adult culture clubs to rural grammar schools and was the one pattern that all Romanians knew and could do together.

Alunelul arrived in North America with the first Oltenian immigrants. It was introduced into the U.S. folk dance community in 1955, when a Romanian dance specialist, Larisa Lucaci, taught it at the Hermans' Folk Dance House in New York City. (This house was an important source of international dances in the early years of the folk dance movement.) Dick Crum, well-known Balkan dance researcher, learned *Alunelul* there and taught it the next year at Stockton Folk Dance Camp at University of the Pacific, Stockton, California. (The camp was another source for numerous dances in the international dance repertoire.)

Many dances include "alunelul" in their titles, such as *Alunelul Batut*—the stamping *Alunelul*, or *Alunelul de la Goicea*—*Alunelul* from the town of Goicea. The *Alunelul* in *TFD* is identified by the single name and has no other versions. The little hazel tree or hazelnut, for which most researchers say it is named, is typical of the everyday subjects of Romanian dance titles. Madame Eugenia Popescu-Judetz, a Romanian choreographer and researcher who along with her renowned husband, Gheorge Popescu-Judetz, collected hundreds of Romanian dances, wrote that the word "alunelul" means little hazel tree, a magical symbol whose branches are supposed to divine water sources and precious metals. Michael Kuharski, a Balkan dance researcher, comments that hazelwood switches, or rods, often appear in Romanian and Bulgarian folk customs. In another view, however, Romanian dance experts Anca Giurchescu and Sunni Bloland argue that "alunelul" is not the diminutive of hazel tree, but a contracted form of a word meaning Nelu's dance, "Nelu" being the diminutive of the name "Ion" (John).

The song that was sung during the dance is typical of the improvised shouts that accompanied horas in the old days. Here is one version:

Alunelul, alunelul, hai la joc,   Little hazel, come and dance,
Să ne fie, să ne fie cu noroc!   Bring all of us luck.
Cine joacă şi nu strigă,   Whoever dances without shouting,
Face-i s-ar gura pungă!   May his mouth become dried out!
Cine n-o juca de fel,   Whoever won't dance,
Să ramîie mititel!   May he never grow up!
Cine n-o juca cu noi,   He who won't dance with us,
Crească-i coarne ca la boi!   May he grow horns like an ox!

Good dance styling for *Alunelul* is the same as for many Romanian horas. The body is carried upright and well-balanced, facing center with toes turned slightly out in the direction of movement, to keep an open posture. Arms are in shoulder-hold (T-position), hands placed lightly on top of adjacent neighbors' shoulders (not on their neck or upper arm). When arms are in the T-position, it is more comfortable to dance in smaller circles—ones of 8 to 10 people. Originally, in Oltenia, *Alunelul* was done in an open, curved circle. Larisa Lucaci, however, taught it in a closed circle in New York, and that's the way it has been done in North America ever since.

There is much stamping in the pattern, as there is in many Romanian dances, but this is not a clumpy dance. Steps should be small and light, with slight leaps on the SIDE/STAMPs in Part III. Stamps are also fairly light, not noisy, although done on the full foot.

Two recreational folk dancers at a folk dance camp wear t-shirts expressing their appreciation for some of the characteristic footwork of Romanian dances.

Romanian Dances

Joined in a shoulder-hold, or T-position, recreational folk dancers doing a Romanian dance bring their knees macho-high.

Photo by Zoltan Horvath

Other easy horas in TFD

Besides *Alunelul,* there are three other fairly easy and enjoyable horas in *TFD* to help develop the movement skills required by Romanian dances: *Ciocărlanul, Frunza,* and *Hora Pe Gheaţa.*

Ciocărlanul (the lark) was presented by Larisa Lucaci at the same time as *Alunelul.* She said that female larks sing and male larks dance, but apparently both human genders may join in this dance. The earliest notes for *Ciocărlanul* describe the dance as being performed in a closed circle with dancers' hands joined in the W-position throughout the pattern. Many people, however, use vibrating arm movements that add emphasis to the footwork; such arm movements are described in other *Ciocărlanul* notes and are not uncommon in Romanian dances. The *TFD* version begins with adjacent dancers' hands joined in the W-position and tucked up close to the shoulders and with their elbows touching. The arms come down sharply on beat 1 of the first three measures as the right foot steps IN, and then they come up on beat 2. In Part II, dancers hold their joined hands in the V-position.

When executing the footwork, note that beats 1–4 are a modified version of the Cherkessiya pattern: Instead of IN, STEP, <u>OUT,</u> STEP, do IN, STEP, <u>STEP IN PLACE,</u> STEP. The IN is an accented right step, crossing in front of the left

262 Cultures and Styling in Folk Dance

foot. The left foot does indeed lift up behind but not so much that balance is upset. Beats 13 and 14 are tiny, accented steps in place—do very slight crosses, if at all. These are small differences and easily lost in the heat of the action, but they are more in keeping with the styling and intent of *Ciocărlanul*.

Frunza, another hora from Oltenia, is a natural extension of *Ciocărlanul* with a similar pattern but faster and lighter steps to imitate the leaf for which it is named. It is usually done in an open circle and was originally taught with arms in the T-position. The shoulder-hold, however, is not always comfortable, and thus the T-position is often naturally modified to the V-position. *Frunza* was introduced by Sunni Bloland, a well-known U.S. specialist in Romanian dance who has contributed a number of excellent dances to the repertoire. Many of the dances discussed here are hers, learned in Romania and presented at workshops in the 1970s and 1980s.

One of Sunni Bloland's most popular dances is *Hora Pe Gheața*, the dance on ice, originally from the Muntenia region of Romania. Every step of this dance should be smooth and elegant, like the ice dancing in the Winter Olympics. It was taught as a single circle but is also done in an open circle, which is a natural modification that gives dancers a little more "skating" space.

The Brîul

Besides the hora, another major type of Romanian dance is the *brîul*, or belt dance, represented in *TM&D* by *Brîul Pe Opte*. There are numerous dances with "opt" (meaning the number 8) in their name, and they are mostly from southern Romania. Every village had its own variations on the main 8-count theme, and every ensemble has its own choreography. According to John Omorean, because they are too difficult, brîuls are no longer done in the émigré communities.

Brîuls are made up of a number of fast, syncopated patterns, sometimes with the dancers' feet moving so quickly that all one can see is a white vibration. The 4-figure brîul presented in *TM&D* is part of an 11-figure *Brîul Pe Opt* introduced by Balkan dance expert Martin Koenig with steps he learned from Gheorge Popescu-Judetz. (Madame Judetz once taught a brîul in Chicago with 19 figures!) Martin Koenig suggests slowing down the recording when teaching this dance, and so do we.

Dancing with a belt-hold requires special skill. Dancers should be arranged in short, fairly straight lines of about three to eight people. Each holds the immediate neighbors' belts, more toward the front than the side; some Balkan dance teachers even say to hold the belt "above the navel." Having such close connection helps the line to move as one unit. In this brîul, the left hand is over, and the right is under, but this is not a hard and fast rule. If two people are of different heights, they can adjust the belt hold to whatever is comfortable. In the village, dancers just take hold in whatever is the most natural way.

Other Fast Dances

Most of the other Romanian dances listed in this chapter are exciting and lively and were introduced by either Sunni Bloland or Mihai David. David is a Romanian dancer and teacher, now living in the U.S., who learned the dances when he was a member of the Romanian State Folk Ensemble in the mid-1960s. There are also many other dances—traditional versions, recreational arrangements, or stage choreographics—named *Bătuta, Boeraesca, Floricica, Paidușca, Pomolețul, Rustemul,* and *Trei Păzeşte.* Most of these dances come from the Romanian regions that share the Danube River borders with northern Bulgaria and eastern Yugoslavia (Serbia), so it is no coincidence that they also share movement characteristics with the dances of these neighboring countries. In fact, the popular Romanian *Sîrba* is named for Serbia, while the very similar Serbian *Rumunjsko Kolo* means Romanian kolo.

Slow Dances

Not all Romanian dances are fast and light. Some of the most beautiful ethnic dances in the world are the slow, contemplative women's dances of Romania. The two in this series, *Dragaicuța* and *Mîndrele,* were both introduced by Sunni Bloland. Like most women's dances, both dances had ritual functions in their original settings: *Dragaicuța* is a girls' dance originally from the Dobrogea region, and *Mîndrele* is a ceremonial dance for older women performed at weddings in Oltenia.

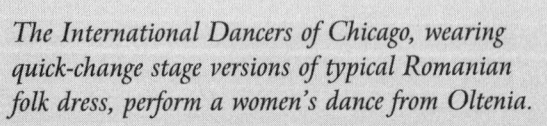

The International Dancers of Chicago, wearing quick-change stage versions of typical Romanian folk dress, perform a women's dance from Oltenia.

These two dances are performed in a smooth and stately manner and with a solid and serene demeanor. The heavy feeling of the music encourages the dancers to step almost behind the beat. When all the women move as one, there is an extraordinary feeling of community. The steps are not difficult, but these dances will be most appreciated by adults and mature teens. Though the women's dances can be taught to a mixed group, once learned, the dances should be done by men and women dancing in separate circles. In staged performances, the dances should be for women only.

MODIFICATION AND TEACHING TIPS. One modification we can recommend for the three easy horas described in this chapter is to change the T-hold to a V-hold. Since most of the horas have only two parts, there is not much to omit. Students will find these dances are achievable after some skill-building, and the challenge will be worth the effort, because these dances are great fun and their music is enchanting. See the dance descriptions in *TFD* and *TM&D* for some initial simplifications to help students gain the ability to do the dances as intended. As mentioned earlier, joining the hora was the entré to adulthood. Therefore it is no surprise that except for *Alunelul,* there are few Romanian dances for young children. As in almost all traditional societies, children learn dances under the tutelage of their elders or simply by imitating adults at the hora and other occasions.

Once students can do the five simple horas well, they may move on to the other kinds of dances. At that point, omitting figures from the longer dances is a natural way to modify them. Also, we recommend waiting a bit before introducing the belt-hold in the brîul. Once dancers are comfortable with the steps (it may take a while), then the belt-hold can be introduced. Although it may feel natural to at first substitute a front basket-hold for the belt-hold, this is not correct in a Romanian dance; front baskets belong to other cultures. However, joining hands in a V-position *is* an acceptable substitution, even though it changes the feeling of connection.

MUSIC. One of the most important instruments in Romania is the human voice that yells, whistles, shrieks, and shouts commands during the dance. In almost all cultures, vocalizing is an integral part of dancing, and in this culture it is essential. Traditionally, rhythmic verses called *strigaturi* were chanted during the hora. It might be fun to create some strigaturi as part of a multicultural unit. For examples, see the verse in the *Alunelul* discussion earlier in this chapter, or these verses:

> Pay no 'tention to my clothes,
> Rather watch my nimble toes.

> A new year with happiness
> And in everything success.

Easy does it, partner mine,
For I dined on soup and wine,
And on baked sparerib divine.

Romania's music has distinct moods. Much of it is energetic, bright, intense, and lyrical, with syncopated rhythms. Some of it, however, is heavy and mournful, calling up centuries of sadness. The most characteristic is the *doina,* a melancholy lament originally sung by shepherds and now a basic part of the Romanian musical culture.

Dance meters are duple (2/4) for the most part, although the *Paiduşca* is in assymetric (5/8) meter like the Bulgarian *pajduško,* and *Rustemul* is in duple (6/8) meter when it isn't in 3/8 or asymmetric 5/16, depending on how the musicians are feeling that day. Romanian music is often associated with Gypsies, and for good reason. Folk musicians of eastern Europe and the Balkans generally have been and still are Gypsies, and they have had enormous influence on the color, dynamics, and improvisation of Romanian music.

The Gypsy violin is what comes to mind when thinking of instruments, but trumpets, clarinets, and accordions are also popular. Two characteristic older instruments are the *cimbalom,* which is the hammered dulcimer played in so many cultures, and the *naï,* the Romanian flute, or panpipe, made famous and played so beautifully by Gheorghe Zamfir.

CLOTHING AND COSTUMES. As in so many things Romanian, even clothing is reminiscent of the people's ancient ancestors, the Romans. It is possible to see on the historic Trajan Column in Rome outfits very similar to Romanian traditional dress. Influences of the Ottoman Turkish occupation are also obvious in the embroidery colors and rich decorations that make Romanian folk clothing so distinctive.

For a generic costume in a dance program, girls can wear a white blouse with collarless round neck and short puffed sleeves or long full ones. The blouse's special Romanian look includes bands of embroidery across the upper part and down the sleeves, on the cuffs, around the neck, and down the front of the bodice. Students might design their own faux embroidery with fabric markers. The skirt is not full, but quite straight or pleated, at about knee length, and usually a dark color. Over the skirt is an apron, often red, with horizontal stripes or a bright geometric design—another chance to use those fabric markers. A nice touch for young girls is a white veil off the face, held by a headband and draped partway down the back, with maybe a red flower tucked on one side. White tights and low black shoes can complete the outfit.

Boys, too, can wield the fabric markers by creating geometric designs around the collar and on the cuffs of their long white shirt, which can be worn over their white trousers (maybe add a little design on the trouser cuffs, also).

A member of the International Dancers of Chicago poses in an authentic outfit from the Romanian Folk Arts Museum.

Around the waist is a colorfully embroidered wide belt, or cummerbund, and over everything, perhaps a white "sheepskin" vest with dark bands drawn around the neck, down the front edges, and around the sleeve openings to depict fur and with some designs on the front panels. On the head, boys could wear a Russian-style lambskin hat, and on the feet, black shoes or black boots in which to tuck their trousers.

A Romanian woman's headdress appropriate to the Transylvania region is a flowered kerchief tied behind the head.

Romanian Dances

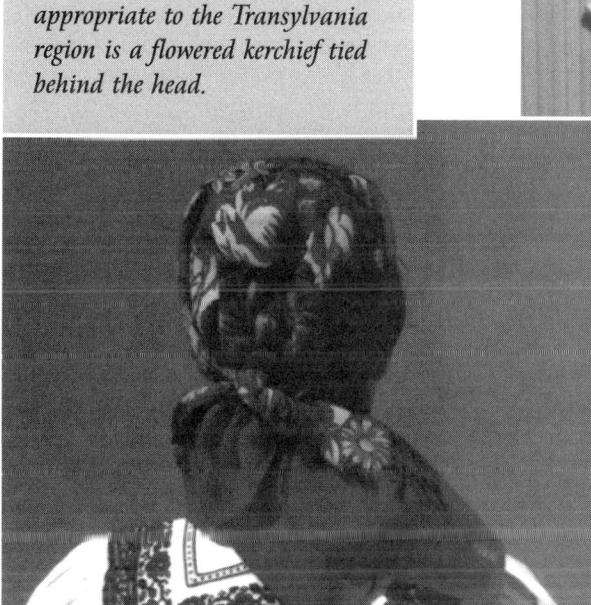

Resources Used for Chapter 23

Bloland, Frances (Sunni). 1970–90. Romanian dance workshops at University of Chicago; University of Illinois–Champaign/Urbana; Buffalo Gap Camp in Capon Bridge, WV, and Evanston, IL.

Bloland, Frances (Sunni). 1980–95. Conversations and correspondence.

Crum, Richard (Dick). n.d. "About *Alunelul.*" *Mixed Pickles.* This is an article in a newsletter published in New York City by Steve Zalph in the 1970s.

Crum, Richard. 1965. "Balkan Dance." In *Folk Dance Progressions,* Miriam D. Lidster and Dorothy H. Tamburini, eds., 2–15. Belmont, CA: Wadsworth. This is an excellent overview by one of the most respected North American Balkan dance experts.

David, Alexandru. 1974–88. Romanian dance workshops held in Chicago, IL.

David, Mihai. 1972–94. Romanian dance workshops at University of Chicago; University of Illinois–Champaign/Urbana; Buffalo Gap Camp in Capon Bridge, WV; and Evanston, IL.

Eastern Europe Phrasebook. 1992. Victoria, Australia: Lonely Planet Publications. This is a handy book for an overview of the language and how to pronounce it.

Folk Dance Federation of California Research Committee. 1957. *Folk Dances from Near and Far,* Vol. VIII. San Carlos, CA: Folk Dance Federation of California, Inc. This book contains one of the earliest U.S. dance descriptions of *Alunelul.*

Folk Songs from Romania. This is a Laserlight CD with renowned pan flute artist Georghe Zamfir and friends playing the original renditions of the music for dances in this chapter. It is available in commercial music stores.

Gheorghe and Eugenia Popescu-Judetz Collection of Romanian Folk Dance and Music. Housed in the Archive of Folk Culture at the U.S. Library of Congress, this collection includes photos, films, thousands of dance notes, notated music, and recorded melodies. The guide to the collection is loaded online on LCMARVEL. To access: Use gopher to access <marvel.loc.gov>, look under "Research and Reference," then under "Dance Heritage Coalition."

Giurchescu, Anca, and Frances (Sunni) Bloland. 1995. *Romanian Traditional Dance.* Mill Valley, CA: Wildflower Press. This is a serious and fascinating study of all aspects of the subject, with a clear description of the Romanian Rapid Dance Notation System (RDNS) and excellent photographs.

Grindea, Miron, and Carola Grindea. 1952. *Dances of Rumania.* London: Max Parrish & Co. One of the Handbook of European National Dances series, this book gives good background information, including music, instrumentation, and costumes for a few characteristic dances.

Houston, Ron (ed.). 1987. "Alunelu(l)" *Folk Dance Problem Solver,* 5. Austin, TX: X-Press.

Houston, Ron (ed.). 1993. "Ciocârlanul." *Folk Dance Problem Solver,* 8. Austin, TX: Society of Folk Dance Historians.

Houston, Ron. 1994–97. Correspondence and conversations. Houston is founder and trustee of the Society of Folk Dance Historians, Austin, TX.

Joukowsky, Anatol M. 1965. *The Teaching of Ethnic Dance.* New York: Pratt & Co. Joukowsky is a pioneer in eastern European staged dances. Note his chapter on Russia, pp. 82–92.

Kaplan, Robert D. 1994. *Balkan Ghosts: A Journey Through History.* New York: Vintage Books. This author's seven chapters on Romania give fascinating information on this culture.

Koenig, Martin. 1980–90. Romanian dance workshops.

Kuharski, Michael. 1996. E-mail comments, 3 October 1996, about *Alunelul.*

Lucaci, Larisa. 1968. "Romania—Historic Outline." *Viltis* (March): 4–6.

Lucaci, Larisa. 1968. "Romanian Dances and Shots." *Viltis* (December): 6–7.

Omorean, John. 1994, November. Workshop in Romanian dance, Chicago.

Popescu-Judetz, Eugenia. 1974. "Regarding *Alunelul.*" *Viltis* (October–November): 21.

Popescu-Judetz, Eugenia. 1979. *Sixty Folk Dances of Romania.* Pittsburgh: Duquesne University Institute of Folk Arts.

Popescu-Judetz, Eugenia. 1981. "Romanian Folk Dancing." In *International Folk Dancing USA,* Betty Casey, ed., 241–45. Garden City, NY: Doubleday.

"The Rumanian Folk Costume." 1970. *Viltis* (May): 12–13.

Russian Dances

Chapter 24 — Russian Dances

Russian Dances in Phyllis S. Weikart's Books

Katia, also *Our Katia*   [KAH-tyah] (a girl's name) *TFD, CD6*

Kohanochka   [kah-HAH-nutch-kah] (Sweetheart, or beloved) *TM&D*

Korobushka   [kah-ROH-boosh-kah] (The peddler's pack) *TFD, RM8*

Troika   [TROY-kah] (Threesome, or three-horse sleigh) *TFD, RM2*

Russia, or the Russian Federation, is geographically the largest nation in the world. Sprawling across 11 time zones with 89 territorial units, it covers part of eastern Europe and a good deal of northern Asia. Once the most dominant republic in the former Union of Soviet Socialist Republics (U.S.S.R.), Russia became an independent state in late 1991.

Russia's neighbors are a varied lot. They include Norway and Finland at the northwest corner; Estonia, Latvia, and Lithuania in a little Baltic bulge; Belarus, Ukraine, Georgia, and Azerbaijan down the western edge; Kazakhstan across half of the southern boundary; and Mongolia and China's Manchurian region along the other half. In addition, a tiny southeastern finger of Russia almost touches Japan, and Russia's northeastern tip is surprisingly close to the United States—Alaska is just across the Bering Strait. Russia also borders on many seas—among them the Black, Caspian, Okhotsk, Bering, and East Siberian. (See the map on p. 274.)

The Russians are a Slavic people who have occupied most of the same land for more than 15 centuries. There are also hundreds of other ethnic groups, such as Tatars, Yakuts, Ossetians, and Buryats, who live within Russian borders. The Russian church, which was established in 988 C.E., is the largest of the Eastern Orthodox churches, and after the demise of the Soviet Union, it is experiencing a revival. For example, it is again possible, after 74 years of prohibition, to officially celebrate Christmas in Russia.

Russia's ancient history has been traced back to the Stone Age. Its modern history began in 1547, when Ivan the Terrible was crowned czar of all Russia, starting centuries of czarist rule. The Russian Revolution in 1917 brought the Bolsheviks to power, and Vladimir Lenin, head of the new government, tried to set up an experimental Communist state based on the ideas of economist Karl Marx. After a bitter civil war, the U.S.S.R. was established in 1922, and soon after that, Joseph Stalin succeeded Lenin as dictator of the Soviet Union. During World War II, the Soviet Union sided with the West; however, shortly after the war's end, the former allies became embroiled in an East-West struggle known as the Cold War. This volatile situation alternately flared up and cooled down over the next 40 years, as all of us who lived during those decades know. In the late 1980s the political climate began to change when Mikhail Gorbachev introduced governmental reforms and restructuring through his policy of *glasnost*. This led to the final breakup of the U.S.S.R. in 1991. Russia's first free elections, in December 1991, made Boris Yeltsin president, and two years later, in an interesting historic irony, Russia adopted a democratic constitution using as its model the United States of America.

During this turbulent history and in spite of horrific ethnic purges and repressions, the many separate cultures of Russia survived, partly because the Communist ideology encouraged the support of folklorists and folk artists. It was through the traveling state dance and music ensembles that the rest of the

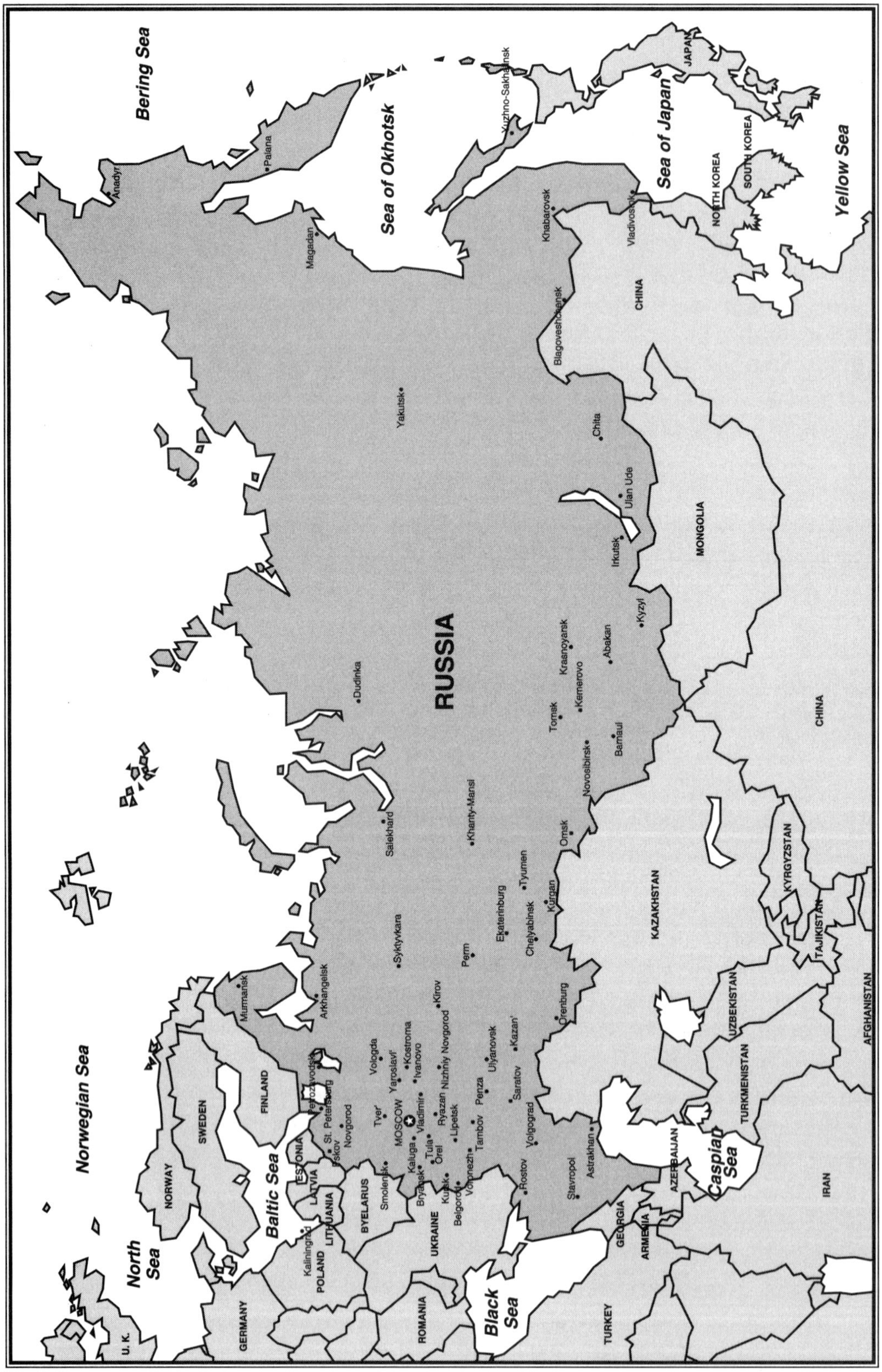
Bering Sea
Sea of Okhotsk
Sea of Japan
Yellow Sea
Norwegian Sea
North Sea
Baltic Sea
Black Sea
Caspian Sea
RUSSIA
JAPAN
NORTH KOREA
SOUTH KOREA
CHINA
MONGOLIA
KAZAKHSTAN
KYRGYZSTAN
TAJIKISTAN
UZBEKISTAN
TURKMENISTAN
AFGHANISTAN
IRAN
AZERBAIJAN
ARMENIA
GEORGIA
TURKEY
ROMANIA
UKRAINE
BYELARUS
POLAND
LITHUANIA
LATVIA
ESTONIA
FINLAND
SWEDEN
NORWAY
GERMANY
U.K.
Anadyr
Palana
Magadan
Yuzhno-Sakhalinsk
Khabarovsk
Vladivostok
Blagoveshchensk
Yakutsk
Chita
Ulan Ude
Irkutsk
Kyzyl
Abakan
Krasnoyarsk
Kemerovo
Tomsk
Barnaul
Novosibirsk
Dudinka
Salekhard
Khanty-Mansi
Omsk
Tyumen
Kurgan
Chelyabinsk
Ekaterinburg
Perm
Syktyvkara
Orenburg
Kazan'
Ulyanovsk
Kirov
Murmansk
Arkhangelsk
Petrozavodsk
Vologda
Kostroma
Ivanovo
Yaroslavl'
Nizhniy Novgorod
Vladimir
Tver'
St. Petersburg
Novgorod
Pskov
MOSCOW
Ryazan
Lipetsk
Penza
Saratov
Tambov
Kaluga
Tula
Orel
Smolensk
Bryansk
Kursk
Belgorod
Voronezh
Volgograd
Rostov
Stavropol
Astrakhan
Kaliningrad

world was able to get a glimpse of the Soviet Union's multinational folk cultures. The view given the world, however, was a carefully chosen, highly romanticized, and professionally polished version of what actually goes on in the villages.

The most famous of these troupes was the Moiseyev Dance Company established in 1937, which was later honored with the title of The State Academic Ensemble of Popular Dance of the Soviet Union. For this company, Igor Moiseyev created suites of dances and music intended to showcase the cultural regions of the U.S.S.R. Through Moiseyev productions, people on the other side of the Iron Curtain were able to enjoy the more familiar songs and dances of Russia, Poland, Ukraine, and other Eastern European peoples while also being exposed for the first time to the lesser known music and movements of such ethnic groups as the Kazan Tatars, the northern Nanayans, and the nomadic Turkmen.

This multicultural mosaic was often referred to as *Russian* because Russia was the largest and most dominant of the Soviet republics. When much of the world thinks of Russian dance, for instance, they may picture the breathtaking leaps and soaring flights of the Ukrainian *Gopak* or the fiery motions and amazing toe-dancing of the Georgian mountaineers. *Russian,* however, is not a generic label for the folklore of all the former Soviet peoples; rather, it refers to the unique music and dance of a single culture. Similar to Ukrainian dances, Russian dances can be acrobatic and strenuous for both men and women. Russian dances can also be dignified and elegant, as we shall see in the descriptions that follow.

Traditional Russian dances, like the traditional dances of almost all peoples, have no fixed sequences. Within a basic framework they are improvisational, which may account for the various versions of the dances listed on p. 272. We will describe some of the discrepancies between versions, in case some readers have been doing one or another version of particular dance. We advise not worrying about which version is the "right one" to teach, but just being consistent. Because it may be difficult for you to unlearn a familiar pattern, when choosing among syllabus notes, teach what is most comfortable for you.

The four Russian dances listed on p. 272 are not truly authentic village dances. They may not be truly Russian, either, but both Russian and Ukrainian. By now, however, they can be called folk dances. The first one, *Katia,* is a choreographed pattern representing the *horovodnaya pliaska,* or circle dance, the oldest Slavic dance formation, and the last one, *Troika,* is an urban Russian-American folk dance. *Kohanochka* and *Korobushka* are known as old-time Russian ballroom dances that were choreographed by nineteenth-century dance masters for a society that loved to dance. It is interesting to note that even today, in spite of the inroads made by rock-and-roll, Russian youngsters are flocking to ballroom dance classes sponsored by such organizations as the Russian Dance Sport Association. Modern Russian society still understands that such skills promote grace, poise, self-confidence, and good physical training—other societies take note!

The great variety of cultures within Russia can be seen in the contrast between the fur-wrapped woman (at right) from the northern Russian region of Komi (at the International Folkfest in Murfreesboro, Tennessee) and the summery scene (above) staged by the Vesennie Zori group from the southern Russian city of Voronezh (performers at Folkmoot USA in Waynesville, North Carolina).

Katia, or Our Katia

Katia is one of many dances that exist in several variations and occasionally cause confusion among long-time folk dancers. One version was arranged by Anatol Joukowsky, a pioneer in ethnic dance research as well as a ballet dancer and choreographer in European companies before emigrating to the U.S. in 1951. He introduced *Our Katia (Nashy Kate)* at the 1964 Stockton Folk Dance Camp at University of the Pacific in California. A similar but not identical version of *Katia* was taught as a Ukranian dance in the early 1970s by Vincent Evanchuk, a professional dancer and teacher of Ukranian and Georgian dances. Another slightly easier version evolved through the folk process when people who learned and taught the dance third- and fourth-hand smoothed out some pattern parts to better fit the musical phrasing. There are at least five different sets of notes, all using the same record but showing variations in formation, starting foot, hand-holds, and pattern. Our advice is to choose your favorite and then be consistent; if someone questions your version, simply explain "This is the way I learned it."

The version of *Katia* notated in *TFD* was learned at a workshop and seen at regular folk dance evenings. It uses the original, closed-circle formation. Some groups use an open circle with the leader on the left, which originally had been one of several suggested variations.

The meter is duple (2/4), typical of polkas, and indeed, the basic step of *Katia* is the so-called Russian polka. This FORWARD/CLOSE, FORWARD, or quick/quick, slow, pattern is more like the two-step than like the HOP/FORWARD/CLOSE, FORWARD central European polka step. For a touch of Russian choreographic styling, try Joukowsky's original description of placing weight on the heel, rather than on the full sole, of each forward step.

Hand-holds vary in different interpretations. Most are in the simple V-position rather than straight toward center; one version has joined hands coming up to the W-position in Part II. The airplane turn at the end has arms extended to the sides, with left high and right low, palms out, and elbows straight.

The pattern of Part II offers possibilities for choice. When enjoying the dance in a classroom or recreational situation, dancers can create variations by adding step-stamps within the structure, as long as they do so without disrupting their neighbors. When the dance is being done for a program, it is exciting when everyone stamps simultaneously.

Kohanochka

Kohanochka was choreographed by a dance master in the late nineteenth or early twentieth century. It was popular in the ballrooms of Russia and Ukraine, where it was also called *Polka Kohanochka*. The version in *TM&D,* which came from Russian and Ukranian immigrants who lived in the New York area during the 1930s, was taught to folk dancers first by Michael and Mary Ann Herman and later by Dick Crum. It is the simplest and probably truest version of the dance. A few nonauthentic frills have been added over the years by folk dance groups, turning it into more of a peasant dance than it was intended to be.

The *Kohanochka* pattern is based on the Russian polka step. In this and other ballroom dances, the polka resembles a running two-step with a small initial leap: LEAP/RUN, RUN, in a quick/quick, slow rhythm. The movement should be smooth rather than bumpy, and dancers should surge ahead rather than polka in place. On the turning polka, beats 5–8, partners progress together forward along the line of dance instead of revolving in one spot.

Hands and arms for the *Kohanochka* are strong and graceful and as purposeful as the feet. They should not be merely flung out and forgotten, or hung out to dangle dispiritedly, but should move in and out with the phrasing of the music. The dancer's free outside arm is smooth and flowing, the partners' joined inside hands work as a lever as they move forward and down and then up, and the movements of both inside and outside arms are coordinated. In the varsouvienne (also spelled "varsovienne") position, be sure that both partners hold up their own arms and that neither pulls or pushes down on the other. When the boys and men fold their arms across their chest, they point elbows out and hold chin and chest proudly upright. Girls and women also dance proud and tall, knuckles on hips, with fingers pointing backward. Partners should communicate with their expressions, being sure to look at each other as they pass shoulders.

Korobushka

Like *Kohanochka, Korobushka* was created in the late nineteenth century by a dance master. Because of some Hungarian-style movements in *Korobushka,* several researchers have surmised that its choreographer was either Hungarian or trying to give a Hungarian flavor to the dance. The history is not clear—the dance either began in Russia and came to the U.S. with the early twentieth-century immigrants, or it was first danced in the U.S. expatriate communities and then, by reverse migration, traveled back to Russia.

What *is* clear is that *Korobushka* was very popular from the turn of the century into the 1920s, not only in Russia but in Ukraine, Belorussia (now Belarus), and other occupied areas, even in the Jewish settlements. Vyts Beliajus remembered dancing *Korobushka* and other urban ballroom dances as a youngster in Lithuania before emigrating in 1923, and Michael and Mary Ann Herman learned it just a bit later in New York City as members of the Ukranian immigrant community. Others learned it decades later in the Latvian-American community of Chicago. What is special about this dance is that it continues to be one of the most popular in the North American international folk dance repertoire more than 100 years after its introduction. That is an incredible achievement for any choreographer!

How did a consciously created ballroom sequence spread so quickly through such a vast geographic area in the days before radios and recordings? The music, of course, has a great deal to do with *Korobushka's* popularity, as is true of most long-lived dances. The dance is choreographed to a nineteenth-century Russian folk song about a young peddler who shows his wares to a pretty girl. According to Dick Crum, people brought the dance from the cities back to the villages and passed it on to other villages by whistling the melody for musicians to play. In this process, the pattern naturally changed somewhat, but it is remarkable how similar were the various versions of *Korobushka*.

The pattern presented in *TFD* is in the courtly style of the Russian and Ukranian émigrés and is the one danced in New York in the 1930s. It is similar to the Hermans' descriptions, with some added flourishes in Part I, beats 13–16. This TOUCH, APART, TOGETHER, REST is reminiscent of the closure step in many Hungarian dances. In the Russian old-time ballroom styling, which is graceful and flowing, these beats are more gentle, with a step, a point, and a close. Folk dancers have made this measure more vigorous, in the style of the Hungarian *bokázo*, with the jumps and heel-click.

We mention other variations here not to confuse, but to prepare teachers for finding other descriptions and seeing other ways of doing the dance. When Vyts Beliajus danced *Korobushka* in the old country, for the schottische steps of Part I, beats 1–12, dancers moved forward and backward facing counterclockwise instead of moving out of and into the circle. We have also seen this in the 1990s when the dance is done by Russian-Americans. Dick Crum's notes describe the initial formation with the woman's back to the center and the man facing in.

In Part II, partners should be aware and appreciative of each other as they move to their own right and left. Arms move freely, perhaps spread diagonally overhead (as described in *TFD*) or with the right hand leading to the right and the left hand leading to the left. The changing-places part in beats 9–16 should be done with dignity, in keeping with the dance's original spirit.

Young people may prefer the more vigorous but less traditional version of *Korobushka* that is danced in many recreational folk dance groups. Somehow, when brought from New York to California in the mid-1940s, the dignified, courtly Russian ballroom dance changed to a swirling, noisy mixer done in the style of what people pictured as "Russian Gypsies." In Part I of the version, hands crank as partners move in and out of the circle. The first eight beats of Part II become a turn to the right and a turn to the left, with dramatic claps on beats 4 and 8. When changing places, the man turns the woman under their joined right hands as they pass each other. Some men with good knees even do *prisyadki,* or squats, while their partners turn to the right and left.

The optional mixing part occurs during the repeat of Part II, when partners turn to their own right and left (beats 17–24). Finish the full turn to the right by facing the next person along the circle; instead of turning back to the original partner, execute the turn to the left *in place* in front of the new partner. Then join right hands with that person, as in beat 9, and continue to the end of the pattern.

Troika

Troika continues to be popular in recreational folk dance groups as well as at Russian-American parties. Many teachers may remember it from their own school days. Researchers believe that it was created in the Russian immigrant community in the 1920s or 1930s. As its name indicates, the dance pattern depicts the *troika,* which was originally the three-horse sleigh or carriage used by the Russian nobility; the term *troika* later was used to describe a governing group of three.

The description of *Troika* in *TFD* shows one of the original ways the dance was done, again, the way it was done by the Hermans in New York City. Since *Troika* is a popular living dance, however, it is not surprising that there are variations in its patterns. In Part I, for example, some early notes (of the California Federation and others) describe beats 1–4 as moving diagonally forward to the right, beats 5–8 as moving diagonally forward to the left, and beats 9–16 as moving straight forward around the circle.

These light running steps were changed through youthful enthusiasm to kick-steps, or "goose steps," with arms raised high, even though (probably *because*) this was often disapproved of by dance teachers. Although kick-steps are still seen today, many long-time dancers now are relieved to lower their tired arms and legs into the original step pattern. In a more difficult and more dangerous variation—which is thus more popular among elementary school boys—some groups move forward on the first eight beats and *backward* on the second eight beats.

The arches pattern in Part I is similar to that in other cultures and always a favorite part of every dance. The smooth flow from one arch to another requires a coordinated, cooperative effort, which is a good reason to teach this dance to today's students. It also requires the center person to have a flexible wrist and flexible fingers.

The simple circles in Part II, beats 1–12, are often done in the more complex grapevine pattern (CROSS, SIDE, BACK, SIDE three times). This way is more challenging and makes it imperative that the correct foot is used—

crossing the right foot when circling left and vice versa. Correct footwork is not actually necessary in the original, easier version.

Another variation—one that raises the excitement level of this already energetic dance—involves doing *Troika* as a mixer. At the end of the pattern on the last three stamps, the center person runs ahead to join the next group. To add even more spice, the two outside people may raise their joined hands and "shoot" the center person under to the next group.

MODIFICATION AND TEACHING TIPS. These four Russian dances probably should not be modified. *Troika* in its original form, without the kick-steps and grapevine pattern, is appropriate and fun for second grade and up. The slower, traditional *Korobushka* could be taught to fourth grade and up, since the movement skills required are not difficult; however, children of that age usually are not sophisticated enough to appreciate the beauty of this version. Perhaps *Korobushka* should be saved until students can achieve the steps of the more exciting version, at which point they will probably be emotionally ready for the courtly variation, also.

Katia and *Kohanochka* should wait until students are comfortable with the two-step, which leads to the Russian polka. If the polka step is modified in the interests of simplifying the dances, these dances will lose their basic spirit and character.

MUSIC. Nothing evokes the sounds of old Russia as much as the traditional *balalaika*, a three-stringed triangular lute. Balalaikas come in many sizes, ranging from the tiny tinny ones to the huge bass ones. Other traditional instruments include the psaltery, a plucked board zither; the *domra*, a three-stringed mandolin; the shepherd horn and pipe; and the tambourine. Russian folk musicians also do marvelous percussion with wooden spoons as well as with other little items that clack, whirr, rattle, squeak, bang, and scrape. The most popular modern folk instrument is the *bayan*, a Russian button accordion. Violins, bass fiddles, guitars, and flutes also are used for dance music.

It is characteristic for Russian musicians to accelerate the tempo for the pleasure of the dancers. Traditional renditions of *Korobushka*, for example, usually begin slowly and deliberately, but work up to a furiously fast finish.

All the sounds of the songs from this culture—from the open, archaic harmonics of the Byzantine chants to the strong, earthy, chest sounds of the folk melodies—are unmistakably Russian. It is not uncommon to have abrupt mood changes when lively, cheery passages suddenly shift to a melancholy minor key.

CLOTHING AND COSTUMES. For a staged program, girls could wear a version of the simple but elegant nineteenth century regional outfit—a jumper called a *sarafan* worn over a long chemise or blouse. The jumper can be

*Russian street musicians, hoping to attract tourist dollars in Munich, play a keyboard, a bass **balalaika**, and the mandolin-like **domra**.*

In the Karelian region of Russia near St. Petersburg, this musician plucks his homemade psaltery.

*Visitors to Russia listen as this talented musician plays his button accordion, or **bayan**.*

red, blue, or gold, and is usually ankle length but also can be worn to just below the knees. It is trimmed down the front and at the edges with bands of gold or bright embroidery. The chemise has a round neck and full sleeves, either three-quarter or wrist length.

The headdress for this outfit is like a small crown made of stiff, colored cloth that often matches the jumper. The crown might be embroidered in braid, pearls, or other "jewels" and should have a large bow in back with long hanging ribbons. Like girls in other cultures, unmarried girls in Russia wore headdresses meant to show off their tresses; married women, however, had to keep their hair covered completely. On their legs and feet, girls can wear flesh-colored or white hose and shoes or boots, preferably red, but black is also appropriate.

For a traditional Russian look, boys should wear a loose, smock-type, full-sleeved shirt with a stand-up collar. The shirt is tied at the waist with a red cord or sash and has bands of embroidery around the high collar and wrist cuffs as well as down the front opening, which is not in the middle, but off a bit to the side.

Russian Dances

The shirts can be white or a bright color, particularly red. On their legs, boys wear long, slightly full black pants tucked into black boots, and on their heads, a black-billed cap that resembles a Greek fisherman's hat.

Balkanske Igre of Chicago has created these easy-to-change costumes for its Tatar dance.

Cultures and Styling in Folk Dance

Two Russian dancers, participants in the World-Fest held each spring in Branson, Missouri, wear an attractive stage version of their traditional outfits.

Resources Used for Chapter 24

Alsberg, Frank, and Dee Alsberg. 1976. *Disc-Criptions,* Vol. 4:15. Evanston, IL: Author.

Beliajus, Vyts. 1968. "Anent *Korobushka* and *Aleksandrovska.*" *Viltis* (January-February): 13. A pioneer folk dance teacher writes in this article about how he danced these two dances when a youngster in Lithuania.

Beliajus, Vyts. 1980. "*Korobushka* and *Alexandrovska.*" (May): 20–21.

Chalif, Louis H. 1921. *Russian Festivals and Costumes for Pageant and Dance.* New York: Chalif Russian School of Dancing. This book has details on customs and wonderful photos of people wearing daily and festive garb.

Crum, Dick. 1989. *Old-time Russian Ballroom Dances.* Syllabus used at Buffalo Gap Camp, Capon Bridge, WV, Memorial Day weekend, 1992.

Folk Dance Federation of California. 1964. Syllabus of University of Pacific Camp, Stockton, CA, July 1964. See "Our Katia" on p. 16.

Folk Dance Federation of California Research Committee. 1945. *Folk Dances from Near and Far,* Vol. I. Berkeley, CA: Folk Dance Federation of California, Inc. See the *Korobushka* dance notes on p. 14.

Gallagher, James P. "Moscow Moms Push Kids to Dance." *Chicago Tribune,* 11 June 1995. Nation/World section. This article describes ballroom dancing as "one of the hottest crazes among Russian youngsters today."

Gault, Ned, and Marian Gault. 1970. *101 Easy Folk Dances,* 12–13. Monte Sereno, CA: Author.

Herman, Mary Ann. 1990. "Costumes of Old Russia." In *Folk Dance Problem Solver,* Ron Houston, ed., 46. Austin, TX: Society of Folk Dance Historians. The author is a member of the between-the-wars New York City Ukranian community; she and her husband, Michael, were early and long-time folk dance leaders.

Herman, Michael. 1953. *Folk Dance Syllabus, Number One.* New York: Folk Dance House. This book includes the author's descriptions of *Korobushka* and *Troika* as originally taught in the U.S.

Houston, Ron (ed.). 1988. "Korobushka." *Folk Dance Problem Solver,* 20–23. Austin, TX: X-press.

Houston, Ron (ed.). 1990. "Kohanochka." *Folk Dance Problem Solver,* 50–51. Austin, TX: Society of Folk Dance Historians.

Houston, Ron (ed.). 1997. "Katia." *Folk Dance Problem Solver,* 33–34. Austin, TX: Society of Folk Dance Historians.

Joukowsky, Anatol M. 1965. *The Teaching of Ethnic Dance.* New York: Pratt & Co. Note the author's chapter on Russia, pp. 144–66.

Oakes, Dick. 1977. *Lighted Lantern Folk Dances Notes,* 22–23. Lookout Mountain, Golden, CO: Rocky Mountain Folk Dance Camp.

Safirov, Andrei G. 1995. Information from lectures by Moscow Academy of Sciences professor of international politics and Russian-American relations, on July 1995 Russian river cruise.

Scottish Dances

Chapter 25: Scottish Dances

Scottish Dance in Phyllis S. Weikart's Books

Road to the Isles   TFD, RM5

Scotland, a small, rocky, western European nation with beautiful lakes and streams, occupies the northern third of the large island called Great Britain. Officially one of the four countries that make up the United Kingdom of Great Britain and Northern Ireland, Scotland is almost entirely surrounded by water, situated as it is between the North Atlantic Ocean and the North Sea. About the size of the state of Maine, its mainland is divided into the Highlands, the Central Lowlands, and the Southern Uplands. The country also encompasses the Inner and Outer Hebrides and smaller islands off its west coast, and the Orkney and Shetland islands off its northern tip. (See the map on p. 98.)

Modern-day Scots, or Scottish people, (not "the Scotch") are descended from the ancient Celts, Romans, and Norsemen who settled the area. The Celtic culture, which goes back over 2000 years in Scotland, is particularly strong and evident in the Gaelic language that many Scots still speak today.

The Scots, always a fiercely independent people, have resisted for centuries coming under the domination of any one power. Their strong loyalties were tied to specific clans rather than to a ruling sovereign. In 1295, John de Baliol, a Scottish baron whom Edward I of England recognized as King of Scotland, refused to recognize King Edward's rule and instead formed an alliance with France. This alliance continued for several hundred years and was the start of a longstanding French influence on Scottish culture. England became the common enemy, leading to much intrigue and many bloody battles. Scotland finally came under the British crown in 1603, when James VI, son of Mary Queen of Scots, succeeded to the English throne. England, Wales, and Scotland united as the United Kingdom of Great Britain in 1707, with Scotland retaining her own courts, laws, and Presbyterian Church.

The strong French influence on Scottish culture can be seen very clearly in its various forms of traditional dance. The popular longways formations called country dances are found all over the British Isles. However, the Scottish country dances are unique, because their presentation and technique is closely allied to French classical ballet and goes back to the days of the "Auld Alliance" between Scotland and France. Many of the commonly used Scottish dance terms, such as *pas de basque* and *poussette,* come from France, where there are similar types of set dances. Indeed, even the name "country dance" is a modification of the French prefix "contra," meaning opposite or opposing; traditional U.S. dances in similar opposing-line formations are called contra dances.

There are many Scottish country dances, both traditional and modern, and many thriving Scottish country dance groups in North America, the United Kingdom, Japan, and other parts of the world. Most of the various groups, at least outside the British Isles, belong to the Royal Scottish Country Dance Society (RSCDS). Formed in 1923, the RSCDS aims to restore the country dances, which disappeared in the Jazz Age after World War I, and to certify teachers, so dances will be taught true to tradition. Miss Jean Milligan, a founder of the RSCDS who is known as the grand old lady of Scottish country dancing, admonished that

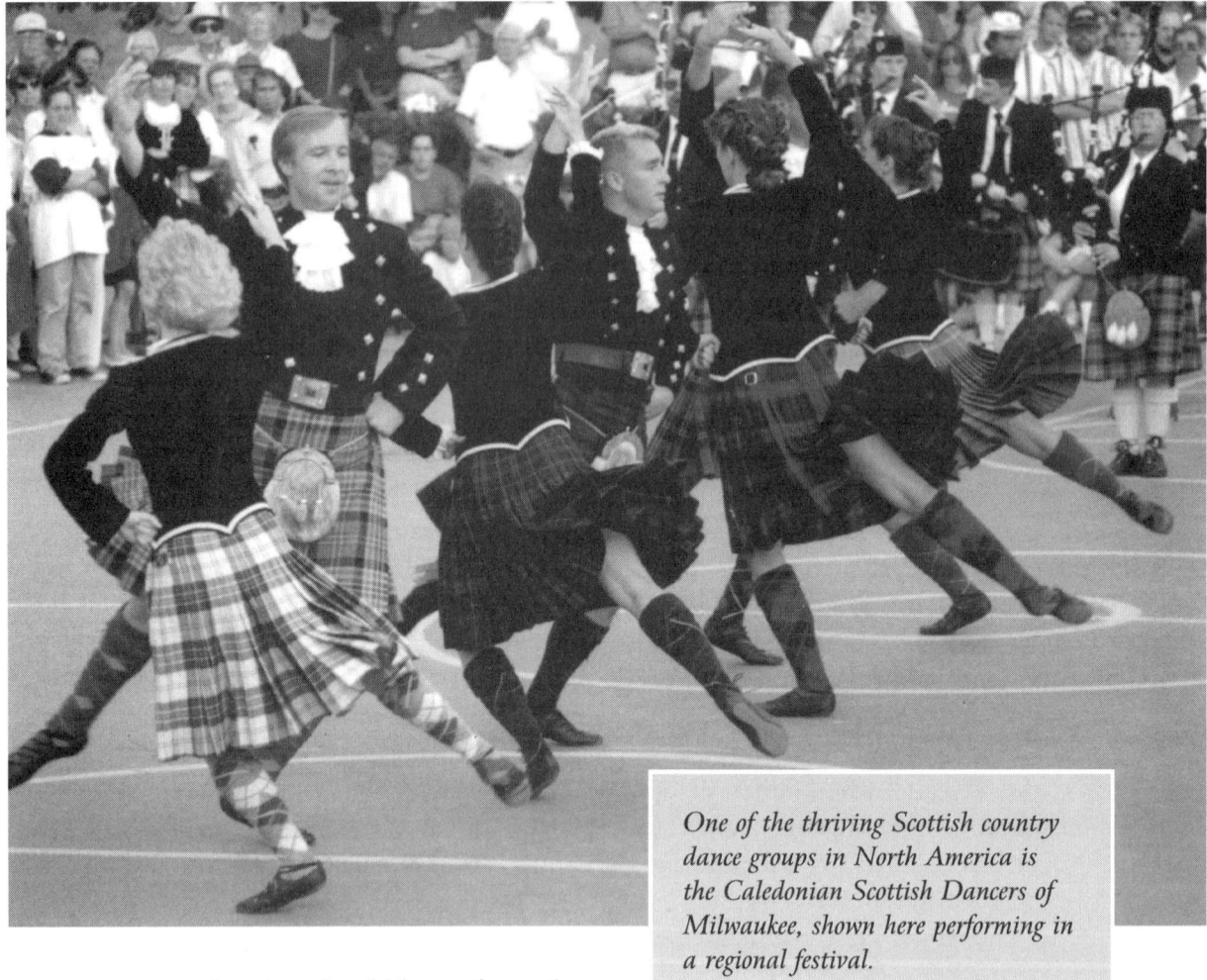

One of the thriving Scottish country dance groups in North America is the Caledonian Scottish Dancers of Milwaukee, shown here performing in a regional festival.

Photo by Norman Lieblein

country dancing should be performed with "controlled abandon" and never degenerate into a "disorderly romp."

The influence of the French court can also been seen in the vigorous Highland dances with their vertical posture, light carriage, careful placing of the toe, and prescribed curve of the arm. Scottish military men warmed up with these strenuous dances before battle to ensure strength, effort, grace, teamwork, and comraderie. The *Highland Fling* and others today are performed competitively at the annual Highland Games, along with other active skills.

Road to the Isles, the single Scottish dance in Phyllis S. Weikart's books, is neither a Highland nor a country dance. It belongs to the group of old-time English and Scottish ballroom couple dances called round dances, many of which date from the early nineteenth century. The name "round dance" distinguished such a dance from dances done in long lines, where partners do not place their arms around each other (in other words, country dances). These round dances

Milwaukee's Caledonian Scottish Dancers demonstrate Highland dance styling—the vertical posture, light carriage, careful placement of the toe, and prescribed curve of the arm.

Photo by Norman Lieblein

illustrate how dances that we now label as "folk" may have been the trendy ballroom dances of the past. In fact, they may be trendy again, as ceilidh (or ceili) parties featuring these same dances have become popular in Scotland and parts of England.

Road to the Isles, which dates from the early 1900s, is considered more modern than some of the others. In Scotland and England, the pattern described in *TFD* is called *Palais Glide* or the *Douglass Schottische* and is done to a variety of different tunes. International folk dance groups generally do this choreography to a melody called *Road to the Isles,* so it has come to be known in the U.S. by that name. This melody, a favorite marching song of the pipe bands, is actually *Bens of Jura,* composed by Pipe Major MacLellan about 1890.

Although *Road to the Isles* is still a staple in international dance group

Scottish Dances

repertoires, it no longer appears regularly on many ceilidh programs. However, a Scottish friend remembers dancing the *Palais Glide* at weddings and socials in her hometown of Dundee, Scotland, as well as during the annual Robert Burns celebration, when all Scottish people gather to recite his poetry, pipe in the haggis (a traditional Scottish dish), and toast the laddies. She says it is done in other parts of the British Isles also, and this is corroborated by an English friend who remembers dancing it during her school days in a suburb of London. Whatever its background, what we know as *Road to the Isles* is a charming dance that offers much enjoyment and learning.

FORMATION. *Road to the Isles* is a partner dance, originally meant to be enjoyed by women and men dancing with each other. Couples move around the dance space in a counterclockwise direction, but they do not have to be in a precise circle, one pair behind another. It is more traditional, more exciting, and a more efficient use of the space if they are scattered around the room, as long as everyone is going in the same direction.

STEPS AND MOVEMENTS. This simple little pattern encompasses a number of basic movement skills that make it useful for learners and even a challenge for some. Part I includes touches and steps that require knowing about change of weight and knowing how to do a modified grapevine step. The French influence is seen in the touching of the toe for both partners, although in some international dance groups, the male partners touch with their heels, as reflected in the dance description in *TFD*.

The second half of Part I is a series of movements known internationally as schottische steps. (The German adjective "schottische" literally means Scottish.) Although the origins of this step pattern are not clear, researchers believe it appeared for the first time in northern Europe at the beginning of the nineteenth century and was probably named for what people thought was a typical Scottish step or rhythm. The same pattern shows up in dances of many other cultures, particularly in the Swedish *schottis*.

The half-turn to the right on beat 12 and the half-turn to the left on beat 14 are a gentle variation on the second and third schottische steps, which just as easily could continue in a forward direction as does the first schottische step (beats 9–10). Other variations are also possible.

When teaching the schottische step in this dance or any other, first have students clap the beat of the music to understand that there will be three steps in a four-count measure. Then have them try the steps in place, without partners, giving a little lift on the fourth beat. When all are comfortable with that, they may start moving forward with the same pattern.

HANDS AND ARMS. The varsouvienne position was named by the French for a partner hold that a dance instructor brought back from Warsaw,

Poland. It is one of the more comfortable partner positions: The man does not have to put his arm around the woman; in fact, they do not even have to look at each other. The arms and hands are as illustrated in the Glossary of *TFD*, although usually the woman holds both hands up. This way her partner can lead and turn her with gentle push-and-pull motions.

It is important, when partners are in the varsouvienne position, that each person remembers to keep his or her own hands and arms raised all the way through the dance, so there is no leaning or yanking on the other person.

MODIFICATION AND TEACHING TIPS. *Road to the Isles* should probably not be modified for less able learners. If students are socially ready to do a dance in this position, then they will be likely to have the requisite movement skills. However, the pattern can be modified during the teaching process, as is often a good idea for many dances. For example, it will promote success to have students learn the steps without partners, as individuals moving around the circle. Then, when the anxiety-provoking concept of partnering is layered on—especially if partners are of opposite gender—the dancers will at least be comfortable with the footwork.

For teaching purposes, another useful temporary modification is to omit the half-turns mentioned earlier (beat 12 and beat 14) and simply continue the pattern forward until students are comfortable with the three schottische steps.

MUSIC. This simple tune can be played in the classroom by using a pipe-type instrument for the melody and using percussion to keep the steady beat. The version on *Rhythmically Moving 5* also reproduces the sound of a bagpipe drone. Appropriate modern instruments include the fiddle, accordion, and string bass.

CLOTHING AND COSTUMES. If the ballroom dance *Road to the Isles* is to be done in a program, it is not necessary to have the boys dress in full Highland outfit, as they should if performing a Highland or country dance. They may wear long dark pants or wear breeches and knee socks along with a short jacket and soft black leather shoes. Sartorial splendor can be added with a tartan tie or a lace jabot at the throat.

If it is possible, however, having the boys wear the kilt would certainly leave no doubt as to which culture was being represented. Scottish men often wear the kilt in everyday activities as well as when dancing or when with their Highland regiments. For the ball, the kilt is worn with a short jacket, or coatee, (in blue, wine, green, or black) over a white shirt, topped off by a lace jabot, black bow tie, or tartan tie at the neck. On their legs, men wear heavy patterned knee socks and, especially for dancing, soft black leather laced shoes similar to ballet slippers, called *ghillies*. This footwear allows for flexibility of ankle and instep when doing the ballet-like movements.

Shown here onstage at the Milwaukee Summerfest, the Caledonian Scottish Dancers wear full Highland outfit.
Photos by Norman Lieblein

294　　　　　　　　　　　　　　　　*Cultures and Styling in Folk Dance*

The outfit is not complete without the *sporran,* a pouch that hangs down in front from the man's belt, made of leather (for everyday) or of fur (for dress). It was used as a purse and as protection for the body.

The kilt is, of course, in the colors of the person's clan tartan. Instead of just picking out some attractive plaid, it would be respectful to this culture for students to research the history of their chosen tartans and wear them proudly. If a person has no clan tartan, they may wear a kilt of gray or the Jacobite or Caledonian tartan (more research). The knee hose may match the tartan or be of checks in the tartan's prominent colors.

At the dance, whether country, Highland, or ballroom, women usually wear a white or light-colored long dress with a plaid sash draped diagonally across the chest and pinned with brooch on the left shoulder. (Long ago only women chiefs—yes, they had them—or wives of chiefs were allowed to wear the sash on the left shoulder, but now everyone is permitted to do so.) In contests and performance today, knee-length tartan skirts are worn, with dark vests and white blouses. Women and girls also wear ghillies or ballet shoes.

Don't let the students think that there is anything nonmasculine about wearing a skirt-like kilt and ballet-type shoes. Scottish Highland and country dancing is extremely strenuous and requires as much strength as any team sport to keep the pace and the pattern while performing on the toes with balance and agility. Any student would be inspired by the sight of eight kilted Scotsmen swirling vigorously on their well-muscled legs through the intricate formations of the *Reel of the 51st Regiment,* a dance created by Scots in a German military prison during World War II and performed at festivities today only by men having the greatest skill and stamina.

Resources Used for Chapter 25

Donald, Emily Ann. 1986. *The Scottish Highland Games in America.* Gretna, LA: Pelican Publishing Co. This book provides details on national events, history, excellent photos, and a chapter on Highland dances.

Duggan, Anne Schley, Jeanette Schlottmann, and Abbie Rutledge. 1948. *Folk Dances of the British Isles.* New York: Ronald Press.

Emmerson, George. 1967. *Scotland Through Her Country Dances.* London: Johnson.

Fiebig, Heidi. 1975. "A Wee Drap o' Scotch." *Ontario Folkdancer,* (Vol. 6, #2): 26—35. A reprint of an article giving information on the history of Scottish dance and dress.

Harris, Jane A., Anne M. Pittman, and Marlys S. Waller. 1994. *Dance Awhile,* 7th ed. New York: Macmillan International. See the *Road to the Isles* description on p. 274.

Hood, Evelyn M. 1980. *The Story of Scottish Country Dancing.* London: Wm. Collins and Sons.

Lamb, Sandra. 1995, June. Conversation in Wilmette, IL, with this native of Dundee, Scotland, who was an RSCDS-certified teacher and leader of a Scottish country dance group in Chicago until her return to Scotland.

Smith, Kent. 1980–95. Conversations with this active Scottish dancer who is an RSCDS-certified teacher and former leader of a Scottish country dance group in Chicago, now living in Hartford, CN.

Thurston, Hugh. 1984. *Scotland's Dances.* Kitchener, Ontario: The Teachers' Association.

Zielke, Reuel. 1995, November–December. Conversations with this Scottish dance expert, teacher, and performer from Milwaukee, WI.

Swedish Dances

Chapter 26: Swedish Dances

Swedish Dance in Phyllis S. Weikart's Books

Fjäskern   [f-YESS-kehrn] (also known as *Hurry Scurry*) TFD, RM2

*O*ne of the largest nations in Europe, Sweden stretches from the Baltic Sea to far above the Arctic Circle. The southern part of Sweden has a temperate climate, but the northern part lies in the Land of the Midnight Sun, where there are extended dark winters contrasted with two summer months of continuous daylight. Sweden is part of the northern European region known as Scandinavia, which also includes the countries of Denmark and Norway, with whom Sweden shares a common language root. Although Finland and Iceland are not true Scandinavian nations, they are also usually categorized as Scandinavian in the cultural dance field. A look at the map will show that Sweden shares much of its western border with Norway, and its northeastern corner borders on Finland; its southern tip is close to Copenhagen, and the rest of the boundaries are splashed with water from various cold seas. (See the map on p. 300.)

Early inhabitants of Sweden have been traced back to the melting of the last of the ice covering most of Europe, 8,000 years ago. Along with their Scandinavian neighbors, the Swedes made history in about 800 to 1000 C.E. as Vikings, the pirate Northmen who traveled both east and west, beginning from the Baltic and North seas. These forays, which extended as far west as the North American continent and as far east as Russia, led the Vikings to various coastal lands, where they eventually began to start colonies. For example, a Danish Viking chief and his followers were early settlers in the northern region of France known as Normandy ("Norsemen" and "Northmen" became "Normans"), and a group of Norwegian Vikings founded Dublin, Ireland, in 841. The Swedish Vikings traveled eastward as far as the Black and Caspian seas. The name they were called by there, the *Russ,* is thought to be the source of the name *Russia.*

At home in Sweden, the Scandinavian countries were separate kingdoms for a time, then were all three united in 1389 under Queen Margrete of Denmark and Norway—a union that lasted throughout most of the fifteenth century. Sweden finally broke away to become an independent nation in 1523.

Sweden had first been introduced to Christianity in the ninth century; eventually, Lutheranism became the state religion in the sixteenth century, when King Gustavus I gave protection to the followers of Martin Luther. The Swedish people today still enjoy some pre-Christian festivals, such as May Day Eve and Midsummer's Eve, as well as the more modern December 13 holiday of Santa Lucia Day, the Festival of Light.

Present-day Sweden continues to have a king, although his power is mainly ceremonial; as a constitutional monarchy, the country is ruled by a prime minister and parliament. An interesting fact about this important industrial nation is that it managed to stay neutral during both world wars.

Fjäskern, also known as *Hurry Scurry* in English-speaking places for reasons that soon become obvious, is a fairly modern recreational dance from southern Sweden. It was learned in Sweden by noted Scandinavian dance researcher and teacher Gordon Tracie, who introduced it into the U.S. folk dance repertoire in

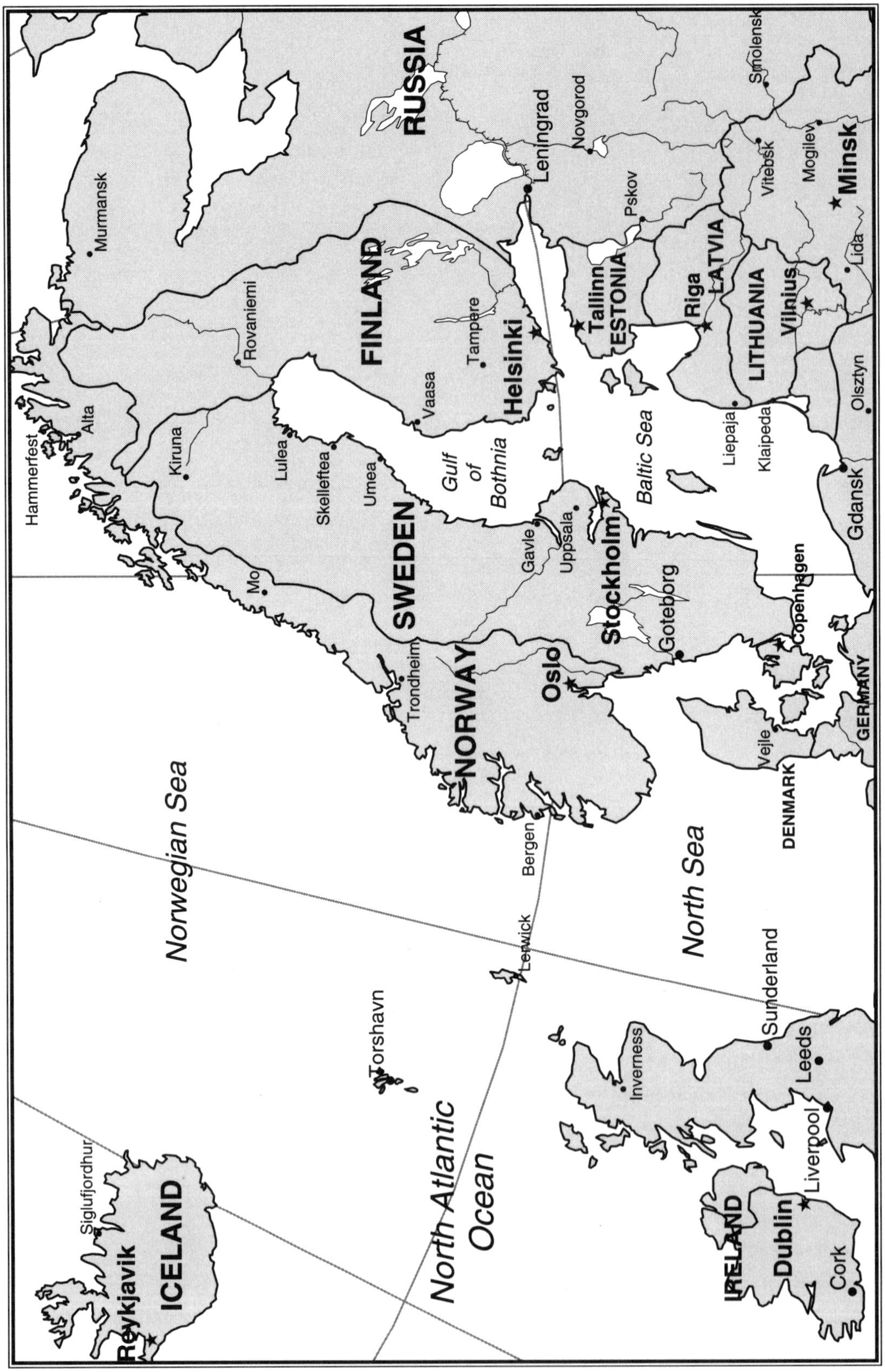
ICELAND
Reykjavik
Siglufjordhur
Norwegian Sea
North Atlantic Ocean
Torshavn
Lerwick
North Sea
Bergen
NORWAY
Trondheim
Oslo
SWEDEN
Mo
Hammerfest
Alta
Kiruna
Lulea
Skelleftea
Umea
Gavle
Uppsala
Stockholm
Goteborg
Gulf of Bothnia
FINLAND
Rovaniemi
Vaasa
Tampere
Helsinki
RUSSIA
Murmansk
Leningrad
Novgorod
Pskov
Smolensk
Vitebsk
Mogilev
Minsk
Lida
ESTONIA
Tallinn
LATVIA
Riga
LITHUANIA
Vilnius
Liepaja
Klaipeda
Olsztyn
Gdansk
Baltic Sea
Copenhagen
DENMARK
Vejle
GERMANY
IRELAND
Dublin
Cork
Liverpool
Leeds
Sunderland
Inverness

1950. The dance was also popularized by Jane Farwell, the well-known recreation leader.

Fjäskern belongs in the Swedish and Norwegian dance family called *turdanser*. These are choreographed figure dances that include quadrilles and longways sets, which migrated from western European courts to the Scandinavian cities and then were adopted and adapted by the villagers. A more ancient type of dance, presumed to be pre-Christian, is the *långdans* (longdance), a type of group singing dance. Another type, known as *bygdedans* (regional or village dance), with roots in the Renaissance, includes the Swedish *polskas* and Norwegian *springars*. These dances, with their regional variations, are popular today not only in Sweden and Norway and in expatriate communities but also in North American international folk dance clubs.

A fourth family of Swedish and Norwegian dance, also very popular with contemporary folk dancers, is the *gammaldans* (old or round dance) that includes regional Swedish versions of waltzes, schottishes, polkas, and mazurkas. The most popular village

*Dancers from Sweden performing at Folkmoot USA demonstrate a choreographed figure dance—from the dance family called **turdanser**. Many of these migrated from western Europe to Scandinavian cities and then were adopted and adapted by the villagers.*

Two young Swedish dancers concentrate on a schottische pattern during a performance at Folkmoot USA.

dance is the 3/4 meter *polska*. It evolved about 400 years ago during a period when Sweden and Poland (thus the name) were politically connected. The beautiful *hambo,* which many folk dancers know or at least aspire to, is considered to be a polska. Hambo contests are held each year, with Swedes and participants from a few other countries gathering to compete and enjoy hours of hamboing.

The era of Romantic nationalism all over Europe at the end of the nineteenth century encouraged an interest in Swedish peasant culture that included research into old-time dances and soon led to the establishment of dance clubs. Contemporary students might be intrigued to know that when the dances were performed on stage, men would be each other's partners because women were not allowed on stage at that time. In the 1970s, there was a revival of interest in the regional dances in the international dance community as well as in Sweden, and this led to recreational dance groups in Europe and North America that specialize in Scandinavian dance, music, and culture.

Gordon Tracie, who introduced *Fjäskern,* is known as the grandfather of Swedish dance in the U.S. A native of Seattle whose grandparents were from Dalarna, Sweden (it is said he was bounced on their knees in a polska rhythm), he first became interested in traditional fiddle music while studying in Sweden in 1947. Through his subsequent research, he sparked the Swedes' interest in their own music. In addition, he introduced Swedish dances to U.S. dancers during the 1950s and 1960s, at least a decade before the Swedes themselves began similar activities. As a cultural exchange, Tracie toured Sweden teaching square dancing, thus also leaving a legacy of square dance clubs.

Roo Lester is another person who has been responsible for the present level of interest and skill in Swedish and Scandinavian dancing around North America. She is especially known for her clear and enjoyable teaching of these sometimes complex patterns.

When Gordon Tracie first presented *Fjäskern,* it was done at a steady running pace. The special humor was added by a folk musician in Upsala named Nils Presto, who lived up to his name by speeding up the tempo. It is a wonderful dance for getting students to really listen to the music as they move and to keep a steady but accelerating beat. To add to its versatility, *Fjäskern* may be done as a mixer as well as a couple dance.

FORMATION. *Fjäskern* begins in a circle of couples, with partners side by side, facing counterclockwise (CCW). Traditionally, like most Swedish dances, it is done in female-male pairs, with men on the inside and women on the outside. However, given elementary classroom realities, same-gender partners are perfectly acceptable. If done as a mixer, a person of the opposite persuasion will inevitably appear as the dance progresses.

STEPS AND MOVEMENTS. As Gordon Tracie has described, the dance style is "sprightly and with humor." In Part I, although the pattern is simply to alternate one foot after the other, one challenge comes in matching the dance steps to the quickening tempo. Students might practice making their steps shorter and lighter as the music gets faster, to feel how the initial plodding walk finally ends up as a rhythmic run.

The other challenge in Part I is to know when to turn in the opposite direction. Many students—adult folk dancers, too—think that instead of simply allowing a certain amount of time, they must cover a certain amount of space before facing the other way. However, the turn comes after moving 16 beats in each direction, no matter how fast those beats go. And as always, students must be instructed to *begin the turn on the first beat of the fourth measure* (beat 13), so the pieces of the pattern flow together; this is preferable to waiting until the last beat and then whipping around the other way.

In Part II, it is best to use the cue "scissors" (as described in beats 1–4) rather than "kick," while teaching children. One common error when partners are changing places is for them to execute a half-turn to the left when passing shoulders, rather than to simply pass by and then turn right (CW) to face one another. Although it does not ruin the dance, this mistaken half-turn can cause disorientation and unnecessarily adds an extra layer of difficulty. To practice the pass-by, partners might try joining hands at first as they change places.

In Sweden and in folk dance groups, *Fjäskern* is generally danced as a mixer. When the pattern starts again, during the first four to eight beats, one person moves ahead to the next person forward. It is easier for the person on the inside, traditionally the man, to be the one who moves ahead, since he has a shorter distance to cover. In Sweden, however, it is often the woman who moves ahead.

HANDS AND ARMS. In Part I, whether moving counterclockwise (CCW) or clockwise (CW), partners hold inside hands at shoulder level. Free hands are on hips, in the Swedish style with fingers forward and thumbs back. In Part II, each person places hands on his or her own hips while kicking. Be sure to emphasize that the clap comes on the first beat when partners change places past right shoulders.

MODIFICATION AND TEACHING TIPS. As shown in *TFD*, *Fjäskern* can easily be modified by keeping it in a single circle, without partners. This is indeed a good method of teaching any partner dance. The single circle is appropriate when using this pattern to demonstrate, for example, the idea of moving to an accelerating beat. When teaching the dance as part of a recreational or multicultural curriculum, however, it is best to add the partner part as soon as possible, for that turns a movement exercise into a real people's dance. In addition, once they master the skills involved, students are often more successful dancing with one friend instead of trying to relate to an entire circle of classmates.

MUSIC. The most common instrument for Swedish folk music is the fiddle. Fiddle-playing is so common that there is this popular saying: "If you meet two people from Rättvik, three of them will play the fiddle." There are also many good Swedish musicians in the U.S. The ornamentation and accents are what make the *Fjäskern* music special and Swedish. Each region has its own musical style, and every musician adds his or her own personal embellishments.

Playing their fiddles, musicians from Sweden lead a grand march at Midsummer Scandi Fair in Estes Park, Colorado.

Other popular old-time instruments include the *nyckelharpa,* an unusual relative of the hurdy-gurdy that plays a drone as well as a melody; Swedish bagpipes; and rural soundmakers such as cow and goat horns and herding flutes. The accordion has been the bridge from old-time to modern music and is now a regular part of the folk music scene, along with saxophones, clarinets, guitars, basses, synthesizers, and instruments from Latin and African cultures.

The music for *Fjäskern* is what makes a somewhat pedestrian pattern become a humorous and often-requested dance. It sounds best when played by a fiddle accompanied by a bass or some other instrument that can furnish the quickening pulse.

CLOTHING AND COSTUMES. The revival of interest in Scandinavian folklore has also focused on traditional clothing. People show pride in their background by weaving and wearing the attire of their forebears for festive occasions. Both men and women carry on the traditions by knitting special socks to wear at their own weddings. There are many local variations, but some general similarities may offer guidelines for school programs.

Swedish Dances

Guests from Sweden wear their own regional clothing at the Midsummer Scandi Fair in Estes Park, Colorado.

The International Dancers of Chicago put together quick-change costume pieces to simulate Swedish folk clothing. Note that the man has created "knickers" by pulling long white socks up over his trouser legs.

Simple generic Swedish folk costumes for girls may include a short bodice that laces up the front and is worn over a high-necked, long-sleeved white chemise or blouse. The full skirt is about calf length and always worn with a white or vertically striped apron. Common colors for clothing are blue, red, green, yellow, or black. On the girls' legs are plain red or white hose and low-heeled black shoes. Sometimes Swedish women wear short, fringed and flowered shawls like capes, fastened in front with a brooch of silver, tin, or brass. Married women cover their hair with small bonnets or caps sometimes turned up in the back, but girls can be bareheaded.

Boys can wear a white, long-sleeved chemise or shirt under a high-necked red, checked, or striped waistcoat that is fastened down the front with metal buttons. Long trousers can be worn, but knee breeches or knickers are also characteristic—usually yellow or dark blue and tied below the knee with red braid and pom-poms. The boys can wear plain white or dark hose and black shoes with silver buckles. Men also wear a variety of caps or hats, depending on the region represented. Costume books will give good ideas on this.

Swedish Dances

Resources Used for Chapter 26

Backstrom, Magnus, and Phillip Page. 1994. "The Midnight Sound: Scandinavia's Finn-led Folk Revival." In *World Music, The Rough Guide,* Simon Broughton, Mark Ellingham, David Muddyman, and Richard Trillo, eds., 48–50. London: Rough Guides, Ltd.

Bacon, Eleanor. 1981. "Swedish Costumes." *Let's Dance* (January): 10–11.

Berg, Inga Arno, and Gunnel Hazelius Berg. 1975. *Folk Costumes of Sweden: A Living Tradition.* [in English] Västerås: ICA bokforlag. Excellent book for costumes.

Boorstin, Daniel J. 1983. *The Discoverers.* New York: Random House. This excellent history book has a good section on the Vikings, describing everything from their raids on Europe in the eighth century to their accidently bumping into North America in the tenth.

Deny, Sharron. 1981. "Scandinavian (Danish, Norwegian, Finnish) Folk Dancing." In *International Folk Dancing USA,* Betty Casey, ed., 265–67. Garden City, NY: Doubleday.

Folestad, Agnetha. 1995. "How to Teach Children Traditional Dance: Recent Thoughts in Sweden." *Viltis* (May–June):8–9. Dr. Folestad is an orthopedic surgeon and active folk dancer.

Houston, Ron. 1995, November. Information about *Fjäskern* provided from the archives of the Society of Folk Dance Historians—pages from a syllabus put together by Gordon Tracie.

Lester, Roo. 1992. "The United States Scandinavian Dance Community and Norsk *bygdedans,*" Master's thesis, University of California–Los Angeles.

Lester, Roo. 1995–97. Conversations with this Scandinavian dance expert, Chicago, IL.

Lester, Roo. 1997. "Some background of Swedish and Norwegian Folk Dance." From the Internet: <http://members.aol.com/Dancing Roo>.

Salvén, Erik. 1949. *Dances of Sweden.* London: Max Parrish & Co. Part of a series of books, with much cultural information on some of the country's basic dances.

"Sweden." 1994. In *World Music, The Rough Guide,* Simon Broughton, Mark Ellingham, David Muddyman, and Richard Trillo, eds., 48–50. London: Rough Guides, Ltd.

Tracie, Gordon. 1965. "Scandinavian Dance." In *Folk Dance Progressions,* Miriam D. Lidster and Dorothy H. Tamburini, eds., 23–27. Belmont, CA: Wadsworth.

Tracie, Gordon. 1981. "Gammal Polska." *Let's Dance* (January): 8–9.

Tracie, Gordon. 1981. "Swedish Dance Preface." In notes of 1981 Stockton Folk Dance Camp, University of the Pacific, Stockton, CA, and syllabus of University of Chicago's 1981 Folk Dance Festival.

Turkish Dances

Chapter 27: Turkish Dances

Turkish Dances in Phyllis S. Weikart's Books

Ali Paşa   [AH-lee pah-SHAH] (General Ali) *TM&D*

Güzelleme   [gu-ZEL-leh-meh] [song of praise] *TM&D*

Işte Hendek   [ISH-teh HEN-deck] (Dig a ditch) *TFD, RM6*

Karşilama   (*Karsilimas*—the Greek spelling—is used in *TM&D*) [kar-shuh-la-mah] (Face to face) *TM&D*

Kendime   (*Kendimé* in *TFD*) [KEN-dee-meh] (To myself) *TFD, RM5*

Turkey has a special and important geographic location as the bridge between two continents, southeastern Europe and southwestern Asia. (See map on p. 48.) Most of Turkey is on a large peninsula called Asia Minor, known historically as Anatolia. It lies between the Black Sea to the north, the Mediterranean Sea to the south, and the Aegean Sea to the west; on the east, its neighbors are the republics of Georgia, Armenia, Iran, Iraq, and Syria. The northwestern part of Turkey lies in Europe across the Straits of Bosporus, the boundary between the two continents. This little piece of Turkey borders Greece and Bulgaria and contains the beautiful city that was called Byzantium from the seventh to the fourth century B.C.E., then renamed Constantinople after the Roman emperor Constantine. In 1453, the city's name changed once again, to Istanbul and that is the name we know it by today.

Besides being a geographic bridge, Asia Minor has also been a cultural bridge in its long history. Around 2000 B.C.E., ancient nomadic Hittite peoples migrated to this location from central Asia, and over the ensuing 500 years, they were able to create a powerful empire in this region. As they did so, while making their way across the continent, these barbaric horsemen were so troublesome that the Chinese built the Great Wall of China for protection from them. Over the remaining centuries before the Common Era, other groups—Phrygians, Lydians, Persians, and Greeks, also conquered parts of Asia Minor. The Greeks took their turn in dominating the region during the last three centuries B.C.E., and their influence is still evident today. Visitors to the area can see former sites of the underground cities into which early settlers disappeared when yet another group of invaders came sweeping across Asia Minor. The Romans took over in the first century B.C.E., and the next 400 years of peace under Roman rule brought roads and unification as well as Christianity. For a period of nearly 800 years, many religions—including paganism, Hellenism, Judaism, and Christianity—were able to coexist and take root in the region. Along with the various religions came Greek, Roman, and Oriental arts and culture; libraries and medical knowledge; and the development of great trade routes between continents.

The coveted Asia Minor was conquered again around 1000 C.E. by the Seljuk Turks, Islamic peoples from Persia, who have maintained the longest and strongest hold on the area. Even today, more than 90 percent of the Turkish people are Sunni Muslims of the Islamic faith. During the eleventh, twelfth, and thirteenth centuries, Christian military expeditions known as the Crusades were launched from central Europe and fought their way six times across Asia Minor to "save Jerusalem from the infidels." As in most wars, no one was truly the final victor in the Crusades, with the Anatolians suffering as much as the others. Not long after dealing with the crusaders, the Turks also had to face the armies of Ghengis Khan, but they recovered from these Mongol invasions and, during the 1300s, began to build what was to be known as the Ottoman Empire. (It was in the course of building this empire that the Turks conquered Byzantium in 1453 and renamed it Istanbul.)

At its height, the vast Ottoman Empire stretched from southern Arabia through western Asia, across some of northern Africa, and across most of southeastern Europe up to Hungary and even Russia. This Islamic sovereignty dominated the region for almost 600 years, until the early twentieth century, and permanently imprinted its legacies on many peoples. Most of these subjugated cultures were not able to participate in the Renaissance of western Europe and the progressive ages that followed, so they carried much of their agrarian peasant life into the twentieth century. Some are still trying to come to terms with their past history as they approach the next millennium.

After the collapse of the Ottoman Empire following World War I, a military leader named Mustafa Kemal was able to defeat Turkey's enemies and politically guide his people during their awakening to the new age. Known as *Atatürk*, father of the Turks, he worked to modernize his nation. He created the Republic of Turkey in 1923 and established the more centrally located city of Ankara as the new capital, instigating reforms of government and society. The country has been through political turmoil and military rule since then but has now returned to a civilian democratic government and is entering into the economic life of Europe.

In his attempts to modernize his country, Atatürk tried to forbid the playing of traditional Turkish music on the radio. In this he went too far—there was great protest, and he was forced to lift the ban. (Ironically, in private he enjoyed music and dance from his native region and invited folk musicians to play for him in the palace.) Traditional dancing and music are still important to the Turkish people, although the young Turks, like young people everywhere, also love jazz and American rock-and-roll—a modernization even Atatürk might have regretted.

Turkey's fascinating history has not been lost, however, and visitors can view carefully preserved edifices, archeological ruins, and opulent palaces, as well as the Anatolian landscape, animals, and plant life that combine characteristics of Africa, Asia, and Europe.

The dances discussed in this chapter were presented by Bora Özkök, the foremost and earliest teacher of Turkish folk music and dance for the international dance community. A native of Adana, Turkey, and an excellent folk musician, Özkök in about 1970 began teaching Turkish dances at major folk dance camps, and the dances listed here were some of the most popular he taught. Still solidly entrenched in most groups' regular repertoires, they are fixed forms of dances that come from the village and folk communities.

Another basic type of Turkish dance incorporates the expressive rotating movements of some religious orders, such as those of the Sufi sect called *Mevlevi*, known as whirling dervishes. This meditative dance symbolizes the cycle of the seasons and the motions of the heavens. A third main type of dance is that meant especially for entertainment, which includes Oriental dance popularly (but not respectfully) known as belly dancing.

As in most traditional cultures, true Turkish folk dances are improvisational within the parameters of the music and the styling. Like most international folk dances, however, the Turkish dances in *TFD* and *TM&D* are not improvisational but have been arranged by Bora Özkök from authentic steps and patterns to fit the music he recorded (the *Rhythmically Moving* recordings use his melodies for *Işte Hendek* and *Kendime*).

Ali Paşa comes from western Turkey and is named for the man who governed the southwest Balkans for the Ottoman Empire in the late eighteenth and early nineteenth centuries. Apparently an exceptionally cruel ruler at a time when cruel rulers were not unusual, he caused enough trouble that the Sultan had him murdered. Özkök learned *Işte Hendek* from the University of Istanbul Ethnic Dancers in 1970 and introduced it to U.S. folk dancers in 1972. Also introduced in 1972, *Güzelleme, Kendime,* and *Karsilima* are authentic dances with patterns arranged by Özkök for recreational enjoyment.

FORMATION. Most Turkish folk dances are done in open lines or circles; often several lines of medium length move at the same time. Some dances are for men only, and some for women only. Leaders are at the right end, wielding a kerchief and calling the pattern changes by shouting *geç, geç* (change, change)! *Ali*

Turkish men dancing in an open line demonstrate a dance from the Black Sea region during Folkmoot USA.

Cengiz photo

Paşa can be done in a closed circle as described in *TM&D*, but it and *Işte Hendek* are usually performed in shorter lines (no more than 10) having a leader at both ends. Both *Güzelleme* and *Kendime* have a single leader, on the right.

Karsilama is an example of a couple dance from this area. It comes from the region called Trakia, or Thrace, that spreads over the contiguous corners of Turkey, Greece, and Bulgaria. Actually, "karsilama" is a generic dance name like "schottische" or "tango," and it denotes a dance that can have a variety of patterns. When teaching such a freestyle dance, it is useful to start with a definite pattern like the one described in *TM&D*. After learning this pattern, students can try creating their own appropriate movements.

There are few partner dances that are traditional in the cultures of the Moslem-based Ottoman Empire, since men and women usually danced separately because of religious and societal injunctions; other reasons for this separation were mentioned in the chapter on dances of the Armenian people. In the couple dances that do exist, such as *Karsilama*, partners do not touch, even to hold hands. In fact, the two people dancing together are often of the same gender.

STEPS AND MOVEMENTS. Turkish dances, like those from all cultures, have regional styling variations. Those in this series are all of the same type—done with small, light, precise steps, but with much spirit and vigor and rhythmic vocalization. Generally, when the pattern calls for a foot touching, the touch is done with the whole sole rather than with just the toe or heel. Not only the feet move, however, in dances from this culture. It is important that knees are kept flexible, so trunk and arms can bounce with the beats.

In addition, the body often leans forward or backward. For example, in *Ali Paşa,* Part I, beats 4–5, and Part III, beats 14–15, lean backward slightly when touching the left foot in. Also lean backward when hooking one foot behind the other knee as in *Işte Hendek,* Part I, beat 4, and in Part I's variation, beat 4&, or on the last beat of *Kendime*. Lean forward, however, on the chug in Part II, beat 4, of *Işte Hendek* and its variation.

In *Güzelleme*, the dipping movement described in beat 3 is the culmination of a soft forward-rolling movement that begins with a left knee-bend as beat 1 begins. In *Karsilama*, partners are facing each other, about three feet apart to begin. Partners should relate to each other with their body language and feel free to move around the space, as well as to improvise other patterns.

HANDS AND ARMS. Two characteristic hand-holds of Turkish folk dances are represented in these dances. For the first, shown in *Ali Paşa* and *Kendime,* hands are joined by little fingers (the pinkie-hold) with arms bent in the W-position. People at each end of the line hold handkerchiefs in their free hand. In *Kendime,* arms make small circles during the simple movement pattern.

The second characteristic hand-hold is quite different and is shown in

A visiting Turkish group at the Folkmoot USA festival perform a partner dance from the northeast area of Turkey. Partner dances are uncommon, since Turkish men and women usually danced separately because of religious and societal injunctions.

Cengiz photo

Güzelleme and *Işte Hendek*. Arms are held bent or straight down, with adjacent dancers' fingers interlocked or with their hands clasped. Dancers are tight together, shoulder to shoulder. When arms are straight down, one dancer's right arm is tucked behind the other dancer's left, and all arms are held a bit behind the hips so no arms show in front. The lines are short, and there is (gentle!) inward pressure by all dancers to keep the line close together.

This shoulder-to-shoulder position, of course, is difficult to maintain, especially with young learners. For classroom dancing, it would be easier for everyone to hold hands down at the side; if preparing these dances for a program, however, the traditional hand-hold would be a good learning challenge and very effective.

Karsilama being a more improvisational dance gives choices of hand and arm positions. Men usually open their arms to the side or in front, at shoulder

Doing a Turkish dance from the Black Sea region, men of the Brigham Young University International Folk Dance Ensemble clasp hands and dance tightly together, shoulder to shoulder.
Photo by Mark Philbrick

height or above, using their hands expressively. Women use this arm position, too, but they may also dance with the backs of their hands on their hips. Sometimes, as they dance facing their partner, women hold a triangular kerchief by two corners, at about face height, to symbolize the veil formerly worn.

MODIFICATION AND TEACHING TIPS. The footwork of these dances should not be modified. The arm positions and hand-holds actually are more difficult than the step patterns; perhaps the pinkie-hold and the shoulder-to-shoulder position could be changed to a plain W-hold or V-hold until students are comfortable moving together to these steps. When they are finally ready for the traditional hand-holds, these should be practiced a lot while standing or bouncing in place—there is a tendency to stretch out arms or squeeze fingers. It may also help to keep the lines fairly short, with people of similar sizes (and who are fairly friendly) next to each other.

When teaching the asymmetric meters, pat the stepping beat on knees or thighs. This leads to stepping the beat in place, followed by moving in the same step pattern in and out of the circle, then forward in the line of direction. At this point, steps in the asymmetric 5/4 and 9/8 meters can be combined with the pattern. Perhaps first singing songs in these asymmetric meters would also help. See *TFD* p. 78 for more information on presenting asymmetric meter (which *TFD* terms "uncommon" meter).

MUSIC. Much traditional Turkish music has asymmetric meter (for example, *Ali Paşa* is in 5/4, and *Karsilama* is in 9/8). When dancing to such meters, all that is required is to hold the last beat in each phrase.

In *TM&D*, the music for *Karsilama* is a song called *Rampi Rampi*. (*Karsilama* should not be confused with the Greek line dance called *Rampi Rampi*, however.) This is a favorite song to which people enjoy doing various versions of the karsilama; the dance can also be done to many other melodies. *Güzelleme, Işte Hendek,* and *Kendime* are some other Turkish patterns that can appropriately be danced to more than one tune. The melody for *Ali Paşa*, however, is generally the only one used for this specific choreography.

To unaccustomed ears, the sounds of Turkish village music might be startling at first, but the exciting, driving rhythms are infectious. A basic instrument is the *zurna,* a shrill reed that is ancestor to the oboe—this is what the snake charmers use in India. It is usually accompanied by the two-sided *davul,* played with a beater and stick, and the *darbuka,* a hand drum played with the fingers. Tambourines and wooden spoons also add percussion. Other popular instruments are the *saz,* a long-necked guitar; the *kaval,* an end-blown shepherd's flute; and a bagpipe called the *tulum.* Just as important is the voice as it sings, chants, calls, and makes rhythmic sounds.

CLOTHING AND COSTUMES. Each province has its own style, but typical attire for Turkish women that will work for school programs might begin with the full, baggy trousers that close at the ankle; they are called *şalvar* (sometimes known in the west as harem pants). These can be worn with a long-sleeved blouse worn with a short sleeveless vest or with a long-sleeved, waist-length jacket and a colored, fringed sash. The soft leather shoes with turned-up toes might be difficult to duplicate; if so, black or red ballet shoes would work fine, although nowadays Turkish women often dance in high-heeled pumps.

Until recently, women covered their faces with veils and draped scarves, but this is not necessary, as long as the hair is hidden. A long scarf can be tied around the head in various ways. Or instead, a pill-box type hat, the *fez,* can be worn with a scarf put over it, then tied around the neck and under the chin and draped with coins across the forehead and around the face.

Men's dress is similar to women's. The şalvar is appropriate for the boys, also, with a high-necked, long-sleeved shirt and a short sleeveless vest or long-sleeved jacket. They may wear a long, wide sash tied around the waist, and for an added touch, a leather belt over the sash, with a dagger or sword thrust into it. On their feet are the turned-up shoes or ballet-type shoes, or soft, black boots. Men also cover their heads with a fez and/or a scarf that is wound around the head or hat, then tied in a knot at the back, with material left to hang down the side of the neck.

Turkish clothing is vibrant and vivid because of the variety of materials, colors, patterns, and pieces that are put together. The clothing does not have as much embroidery as in some other cultures, although stripes are popular, and gold braid is often seen.

Resources Used for Chapter 27

Blumenthal, Laura. 1997. E-mail messages on the subjects of Turkish language and dance.

Boratav, Ferhat, and David Muddyman. 1994. "Rondo á la Atatürk." In *World Music: The Rough Guide,* Simon Broughton, Mark Ellingham, David Muddyman, and Richard Trillo, eds., 160–66. London: Rough Guides, Ltd. This chapter in a small encyclopedia is about traditional, classical, and contemporary music in Turkey.

McGowan, Bruce. 1968. "Turkey's History." *Viltis* (March): 4–7.

McGowan, Kate (Süheyla). 1981. "Turkish Folk Dancing." In *International Folk Dancing USA,* Betty Casey, ed., 285–88. Garden City, NY: Doubleday.

Özkök, Bora. 1972–90. Dance notes and record covers from many workshops.

Dances From the United States

Chapter 28: Dances From the United States

U.S. Dances in Phyllis S. Weikart's Books

Alley Cat	TFD, RM3
Amos Moses	TFD, RM8
Bossa Nova	TFD, RM7
Good Old Days	TFD, RM6
Hot Pretzels II	TFD, RM8
Jessie Polka	TFD, RM8
The Little Shoemaker	TFD, RM3
Twelfth Street Rag	TFD, RM5

The dances in this chapter are twentieth-century urban social dances of the United States. They illustrate the freedom of dance styles in this country as well as a few of the fads, with each decade seeming to have its signature dances.

The most represented dance style here is the Charleston, which illustrates more than just U.S. dance history. It was in the 1920s, shortly after the end of World War I, that clothing fashions began to relax. This was a milestone for women particularly: They cut their hair, shortened their skirts, simplified their fashions, and most important, took off their constraining corsets forever. For the first time in history, women could literally fling out their arms and kick up their heels. The Charleston and other vigorous dance styles were direct results of this unprecedented personal freedom.

The Charleston pattern is the basis of a number of this chapter's dances, which are called novelty, rather than traditional or historic, dances. "Novelty" implies that the dance is a choreographed pattern without any cultural connotations, arranged to a popular melody and meant to be for fun. While "novelty" is a useful label for such dances, one could argue that historic dances such as *The Virginia Reel* and traditional singing games like *Sally Down the Alley* were also once novelty dances—arranged by someone to popular songs and meant to be just for fun. One could also argue that the steps of the novelty dances in this chapter do indeed have cultural roots, because, like the Charleston, they come from quintessential U.S. movements or because they come from ethnic cultures in the American melting pot. Moreover, most of the "folk" dances in the international dance repertoire were not handed down through the ages but have been recently choreographed by ethnic dance teachers, most of them living in North America and using popular music and movements from their original cultures.

Taking all of this into account, we must admit that this chapter's dances, which have been enjoyed for a number of decades, probably have now graduated from being novelty dances to being U.S. folk dances. However, let's not argue—let's just enjoy these dances!

The music for most of the dances was composed in the 1940s and 1950s. Many were popular with the general public for a number of years and have remained in the folk dance repertoire even longer. Their timeless appeal is still attractive to contemporary youngsters and adults, who request them again and again.

Alley Cat

A proven success for many levels of learners, *Alley Cat* is a good dance for reinforcing rights and lefts. It was originated by Dottie Dicks of the Methodist Recreational Lab in Leesburg, Florida, and Marie Armstrong of Port Richie, Florida, probably in the 1950s. It may be one of the original so-called four-

All ages can enjoy traditional U.S. singing games.

corner dances, in which dancers make a quarter-turn at the end of the pattern to begin the dance again facing in a different direction.

Alley Cat is an individual dance—country/western dancers call this a line dance—with dancers all facing one way or individuals facing different ways. Sometimes it is better to have students all in a circle around the teacher when they are first learning an individual dance, so everyone can see the teacher and, more important, so the teacher can see them. After dancers are comfortable with the pattern, then all may face one way or as they wish.

Amos Moses

The music for one of the more recent dances on the list, *Amos Moses,* was recorded in the late 1960s by Jerry Reed. This is another four-corner individual dance and is particularly attractive to youngsters because of its rock rhythms and short eight-beat pattern. However, the pivot to the left and then to the right is tricky for inexperienced dancers and may require careful preparation. The pattern also lends itself to variations and creativity, which should be encouraged. Claps, particularly on the last beat, are usually the first added embellishment.

For young students, individual dances provide good practice with rights and lefts—or, oops, lefts and rights.

Photo by Zoltan Horvath

Bossa Nova

Based on the compelling Latin rhythms, this *Bossa Nova* pattern was arranged by Henry ("Buzz") Glass, a long-time leader in movement education, to the once popular *Blame It on the Bossa Nova* song. The description in *TFD* is for a couple mixer, but the same pattern may also be enjoyed as a non-mixing partner dance, as an individual dance with women lined up on one side and men lined up facing them, or as a solo dance with individuals facing the same or different ways. Note that the footwork instructions are for the inside person; the outside person uses the same instructions but opposite feet.

The SIDE/CLOSE; SIDE/TOUCH on beats 1–8 and its variation on beats 9–16 should be done in rhumba style, with knees bent and close together to give a modest sway to the hips. Good Latin dancers keep their upper body fairly still, so most of the movement occurs below the waist. The Charleston pattern on beats 17–24 should be not too vigorous, to continue the Latin flavor of the dance through the movements on beats 25–32.

Good Old Days

Here's a Charleston pattern that not only may be done with vigor and enthusiasm but also may be accompanied by the heel and toe swivels of the original dance. This partner mixer was arranged by Nina Reeves in the 1960s. Note, again, that the footwork description is for the partner on the left; the other person uses opposite footwork. There is also a solo hand-jive dance that has been choreographed to this music.

Hot Pretzels II

Hot Pretzels II was once a staple of the recreational dance repertoire as well as a popular dance with cheery music evoking an earlier era. It can be done as a solo dance, but the particular fun of this pattern is to move side by side and in unison with friends. Short lines can be formed, with dancers' hands or arms joined in back at waist-level. On each beat where a heel is extended (beats 1, 4, and 7), the upper body leans backward to create a straight line from neck to ankle. The "pedal backward" on beat 14 is executed by lifting the right knee with right toe up and making a small counterclockwise circle backward with the foot.

Jessie Polka

The *Jessie Polka* has a longer history than the others in this chapter and came originally from the U.S. Southwest, so it can be labeled a truly traditional

The heel-toe swivels of the Charleston-type dances require some concentration.
Photo by Zoltan Horvath

rather than a novelty dance. As in many authentic dances, the dance pattern may be done to a variety of tunes and may be known by other names, for example, the *Cowboy Polka* or the *Eight-Step Shuffle*.

Also, like most authentic dances, *Jessie Polka* has several variations developed through the folk process. For example, the same pattern is done with dancers in short lines forming a wheel formation; as a partner dance with partners holding inside hands or in the closed ballroom position; as an individual dance with dancers in a circle, moving counterclockwise around the dance space, or in a line, all facing the same wall; in a conga line; and even in a chorus line, like the Rockettes.

As in *Hot Pretzels,* dancers in the *Jessie Polka* may lean backward while extending the heel diagonally forward (beats 1, 5, and 7), and lean forward while extending the toe diagonally backward (beat 3). The polka in the second half of Part 1 can also be a two-step without the preliminary hop, which is one way it was done traditionally.

The Little Shoemaker

The Little Shoemaker is based on European polka dances, with clapping sequences and hand movements that symbolize the shoemaker's work. As described in *TFD*, with its new Part III choreography, this is the easiest pattern in the novelty dance category and can be enjoyed by quite young children. It can, however, be made more interesting for experienced dancers by changing the march in Part I to a two-step or polka and by ending the pattern, as noted, with one partner moving ahead to join another person.

Twelfth Street Rag

This is another dance that shows the Charleston to be a traditional U.S. step pattern. Arranged to a tune recorded in the 1940s, it has been subjected to the folk process just as many another dance that has been popular for generations. The pattern may be done, as in other dances described here, in short lines with people joining hands in back at waist-level. In folk dance groups, it is often done as a dance for two people, and in classrooms, it is done in a free formation or with individuals in a circle.

Part IB is done as described in *TFD* or, as described in other notes, by moving sideways toward the center with seven steps and a hold, then repeating the pattern sideways out from center. On the hold, people may quickly brush or lightly stamp. This pattern simulates the original Charleston "Susie-Q" movement, with the swiveling feet and the hands crossing on knees. The bridge can be the creative part. Some early notes describe the first jump with "hands overhead" and the second jump with "hands thrown back" and sometimes knees bent. Often people clap their knees on beat 7 and clap their own or their partner's hands on beat 8.

Preteens especially like this dance, but it is not easy for today's students. Spending time on the transitions from one part to another gives them a chance for greater success. Once students can achieve *Twelfth Street Rag*, it is one of their most requested dances.

Resources Used for Chapter 28

Duree, Richard. 1995. "American 'Vintage' Ballroom Dance." *Quo* (September): 4–5.

Eden, Ya'akov. 1988. *Moving in International Circles.* Dubuque, IA: Kendall/Hunt.

Evans, Jane. 1985. *Let's Dance.* Toronto: Can-Ed Media.

Gilbert, Cecile. 1970. *International Folk Dance at a Glance.* Minneapolis: Burgess.

Harris, Jane A., Anne M. Pittman, and Marlys S. Waller. 1994. *Dance Awhile,* 7th ed. New York: Macmillan International.

Herman, Michael, and Mary Ann Herman. 1957. Syllabus from workshop in Chicago. New York: Folk Dance House.

Kraus, Richard. 1962. *Folk Dancing.* New York: Macmillan.

Mynatt, Constance, and Bernard Kaiman. 1975. *Folk Dancing for Students and Teachers.* Dubuque, IA: Wm. C. Brown.

Dances From the Former Yugoslav Republics

Slovenia, Croatia, Serbia, & Macedonia

Chapter 29: Slovenia, Croatia, Serbia, & Macedonia

Dances From the Former Yugoslav Republics: Slovenian, Croatian, Serbian, and Macedonian Dances in Phyllis S. Weikart's Books

Slovenian Dance
See page 337.

Croatian Dances
See page 340.

Serbian Dances
See page 349.

Macedonian Dances
See page 358.

The fortunes and misfortunes of this fascinating and turbulent region emphasize once again that the culture more than the country is important when describing ethnic dance background. From 1929 until June 1991, the nation of Yugoslavia (an older English spelling is "Jugoslavia") included the peoples whose dances are described in this chapter—Slovenians, Croatians, Serbians, and Macedonians. Since then, the borders have changed, and the political situation is chaotic, but the centuries-old characteristics of dances and societies remain the same.

Geographically, the republics of the former Yugoslavia occupy only a small corner of southeastern Europe, part of what is called the Balkan Peninsula. (See the map on p. 66.) The other Balkan states are Albania, Bulgaria, Greece, and Romania (some sources also place the European part of Turkey in the Balkans, but ethnochoreographically speaking, Turkey is considered western Asian). Politically and culturally, however, this little corner looms large in world history, as it is in the center of the "Powder Keg of Europe." The boundary between Eastern and Western civilizations, a deep cultural chasm, bisects southeastern Europe and cuts the former Yugoslavia almost exactly in half.

To the west of this imaginary but significant line are Croatia and Slovenia, which are populated with Roman Catholic Slavic people who share much of western European history, including the Renaissance, the Reformation, and the Industrial Revolution. These people experienced political and economic domination by the Austro-Hungarian Hapsburg Empire until World War I, and Austrian cultural domination lasted even longer than that.

To the east of the boundary between eastern and western civilizations are Serbia and Macedonia, populated mostly by Eastern Orthodox Christians and Islamic Muslim Slavs. These peoples were conquered successively by the Roman Empire, by the Byzantine Empire, and in the late 1300s, by the Ottoman Turks. The Ottoman Empire ruled that part of the world for the next 500 years. Although their influence began to wane during the nineteenth century, the last Ottoman rulers did not actually leave the region until 1912, within memory of many living inhabitants. Thus, because they were immersed in a western Asian society for so long, the Serbs and Macedonians developed a cultural mentality different from the central European one of their closest Slav neighbors.

A basic reason for the revived and vicious hostilities among former Yugoslav republics is this apparently irremediable rift between the Western and Eastern cultures and religions. For all of their history, the southeastern European peoples have been dominated by separate but equally strong rulers—the Muslim Ottoman Turks, the Austro-Hungarian Hapsburgs, the Roman Catholic popes, the German and Italian Fascists, the Soviet Communists. Faced with such oppression, the overriding goals of the subjugated peoples were survival of their own cultures and liberation.

One of the most explosive events in the Powder Keg of Europe was the assassination in 1914 of Archduke Franz Ferdinand, heir to the imperial crown of the Austro-Hungarian Empire. While on an official visit to Sarajevo, the capital of Bosnia, he was killed by a Bosnian Serb who hated the Hapsburg rulers. Although the gunman acted as a private individual, the Austro-Hungarian Empire's subsequent decision to declare war on Serbia became the opening salvo of World War I.

Following that war, these disparate Slavic peoples with their wide range of cultural and economic conditions were officially formed in 1918 into a nation known as the Kingdom of Serbs, Croats, and Slovenes, which comprised Bosnia-Herzegovina, Croatia, Dalmatia, Montenegro, Serbia, and Slovenia. Fighting among the ethnic groups led King Alexander I Karageorgevitch, head of the Serb royal house, to declare himself dictator in 1929. He changed the country's name to Yugoslavia, the Kingdom of the South Slavs, which comprised the republics of Bosnia-Herzegovina, Croatia, Montenegro, Serbia, and Slovenia. Macedonia became a distinct republic in 1945 and was added to Yugoslavia after World War II. Tragically, Alexander's leadership did not prevent further animosities, and he himself was assassinated in 1934 by a Croatian nationalist.

These violent Balkan deaths obsessed Rebecca West, an English writer whose travels through Yugoslavia in the late 1930s resulted in an 1,150-page two-volume book, *Black Lamb and Grey Falcon,* one of the classic works of literature about this region. "Such a terrible complexity," she wrote in 1937, "in which nobody can be right and nobody can be wrong, and the future cannot be fortunate" (p. 112).

Dame Rebecca, sadly, had great foresight—the future of Yugoslavia has been far from fortunate. During World War II, in spite of the brutalities of outside enemies, within Yugoslavia terrible atrocities were carried out by Serbs and Croats, brother Slavs, against each other. After the war, Yugoslavia became a Communist republic under the leadership of Josip Broz, called Marshal Tito, who kept a tight lid on the complex historical animosities by suppressing ethnic rivalries and enforcing communal life. After Tito's death in 1980, however, violence again began bubbling to the surface and boiling over. When this last oppressive empire was finally vanquished, most of the southeastern Euuropean groups were wary, suspicious, and desperate for autonomy. In mid-1991, the Yugoslav federation started to break apart as Croatia and Slovenia declared their independence, followed by Macedonia and then Bosnia-Herzegovina, leaving a mini-Yugoslavia consisting of only Serbia and Montenegro.

This unstable region continues to be embroiled in a vicious civil war that divides neighbors and families. For those who are interested in learning more about the situation, two books are helpful. One is *The Fall of Yugoslavia* by British journalist Misha Glenny (1994), who wrote that it is as though animosities had been put into an historical deep freeze during the Tito years, but now the memories have thawed and are as fresh as ever. The other is *Balkan Ghosts* by U.S. journalist Robert Kaplan (1993), who gives much historical background of the region and describes the situation as "ethnic subtlety atop subtlety." This is indeed a desperate and confusing time for the people of the republics of the former Yugoslavia.

General Dance Background

Despite this dark history, or perhaps because of it, music and dancing are still a living part of Slavic societies. Their own traditions are vitally important to them, particularly after millennia of oppression and repression by conquerors from other cultures. This is especially true of the expatriate communities, those who have left their homelands to settle in North America and other foreign places. Unlike most central and western Europeans, whose dances generally are seen only at seasonal folklore events, natives of the former Yugoslav republics naturally include dancing at almost all of their festive occasions. Though industrialization and urbanization have changed people's pace and priorities, the old songs and dances are still important. Even the younger generations enjoy traditional circle dances alongside the latest rock-and-roll importations from the West.

As a result of such a vital heritage and of government efforts up until recently to preserve the folk arts, there is an amazing abundance of dances available from Croatia, Macedonia, and Serbia; there are fewer, but still a goodly number, from Slovenia. Starting in the 1930s and continuing to the present, many of these dances have entered the international folk dance repertoire through workshops and recordings by native and North American ethnochoreographers and folklorists.

The dances described in this chapter have been enjoyed by the folk dance community for decades. Most are arranged patterns or modified versions of stage choreographies based on dances observed in towns and villages. In their native settings—which might range from the central square in the Macedonian village of Dolneni to the community hall of St. Sava's Serbian church in Chicago—the dances are almost always improvisational. Participants take the basic patterns, which are guided by rhythms that they have known since early childhood, and play with them by incorporating turns, syncopations, changes of direction, dynamics, arm movements, and other ethnochoreographical embroidery. In lines and open circles, leaders decide when to change the step; there are even dances in which everyone in the line simultaneously and spontaneously creates his or her own versions while staying within the basic structure. In partner dances, each couple may be doing different movements to the same rhythm, as in a South American tango or a North American jitterbug.

All of the Croatian, Macedonian, and Serbian dances described in *TFD* and *TM&D* are open- or closed-circle, chain, or line dances that do not require partners. These dances are called by the generic name of *kolo* in Croatia and Serbia (also in Slovenia, although the Slovenian dance described here is not a kolo, but a couple dance) and by the name *oro* in Macedonia. The word *kolo* also refers to an entire festive event that includes other social activities, like eating, drinking, singing, gossiping, and flirting. As renowned Balkan dance expert Dick Crum has observed, it is possible to "go to the kolo" and not dance at all!

To describe dances of the peoples of the former Yugoslavia, we have treated the four cultures—Slovenian, Croatian, Serbian, and Macedonian—in different sections of this chapter, beginning at the north and moving south.

Dances of the Slovenian People

Slovenia is tucked into a little triangle in the northern part of what used to be Yugoslavia. Now an independent nation, Slovenia should not be confused with Slovakia, another recently recognized country, or Slavonia, an eastern region of Croatia. A culture about 15 centuries old, the Slovenians have been under control of Germanic rulers for most of their history. In spite of this, they have managed to retain their customs and their language, which is considered one of the oldest in Europe, although in many ways their lives are somewhat similar to that of their northern neighbors.

Slovenia came under the control of the Hapsburgs in the late 1200s and remained part of the empire for 700 years, until after World War I, when it was included in the fledgling Yugoslav state called the Kingdom of Serbs, Croats, and Slovenes. After some very difficult years under Nazi Germany during World War II, Slovenia then became part of the Communist Federal People's Republic of Yugoslavia. It separated from Yugoslavia in June 1991, and this declaration of independence was one of the catalysts of the breakup of the Federal People's Republic of Yugoslavia. An industrialized nation with most of its people having a common ancestry and religion, Slovenia is more homogeneous than the rest of the region and able to make changes more peacefully.

Although *Zibnšrit* is the only Slovenian dance represented here, it is typical in that it is a hearty partner-dance similar to others of central Europe, and yet it has the "7s and 3s" pattern characteristic of many southeastern European dances. In fact, most dance specialists believe that *Zibnšrit* introduced the "7s and 3s" to Croatia. Slovenians do more couple dances than the rest of the Slavic cultures, but they also enjoy kolos, some in the medieval serpentine formations. In addition, a few interesting, archaic longways dances are still being done by Slovenian people who live across the border of Italy in the Rezia mountains of the Alps.

Zibnšrit was introduced to folk dancers in the 1950s by Dick Crum. He learned this version (and other dances) from a Slovenian-American couple when it was still a living and popular dance among the émigrés in North America. In the nineteenth century, this dance swept Europe, from Scandinavia to the Baltic countries, down through Italy and Austria, into Transylvania and Croatia. It is considered to be of German origin and became a favorite in both rural and urban Slovenia.

FORMATION. *Zibnšrit* is a couple dance similar to those in central and western Europe in which partners hold each other; thus it is unlike the few part-

Slovenian Dance in Phyllis S. Weikart's Books

Zibnšrit   [ZEE-bn-shrit] (Seven steps) *TM&D*

ner dances of the southern Balkans that are done with no contact. It is the descendent of a late nineteenth-century dance and similar to other dances done by Slovenian, northern Croatian, and central European people on their native soil and in expatriate communities.

The couples can be scattered around the dance floor rather than in a double circle. If dancers are in a circle, as the directions in *TM&D* assume, men face counterclockwise, and women face clockwise.

STEPS AND MOVEMENTS. This jolly little dance should be done in a relaxed, natural manner. Steps are small and clean, not exaggerated or scraped on the floor, and partners must work together as a compact unit for the most success and enjoyment.

HANDS AND ARMS. Partners face each other with their right hands joined just below face-level and with each person's left hand on the other person's right hip or waist. During beats 13–16, while the woman turns under the man's arm, both partners may place their left hand on their own left hip, with fingers forward.

MODIFICATION AND TEACHING TIPS. *Zibnšrit* probably should not be modified. When students are comfortable with the step-hops, they will have no trouble physically with the rest of the pattern. Socially, however, if they are not ready for the pleasures of interacting with a partner, they will not find this a very interesting dance. It should be saved for a group that is sophisticated enough to appreciate simple dances such as this one.

MUSIC. Like many Slovenian dances, *Zibnšrit* is in the common duple meter (2/4); there are also some in triple meter (3/4), which is rare in the rest of the Balkans. The music is played by the popular pan-European instrument, the accordion, which in Slovenia is a "button-box," rather than one with keys. The steady beat of this dance creates the kind of pulse that leads to other movement activities. For example, dancers and musicians used to compose nonsense songs to its rhythm, such as this translation by Dick Crum:

Pes pa nema repa več.	The dog no longer has a tail.
Kdo mu ga j'odsekau preč?	Who could have cut it off?
Kaj pa bo, kaj pa bo,	What will happen, what will happen,
Če mu zrastu več no bo!	He won't grow another one!

The Penn State International Dance Ensemble demonstrates their spirited Slovenian dance suite.

338 Cultures and Styling in Folk Dance

CLOTHING AND COSTUMES. Like the dances, the Slovenian dress is less diverse and ornamented than that of other Slavic peoples. For programs, girls might wear a long-sleeved, high-necked white blouse with a full, calf-length skirt of one color, such as black, brown, or red. Over the blouse is a vest that matches the skirt, and over that might be a flowered shawl. Over the skirt is a long apron of contrasting color. On the legs are white hose and low-heeled black shoes. A popular feminine head covering for married women is a little snood made of a broad gold band fastened at the back with a bow, with cotton or linen material gathered into it. Young girls wear braids, perhaps threaded with ribbons.

Boys may wear a long-sleeved white shirt with full sleeves if possible, a sleeveless dark vest (with silver buttons perhaps), long dark trousers tucked into high black boots, and a black felt hat with either a large or a small brim.

Dances of the Croatian People

After centuries of division and domination, Croatia declared itself independent from Yugoslavia in June 1991. Shaped somewhat like a wishbone across the northern and western Balkan region, the nation borders on Slovenia, Hungary, Serbia, and Bosnia-Herzegovina and has a spectacular and famous coastline on the Adriatic Sea.

Croatia's geographic boundaries form the transition between the historic Western and Eastern empires, and this transition is reflected in the Croatian culture. Because of their long connection with Germanic regimes and their early acceptance of the Roman Catholic Church, the Croatian people are among the more Western-leaning Slavs. Although the Croatians use the Roman alphabet while the Serbs use the Cyrillic, both Croatians and Serbs share the Serbo-Croatian language, as well as much of music, dance, and other cultural aspects.

Almost all the Croatian kolos listed on p. 340 were introduced into the folk dance repertoire in the 1950s and 1960s by master teacher Dick Crum. He learned them while dancing in Yugoslavia and in North American immigrant communities, particularly the one in Pittsburgh that is home to the largest U.S. societies of Croatian and Serbian people. The patterns described here are for mixed groups of men and women, but they can also be done in couple forms and even in groups of three. One of the most popular performance numbers is a dance for one man and two women, known as *Bunjevačko Momačko Kolo.* In addition, Croatians enjoy partner dances similar to the more modern nineteenth-century ballroom dances of central and eastern Europe, such as the polka, waltz, mazurka, and csardas.

The kolos here are arranged sequences based on choreographies performed by the Yugoslavian national ensemble Lado, the Duquesne University Tamburitzans, and other dance troupes. Originally, such dances were more freestyle, with the steps changing at the shouted direction of a leader or the spontaneous whim of the dancers. Often, the dance had a social function. For example, *Sukačko Kolo*

> ### Croatian Dances in Phyllis S. Weikart's Books
>
> | | |
> |---|---|
> | *Ajde Noga Za Nogama* | [AY-day NOH-gah zah NOH-gah-mah] (Let's go, foot behind foot, or one foot after another) *TFD, RM5* |
> | *Drmeš Iz Zdenčine* | [DER-mesh eez ZDEN-chee-neh] (Drmes [shaking dance] from Zdenčina) *TM&D* |
> | *Drmeš Medley* | [DER-mesh] (Combination of shaking dances) *TM&D* |
> | *Dučec* | [DOO-chets] (Jumping) *TFD, RM8* |
> | *Hopa, Hopa* | [HOH-pah, HOH-pah] *TM&D* |
> | *Kiša Pada* | [KEE-shah PAH-dah] (Rain is falling) *TM&D* |
> | *Kriči Kriči Tiček* | [KREE-chee KREE-chee TEE-check] (Whistle, whistle, or chirp, chirp, birdie) *TFD, CD6* |
> | *Moja Diridika* | [MOY-yah DEE-ree-dee-kah] (My sweetheart) *TM&D* |
> | *Slavonsko Kolo* | [SLAH-vohn-skoh] (Dance from Slavonia) *TM&D* |
> | *Sukačko Kolo* | [SOO-kahch-koh] (Dance done to the song about the *sukačice*) *TM&D* |

was done at weddings in the Prigorje district during the feast following the church ceremony. When the sumptuous meal was brought from the kitchen by the *sukačice* (the women who had been doing the cooking) the guests would sing a humorous song to them. Sometimes people would spontaneously leap up and start dancing a kolo, or some dancer would take a sukačica to whirl around as a partner. (In the recreational repertoire there is also a couple dance called *Sukačica* using the same music.) There were no set sequences, as we have now, from arranged choreographies.

Today, when kolos are done at occasions in Croatia or expatriate communities—which is not as often as formerly—they tend to be danced in couples or as folklore exhibitions. One dance has survived as a trio dance. The circle kolos, however, because of the teaching of Dick Crum and others, are still enjoyed by North American recreational folk dance groups, so this tradition has not yet been completely lost.

FORMATION. Croatian kolos are generally closed circles that start to the left, or clockwise, in contrast to Serbian kolos, which are usually open circles that move to the right. A Croatian exception is *Ajde Noga Za Nogama,* which is a simple processional pattern that, although it moves to the left, is done in an open, not a closed, circle. The Croatian *Dučec* is described in *TFD* as a free formation, but originally it was probably a closed, joined circle before evolving into a stage choreography and then a recreational arrangement.

The other kolos on the list are done in the traditional closed-circle formation. It is more comfortable to keep the circles somewhat small, perhaps with five to eight people.

At Folkmoot USA, dancers from Croatia perform a popular dance done in trios—by one man and two women dancing together.

STEPS AND MOVEMENTS. The Croatian kolos listed in this chapter are of the type called *drmeš* [DRR-mesh], which means shaking dance. Each choreography usually consists of a traveling part and a bouncing, jiggling, trembling part. Some include a "flying" part—but don't worry, not the ones listed here! When doing the drmeš step, shoulders should be back, and "earlobes upright," says Dick Crum. The main thing to remember is that the trunk does not dip but remains erect. It helps to tighten the center of one's body as the knees and thighs guide the bounce. Feet should be flat on the floor and close together, and the body should be alert but relaxed, so the jiggle can travel through it.

Slovenian, Croatian, Serbian, & Macedonian Dances

During a street festival in Chicago, three men of the International Dancers hold tightly to their partners as the women lift their feet and fly in a Croatian kolo (top photo). At Folkmoot USA, a dance team from Croatia shows an even more acrobatic flying routine (bottom photo).

342   *Cultures and Styling in Folk Dance*

Several versions of these dances have been introduced at various times, so the arrangements of the *drmeši* in *TFD* and *TM&D* may be different from others in the repertoire. The *Drmeš Medley*, for example, is a combination of three that are also listed separately: *Drmeš Iz Zdenčine*, *Kiša Pada* (sometimes called *Posavski Drmeš II)*, and *Kriči Kriči Tiček*. The versions in the medley, however, are not the same as those noted separately.

Many drmeš steps are done in the common Balkan rhythm of slow, quick/quick or one, two/and (♪♪♪). Dick Crum uses the rhythmic phrases "mixed-pickles" or "dash-dot-dot" for this step. The "mixed-pickles" is shown in the drmeš step of *Moja Diridika* (Part III) and *Slavonsko Kolo* (Part V), as well as in parts of most of the other dances. In *TFD*, the term "reverse two-step" is used for this step.

These slow, quick/quick steps should be a bit springy and done on flat feet, with flexible knees. The top part of the body is not rigid, so there is a subtle "mixed-pickles" movement above the waist also. Try not to kick out to the side and not to add extra movements; the energy is internal.

HANDS AND ARMS. A characteristic styling aspect of Croatian dance is the basket-weave, or basket-hold, position, which has the arms either in front (typical of Croatia's eastern Slavonian region) or in back, the reverse basket (typical of western Croatia). Dancers reach out to the sides to grasp hands or middle fingers with the people next to their immediate neighbors, so alternate dancers are joined. Arms should be straight but not stiff. When introducing this position, avoid describing it as "crossed arms," or some students will inevitably get tangled in their own limbs.

Most descriptions of the front basket say to put the left arm under when the dance begins to the left and to put the right arm under when the dance begins to the right. This is generally the more comfortable way to travel, but it is not a carved-in-granite rule. In the village, no one consulted the syllabus; they just reached out and grabbed. If there is a wide range of heights in the classroom or dance group, suggest that students find a place in the circle near others of their own height.

For the back basket, in the native setting women tended to join their hands over the men's. Some recreational groups have found the back basket awkward, so there are dances that began life as a reverse basket but are now done with arms woven in front. Examples of the folk process at work in this regard are *Kriči Kriči Tiček* and *Sukačko Kolo*.

MODIFICATION AND TEACHING TIPS. These dances are easily modified by omitting one or more parts and then adding them later (or not). Do not eliminate so many parts as to make them boring, however. Note that even with fewer parts, a drmeš requires good movement skills; it is especially important to be able to take small steps and move well with others. We do not recommend

A characteristic styling aspect of Croatian dance is the front basket-hold, demonstrated here by a group of recreational dancers.

Photo by Zoltan Horvath

omitting the basket-holds or the shaking, as these are what give the dance their specific ethnic character. They can be added, of course, after students are comfortable with the steps. These two styling points also require good social skills and can be used to help a group achieve cohesiveness.

MUSIC. Most Croatian dance music is in duple (2/4) meter, but the step patterns can be subtle and are often embellished, adding to the rhythmic complexity.

One of the most characteristic traditional Croatian and Serbian instruments is the *tambura,* or *tamburitza* (the diminutive), a four-string, fretted, long-necked type of guitar or mandolin. Today's tamburitza is a mid-nineteenth-century adaptation of a primitive lute used by shepherds and village bards that probably arrived in this region in the wake of fourteenth-century Ottoman Turkish armies. It is common to

*Joined in a back basket-hold, women from Brigham Young University's International Folk Dance Ensemble perform a Croatian dance—a **Posavski Drmeš** choreography.*
Photo by Mark Philbrick

find entire musical ensembles made up of various sizes of this instrument; they are called tamburitza orchestras, and the instrumentalists are called *tamburashi*. Many people know of this music through the internationally known performing folk troupe called the Tamburitzans, based at Duquesne University in Pittsburgh. More modern instruments that are often used are the violin, accordion, and double bass, and contemporary tamburashi are developing their own styles, as happens with most younger musicians in all societies.

As is true in all the Balkan cultures, another important instrument in Croatia is the voice. Singing accompanies many of the dances and is often the only accompaniment. There is a special style of Balkan singing that is particularly strong in the region of the Dinaric Mountains in western Croatia. The style, which consists of full-bodied, vibrant voice-production, was developed by people who communicated from mountain to mountain and is a reminder that the human voice was the first musical instrument.

During the kolo, it was traditional for the dancers to sing or shout across the circle, using improvised satiric, sometimes insulting, verses; the verses concerned the dancers themselves or village scandals, and an insulted dancer's only possible retaliation was to make up another verse. On one of the classic *Slavonsko Kolo* recordings, according to Dick Crum's translation, the women taunt the men:

Bolji mi nego vi,	We are better than you are,
vi ste malo šašavi,	you are a little crazy,
vidi vam se po nogama	one can see by your feet
da ne znate složit s nama!	that you can't keep in step with us!

And the men answer:

| *Bolji naši nego vaši,* | Our dancers are better than yours, |
| *naši vaše nadigraši!* | ours have out-danced yours! |

CLOTHING AND COSTUMES. Clothing styles vary in Croatia according to which border is closest. There are styles in which Hungarian and Italian influences can be seen, as well as styles with veils, fez, and soft slippers that show the centuries of Turkish proximity. The style adopted by many folk ensembles is the one from around Zagreb, Croatia's capital city, which is closer in geography and fashion to the Austro-Hungarian part of Croatia's history. Clothing is white for both women and men and includes pleated skirts with aprons and wide long trousers, embroidered mostly in red with a dense flower pattern. In some regions, men wear long fringes, and women wear shimmery fabrics, all of which lend themselves beautifully to the jiggling, shaking motions of the drmeš.

To approximate this for a program, girls might wear a long-sleeved white blouse and long white skirt covered with a long white apron, with red rickrack or fabric-marker designs all down the full sleeves and across wide borders on the apron and skirt. For an added touch, tie red ribbons around the upper arms and

Singers from the Penn State International Dance ensemble, dressed in regional costumes from Petrinja, Posavina, and Slavonija, sing a Croatian song.

put on strands of red beads. A red flowered head scarf can be knotted under the hair at the back of the head. White or red tights complete the outfit, until we get to the shoes, described in the next paragraph. Boys can wear a long-sleeved white shirt topped with a short red vest, and long white trousers.

Traditional footwear in the Balkans is a type of leather moccasin called, variously, *opanci, opanki, opinci, opinki*, with slightly different shapes for each culture (see p. 356). The Croatian opanci may have woven tops, often in colorful designs. However, unless everyone has these, it is probably best to use low black shoes or black boots (for the boys).

Dances of the Serbian People

Along with Montenegro, Serbia makes up most of what is still Yugoslavia. However, Serbian people live across many of the current national borders. A nationality group since the 1200s, the Serbs every year commemorate the date when the Ottoman Turks conquered but did not crush them in the Battle of

Kosovo in 1389. Calls for Slavic unity began in the early nineteenth century, and Serbia at last gained independence in 1878, after almost 500 years of Ottoman rule. Its modern history was that of the other South Slavs, until the breakup of Yugoslavia in 1991–92. Currently, the region is extremely unstable, with much fighting on all sides for nationalistic reasons.

When they have the time and the heart for it, Serbian people celebrate with a kolo, as do their Croatian cousins. The Serbs who now live in North America probably do more traditional dancing than those in the homeland, for as with all émigrés, it is especially important for them to keep their traditions alive while living among other cultures. In addition, there was renewed interest in kolo dancing in the 1950s, when the third and fourth American-born generations, in the process of seeking their roots, revived the dancing they had learned from their parents and grandparents.

Kolos and other line dances soon found their way into the recreational folk dance repertoire through the field research, choreographies, and workshops of traveling teachers, as well as through the recordings of kolo music and tamburitzan orchestras. Indeed, by the late 1960s these dances were so popular that afficionados were disparagingly labeled "kolomaniacs" by those who did not appreciate the joy of truly communal dances.

Serbian kolos have been among the basic dances in the international folk dance repertoire since they were introduced in the 1940s and 1950s by pioneering teachers such as Vyts Beliajus, Dennis Boxell, Dick Crum, John Filcich, Michael and Mary Ann Herman, and Anatol Joukowsky. Many of the dances in the list here were learned from first- and second-generation Serbian-Americans, particularly during the North American kolo revival that began in Pittsburgh in the 1950s; some others were brought back from travels in Yugoslavia; and some are stage arrangements using traditional folk materials.

One of the most popular even today is *Šetnja,* which Dick Crum learned in Belgrade (the Serbian and Yugoslavian capital) and observed on many occasions in the villages of the Sumadija region. Often it was the dance that opened the festivities, and this is still its role at North American recreational folk dance groups today. In *Šetnja's* native setting, at the Sunday kolos or special events, one man would pay the musicians to play the song or another like it, and people would join and follow as he led the line for as long as he chose—and could afford.

Other dances listed here also have interesting histories. *Srbijanka* is one of the first kolos to arrive with immigrants to North America, and *Žikino Kolo* was by far the most popular for decades. Dances such as *Jeftanovičevo Kolo* and *Kokonješte* were brought to the U.S. before World War I and survived until the 1950s, when Dick Crum saw them in Pittsburgh and other South Slavic communities. Some dances, such as *Nebesko Kolo,* are not old-timers at all but sprang up during the 1950s kolo revival. *Orijent,* one of the most endearing and enduring of the recreational repertoire, is a fixed sequence by Dick Crum for a stage choreography. He first saw it in Serbia between 1954 and 1957, where it was a new dance,

Serbian Dances in Phyllis S. Weikart's Books

Ajde Jano	[EYE-deh YAH-noh] (Come on, Jana)	*TFD, CD4*
Bosarka	[BOH-sar-kah]	*TM&D*
Čarlama	[char-LAH-mah] (Means to an end)	*TM&D*
Djurdjevka Kolo	[jer-JEF-kah KOH-loh] (St. George's Day kolo)	*TFD, RM2*
Ersko Kolo	[AIR-skoh] (Dance of the Ero [people from Užice region])	*TFD, RM4*
Fatiše Kolo	[fah-TEE-sheh] (Join the kolo)	*TFD, CD6*
Gružanka	[GROO-zhan-kah] (From Gruze village)	*TM&D*
Jeftanovičevo Kolo	[yef-TAHNO-vee-CHAY-voh] (Kolo named in honor of Jeftanovič)	*TM&D*
Kokonješte	[koh-kone-YESH-the] (In the style of a young noble)	*TM&D*
Makazice Kolo	[mah-KAH-zee-tseh] (Little scissors)	*TFD, RM7*
Milanovo Kolo	[MEE-lah-noh-voh] (Milan's kolo [a man, not a city])	*TFD, CD3*
Nebesko Kolo	[NEH-beh-skoh] (Heavenly, or blue sky, kolo)	*TFD, RM9*
Neda Grivne	[NEH-dah GREEV-neh] (Opening line of song says *Neda grivne izgubila*—"Neda lost her bracelets")	*TFD, CD2*
Orijent	[OR-ee-yent] (The Orient, or possibly, Orient Express)	*TM&D*
Pinosavka	[PEE-noh-saf-kah] (Kolo from Pinosava)	*TM&D*
Pljeskavac Kolo	[PLYES-kah-vats KOH-loh] (Clapping dance)	*TFD, RM3*
Preplet	[PREHP-leht] (Interwoven); sometimes *Mangupsko Kolo* [MAHN-goop-skoh] (Idler's dance)	*TM&D*
Rumunjsko Kolo	[roo-MYOON-skoh] (Romanian kolo)	*TFD, CD4*
Sarajevka Kolo	[sah-rah-YEHF-kah] (The girl [or the dance] from Sarajevo)	*TM&D*
Savila Se Bela Loza	[SAH-vee-lah seh BEH-lah LOH-zah] (A grapevine entwined itself)	*TFD, RM6*
Seljančica Kolo	[sell-YAHN-chee-tsa] (Village girl)	*TM&D*
Šestorka from Bela Palanka	[SHEHS-tor-kah BEH-lah PAH-lahn-kah] (Dance in six)	*TM&D*
Šetnja	[SHEHT-nyah] (Walking)	*TFD, RM9*
Srbijanka	[SER-bee-yahn-kah] (Serbian woman)	*TM&D*
U Šest	[OO shest] (In six steps)	*TM&D*
Vranjanka	[vrahn-YAHN-kah] (Dance from Vranje—the dance pattern); *Šano Dušo* [SHAH-noh DOO-shoh] (Shana, sweetheart—the melody)	*TFD, RM8*
Vranjsko Kolo	[VRAHN-skoh KOH-loh] (Kolo from Vranje)	*TM&D*
Zaplanjski Čačak	[ZAH-pline-skee CHAH-chahk] (Čačak from Zaplanje)	*TM&D*
Žikino Kolo	[ZHEE-kee-noh] (Žika's kolo)	*TM&D*

Slovenian, Croatian, Serbian, & Macedonian Dances

apparently of Gypsy origin and popular with the young people. He observed many versions among different peer groups and chose three for the pattern of what we know as *Orijent,* although in its native setting, dancers would repeat a single variation throughout the music.

A number of the dances in this section may be Serbian by culture but not by geography, or they may disregard national boundaries entirely. Eastern Serbia, southwestern Romania, and northwestern Bulgaria have a number of similar dances in what is called the Danubian style, because these regions come together at the Danube River. For example, the Serbian *Rumunjsko Kolo* means Romanian dance, and it is almost the same as the Romanian *Sîrba,* a popular dance named for the fast dances of Serbia. *Pljeskavac* is sometimes labeled Romanian-American or pan-Balkan, because it was played by the Banat Tamburitza Orchestra, a group of Yugoslavs from the Banat region of Romania, which borders Serbia. Dick Crum learned this version of *Pljeskavac* from them in New York City in the 1950s, naming it *Pljeskavac II,* since he knew of at least one other pattern. (Incidentally, he says there should be no diacritical mark on the "s"—the original record label on the orchestra's recording made that mistake.)

Other dances, although called Serbian, have different cultural backgrounds. Those labeled South Serbia, such as *Fatiše Kolo* and *Vranjsko Kolo,* are from the Vranje region close to Macedonia. *Vranjanka,* from the same area, has been called both Macedonian and Serbian. *Čarlama* is known as Serbian and Bosnian, but *Sarajevka Kolo* is actually Serbian although named for the Bosnian capital. *Nebesko Kolo* has two distinct arrangements, the Serbian one done in the open, counterclockwise formation described in *TFD,* and a Croatian version done in a closed circle moving clockwise.

All this seeming confusion illustrates that it often is necessary to take a broader view when identifying folk material. Political boundaries may divide nations and change over time, but across the borders people intermingle and are often from the same culture.

Almost all the Serbian dances listed here are arranged patterns for stage or teaching purposes. The exception is *U Šest,* a traditional kolo that is like a true village dance—improvisational within a basic structure. The dance notes on *U Šest* in *TM&D* describe two parts that are usually done and three variations. We encourage students and teachers to rearrange them in any order, as many times as desired, and then to try out some other steps. Instead of having a leader call the changes, every dancer in the *U Šest* line creates her or his own personal variations on the basic theme while keeping within the main pattern and feeling of the dance. The main kolo done at Serbian parties at home and abroad, it is often called simply *Kolo* or *Kolo U Šest.*

FORMATION. Most of the Serbian kolos in this chapter are done in the characteristic Serbian open- or broken-circle formation with a leader on the right. The exceptions are the three East Serbian belt dances, which are done in small, straight lines: *Bosarka, Šestorka from Bela Palanka,* and *Zaplanjski Čačak.* These were originally danced only by men, as were *Čarlama* and *Preplet,* and the dances from the Vranje region were done only by women, because in the Muslim Ottoman Empire, men and women danced separately. Now all of these dances are done in mixed-gender groups.

There are almost no traditional Serbian couple dances as we know them, but people did dance in twos, face to face, with no physical contact. In addition, because originally there were variants of given dances in every village, a number of the dances in Phyllis S. Weikart's books exist in other versions—a result of the true folk process.

STEPS AND MOVEMENTS. Serbian dance styling varies, depending on where the dances originated. Generally in kolos, however, bodies are proudly erect—with "earlobes upright," according to Dick Crum, whose pithy word pictures create instant comprehension and have been quoted often on this subject. Steps should be small and clean with no scraping sounds, and movements are sort of up-and-down rather than covering a lot of space. Dick Crum advises us to "dance inside our shoes" and keep an unconcerned expression on our faces, as though we've been doing it this way all our lives. Steve Kotansky, another well-respected Balkan dance expert, suggests that we "see what our feet can do without moving them."

Here is a true story to illustrate these styling points: A few years ago, a Hollywood choreographer came to Chicago to find people to dance in the picnic scene of a motion picture about some young Serbian-American men. She went to a Serbian festival, where she observed the kolo dancers and later complained to a local folk dance leader that all they did was "hold hands and move up and down in the same spot." "That's what Serbian dances look like," she was informed, which did not prevent her from choreographing some head-bobbing, foot-stamping, hand-waving movements for the movie. Before the filming was over, however, all the members of the local South Slavic community had walked out of the rehearsals, announcing "This is not Serbian dancing!"

Dances from the Vranje area have a somewhat oriental feeling and should be done with soft knees and movements that are more flowing than those of the Šumadjian kolos just described. With each step, the whole foot is not plopped down but is placed on the floor, feeling the ground from heel to toes. Arms, which are up in the W-position, follow the flowing motion of the rest of the body.

In contrast, the East Serbian dances are closer in feeling to those of Bulgaria, with strong, vigorous movements in unison with the other dancers in the line. Men raise their legs sharply so thighs are parallel to the floor and lower legs are perpendicular. Women, who did not do these dances in the old days, should be more restrained but no less energetic in their movements.

There are three basic kolo patterns that occur in many of the dances, and once these are learned, quite a few dances can be achieved. The patterns are (1) *malo kolo,* or HOP/SIDE, CLOSE; SIDE, HOP; (2) *kokonješte,* or FORWARD,

Dancing in separate men's and women's lines, the Penn State dancers perform a dance from East Serbia. The men raise the leg sharply, while the women use a more restrained movement.

FORWARD; SIDE, TOUCH; SIDE, TOUCH; SIDE, TOUCH; and (3) HOP/STEP, STEP. All three can be seen in *Jeftanovičevo Kolo*. There are also other connections between dances, such as the fact that *Žikino Kolo* is a fast version of the *Vranjanka* pattern.

In *Orijent*, there is a common Serbian step. On beat 1 of Part I, when extending the left foot forward, actually touch it to the floor with no weight. On beat 2, place weight on it, just where it was touching. The touch may be on the ball of the left foot, or what is trickier but more traditional, on the full sole. The cue could be TOUCH (FORWARD), *PRESS;* SIDE/BACK, SIDE. This is more in keeping with the styling than letting the left foot hang in the air on beat 1.

A good method for enjoyment and success is to encourage students, especially the boys, to lead the open circles and lines. Leading is a responsibility but also an honor. Traditionally, it was the men who led the dances, although nowadays in North American South Slavic communities, it is often the women. Remind students that in other cultures, the most popular young people were also the best dancers, like our athletes. Dances such as *Ersko Kolo* and *Savila Se Bela Loza* are doubly useful because they require a strong leader at each end of the circle.

HANDS AND ARMS. The majority of Serbian kolos use the V-position, with hands joined down at sides. Dancers should be close to their neighbors on either side, almost shoulder to shoulder, in narrow compact V's instead of wide stretchy V's.

Some dances, such as *Šetnja* and *Pinosavka,* start in the escort-hold with slower music, then when the tempo begins to accelerate, hands drop down into the V-position for ease of movement. To "escort" one's neighbor, bend the left elbow with left hand at waist, hip, or belt, and hook the right hand into the left elbow of the person ahead.

For the East Serbian belt dances, the dancer holds each adjacent neighbor's belt closer to the front than to the side, so dancers move together as a cohesive unit. Buckle the belts firmly rather than floppily. Lines should be straight and made up of no more than five or six people. Since these dances all move to the right, for comfort and choreography, put each dancer's right arm under the next dancer's left arm. (As Aunt Draga said when you were scrounging in the refrigerator for the last piece of baklava, "It's right under the leftovers" [a David Henry quote].) The South Serbian dances, closest to Macedonian styling, are done in the W-position with hands at shoulder height and a bit forward, forearms close to those of one's neighbors.

In an open circle, leaders may hold their belt or their "vest" with their free hand or, to be really cool, put their right hand in their pocket. They also can carry a handkerchief to twirl at appropriately enthusiastic junctures. For the person at the other end of the open circle, the convention is to place the left fist at the small of the back.

MODIFICATION AND TEACHING TIPS. When starting to teach kolos, teachers might omit the hops in such dances as *Pljeskavac* and *Savila Se Bela Loza,* which is the most natural way to simplify. However, students who are mature enough to appreciate these dances should be developmentally ready to achieve step-hops. By the time they have mastered and enjoyed the beginning kolos in *TFD*, they will be ready for most of the intermediate ones in *TFD* and *TM&D*, which by then should not need much modifying.

Teachers, no matter how enthusiastic, should realize that dances with one pattern that is repeated and repeated can be BOOOORing to youngsters who are used to responding to 15-second flashing, smashing sound bites. Consider developing some context when adding kolos to the classroom or when beginning recreational group repertoire. Instead of moving round and round on the gym circle or the music room carpet, perhaps the lines could snake among chairs and tables set up for a special "festival." Maybe students could choose village personae and form family groups or wedding parties. Young men could compete to "pay the band" and lead the dances. Young women could huddle in a self-conscious group and giggle. It would be fun to somehow show how kolos are not just dance patterns but part of an entire event.

MUSIC. Most of the kolos discussed here are in duple meter (2/4 or 4/4). The triple meter (3/4) is unusual but is found in *Žikino Kolo,* which is sometimes played the old-time way, with a slight hold on beat 1. Most of the South Serbian dances, such as *Ajde Jano* and *Vranjanka,* are in the asymmetric 7/8 meter, which we will hear more of as we get closer to the fascinating Macedonian rhythms. (*Vranjanka* has also been recorded in 3/4 meter.) *Fatiše Kolo* illustrates one of these with its 9/16 meter.

In Balkan and Middle Eastern dances, often there is no direct correlation between musical phrases and dance patterns. In *Vranjanka,* for example, there is a 5-measure movement pattern on the 4-measure melody of *Šano Dušo,* although it all comes together after every 20 measures and at the end. Sometimes there are tempo changes, as in *Seljančica,* in which the music accelerates greatly by the end, and as in *Sarajevka Kolo,* which alternates slow and fast rhythms.

Serbian folk instruments include the *frula,* or shepherd's pipe; the *gajda,* or bagpipe; the *gusla,* or fiddle; and the *tupan,* or double-headed bass drum. These can still be found in folk ensembles today alongside clarinets, flutes, guitars, and double basses. Serbs also play the *tambura,* as do the Croats. However, the instrument that has now come to be associated with kolos is

A very young musician plays his accordion for a kolo performed on the grass in South Serbia.

Cultures and Styling in Folk Dance

the accordion, which can be played with astonishing virtuosity. Another modern instrument that has become popular is the horn—trumpet, trombone, tuba—leading to international appreciation of the brass band music of Serbia.

In Serbia and the rest of the Balkans, much of the music is played by Gypsies, the Romany people with original roots thought to be in India who live in many parts of the world. As professional musicians, their interpretation of the music, as well as their dancing, has had great influence in the regions in which they live.

The most basic Balkan instrument is the voice. Some kolos are accompanied by songs, many of which are so familiar to even non-Serbs after decades of dancing that it is natural to at least la-la-la along with the music to *Ajde Jano* ("Come on, Jana, let's dance the kolo—let's sell the horse and the house just so we can dance"), *Žikino Kolo,* ("Dance, kids, *Žikino Kolo,* who wouldn't like it, Žika will play for you solo"), and *Šetnja* ("Come, Mile, to our place to see what paradise is like"). *Seljančica* has a wonderful melody, but the lyrics are seldom sung. Here they are now, for our edification: "Annie, stay clear of the students from Karlovac; the students are wily, the professors are worse, and the director is worst of all, only I can't talk about it!"

Shouts, called *poskočice,* are often used for excited rhythmic punctuation—"hey hey," "*veh-seh-loh,*" and "*hopatsoop, hopatsoop, tri su babe, jedan zub* (three old ladies with one tooth)!"

CLOTHING AND COSTUMES. Serbian clothing varies as the regions do. To simulate an outfit from the Šumadija region, which many kolos come from, the girls might wear a long-sleeved white blouse and a pleated, knee- or calf-length skirt with dark horizontal stripes. A red vest over the blouse and a red apron with stripes or geometric patterns are also appropriate, and perhaps a striped sash. Around the head, girls may wear a long white scarf tied at the back to drape down the neck. On their legs are dark knee socks with bright flower designs.

Boys may wear a long-sleeved white shirt with cuffed full sleeves and a dark vest. Their baggy dark trousers should be tucked into high, brightly decorated socks, and topped with a wide leather belt. Serbian men wear round black sheepskin hats, somewhat like the Russian ones.

The Serbian opanci, like the Croatian ones, are flat leather sandals or moccasins. What distinguishes them as Serbian are the pointed toes that curl up in a small or large hooked shape. If these are not available, flat leather shoes will work; if anyone has brown ones, these would give more of an impression of opanci.

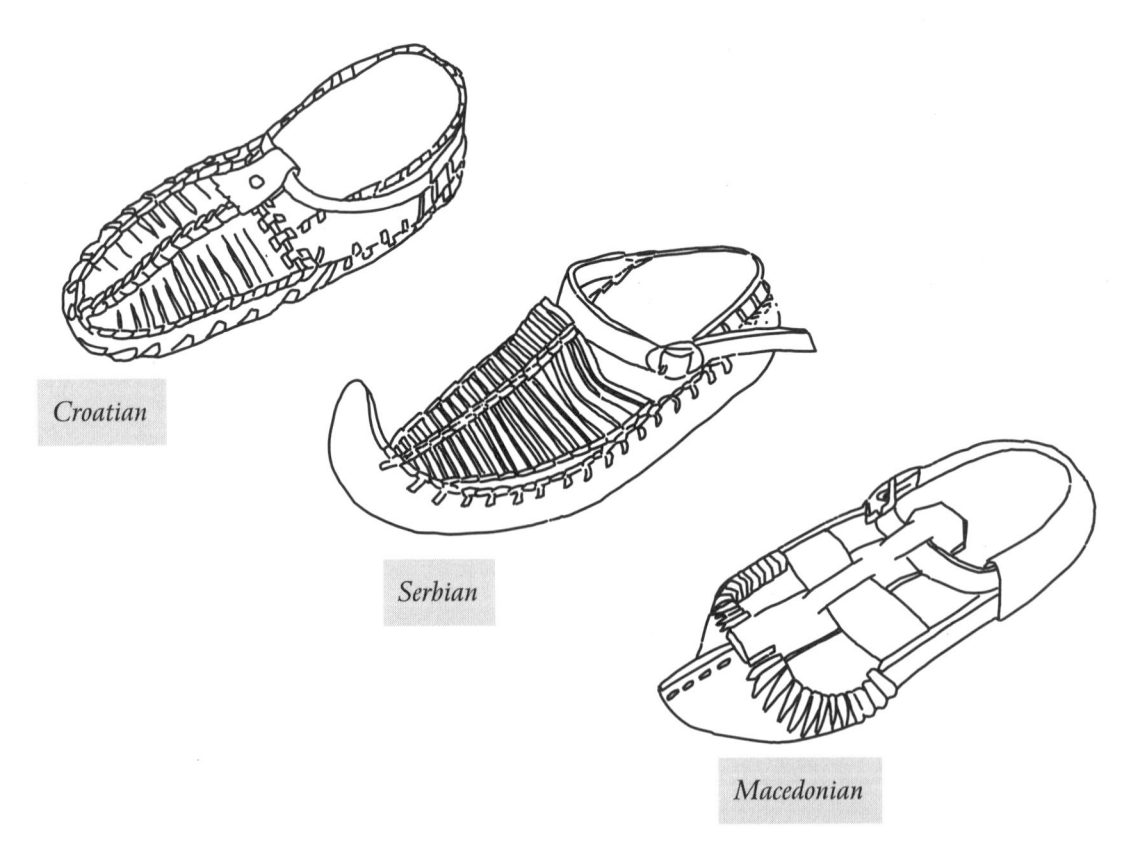

Girls wearing the dress of the Sumadija region present a special wedding kolo during an international festival in Szeged, Hungary.

Croatian

Serbian

Macedonian

356   *Cultures and Styling in Folk Dance*

Dances of the Macedonian People

Macedonia is a small country encircled by Greece, Bulgaria, Yugoslavia, and Albania. Known officially as the Republic of Macedonia, it has been independent from Yugoslavia since late 1991, shortly after Slovenia and Croatia also declared independence.

Being at the geographic center of the invasion routes between Europe and Asia, both in ancient and modern times, the Macedonians have been subjugated by one ruler after another. As descendants of the southern Slavic people who migrated to the area in the sixth century C.E., they were conquered by the Ottoman Turks in 1389 and remained under their rule until the Ottoman Empire was finally vanquished after the First Balkan War in 1912. After the Second Balkan War a year later, the Macedonian homeland was spread over the three countries of Serbia, Greece, and Bulgaria. Aegean Macedonia is in the northern part of Greece, and Pirin Macedonia is the southwestern region of Bulgaria. Vardar Macedonia was part of Serbia until 1945, when it became the Yugoslav republic of Macedonia. This was the first time Macedonians were free in their own state with their own government, and equally important, free to speak and write in the Macedonian language, which together with Serbo-Croatian and Slovenian made up the three officially recognized languages of the former Yugoslavia.

The Macedonian people are very proud of their cultural heritage, especially their folk arts. Detailed frescoes dating from before the eleventh century have been preserved in their churches and monasteries. The rich ornamentation and embroidery on the national dress show the skill of the culture's fabric designers and artisans. And Macedonia's music and dance, among the most subtle and complex of southeastern Europe, is particularly interesting and unique.

Each Macedonian village and town has its own dances, and every dancer in those villages and towns may have his or her own distinctive style, which might vary even more, according to the dancer's mood. In fact, the best native dancers are proud of never doing a dance the same way twice. Macedonian dance teachers have been known to change a choreography from workshop to workshop, because a particular choreography felt better at the moment; this vastly confuses conscientious folk dancers who cannot find each new variation in the syllabus. However, when dance is a living part of a culture as it is for the Macedonians, it can change and develop just as other living entities can, and it should be valued for that very reason.

The Macedonian dances listed on p. 358 may appear in a multitude of versions at a *sobor* in the homeland (a village gathering that celebrates a saint's day or other holiday) or at a wedding reception in an émigré community. They have been arranged in sequences, however, by native and North American ethnochoreographers wishing to teach them to non-Macedonian groups and have thus entered

Macedonian Dances in Phyllis S. Weikart's Books

Arap	[AHR-ahp] (Arab) *TM&D*	
Belasičko Oro	[BELL-ah-seetch-koh ORE-oh] (Named for the Belasica Mountain) *TM&D*	
Četvorka	[CHET-vor-kah] (A foursome) *TM&D*	
Deninka	[DEN-ink-ah] *TM&D*	
Dimna Juda	[DEEM-nah YOO-dah] (Dimna Juda, or Smoky Juda, is the name of a nonhuman troublesome female who lives in the mountains) *TFD, RM6*	
Dimna Juda Mamo	[DEEM-nah YOO-dah MAH-moh] (Dear Smoky Juda) *TFD, RM6*	
Gaida Avasi	[GUY-dah ah-VASEE] (Loudly sounding bagpipe) *TM&D*	
Ivanica, or *Ivanice*	[EE-vah-neet-seh] (A song about Macedonia) *TFD, CD3*	
Jovano Jovanke	[YOH-vah-noh YOH-vahn-keh] (Oh, Jovana, little Jovana) *TM&D*	
Kasapsko Oro	[KAH-sahp-skoh] (Butcher's dance) *TM&D*	
Katushe (or *Katuše*) *Mome*	[KAH-too-sheh MOH-meh] [Maid Katushe] *TM&D*	
Kosovsko Lesno Oro	[KOH-sof-skoh LEH-snoh OH-roh] (Easy dance from Kosovo) *TM&D*	
Kostursko Oro	[KOE-stur-skoh OH-roh] (Dance from Kostur) *TM&D*	
Legnala Dana	[LEG-nah-lah DAH-nah] (Dana was lying down) *TFD, CD6*	
Lesnoto Oro	[LEH-snoh-toh OH-roh] (The easy dance) *TM&D*	
Makedonsko Bavno Oro	[MAH-keh-DOHN-skoh BAH-vnoh OH-roh] (Slow Macedonian dance) *TM&D*	
Makrinitsa	[mah-kree-NEET-sah] *TM&D*	
Povrateno	[poh-VRAH-the-noh] (Forward and back, or returning) [Linguistic note: In Serbian, this means throwing up] *TM&D*	
Skudrinka	[skoo-DRIN-kah] *TFD, CD6*	
Tino Mori	[TEE-noh MOH-ree] (Oh, Tina) *TM&D*	
Tri Godini Kate	[tree go-DEE-nee KAH-the] (Three years, Kathy) *TM&D*	
Vrni Se Vrni	[VER-nee seh VER-nee] (Come back, come back) *TM&D*	
Žalna Majka	[ZHAHL-nah MYE-kah] (Sorrowful mother) *TFD, CD5*	

the international folk dance repertoire in various versions, including those described in Phyllis S. Weikart's books.

Several of the Macedonian dance regions are represented by the dances listed. For example, *Kostursko Oro, Makrinitsa,* and *Gaida Avasi* are from Greek Macedonia. *Arap,* the two *Dimna Juda* dances, and *Povrateno* show the styling of the eastern Macedonian area in and near Bulgaria. *Deninka* is from western Macedonia near Albania, and *Kosovsko Lesno Oro* is named for Kosovo, an Albanian Muslim province of present-day Yugoslavia that borders Macedonia to the north.

The Lesnoto

The *lesno,* or *lesnoto,* can be called a pan-Macedonian dance, for versions of it are done in all regions of Macedonia and all countries where Macedonians live. Many dances in this series are variants of the lesnoto, which is also called *lesnoto oro,* or just *oro* alone, to indicate its role as the basic dance form. Other names that might be used are *pravo* and *pravoto* (meaning straight, or plain, dance), and *zaramo* (holding shoulders). In Greek Macedonia, this dance form is referred to as *prava* or *za rakas* (holding hands). Ethnic dancers often call the dance by the name of the specific music played (such as *Makedonsko Devojče,* the beautiful song composed by renowned musician Jonche Hristovski about a Macedonian girl that is the melody for *Kosovsko Lesno Oro* and other lesnotos).

The three-measure lesnoto pattern is similar to the hora step that appears in numerous Balkan and Middle Eastern dances. Several of the Macedonian dances listed here are variations of the lesnoto, including *Kosovsko Lesno Oro, Lesnoto Oro, Jovano Jovanke,* and *Žalna Majka.* More complex lesnoto choreographies are found in *Legnala Dana, Ivanice,* and *Makedonsko Bavno Oro.* (There is also a four-measure pattern, not in *TFD* or *TM&D,* called *Lesnoto Oro* or *California Lesnoto.*) Generally, this common three-measure pattern is danced to a four-phrase melody, like the hora, showing the nonconcordance between dance pattern and musical phrases.

The asymmetric meter of lesnotos is usually 7/8, although it sometimes speeds up and becomes 2/4 (*Gaida Avasi* is actually a lesnoto, or a hora, in 2/4). This asymmetric meter, sometimes called "the Macedonian seven," can be described as *slow,* quick, quick or 3/8, 2/8, 2/8 (♩. ♩ ♩).

Since its step description seems quite short and simple, teachers might be tempted to teach the lesnoto early and often. However, the asymmetric meter and the irregular pattern, plus the characteristic *čukče* step (described under "Steps and movements" on p. 360), make this dance and its variants much more subtle than they appear on paper. In addition, context is very important, as has been mentioned before about the deceptively easy Balkan dances. Such dances are meant to be an integral part of a larger event at which other activities are also going on. Although it may not be practical to set up a village in the gym or music room (it might be fun to try sometime!), students could be encouraged to gossip and tell jokes as they dance, to create a bit of the community ambience.

The lesnoto is a good dance for recreational folk dance groups, as long as there are enough people to create a friendly energy. *Ivanice,* one of the lesnoto choreographies, is an excellent one to teach to those who are not experienced in Balkan dances. It is simple but enough of a challenge to sustain interest, and it has a singable melody—always a good reason for choosing a dance.

FORMATION. The Macedonian oro is usually an open, or broken, circle, with a leader on the right, as are the majority of the Macedonian dances listed here, and it is a dance with men and women intermingled. In the old days under the influence of the Muslim Ottoman Turks, however, men and women danced separately in their own dances, or they were segregated within the circle. Dances that were originally for men alone include *Kasapsko Oro* and *Arap,* and those originally for women alone are *Deninka* and *Ivanice.* Today these are done in mixed groups.

Jovano Jovanke and *Makedonsko Bavno Oro* were brought back from Macedonia by North American researchers in the late 1950s and early 1960s, and they introduced them as they had seen the dances done, with the men at the right end of the line and the women at the left end. As was done in other religiously conservative societies, a kerchief was held between the last man and first woman, so they would not touch. This segregation no longer happens among most Macedonians, but some folk dance groups still keep *Bavno Oro* (as it is called) in separate lines of men and women as described in *TM&D.*

Other dances done in shorter lines instead of large open circles are *Povrateno* and *Četvorka. Vrni Se Vrni* is described as a circle but is also an open circle.

STEPS AND MOVEMENTS. One of the characteristic Macedonian steps is the *čukče* (literally meaning little hammer). This is a slight hesitation step in which the heel lifts before the beat and comes down on the beat. The up-down movement comes from the knee, not the heel. The *čukče* appears in many of the dances here, described in the first slow, quick/quick steps of *Jovano Jovanke, Kosovsko Lesno Oro, Lesnoto Oro, Žalna Majka, Katuše Mome,* and parts of others.

Basic Macedonian styling is restrained and cautious, but sure-footed, with soft, flexible knees. Yves Moreau, an expert on Bulgarian regional dances, calls this the "sneaking back home late at night" style. Do not tiptoe, however, but softly pad, rolling the whole sole from heel to toe—a "catlike tread."

In some of the more challenging dances, particularly in those from the Pirin region, it sometimes seems to take a long time after the foot is picked up before it is allowed to touch the ground again. During this pulsing pause, experienced dancers add extra hops and other movements, which Dick Crum calls choreographic embroidery. Sometimes native dancers add a hesitation, so their foot touches just after the beat, a movement rubato that stretches the musical moment and adds a slight tension to the step. This can be seen in *Kostursko Oro* and *Tino Mori* in the "slower" beats.

Styling for men and women is quite different. Men's movements are large and open, women's more subtle. For example, when knees are raised, men lift theirs high and turn them out so the inner ankle is almost pointed up; women lift their knee only until the toe barely clears the floor. This difference in styling is sometimes a good reason for the genders to dance in separate groups.

It is possible, of course, to do Macedonian dances without paying too much attention to styling details, but these are what make this culture's dances so intriguing. It would be like making a stew without adding the spices—leaving in the pan merely some uninteresting lumps. We encourage those interested in investigating further to go to workshops, folk dance groups, and local Macedonian events, if possible.

HANDS AND ARMS. Macedonian dances employ a variety of hand and arm positions. When dances are done in segregated formations, traditionally men danced in the T-position, or shoulder-hold position, and women used the W-position, or bent-elbow-hold. In mixed lines, usually the W-position is used. In Macedonian dancing, the W-position is usually at shoulder height with arms a little forward and neighbors' forearms close together. Some women's dances have the hands held a little higher, about head height.

Other positions represented are the front basket-hold ("right under the leftovers") in *Dimna Juda* and *Dimna Juda Mamo*, which are variations on the same theme. *Četvorka* and *Makrinitsa* are in the V-position, *Kasapsko Oro* takes the belt-hold, and *Povrateno* and *Gaida Avasi* are done in a T-hold. Some dances, such as *Belasičko Oro* and *Vrni Se Vrni*, change hand positions during the dance.

With the free hand, leaders may wave a kerchief to signal pattern changes, or they may put their free hand, with fingers down, on the back of the right hip; the free hand might also rest up where the vest or suspenders might be. The people at the other end usually close off the circle by holding their fist at the small of the back, as described in the Serbian section.

MODIFICATION AND TEACHING TIPS. Generally, by the time students are sophisticated enough to appreciate these dances, they should be developmentally mature enough to feel comfortable with the steps and movements. The čukče, however, might take practice and experience to achieve, since it requires dancers to inhibit movement, which is difficult for some people. Since this step appears in the easier dances, teachers might want to simplify it when first introducing those dances.

The natural way to modify the čukče is to merely walk with a slight hesitation, as native dancers sometimes do. For example, in *Kosovsko Lesno Oro*, instead

These recreational dancers doing a Macedonian dance are using the W-position, with arms at shoulder height and a little forward. Forearms may be closer.

Photo by Zoltan Horvath

of the SIDE, LIFT, CROSS of measure 1, try SIDE, *AND,* CROSS: Glide the left foot across the right instead of lifting it, and do not bounce with the right knee and foot—yet. It is important to make sure that the left foot does not touch the floor until the second quick/quick, so dancers feel the asymmetric meter. Soon the knee bounce can be added, and then the heel lift.

MUSIC. Macedonian music is known for its exciting rhythms. Most of the dances discussed here are in duple meter (2/4) or asymmetric meter (7/8), although *Katuše Mome* is in 9/16 or quick, *slow,* quick-quick (2/8, 3/8, 2/8, 2/8; ♩♩.♩♩). Other meters can be 5/8, 11/16, 12/16, and more, or the meter may fluctuate with the intensity of the musicians and dancers. When we dance to recordings the music never varies, but when we are lucky enough to dance to a folk ensemble—"live music"—the musicians can provide delightful surprises. The phrasing of some of the melodies is also irregular. The music for *Dimna Juda* and *Dimna Juda Mamo* is a 20-measure song. ("Dimna Juda built a home on the Vlaina mountain; what posts she pounded in were good-looking bachelors.") The patterns described for these two dances in *TFD* are variations of the slow part of a dance known as *Kopačka* (digging). The music for *Tino Mori* is a 16-measure song with a 12-measure interlude. ("May God strike your old mother and father for engaging you to someone so far away; he lies ill, he will die.") Both songs are good for lessons in listening while moving to musical phrases.

Other dances, such as *Jovano Jovanke, Legnala Dana,* and *Tino Mori,* are named specifically for the songs to which they are choreographed. Some are known by the name of either the song or the dance. Thus *Arap,* for example, is the dance pattern to a humorous song about a little rabbit called *Zajko Kokorajko* [ZYE-koh koh-koh-RYE-koh], which is also the name of a more complicated dance. There also are other dances called *Arap* that are done to different music. *Deninka* is sometimes called by the name of its song, *Ordan Sedi* [ORE-dahn SAY-dee] (Ordan sits). *Ivanice* is choreographed to a paean of praise to Macedonia called *Vie Se Vie* (circling around). All this information may not seem necessary just to teach a few dances in a classroom, but anyone who might want to delve more into Macedonian dance will find such background helpful.

The main folk instruments are the *kaval,* an end-blown vertical flute; the *gajda,* a bagpipe made from goatskin; the *tambura,* a strummed type of lute; and the *tapan,* a large, double-headed bass drum played on one side with a heavy mallet and on the other with a light wand. Many ensembles are made up of Gypsy musicians.

Singing is a vital component of Macedonian dance music as it is in the rest of the Balkans. In public, the women carried on the singing tradition while the men were the musicians. Because women's hands were always busy with embroidery or other work, the strong vibrant voice of the mountains became their instrument, although they did play strings and some percussion in private. An interesting feature of Macedonian singing, besides the powerful "outdoor" voice, is the drone—a sustained low note that anchors the rest of the harmony. Nowadays, however, there are women musicians in the instrumental ensembles and men singers recording popular ballads for lesnotos.

CLOTHING AND COSTUMES. Macedonian dress is the most elaborately decorated traditional dress found in any of the former Yugoslav republics. There is embroidery on the long-sleeved, calf-length white smock, on the long vest over it, on the red apron, on the headdress, and on the heavy woolen socks. Men are somewhat less decorated but have designs on vest, sash, and socks. The designs tend to be geometric rather than floral. Costumes for stage productions, however, usually are not as heavily embroidered because of the time and cost involved.

Creating geometric designs on costumes for a dance program might be an interesting multi-arts project. Girls can wear a long-sleeved white blouse, white skirt, and red apron, with designs added with rickrack, fabric markers, beads, or real embroidery; designs should adorn the blouse neck and cuffs, the skirt hem,

Singing is a vital component of Macedonian dance music. These Macedonian women share their singing traditions at Folkmoot USA.

and the entire apron. Put fringe on the apron bottom for a traditional touch, and string coin necklaces at the neck and waist and on the forehead of the white-scarf headdress that is tied behind the head and draped down the back. On the legs are knee socks in colorful patterns. Faux braids add a traditional touch.

Boys can wear a long-sleeved, loose-sleeved white shirt with designs on the sleeve hems; the shirt hangs over long white or khaki pants or is tucked in and worn with a broad, decorated sash or belt around the waist. Over the shirt is a sleeveless vest. Designs of dark braid may be added to the edges of the vest as well as to the seams, front, and cuffs of the pants. If round sheepskin hats are not available, wrap turbans around the boys' heads; turbans can be knotted at the side and draped down a bit. Boys also wear decorated knee socks.

Traditionally, both men and women wear the flat leather moccasins called opanke, or opinci. The Macedonian ones have small straps across the top and come to only a slightly raised point in front (see p. 356). If these are not available, low brown or tan shoes are appropriate.

The aprons on these Macedonian dancers performing at Folkmoot USA exhibit the characteristic geometric designs.

Resources Used for Chapter 29

Atanasovski, Pece. 1972–93. Dance notes from various workshops. A Macedonian musician and dancer, Atanasovski was one of the first teachers of Macedonian dance in the North American folk dance community.

Boxell, Dennis. 1981. *Dances of Greek Macedonia.* Los Angeles: Festival Records. This syllabus, written by one of the early North American researchers of Yugoslav dances, provides notes that are full of interesting details.

Crum, Richard. 1965. "Balkan Dance." In *Folk Dance Progressions,* Miriam D. Lidster and Dorothy H. Tamburini, eds., 2–15. Belmont, CA: Wadsworth. This is an excellent overview by one of the most respected North American Balkan dance experts.

Crum, Richard. 1973–94. Personal letters and published dance notes from various workshops. His notes are always informative, thorough, trustworthy, literate, humane—even humorous.

Dimchevski, Georgi. 1983. *Vie se Oro Makedonsko* (The Macedonian Dance Circles Around). Skopje: Goce Delčev. (Translated by Ostali Muzikaši, Seattle, 1985.) This publication contains much information about Macedonian folk music and dance. It is written by one of the nation's foremost composers and authorities on folklore and translated by a Seattle ensemble of Balkan folk musicians.

Dunin, Elsie Ivancic, and Stanimir Višinski. 1995. *Dances in Macedonia: Ensemble Tanec.* Skopje, Macedonia: Tanec Ensemble. Written in both English and Macedonian, this book describes many Macedonian dances as collected, choreographed, and performed by members of Macedonia's professional performing group Tanec. (Contact Tanec Ansambl Za Narodni Igri I Pesni, ul. V. Macukovski, 91000 Skopje, Macedonia; fax: 389-91-415043.)

Glenny, Misha. 1994. *The Fall of Yugoslavia: The Third Balkan War.* New York: Penguin Books. This is a European journalist's fascinating and almost impartial account of the maze of politics surrounding the events in former Yugoslavia after 1991.

Janković, Danica, and Ljubica Janković. 1934. *Narodne Igre* (Folk Dances), Vol. 1. Belgrade: Prosveta. This classic series of volumes is the first systematic collection of Balkan dances.

Jordanoff, Nicholas. 1991. Notes, lectures, discussions, conversations about dances of former Yugoslavian republics during a course on Balkan dance and cultures at Duquesne University, Pittsburgh, PA, given in July 1991 by this former artistic director of the Duquesne University Tamburitzans.

Joukowsky, Anatol M. 1965. *The Teaching of Ethnic Dance.* New York: Pratt & Co. For those particularly interested in ethnic dance, this book has historic interest and charm. It is written by one of the pioneer choreographers of ethnic dance, who collected dances between the two world wars and introduced early versions of many dances still in the repertoire. See "Macedonia and Greece," pp. 7–28 and "Serbia," pp. 29–62.

Kaplan, Robert D. 1991. "History's Cauldron." *The Atlantic Monthly,* (June): 93–104. This is an excellent article on the complex history of Macedonia.

Kaplan, Robert D. 1994. *Balkan Ghosts: A Journey Through History.* New York: Vintage Books. An American journalist travels through the Balkans in search of the background of events leading up to current animosities.

Koenig, Martin. 1971. "Village Music of Yugoslavia." *The Explorer Series.* Nonesuch Records H-72042. This record is part of an album produced by Koenig, who is a Balkan dance enthusiast and researcher. It was recorded at the famous *Smotra Folklora* festival in Zagreb in 1971. Koenig's notes on instruments and music are particularly interesting.

Kolar, Walter W. 1974. *An Introduction to Meter and Rhythm in Balkan Folk Music.* Pittsburgh: Duquesne University.

Kolarovski, Atanas. 1968–92. Dance notes from many workshops. A native of Macedonia and member of professional ensembles, Kolarovski has taught his art all over the world and introduced many of the dances in this chapter.

Kotansky, Steve. 1981–94. Workshops, dance notes, and culture sessions.

Kuharski, Michael. n.d. Conversations, letters, and helpful advice from this colleague, who is a Balkan dance expert and musician, an artistic director of a folk ensemble, and a caring teacher.

Papantoniou, Ioanna. 1992. *Macedonian Costumes.* Athens: The Peloponnesian Folklore Foundation. This volume has contemporary and historic photographs of traditional attire, with text in English, Greek, and French. (Available from folk-things, POB 13070, San Antonio, TX 78213-0070; 210/530-0694; <folk-things@msn.com>.)

Rice, Timothy. 1982. "A Macedonian Sobor: Anatomy of a Celebration." In *Macedonia* (pamphlet). Toronto: Selyani Macedonian Folklore Group. This article, reprinted from *Journal of American Folklore,* Vol. 93, April–June 1980, is an account of a traditional event in a Macedonian village, observed by Rice in the late 1970s.

Salopek, Vladimir, Nada Mirkovič, and Janet Goring. 1987. *Folk Costumes and Dances of*

Yugoslavia. Zagreb: Niro Privredni Vjesnik. This is a paperback put out by the "Turistička propaganda" with useful text and many beautiful photos of traditional and stage folk outfits.

Stassen-Berger, Rachel. 1997. "Healing Deep Wounds With the Dance of Life." *Chicago Tribune*, 14 September, Womanews Section, pp. 4–6. This article is a moving account of how the Živli ethnic dance troups of Columbus, OH, performed at refugee camps in eastern Europe that shelter people who cannot return to their homes in former Yugoslavia.

Thurston, Hugh. 1967. "Choreogeography." *Viltis* (May): 5–7; (June–September): 5–7; (October–November): 5–7; (December): 4–6. These articles give an interesting analysis of how cultural and historical geographical regions relate to traditional ethnic dances. Not everyone subscribes to the author's main theories, but the articles include much useful cultural and historical background.

Tomov, George. 1973. "Macedonian Folk Dances," "Macedonian Folk Songs." *Viltis* (June–September): 12–13, 14–15. These are articles by a former member of Tanec, the Macedonian state folk ensemble, who is now a resident of the U.S. and artistic director of the Tomov Dance Troupe, which is well-known on the East Coast.

"Welcome to Croatia." 1997. A Web site with information about many aspects of Croatian folklore. <http://vukovar.unm.edu/wtc/wtc.html>.

West, Rebecca. 1941. *Black Lamb and Grey Falcon: A Journey Through Yugoslavia*. New York: Viking Press. These two classic volumes by a renowned writer recount her experiences and views about the Balkan peoples just before World War II; this has great relevance to today's troubles.

Yampolski, Zelig. 1969. "The Dance in Yugoslavia." *Viltis* (October–November): 4–10. This is a detailed article about Serbian dance and customs.

Živli. n.d. Packet of information about former Yugoslav ethnic cultures from Columbus, OH, professional folk ensemble, which performs songs and dances of the former Yugoslavian republics. Contact Melissa Pinter Oberauf, Executive Director, 1753 Loudon Street, Granville, OH 43023.

Žunić-Baš, Leposava, editor. n.d. *Folk Traditions in Yugoslavia—Ten Tours*. Izdavački Zavod Jugoslavija. This attractive book is intended as a travel guide through 10 regions, with much detail on cultural characteristics and wonderful illustrations by Zdenka Sertić showing clothing, folk designs, and traditional scenes.

Dances by Phyllis S. Weikart

Chapter 30 Dances by Phyllis S. Weikart

Phyllis S. Weikart Choreographies in TFD

Big Circle Dance	RM1
Bulgarian Dance #1	RM8
Close Encounters	RM4
Count 64	RM2
Erev Shel Shoshanim	[AIR-ev shell shoh-shah-NEEM] *RM3*
Gaelic Waltz	RM1
Hot Pretzels I	RM8
Hustle	RM9
Instant Success	RM9
Irish Mixer	RM1
Irish Stew	RM2
Jamaican Holiday I	RM5
Jamaican Holiday II	RM5
Joe Clark Mixer	RM1
Limbo Rock	RM2
Little Shoemaker (revised)	RM3
Nigun	[ni-GOON] *RM1*
Oh, How Lovely	RM1
Pata Pata I	[PAH-tah PAH-tah] *RM6*
Popcorn	RM7
Progressive Circle Dance	RM2
Sliding	RM1
Sneaky Snake	RM4
Soldier's Joy Contra	RM2
Spanish Coffee	RM4
Tipsy I	RM6
Tipsy II	RM6
Two-part Dance	RM2
Yankee Doodle	RM2
Zigeunerpolka	[tsee-GOY-nehr-poka] *RM2*

Thirty dances in *TFD* were choreographed by Phyllis S. Weikart in response to the need for sequenced movement material that students can quickly achieve and immediately enjoy. These patterns reinforce necessary skills and are based on *Rhythmically Moving* selections with a steady pulse. They have proved to be successful with beginning dancers of all ages and are a good foundation from which to progress to dances that are more complex and more ethnic.

Educators know that it is best to start students from where they are—to first lead them through a familiar door and then guide them into new pathways. As the great Hungarian composer and educator Zoltán Kodály put it, "To turn the gaze of the people toward high mountains, we must first show them more accessible hills." In terms of classroom folk dances, these Phyllis S. Weikart choreographies may provide some "accessible hills."

Several of the melodies used have other choreographies that teachers may come across as they delve deeper into the general folk dance repertoire. *Limbo Rock,* for example, is a U.S. novelty dance with a samba flavor. There are at least two versions, one by Henry ("Buzz") Glass, both done in recreational groups as a couple mixer. *Zigeunerpolka (Gypsy Polka)* is a German couple mixer that was popularized by Jane Farwell. *Yankee Doodle* has inspired a number of contra dance patterns and community party mixers over the years.

Ethnic folk materials also are the basis of two popular Weikart arrangements that are favorites for ending dance evenings. Her *Erev Shel Shoshanim (Evening of Roses)* is choreographed to a beautiful melody by Israeli composer Josef Hadar with lyrics by Moshe Dor, which has been the source of several creations by Israeli choreographers. Rayah Spivak presented a fairly easy line dance in the late 1950s, and Eliyahu Gamliel provided both a couple and a circle version, each based on Yemenite steps and styling. Phyllis S. Weikart's *Oh, How Lovely* pattern is in the style of the central European *canon valser* (waltz canon), a traditional way to give warm closure to a community event, and an appropriate dance on which to end this book.

General Resources

The sources listed here are on general topics or cover a number of subjects. For more specific cultural references, see the resource list at the end of each chapter.

We suggest consulting more than one source on a given topic, particularly when doing research. You may find a tendency among the earlier U.S. and English authors to romanticize the "colorful ethnic natives," but these sources are interesting historically. You may also find that some publications in our resource lists are out of print. They often can be found in private collections.

General Information

Aman International Music and Dance Co. 1985. *Folk Dances for Use in the Schools.* Los Angeles: Aman Educational Division. This is a dance and music residency handbook, with two cassettes. Besides dance and culture notes, it includes maps, activities, teaching suggestions, even crossword puzzles, for more than 30 folk dances. (Contact P.O. Box 90593, Long Beach, CA; 562/986-4331).

Arbeau, Thoinot. 1589, reprint 1967. *Orchesography.* New York: Dover. This classic dance manual written by an elderly churchman gives not only dance and music notations for European dances of the period but also an authentic view of the social mores of the time. It is written as a relaxed and amusing dialogue between a dance master and his pupil.

Bambra, Audrey, and Muriel Webster. 1972. *Teaching Folk Dancing.* New York: Theatre Arts Books. Written by two British physical education specialists, this book has excellent information on history, style, costume, and music for dances from Austria, Greece, Israel, and France. It includes descriptions in Labanotation for each dance.

Barer-Stein, Thelma. 1979. *You Eat What You Are: A Study of Ethnic Food Traditions.* Toronto: McClelland and Stewart, Ltd. This delightful book discusses the cuisine of 70 cultures. Its usefulness here comes from the concise opening descriptions of each country and culture.

Beliajus, Vytautas Finadar. 1940, 1942. *Dance and Be Merry,* Vols. I and II. Chicago and New York: Clayton F. Summy Co. "Vyts" was a pioneer of the recreational folk dance movement. These books contain dances that he collected in the 1930s, many of which are still part of school and recreational group repertoires.

Beliajus, Vytautas Finadar. 1955. *Merrily Dance.* Delaware, OH: Cooperative Recreation Service, Inc. Another classic from "Vyts," this book has historic interest with some original descriptions.

Broughton, Simon, Mark Ellingham, David Muddyman, and Richard Trillo (eds.) 1994. *World Music, The Rough Guide.* London: Rough Guides, Ltd. This is a compact, paperback encyclopedia with an astounding amount of information about traditional and contemporary music in numerous cultures.

Burchenal, Elizabeth. 1909–42. *Folk Dances and Singing Games, Dances of the People, Folk Dances from Old Homelands,* and others. New York: G. Schirmer. Burchenal is one of the earliest U.S. researchers. Many of her descriptions are still the ones used today.

Casey, Betty (ed.). 1981. *International Folk Dancing USA.* Garden City, NY: Doubleday. This is a well-organized book with concise backgrounds about 25 cultures, clear dance descriptions, and good folk ballet photos. Although the book's notes on camps and teachers are dated, it serves as an excellent recreational folk dancers' history book.

Crampton, C. Ward. 1909. *The Folk Dance Book.* New York: A.S. Barnes. One of the earliest folk dance manuals, this book is interesting for photos of dance formations (all girls) and useful for music notations. Crampton also published *The Second Folk Dance Book* in 1916.

Dance Traditions. Costa Mesa, CA: Dunaj International Dance Ensemble. This is a newsletter of folk and vintage ballroom dance. (Contact Dunaj at P.O. Box 1642, Costa Mesa, CA 92628.)

Dancer's Source Book. 1996. Costa Mesa, CA: Dance Traditions. This book includes such topics as "The 'Folk' in Folk Dance," "American Social Dance History," "Leading and Following," "Class Management for Teachers," "The 'Physics' of Dance Movement," and more. (Contact Dance Traditions at P.O. Box 1642, Costa Mesa, CA 92628.)

Duggan, Anne Schley, Jeanette Schlottmann, and Abbie Rutledge. 1948. *Folk Dances of the British Isles, Folk Dances of Scandinavia, Folk Dances of European Countries, Folk Dances of the United States and Mexico.* (Folk Dance Library Series). New York: Ronald Press. Classic folk dance texts of an earlier generation, these books cover history, step patterns, clothing, and more.

Duggan, Anne Schley, Jeanette Schlottman, and Abbie Rutledge. 1948. *The Teaching of Folk Dance.* New York: Ronald Press. Although a bit dated, this book has much information on organization and activities, plus a chapter on evaluation/assessment and suggestions for three ethnic programs.

Dziewanowska. Ada. 1977. *Let's Play* (Bawmy Sie): *Children's Games, Dances and Songs from Poland.* Watertown, MA: Author. This is a syllabus of charming activities by a renowned Polish dance teacher. (Contact her at 3352 N. Hackett Ave., Milwaukee, WI 53211; 414/964-8444.)

Dziewanowska, Ada. 1997. *Polish Folk Dances & Songs: A Step-by-Step Guide.* New York: Hippocrene Books. This is a 672-page book by one of the most respected and beloved of Polish dance teachers. Descriptions and illustrations have Ada's usual clarity, and she not only describes the traditional form of the dances with much background but also makes suggestions for stage and recreational versions.

Eastern Europe Phrasebook. 1992. Victoria, Australia: Lonely Planet Publications. This is a handy book for a brief overview of the history and pronunciation of Bulgarian, Czech, Hungarian, Polish, Romanian, and Slovak.

Evans, Jane. 1985. *Let's Dance.* Toronto: Can-Ed Media. This book is a movement approach to teaching folk dance. Each of the 86 dance descriptions has a theme, such as "body awareness—gestures," or "space awareness—pathways." It contains old favorites and modern, jazzy dances.

Farwell, Jane. 1960. *Folk Dances for Fun.* Delaware, Ohio: Cooperative Recreation Service, Inc. Written by a beloved advocate of recreational dance and play-party games, Jane Farwell's little book has 25 folk dances and singing games. (Available through Folklore Village Farm, 3210 Co. Hwy. BB, Dodgeville, WI 53533; 608/924-4000.)

Feldman, Reynold, and Cynthia Voelke (eds.). 1992. *A World Treasury of Folk Wisdom.* San Francisco: Harper San Francisco. This is a wonderful book full of sayings that can give a glimpse into the spirit of a people or just liven up a multicultural lesson.

Folk Dance Federation of California Research Committee. 1945–57. *Folk Dances from Near and Far,* Vols. I–VIII. 1945–57. Berkeley, Millbrae, San Carlos, CA: Folk Dance Federation of California, Inc. These eight volumes contain descriptions of dances that are still basic to the folk dance repertoire. They are especially valuable for sources and original notes and for illustrating how dances changed from the East to the West Coast.

Folk Dance Federation of California Research Committee. 1953–55. *Let's Dance,* Vols. A–C. San Francisco: Folk Dance Federation of California, Inc. Volume A contains descriptions of 30 basic dances; Volumes B and C each contain descriptions of 25 intermediate dances.

Folk Dance Phone Book and Group Directory. 1995–. Austin, TX: Society of Folk Dance Historians. This is an annual publication with alphabetical listing of folk dancers worldwide, dance groups, institutions and events, teachers and musicians, and much more. (Contact Ron Houston, 2100 Rio Grande, Austin TX 78705-5513; 512/478-9676; <SOFDH@juno.com> or <ron@ccwf.cc.utexas.edu>.)

The folk♥things Directory. 1996. San Antonio, TX: David Henry. This is an excellent guide to folk dance groups, festivals, camps, teachers, vendors, and more across North America and around the world. It is published annually. (Contact P.O. Box 13070, San Antonio, TX 78213; 210/530-0694; <folkthings@ msn.com>.)

Fonseca, Isabel. 1995. *Bury Me Standing: The Gypsies and Their Journey.* New York: Vintage Books. The author, who lived with and studied the Rom people in eastern Europe, writes about Gypsy history and contemporary life.

Gilbert, Cecile. 1970. *International Folk Dance at a Glance.* Minneapolis: Burgess. A physical education professor at Ball State University, the late Dr. Gilbert understood the importance of folk dance. Her book uses a system of symbols to notate many of the classic dances.

Gottier, Karin. 1991. "Some Thoughts on Folk Dance in the Classroom." Paper from ethnic dance seminar at Duquesne University, Pittsburgh, PA, July 1991.

Hall, J. Tillman. 1969. *Folk Dance.* Pacific Palisades, CA: Goodyear. Another text from the heyday of folk dance teaching, this book has some dances not seen in similar handbooks, like Syrian *Dubka* and a Guam stick dance.

Harris, Jane A., Anne M. Pittman, and Marlys S. Waller (eds.). 1994. *Dance Awhile,* 7th ed. New York: Macmillan International. This is a well-known handbook, useful for a variety of dance types—folk, square, contra, social, and country/western—with some background information.

Hendrickson, Charles Cyril. 1989. *Early American Dance and Music: A Colonial Dancing Experience, Country Dancing for Elementary School Children.* Sandy Hook, CT: The Hendrickson Group. This and Hendrickson's other books and cassettes are useful for anyone doing Colonial U.S. units. (Contact Box 766, Sandy Hook, CT.)

Hendrickson, Charles Cyril, with Frances Cibel Hendrickson. 1989. *Early American Dance and Music: John Griffiths, Dancing Master, 29 Country Dances, 1788.* Sandy Hook, CT: The Hendrickson Group.

Herman, Michael, and Mary Ann Herman. 1940s–1980s. Syllabuses, dance notes, and recordings published and produced in New York City at Folk Dance House. The Hermans were U.S. folk dance pioneers and founders of Folk Dance House in New York City; their dance descriptions are the originals of many in the early recreational repertoire, from both Folk Dance House in New York City and Maine Folk Dance Camp in Bridgton, ME.

Houston, Ron. 1987–. *Folk Dance Problem Solver* series. Austin, TX: Society of Folk Dance Historians (formerly X-Press). This is an extremely useful series of books of folk dance descriptions plus their cultural and choreological backgrounds. (Contact Ron Houston at Society of Folk Dance Historians, 2100 Rio Grande, Austin, TX 78705-5513; fax 512/478-8900; <ron@ccwf.cc.utexas.edu>.

Johnson, Lois. 1993. *Happy Birthdays Around the World.* Detroit: Omnigraphics Press. This book describes different birthday customs in 24 countries, plus other festivities, with birthday greetings in each language.

Jonas, Gerald. 1992. *Dancing: The Pleasure, Power, and Art of Movement.* New York: Harry N. Abrams. This gorgeous book accompanied the PBS television series of the same name. It offers historical and artistic information about a wide variety of cultures and is filled with fascinating illustrations.

Jordanoff, Nicholas. 1991. Notes, lectures, discussions, conversations, during a course on Balkan dance and cultures at Duquesne University, Pittsburgh, PA, given in July 1991 by this former artistic director of the Duquesne University Tamburitzans.

Joukowsky, Anatol M. 1965. *The Teaching of Ethnic Dance.* New York: Pratt. Professor Joukowsky was a ballet dancer and choreographer who arranged many eastern European dances. The dances represented in this book are not for beginners.

Kaplan, Robert D. 1994. *Balkan Ghosts: A Journey Through History.* New York: Vintage Books. This book is a fascinating and contemporary exploration of the Balkan peoples that explains why this area is such a boiling cauldron of animosities.

Kraus, Richard. 1962. *Folk Dancing.* New York: Macmillan. This is a useful book of clear descriptions of more than 100 dances, although what the author considered grade-appropriate in 1960 may be different today.

Lawson, Joan. 1953. *European Folk Dance.* London: Pitman. Besides some dance descriptions and music notations, this book has much in-depth background, including information on development of clothing styles.

Lidster, Miriam D., and Dorothy H. Tamburini (eds.). 1965. *Folk Dance Progressions.* Belmont, CA: Wadsworth. A good source book for folk dance teachers, this book groups dances according to movement patterns (e.g., polka, schottische, grapevine).

Lomax, Alan. 1978. *Folk Song Style and Culture* (First paperback edition). New Brunswick, NJ: Transaction Books. This book came out of the author's systematic scientific surveys of song and dance patterns from 400 world cultures. Chapter 10, "Dance Styles and Culture," discusses his term *choreometrics,* meaning dance as a measure of culture, and illustrates how everyday, work-related movements can become part of a culture's dance patterns.

Lye, Keith. 1996. *The Portable World Factbook.* New York: Avon Books. This is a concise but useful A-to-Z guide to all the world's nations. Illustrations include maps, flags, and stamps of most countries. It is handy for quick information about a country.

Musical Instruments of the World: An Illustrated Encyclopedia by the Diagram Group. 1976. New York: Facts on File. This book has more than 4000 drawings and is an excellent resource for historic, traditional, and modern instruments.

Mynatt, Constance, and Bernard Kaiman. 1975. *Folk Dancing for Students and Teachers.* Dubuque, IA: Wm. C. Brown Co. This is a useful book from two East Tennessee State University professors. It has easy-to-read descriptions and an interesting chapter on "Evaluation in Folk Dance."

National Standards for Dance Education: What Every Young American Should Know and Be Able to Do in Dance. 1996. Reston, VA: National Dance Association (NDA). Developed by the National Dance Association, this publication points up how necessary folk dance is to education. (Contact Judy Oberley, NDA Program Coordinator, 1900 Association Dr., Reston, VA 22091; 703/476-3436.)

NFO News. Milwaukee, WI: National Folk Organization (NFO). This is a quarterly newsletter sent to NFO members that covers topics pertaining to folk dance in fields of education, recreation, performance, and festivals. It includes a national calendar of folk-dance-related events. (Contact NFO, 423 W. National Ave., Milwaukee, WI 53204.)

Ontario FolkDancer. This magazine of the Ontario Folk Dance Association (OFDA) always has interesting articles. Subscription includes membership in OFDA. (Contact Diane Gladstone, 22 Latimer Ave., Toronto, Ontario, M5N 2L8; 416/489-3566.)

Paley Vivian Gussin. 1996. *Kwanzaa and Me, A Teacher's Story.* Cambridge: MA: Harvard University Press. This little book is not about the Kwanzaa holiday but is an inspiring resource for anyone who deals with multicultural education or activities. An award-winning retired Chicago kindergarten teacher, Ms. Paley uses storytelling to share her experiences with integrated classrooms, with her students sharing their own thoughts. This is available in commercial bookstores.

Quo. San Antonio, TX: David Henry. This is a bimonthly newsletter of folk and traditional dance published by David Henry. (Contact P.O. Box 13070, San Antonio, TX 78213-0070; 210/530-0694; <folkthings@msn.com>.)

Roecker, Pirkko. 1986. "Fundamentals of Motion." A paper included in the syllabus of the Stockton Folk Dance Camp, University of the Pacific, Stockton, CA, 1986.

Sachs, Curt. 1963. *World History of Dance.* New York: Norton.

Schafer, Andrea. 1995. *My Harvest Home.* Danbury, CT: World Music Press. This is a book of Polish songs and dances with audiotape; the book is exquisitely illustrated by the author's husband, Peter Schafer, and has a chapter on *wycinanki*, the art of paper cutting. (Contact World Music Press, P.O. Box 2565, Danbury, CT 06813; 203/748-1131.)

Shaw, Lloyd. 1948. *The Round Dance Book: A Century of Waltzing.* Caldwell, IN: The Caxton Printers, Ltd. More than a treatise on waltzing, this friendly book also includes polka, schottische, mazurka, two-step, and circle mixers. Lloyd ("Pappy") Shaw was one of the best teachers and researchers of traditional U.S. dances.

Shenanigans. 1986. *Dance Music of Australia's Many Cultures.* Melbourne: Author. This book has nice dance descriptions of some dances common to international folk dancers and of some dances the Shenanigans arranged themselves. All descriptions are intended for those who teach children. There are accompanying cassettes.

A Teacher's Guide to Folklife Resources for the K–12 Classroom. 1994. Washington, DC: The American Folklife Center. Single copies of this 36-page booklet are free plus postage. Contact American Folklife Center, Library of Congress, Washington, DC 20540, for curriculum guides, videos, recordings, and publications to integrate folklife into schools.

Viltis. 1942–. Milwaukee, WI: International Institute of Wisconsin. This folk dance and folklore magazine was published singlehandedly by folk dance pioneer Vyts Beliajus from 1942 until his death in September 1994. It is now published by the International Institute of Wisconsin, 1110 N. Old World Third Street, Suite 420, Milwaukee, WI 53203; its editor is the Institute's director, Alexander P. Durtka, Jr. *Viltis* is also available in microform from UMI, Dept. F.A., 300 N. Zeeb Road, Ann Arbor, MI 48106.

Weikart, Phyllis S. 1997. *Teaching Folk Dance: Successful Steps.* Ypsilanti, MI: High/Scope Press. This is *TFD*, the companion book to *Cultures and Styling in Folk Dance.* As a comprehensive guide for introducing over 200 folk dances—beginning and intermediate—to dancers of all ages, *TFD*, together with its set of dance notation cards and two teaching videos, is a good resource for teachers of music, elementary and secondary education, physical education, and special education, as well as for persons working with senior citizens. This book (*TFD*) consolidates and expands on Phyllis S. Weikart's two earlier landmark *Teaching Movement and Dance* books, also published by High/Scope Press: *A Sequential Approach to Rhythmic Movement* (1989; 4th edition in press) and *Intermediate Folk Dance* (1984). (For all related movement and music products from High/Scope Press, see p. ii.)

World Facts & Maps: Concise International Review. 1997–. Chicago: Rand McNally. This is an annual handbook on nations of the world. It gives up-to-date information on our confusing world politics and national boundaries. As events and years progress, look for current editions.

Clothing and Costumes

Crum, Richard. 1995. "Costumes." *Viltis* (March–April): 14. Reprinted from an article distributed at a 1980 costume exhibition, this article, by a top Balkan dance scholar, linguist, dancer, choreographer, and teacher, discusses the history of traditional European clothing.

Folk Dance Photos of Europe. 1996. Long Beach, CA: Wenzel Press. Photographed in southern California during dance performances, this book contains many black-and-white photos plus lists of where pictures of national costumes can be found. (Contact Wenzel Press, P.O. Box 14789-V, Long Beach, CA 90803.)

Folk Dance Photos of the World. 1996. Long Beach, CA: Wenzel Press. Photographed in southern California during dance performances, this book contains many black-and-white photos plus lists of where pictures of national costumes can be found. (Contact Wenzel Press, P.O. Box 14789-V, Long Beach, CA 90803.)

Fox, Lilla M. 1971. *Folk Costumes of Eastern Europe.* New York: Plays, Inc. Lilla Fox provides solid information with charming illustrations.

Fox, Lilla M. 1973. *Folk Costumes of Southern Europe.* New York: Plays, Inc.

Fox, Lilla M. 1977. *Folk Costumes of Western Europe.* New York: Plays, Inc.

Gorsline, Douglas. 1952. *What People Wore.* New York: Bonanza Books. This book has nearly 1800 detailed illustrations of clothing styles ranging from ancient times to the twentieth century. After classical Greece, Rome, and Egypt, the book focuses mostly on countries of central Europe, Britain, and the U.S.

Gottier, Karin. 1995. "From A-prons to Z-occoli: The A,B,C's of Native Dress." *Quo* (No. 2):2. This folklore newsletter (see *Quo* on p. 375) article is written by an expert in central European dance and folklore.

Harrold, Robert. 1978. *Folk Costumes of the World.* Dorset, UK: Blandford Press. Although this book has incomplete information, it is useful for the color plates that show clothing of many non-European cultures.

Hedrick, Susan, and Vilma Matchette. 1997. *World Colors—Dolls & Dress.* Grantsville, MD: Hobby House Press. This is a full-color tome to provide a record of the past through doll and costume history. (Available from Hobby House Press, One Corporate Drive, Grantsville, MD 21536; 301/895-3792.)

UNICEF. The annual date books have wonderful photographs of what people wear as they go about their daily lives.

Wilcox, R. Turner. 1965. *Folk and Festival Costumes of the World.* New York: Scribner's. This book has helpful information on how to make costumes.

Music

Campbell, Patricia Shehan, Ellen McCullough-Brabson, and Judith Cook Tucker. 1994. *Roots & Branches: A Legacy of Multicultural Music for Children.* Danbury, CT: World Music Press. This handsome book offers games, dances, lullabies, and songs from 23 cultures, with personal histories and loving photographs of the real people who shared their traditions. A CD or cassette is included. (Available from World Music Press, P.O. Box 2565, Danbury, CT 06813-2565; 203/748-1131.)

Canadian Folkdance Record Service. Carries recordings for the educational and folk market. (Contact 185 Spadina, Toronto, Ontario, M5T 2C6.)

Changing Directions 1–6. Phyllis S. Weikart, creative director. Ypsilanti, MI: High/Scope Press. These are six international folk music recordings (cassettes, CDs) to accompany the dances described in Phyllis S. Weikart's dance book *Teaching Folk Dance: Successful Steps.* (These dances are all discussed in *Cultures and Styling.*)

Festival Records. Carries music for the folk dance market. (Contact John Filcich, 2769 W. Pico Blvd., Los Angeles, CA 90006; 213/737-3500.)

International Folk Rhythms. Carries music, books, videos for the educational and folk dance market, plus tape recorders, etc. Also carries traditional and folksy clothing, accessories. (Contact Joan Amsterdam, P.O. Box 1402, Northbrook, IL 60065; 847/564-2880.)

Music for folk dances written out. (Contact Richard Geisler, 15181 Ballantree Lane, Grass Valley, CA 95949.)

Musica Para Todos (Music for All): *A Catalog of Multilingual Multicultural Music Materials.* 1990. San Antonio, TX: Brain Dance Ink. This is a collection of mostly Hispanic games, songs, dances, and recordings put out by Jim Ryan, a San Antonio music teacher and member of the Osage Indian tribe. The catalog also includes old-time Texas and Louisiana French materials. (Contact Brain Dance Ink, P.O. Box 681264, San Antonio, TX 78268.)

Rhythmically Moving 1–9. Phyllis S. Weikart, creative director. Ypsilanti, MI: High/Scope Press. These are nine international folk music recordings (cassettes, CDs) to accompany the dances described in Phyllis S. Weikart's dance book *Teaching Folk Dance: Successful Steps.* (These dances are all discussed in *Cultures and Styling.*) *Guides to Rhythmically Moving 1–4,* with all dance music written out, are also available from High/Scope Press.

Smithsonian Folkways. 1995, Summer. *Catalogue of Recordings.* The Smithsonian has reissued the Folkways Records on CDs and cassettes and added more. The catalogue includes American Indian Traditions and a variety of World Traditions (Armenian through Tuva). (Available from Smithsonian/Folkways Recordings, Center for Folklife Programs & Cultural Studies, 955 L'Enfant Plaza, Suite 2600, MRC 914, Washington, DC 20560.)

Vancouver International Folk Dancers Music Book, Vols. I–II. 1994. Vancouver, B.C.: Vancouver International Folk Dancers (VIFD). These are books of music transcriptions for musicians who want to play for folk dancing. Volume I emphasizes popular Balkan dance tunes, including many of those in *TFD* and *TM&D,* plus well-known non-Balkan material. Volume II is more international. The books also contain song words, translations, and metronome markings. (Contact VIFD, P.O. Box 2452, Vancouver, B.C., V6B 3W7, or Susan Pinkham at <susanp@gemcom.bc.ca>.)

World Music Press Catalogue. 1996–97. Danbury, CT: World Music Press. Judith Cook Tucker, a multicultural music specialist, has specialized in publishing top-quality multicultural music books with accompanying recordings. Current offerings include Africa to Vietnam and much in between. (Available from World Music Press, P.O. Box 2565, Danbury, CT 06813-2565; 800/810-2040.)

Worldtone Music, Inc. Recordings, equipment, much more. (Contact Kenneth Spear, 230 7th Ave., New York, NY 10011; 212/691 1934.)

Videos

Folk/Ethnic Dance Videos. This is a catalog of videos published by International Dance Discovery, 108½ E. Kirkwood Ave., Bloomington, IN 47401. The emphasis is on Oriental Dance (belly dancing), but it lists a number of other international dance videos.

Latchmo Drom (Safe Journey). 1993. This is the video of an award-winning 103-minute film featuring music and dance of the Rom people, produced by Michele Ray for K.G. Productions and distributed by France Films. (Contact Yves Moreau, P.O. Box 158, St.-Lambert, Québec, J4P 3N8; 514/659-9271; <ymoreau@odyssee.net>.)

Longden, Sanna (producer). 1991. *Favorite Folk Dances of Kids & Teachers.* 1991. Evanston, IL: FolkStyle Productions. This video shows dances for the classroom taught in actual teaching situations; it includes two for Christmas and two for Hanukkah. (Contact FolkStyle Productions, 1402 Elinor Place, Evanston IL 60201; 847/328-7793; fax 847/328-5241; <sannamars@aol.com>.)

Longden, Sanna (producer). 1996. *More Favorite Folk Dances.* Evanston, IL: FolkStyle Productions. This video shows dances for the classroom from a variety of cultures, taught in actual teaching situations. (Contact FolkStyle Productions, 1402 Elinor Place, Evanston IL 60201; 847/328-7793; fax 847/328-5241; <sannamars@aol.com>.)

Longden, Sanna (producer). 1997. *Living Ethnic Dances for Kids & Teachers.* Evanston, IL: FolkStyle Productions. This video shows dances for classroom and recreation groups taught live, juxtaposed with actual scenes from ethnic festivals, picnics, and parties. (Contact FolkStyle Productions, 1402 Elinor Place, Evanston IL 60201; 847/328-7793; fax 847/328-5241; <sannamars@aol.com>.)

Seeger, Mike, with Ruth Pershing (producer). 1992. *Talking Feet.* El Cerrito, CA: Flower Films. This video, funded by the Smithsonian and the NEA Folk Arts Program, shows solo southern dances, including buck dancing, flatfoot, and tap, with personal styles and anecdotes of 24 old-time dancers. (Contact Flower Films, 10341 San Pablo Ave., El Cerrito, CA 94530; 510/525-0942.) There's a separate companion book, also published in 1992. (Available from North Atlantic Books, 2800 Woolsey St., Berkeley, CA 94705.)

Weikart, Phyllis S. (producer). 1988–96. *Beginning Folk Dances Illustrated 1–5.* Ypsilanti, MI: High/Scope Press. These six videos show students performing many of the dances from Phyllis S. Weikart's dance books *TFD* and *TM&D,* which are also the dances discussed in this book.

Weikart, Phyllis S. (producer). 1998. *Teaching Folk Dance: Successful Steps.* Ypsilanti, MI: High/Scope Press. This teaching videotape shows Phyllis S. Weikart, an expert in movement-based active learning, as she teaches a group of fourth-graders nine different folk dances from her book *Teaching Folk Dance: Successful Steps.* The dances are presented in a motor-development progression from simple to more complex and include helpful teaching strategies to use with students of all ages.

Miscellaneous

Dance on Disc [CD-ROM]. This is a complete catalog of the dance collection of the New York Public Library. It includes all aspects of dance, from performing-art to ritual, from all cultures, and can be found in many public and university libraries.

East European Folklife Center (EEFC). The center publishes a newsletter. (Contact EEFC, P.O. Box 3969, Eugene, OR 97403; 541/344-6349; <office@eefc.org>; <http://www.eefc.org/>.)

European Community Folk Culture [CD-ROM]. This contains information for folk festival agents and organizers, folk dress enthusiasts, folk musicians, folk dancers, etc. (Contact Edinburgh Multimedia, 3 Hayfield, Edinburgh EH12 8UJ, Scotland; phone and fax +44(0) 131 339 5374; <k.gourlay@bbcnc.org.uk>.)

Folk Arts Center of New England. The center publishes a newsletter. (Contact 1950 Massachusetts Ave., Cambridge, MA 02140; 617/491-6083; <http://www.facone.org/fac>.)

Folk Dance Federation of California Research Committee. They have many notes, most of which come from syllabuses of the well-respected folk dance camps that this group runs each summer at the University of the Pacific in Stockton, CA. (Contact Bruce Mitchell, Director, 8536 Kenneth View Ct., Fair Oaks, CA 95628-2688; 916/988-7920; <http://www.uop.edu/misc/fdcamp/index.html>.)

Folk dance Web sites. For those comfortable navigating in cyberspace, Web sites are one of the best places for current information as well as historic research. A good source of up-to-date online information is the "On-ramps" column in the *Quo* newsletter (see *Quo* on p. 375).

Folkmoot USA programs. Published by the North Carolina International Folk Festival. The well-known Folkmoot USA festival, established in the mountains of western North Carolina in 1984, each summer brings in dancers from a variety of cultures for a 12-day extravaganza of music and dance. The festival programs give details of each group's performance, with information on culture, dance, music, and costumes.

Interfaith calendar. 1988–. Chicago: National Conference of Christians and Jews. To understand the world's peoples, it is also important to know about their religions. This fascinating 14-month calendar highlights one religion on each page, describing tenets and observances and telling when each holiday is celebrated that year. (Available from The National Conference, Chicago and Northern Illinois Region, 360 N. Michigan Ave., Suite 1009, Chicago, IL 60601-3803; 312/236-9272.)

Society of Folk Dance Historians. Ron Houston is founder and president of this organization, which is a particularly useful resource for people seeking background of international folk dances. The Society publishes a *Folk Dance Phone Book and Group Directory* and has growing archives that include records, syllabuses, costumes, and memorabilia from the collections of many folk dancers. (Contact Ron Houston at 2100 Rio Grande, Austin, TX 78705-5513; fax 512/478-8900; <ron@ccwf.cc.utexas.edu>.)

Thracian Bizarre. Carries traditional clothing, footwear, and accessories. Owner Maria Kaloyanova travels to camps and workshops, sends by mail. (Contact P.O. Box 403, Cary, NC 27511; 919/467-8674.)

University of Chicago Folk Dance Festival syllabuses, 1972–. The dance descriptions for these workshops (later called Fall and Spring Folk Dance Festivals) are invaluable. (Contact John Kuo, 9201 Mason, Morton Grove, IL 60053; 847/967-9822; <jkuo@VNET.IBM.com>.)

Dances Discussed in This Book

(See Index for specific pages where each dance is mentioned.)

African
- Bele Kawe
- Jambo
- Pata Pata II (usually called *Pata Pata*)
- Tant' Hessie

Andean
- Carnavalito

Armenian
- Armenian Misirlou, also *Sirdes*
- Hooshig Mooshig
- Soude Soude
- Sweet Girl
- Toi Nergis, also *Hoy Nergiz*

Assyrian
- Sheikani, or *Sheikhani*

Bulgarian
(Note: Dance names are transliterated from the Cyrillic alphabet, so spelling variations might exist in other sources.)
- Baldâzka
- Bičak
- Bregovsko Horo
- Dajčovo Horo
- Delčevsko Horo
- Dobrolŭshko, or *Dobroluško Horo*
- Eleno Mome
- Jambolsko Pajduško Horo
- Kjustendilska Ruchenitsa, or *Râčenitsa*
- Kulsko Horo
- Lilka
- Neda Voda Nalivala
- Novo Zagorsko Horo
- Osmica
- Pasarelska
- Plevensko Dajčovo Horo
- Porunceasca
- Pravo Horo
- Shopsko, or *Šopsko, Za Pojas*
- Sitno Zhensko, or *Žensko*
- Trŭgnála, or *Trâgnala, Rumjana*
- Za Pojas

Czech and Slovak
- Doudlebska Polka
- Horehronsky Czárdás

Danish
- Danish Masquerade
- Danish Sextur, or *Familie Sekstur*
- Seven Jumps

English
- Cumberland Square (also called *Cumberland Square Eight*)
- Hole in the Wall
- Sellenger's Round

French
- An Dro
- Bannielou Lambaol, or *La Ridée*
- Gavotte d'Honneur
- Le Laridé
- Branle Normand

French-Canadian
- La Bastringue
- Les Saluts

German
- Bekendorfer Quadrille
- D'Hammerschmiedsg'selln
- Man in the Hay
- Sauerländer Quadrille, or *Sauerländer Quadrille #5*
- Zigeunerpolka

Greek

(*Note:* Many of these names are generic; there may be other patterns or choreographies with the same names. Because the names are transliterated from the Greek alphabet, there are likely to be spelling variations in other sources. A tendency among choreographers to drop accent marks leads us to drop them here, also.)

Ais Giorgis
Argos Hasapikos
Chiotikos
Dirlada, sometimes *Dirlanda*
Fissouni
Hasapikos
Hasaposervikos
Iatros
Ikariotikos
Kalamatianos
Kamara
Karagouna
Karagouna (9-part)
Koftos
Kritikos Syrtos
Lakhana
Laziko
Lefkaditikos
Lemonaki
Len Irthe Mais
Makedonikos Horos
Makrinitsa
Misirlou-Kritikos
Nizamikos
Palamakia/Koftos
Pentozalis
Pogonissios
Rebetic Hasapikos
Silivrianos, or *Kykladitikos Syrtos*
Soultana
Syrtaki #7
Syrtos
Tai Tai
Trata
Tsakonikos
Tsamikos
Vari (Varys) Hasapikos
Zagoritikos
Zervos Karpathos
Zonaradikos
Zorba

Hungarian

(*Note:* Spelling and accents of Hungarian dance names may vary slightly from source to source.)

Circle Csárdás, sometimes *Körcsárdás*
Körcsárdás I
Körcsárdás II
Körtánc
Lákodálmi Tánc
Mátrai Verbunk
Oláhos
Palóc Táncok
Somogyi Csárdás
Somogyi Karikázó
Szakacsne Tánc
Ugrós

Irish

Irish Lilt

Israeli and Jewish

Arabic-Influence

Debka Benot Hakfar
Debka Chag
Debka Daluna
Debka Dayagim
Debka Druz
Debka Kurdit
Debka Le Adama
Horat Hasor
Ken Yovdu
Kol Dodi
Marhaba
Mishal
Sapari
Ya Abud

Chassidic-Influence

Bechatzar Harabbi
Hora Bialik
Hora Chadera
Hora Hassidit

Tzadik Katamar
Zemer Atik

European-Influence
Bisdot Bet-Lechem
Cherkessiya, or *Tcherkessiya*
Hora
Romanian Hora
Tarantella
Ve David

Yemenite-Influence
Ahavat Hadassah
Al Gemali
At Va'ani
Betof Utzlil
Dodi Li
Dror Yikra
Haschachar
Hineh Ma Tov
Im Ninalu
Ki Hivshiloo
Le'Or Chiyuchech
Likrat Shabat
Ma Na'vu, or *Ma Na'avu*
Mit Yitneini Ohf
Sapri Tama
Tzlil Zugim

Homeland-Influence
Ana Halach Dodech
Bat Arad
Bat Hareem
Bat Tsurim
Eretz Zavat Chalav
Erev Ba
Hadarim
Harmonica
Haroa Haktana
Hashual
Haya Ze Basadeh
Hora Agadati
Hora Chemed
Hora Eilat
Hora Medurah
Hora Nirkoda
Hora Or
Kalu Raglayim

Kuma Echa
Lamnatseach
Lech Lamidbar
Machar
Mayim
Mechol Hagat
Niguno Shel Yossi
Rav B'rachot
Ronee Bat Tsion
Sham Hareh Golan
Sharm-el-Sheikh
Shibolet Basadeh
Shiru Hashir
Sulam Ya'akov
Te Ve Orez
Uri Zion
U'va'u Ha'ovdim
Yibunei Hamigdash

Italian (Sicilian)
Sicilian Tarantella, or *Tarantella Siciliana*

Japanese
Tanko Bushi

Mexican
Azul Cielo
Corrido
La Raspa
Mexican Mixer
Polka Alegre
Santa Rita

Philippine
Apat-Apat

Portuguese and Brazilian
Fado Blanquita

Romanian
(*Note:* The spellings and diacritical marks used here may vary slightly from those found in other sources.)
Alunelul
Bätuta
Boereasca

Brîul Pe Opt
Ciuleandra
Ciocârlanul
Dragaicuţa
Floricica
Frunza
Hora de la Rişipiţi
Hora Nuţii
Hora Pe Gheaţa
Hora Spoitorilor
Mîndrele
Paiduşca
Pomoleţul
Rustemul
Trei Păzeşte Bătrinesc
Trei Păzeşte de la Bistret
Vulpiţa

Russian

Katia, also Our Katia
Kohanochka
Korobushka
Troika

Scottish

Road to the Isles

Swedish

Fjäskern

Turkish

Ali Paşa
Güzelleme
Işte Hendek
Karşilama
Kendime

United States

Alley Cat
Amos Moses
Bossa Nova
Good Old Days
Hot Pretzels II
Jessie Polka
The Little Shoemaker
Twelfth Street Rag

Former Yugoslav Republics

Slovenian

Zibnšrit

Croatian

Ajde Noga Za Nogama
Drmeš Iz Zdenčine
Drmeš Medley
Dučec
Hopa, Hopa
Kiša Pada
Kriči Kriči Tiček
Moja Diridika
Slavonsko Kolo
Sukačko Kolo

Serbian

Ajde Jano
Bosarka
Čarlama
Djurdjevka Kolo
Ersko Kolo
Fatiše Kolo
Gružanka
Jeftanovičevo Kolo
Kokonješte
Makazice Kolo
Milanovo Kolo
Nebesko Kolo
Neda Grivne
Orijent
Pinosavka
Pljeskavac Kolo
Preplet
Rumunjsko Kolo
Sarajevka Kolo
Savila Se Bela Loza
Seljančica Kolo
Šestorka from Bela Palanka
Šetnja
Srbijanka
U Šest
Vranjanka
Vranjsko Kolo
Zaplanjski Čačak
Žikino Kolo

Macedonian
- Arap
- Belasičko Oro
- Četvorka
- Deninka
- Dimna Juda
- Dimna Juda Mamo
- Gaida Avasi
- Ivanica, or Ivanice
- Jovano Jovanke
- Kasapsko Oro
- Katushe (or Katuše) Mome
- Kosovsko Lesno Oro
- Kostursko Oro
- Legnala Dana
- Lesnoto Oro
- Makedonsko Bavno Oro
- Makrinitsa
- Povrateno
- Skudrinka
- Tino Mori
- Tri Godini Kate
- Vrni Se Vrni
- Žalna Majka

Phyllis S. Weikart Choreographies
- Big Circle Dance
- Bulgarian Dance #1
- Close Encounters
- Count 64
- Erev Shel Shoshanim
- Gaelic Waltz
- Hot Pretzels I
- Hustle
- Instant Success
- Irish Mixer
- Irish Stew
- Jamaican Holiday I
- Jamaican Holiday II
- Joe Clark Mixer
- Limbo Rock
- Little Shoemaker
- Nigun
- Oh, How Lovely
- Pata Pata I
- Popcorn
- Progressive Circle Dance
- Sliding
- Sneaky Snake
- Soldier's Joy Contra
- Spanish Coffee
- Tipsy I
- Tipsy II
- Two-part Dance
- Yankee Doodle
- Zigeunerpolka

Index

(Boldface type indicates the dances from Phyllis S. Weikart's books that are discussed in this book.)

A

Aeschylus, 150
Ahavat Hadassah, 199
Ais Giorgis, 140, 146
Ajde Jano, 349, 354–55
Ajde Noga Za Nogama, 7, 340
Aksak. *See* Assymetric meters
Al Gemali, 199
Ali Paşa, 310, 313–14, 317
Alley Cat, 322–24
Alunelul, 256, 260–63, 265
Alunelul Batut, 260
Alunelul de la Goicea, 260
Amos Moses, 322, 324
Ana Halach Dodech, 203–4
An Dro, 108–10, 112
Apat-Apat, 238, 240, 242
Aquino, Francisca, 240
Arap (Zajko Kokorajko), 358–60, 363
Arbeau, Thoinot, 109–10
Argos Hasapikos, 140
Armenian Misirlou (Sirdes), 46, 49
Armstrong, Marie, 323
Ashkenazi Jews, 188
Assymetric meters (uncommon meters), 70, 150, 154, 266, 317, 354, 359, 362
Assyrians, 57–58
At Va'ani, 199
Austro-Hungarian Empire, 77, 159, 229, 333–34
Aztecs, 229–30
Azul Cielo, 228, 230, 234

B

Balatee, 58
Baldâzka, 64
Balkan Ghosts (Kaplan), 334
Balkans, 65, 257, 333
Ballet Folklorico of Mexico, 13
Bannielou Lambaol (La Ridée), 108–10, 112
Bari-yerker, 52
Barn dancing, 100
Barnes de Angeles, Alura Flores, 230
Bartók, Béla, 160
Bat Arad, 203
Bat Hareem, 203
Bat Tsurim, 203
Bătuta, 256, 264
B.C.E., n. 47
Bechatzar Harabbi, 194–95
Bekendorfer Quadrille, 128–31, 134–35
Belasičko Oro, 358, 361
Bele Kawe, 8, 30–32, 34
Beliajus, Vyts, 49, 247, 278–79, 348
Belly dancing (Oriental dance), 313
Betof Utzlil, 199
Bičak, 64, 70
Big Circle Dance, 370
Bisdot Bet-Lechem, 198
Black Lamb and Grey Falcon (West), 334
Bloland, Sunni, 260, 263–64
Boereasca, 256, 264
Bokázo, 279
Bon odori, 221
Bonuš, František, 77
Bosarka, 349, 351

Bossa Nova, 322, 326
Bourrée, 5
Boxell, Dennis, 58, 348
Bozigian, Tom, 49–50
Branle Normand, 108–10, 112
Branles, 109–10
Bregovsko Horo, 64
Bridge of Athlone, The, 177
Brîul Pe Opt, 256, 263
Bulgarian Dance #1, 370
Bunjevačko Momačko Kolo, 339
Bygdedans, 301
Byzantine Empire, 142, 333

C

Caballito Blanco, 247
Canon valser, 371
Carignan, Jean, 123
Cariñosa, 239
Čarlama, 349, 350–51
Carnavalito, 40–43
Cassatschok, 187
C.E., n. 47
Ceilidh (ceili) dances, 177, 291–92. *See* Set dances
Celts, 97, 109, 177, 289
Četvorka, 358, 360–61
Chain dances, 68, 109, 143, 145, 149
Changing Directions (Weikart), 24
Charleston, 323, 326
Chassidic dance, 194–95, 197
Chassidic Jews, 188
Cherkessiya, 198
Chicano, 229
Chiotikos, 140, 146
Chotis. *See* Schottische

Ciocărlanul, 256, 262–63
Circassian Circle, 198
Circle Csárdás, 158, 162–63, 168–69, ill. 170
Circle dances, 89, 145, 189, 199, 258–60, 275, 335. *See also* Hora
Ciuleandra, 256, 258
Clark, Sibyl, 100
Clogging, 11, 180, 225
Close Encounters, 370
Clothing, traditional. *See also* shoes
  dirndl, 137
  fez, 318
  foustanella, 148
  galabiyeh, 193
  hachimaki, 225
  kafiyah, 194
  kilt, 293, 295,
  kimono, ill. 224, 225
  lederhosen, 137
  masks, 34
  obi, ill. 224, 225
  patadyong, 242
  rebozo, 235
  şalvar, 318
  sarafan, 281
  serape, 235
  sporran, 295
  tabi, 7, ill. 224, 225
  tsamika, 154
  yarmulka (kipah), 204
  yukata, 225
Communism, 159, 161, 239, 257, 273. *See also* Soviet Union
Contra dances, 23, 97, 289
Corrido, 228, 230–31, 234
Cotillions, 119
Count 64, 370
Country Dance and Song Society of America, 100
Country dances, 99–100, 289–90
Country/western dance, 11, 324
Couple dancing, 77, 89, 199, 221, 232, 290, 314, 336
Crum, Richard (Dick), 26, 260, 278–79, 335–36, 339–41, 346, 348, 351, 360
Crusades, 311

Csárdás, 79, 160-61, 163–64, 168, 339
Cueca, 42
Cugat, Xavier, 143
Cumberland Square, 100–101, 103–4
Czárdás, 79, ill. 80, 83.
Czompo, Andor, 161

D

Dajčovo, 70
Dajčovo Horo 19, 64, 70
Dance etiquette, 19–22, 136
Dance figures and movements
  arches, 280
  arming, 102–3
  arm swing, 43, 112, 134
  ballroom swing, 119
  basket turn, 132
  buzz turn, 35–36, 90, 92, 103, 121, ill. 123, 132, 198
  cast-off, 101–2, 104
  do-si-do, 35–36
  doubling, 102
  hallingkast (high kick), ill. 9
  Israeli swing, 204
  kolo, 351
  pas de bas (quick two-step), 169, 233
  pas de basque, 289
  poussette, 289
  prisyadki, 280
  progression, 104
  rhumba style, 326
  right-elbow swing, 121
  saludo, 242
  siding, 102
  skirt work, 233
  slide steps, 132
  underarm turn, 121
Dance hand and arm positions
  back basket-hold, 50, 103, 166, ill. 167, 169, 343, ill. 345
  belt-hold, ill. 15, 69, 149, 263, 265, 353, 361
  clasped hand, 315, ill. 316
  debka hand-hold, 59
  double arm-hold, 36
  elbow turns, 102–3
  escort-hold, 148, 353

front basket-hold, 25, 69, 134, 149, 166, ill. 167, 169, 265, 343, ill. 344, 361
  Kurdish hand-hold, 192
  modified ballroom, 36
  pinkie-hold, 50–52, 112, 314, 317
  promenade hold, 103
  shoulder-shoulder-blade, ill. 91, ill. 168, 168–69
  shoulder-to-shoulder, 59, 192–93, 315, ill. 316, 317
  shoulder-waist, 81, ill. 91, 168
  skater's hold, 121
  T-position (shoulder-hold), 50–51, 69, 148, ill. 149, 152, 166, ill. 167, 168, 192–93, 195, 261, ill. 262, 263, 265, 361
  varsovienne, 103, 278, 292–93
  V-position (hands joined down at sides), 69, 81, 90, 134, 148, 166, ill. 167, 168–69, 192, 195, 200, 204, 248, 263, 265, 277, 317, 353, 361
  W-position (hands joined with elbows bent), 50, 69, 92, 112, 134, 148, ill. 149, 152–54, 180, 242, 262, 277, 314, 317, 351, 353, 361, ill. 362
Dance props, 239–40, 242. *See also* Handkerchief
Dance steps and patterns
  bleking step, 232
  Cherkessiya (Tcherkessiya), 262
  cifra step, 165, 169
  csárdás step, 165
  čukče step, 359–60
  debka hop, 202
  drmeš step, 341
  grapevine, 25, 198, 202, 204, 260, 280, 292
  heel-toe, 234
  hop-step-step, 70
  hora step, 152
  kick-step, 280
  kolo pattern, 351
  Neheimer step, 134
  polka step, 134, 233, 277, 281
  reverse two-step, 59, 153
  rida step, 83, 165
  schottishe step, 43, 134, 248, 251, 279, 292

step-bend, 35
step-hop, 43, 89, 134–35, 337
two-step, 50, 52, 104, 122, 169, 277, 281
Yemenite step, 200, 202, 369
Danish Masquerade, 88–90, 92
Danish Sextur (Familie Sekstur), 88–90, 92
David, Mihai, 264
Debka Benot Hakfar, 191–92
Debka Chag, 191
Debka Daluna, 191–92
Debka Dayagim, 191–92
Debka Druz, 191
Debka Kurdit, 191–93
Debka Le Adama, 191
Debka style, 59
Delčevsko Horo, 64
Democracy, 65, 77, 239, 273, 312
Deninka (Ordan Sedi), 358–60, 363
D'Hammerschmiedsg'selln, 128–32, 134
Diaspora, 47, 57, 187
Dicks, Dottie, 323
Dimna Juda, 358–59, 361–62
Dimna Juda Mamo, 358, 361–62
Dirlada, 140, 146
Djurdjevku Kolo, 349
Dobrolŭshko, 64
Dodi Li, 199
Doina, 266
Dor, Moshe, 371
Doudlebska Polka (Czech Polka), 76–77, 79–84
Douglass Schottische, 291
Dracula, Count, 257
Dragaicuţa, 23, 256, 264
Drmeš, 341
Drmes Iz Zdenčine, 340, 343
Drmeš Medley, 340, 343
Dror Yikra, 199
Drury, Nelda, 232
Dučec, 340

Duncan, Isadora, 189
Dunsing, Gretel and Paul, 133
Duquesne University Tamburitzans, 12, 339, 346

E

El Cinco de Mayo, 229
Eleno Mome, 8, 64
El Jarabe Tapatío. See Mexican Hat Dance
English Country Dance and Song Society, 100
English Dancing Master, The (Playford), 101
Eretz Zavat Chalav, 203–4
Erev Ba, 203
Erev Shel Shoshanim, 19, 370–71
Ersko Kolo, 349, 352
Evanchuk, Vincent, 277

F

Fado, 247
Fado Blanquita, 246–48, 251
Fall of Yugoslavia, The (Glenny), 334
Farwell, Jane, 89, 92, 133, 301, 371
Fatiše Kolo, 349, 350, 354
Ferdinand, Archduke Franz, 333
Festou noz, 109
Figure dances, 103
Filcich, John, 348
Fissouni, 140
Fjäskern (Hurry Scurry), 298–99, 301, 303
Flatley, Michael, 179
Floricica, 256, 264
Folk ballet, 12, 50
Folk Dance Federation of California, 213
Folk Dance Problem Solver (1995, Houston), 79
Folk dances
authenticity of, 11
gender segregation in, 8–11, 23, 232
music for, 23–24
regional identification of, 5
and religions, 8. *See also* Religion
similarities of, 8
Folk process, 19
Freestyle dances. *See* Improvisational dances
Frunza, 256, 262–63

G

Gadd, May, 100
Gaelic Waltz, 370
Gaida Avasi, 357–58, 361
Gamliel, Eliyahu, 371
Gammaldans (round dance), 301
Gankino, 70
Gavotte d'Honneur, 108, 110, 112
Gavottes, 109, 110, 112
Gelman, Morry and Nancy, ill. 137
Gemini, 24
Gender roles, in folk dance, 8–11, 23, 232. *See also* Gender segregation
Gender segregation, 8, 11, 23, 31, 49, 68, 145, 194, 232, 264–65, 303, 313–14, 351, 360–61
Gigue, 119
Giurchescu, Anca, 260
Glass, Henry ("Buzz"), 326, 371
Glenny, Misha, 334
Goobareh, 58
Good Old Days, 322, 326
Gopak, 275
Gottier, Karin, 132
Graham, Martha, 189
Greek Folkloric Celebration, A (Karras), 145
Green, Madelynne, 109
Gružanka, 349
Gurzau, Elba Farabegoli, 211, 213
Güzelleme, 310, 313–15, 317

Index 391

Gypsies, 83, 160, 171, 187, 266, 355, 363

H

Hadar, Josef, 371
Hadarim, 203
Hambo, 302
Handkerchief, use of, 147–48, 154, 240, 314, 317, 353, 360–61
Hapsburg Dynasty, *See* Austro-Hungarian Empire
Harmonica, 203–4
Haroa Haktana, 203–4
Hasapikos, 8, 24, 140, 143, 152–53
Hasaposervikos, 140, 152
Haschachar, 199
Hashual, 203
Haya Ze Basadeh, 203
Hébert, Germain, 109
Helms-Blasche, Anna, 131
Hendrickson, Charles, 104
Henry, David, 353
Herman, Mary Ann and Michael, 79, 89, 133, 278–80, 348
Hermans' Folk Dance House, 260
Highland Fling, 290
"Highlife" dances, 31, ill. 33, 34
Hineh Ma Tov, 199
Hofman, Huig, 35, 131
Hole in the Wall, 8, 96, 101–2, 104
Hooshig Mooshig, 46, 49, 51–52
Hopa, Hopa, 340
Hopsa, 89
Hora (circle dance), 8, 19, 65, 68–69, 198, 202, 258–60, 275
Hora Agadati, 203
Hora Bialik, 194–95
Hora Chadera, 194–95
Hora Chemed, 203
Hora de la Rișipiți, 256
Hora Eilat, 203–4

Hora Hassidit, 194
Hora Mare, 258
Hora Medurah, 203
Hora Nirkoda, 203–4
Hora Nuții, 256
Hora Or, 203
Hora Pe Gheața, 8, 256, 258, 262–63
Horas, 58, 187, 189, 258–60, 262, 265
Hora Spoitorilor, 256
Horat Hasor, 191
Horehronsky Czárdás, 23, 76–77, 79–84
Hornpipes, 104, 177
Horo. See Hora
Horovodnaya pliaska, 275
Hot Pretzels I, 370
Hot Pretzels II, 322, 326
Houston, Ron, 109
Hurry Scurry, (Fjäskern), 298–99, 301, 303
Hristovski, Jonche, 359
Hustle, 370

I

Iatros, 140
Ikariotikos, 140
Ikema, Hiroyuki, 221
Im Ninalu, 199
Improvisational dances, 146–47, 165, 275, 313–15, 335, 350
Inca culture, 41
Individual dances, 31, 35, 324, ill. 325, 328
Instant Success, 370
International folk dancing. *See* Recreational folk dancing
Irish Lilt, 8, 176–79
Irish Mixer, 370
Irish Stew, 370
Irish Washerwoman, 180
Işte Hendek, 310, 313–15, 317
Ivanica, 358–60, 363

J

Jamaican Holiday I, 370
Jamaican Holiday II, 370
Jambo, 30–32
Jambolsko Pajduško Horo, 24, 64, 70
Japanese Folk Dance Federation, 221
Jaques-Dalcroze, Emile, 189
Jeftanovičevo Kolo, 348–49, 352
Jessie Polka (Cowboy Polka), 322, 326–27
Jigs, 8, 104, 119, 177
 couple, 180
 double, 178, 180
 solo, 179
Joe Clark Mixer, 370
Jordanoff, Nick, 12
Jota, 5
Joukowsky, Anatol, 80, 277, 348
Jovano Jovanke, 358–60, 363
Jugentanz, 189

K

Kalamatianos, 140, 143, 154
Kalu Raglayim, 203–4
Kamara, 140
Kaplan, Robert, 334
Karagouna, 7, 140
Karagouna (9-part), 140
Karikázó, 161–62
Karras, Athan, 144–45
Karşilama, 310, 313–14, 317
Kasapsko Oro, 358, 360
Katia, 272, 275, 277, 281
Katushe (or *Katuše*) *Mome*, 358, 362
Kendime, 7, 310, 313–14, 317
Ken Yovdu, 191
Khigga, 58
Kibbutz, 187, 189
Ki Hivshiloo, 199
Kiša Pada, 340, 343

Kjustendilska Ruchenitsa, 64, 70
Klezmer music, 188, 195
Kodály, Zoltán, 160, 371
Koenig, Martin, 263
Koftos, 140
Kohanochka, 272, 275, 277–78, 281
Kokonješte, 348–49
Kol Dodi, 189, 191
Kolos, 8, 335–36, 339, 341, ill. 342, 346, 348–50
Kopačka, 363
Kopanica, 70
Koprivshtitsa Festival, 65
Körcsárdás I, 158, 165
Körcsárdás II, 158, 165
Korobushka, 272, 275, 278–81
Körtánc, 158, 165, 169
Kosovsko Lesno Oro, 358–61
Kostursko Oro, 358–60, 361
Kotansky, Steve, 351
Krakowiaks, 187
Kriči Kriči Tiček, 8, 25, 340, 343
Kritikos Syrtos, 140
Kuharski, Michael, 260
Kulbitsky, Olga, 21
Kulsko Horo, 64
Kumu Echa, 6, 203

L

La Bastringue, 24, 118–21
Lado, 339
La Furlana, 209
Lakhana, 140
Lákodálmi Tánc, 7, 23, 158, 162, 166
Lamnatseach, 203
Landis, Avis, 230
Långdans, 301
La Raspa, 228, 231–32, 234
Laziko, 140

Leading, 9–11, 21, 59, 147, 149–50, 152–54, 314, 335, 352
Lech Lamidbar, 203–4
Lefkaditikos, 140
Legnala Dana, 8, 358–59, 363
Le Laridé (Laridé), 8, 108, 110, 112
Lemonaki, 140
Le Mystère des Voix Bulgares, 70
Len Irthe Mais, 140
Le'Or Chiyuchech, 199
Le Saratoga, 119
Lesnoto, 359–60
Lesnoto Oro, 24, 358–60
Les Saluts, 118–23
Lester, Roo, 303
Let's Dance, vol. C (Folk Dance Federation of California), 213
Likrat Shabat, 199
Lilka, 64, 70
Limbo Rock, 370–71
Lind-Sinanian, Susan and Gary, 49
Line dances, 21, 109, 145, 191, 199, 324, 335
Little Shoemaker, The, 322, 328, 370
Living Ethnic Dances for Kids & Teachers (Longden), 145
Longden, Sanna, 92, 133, 145
Longways dances, 22, 97, 177, 289, 301, 336
"Lord of the Dance," 179
Lucaci, Larisa, 260–61

M

Machar, 203–4
Macrobeat, 135
Magtanim, 240, 242
Magyar, Judith and Kálmán, 161
Makazice Kolo, 349
Makeba, Miriam, 35–36
Makedonikos Horos, 140

Makedonsko Bavno Oro, 8, 358–60
Makrinitsa, 140, 358–59, 361
Malo kolo, 350
Ma Na'vu (or *Ma Na'avu*), 199
Man in the Hay, 128–32, 134
Marhaba, 191–92
Mariachi, 234
Mátrai Verbunk, 23, 80, 158, 162, 164, 167
Mayan culture, 229
May Day Eve, 299
Mayim, 189, 203–4
Mazurka, 77, 230, 339
Mechol Hagat, 203
Men's dances. *See* Gender segregation
Messager, Jeanne, 109
Mestizo, 41, 229
Methodist Recreational Lab, 323
Mevlevi, 312
Mexican Hat Dance, 230–31
Mexican Mixer, 228, 232, 234
Milanovo Kolo, 349
Milligan, Jean, 289
Mîndrele, 256, 264
Minuet, 11, 99
Mishal, 191
Misirlou, 25
Misirlou-Kritikos, 140, 143
Mit Yitneini Ohf, 199
Mixers, 82, 89, 119, 232, 240, 279, 281, 326, 328
Modifying dances, general guidelines, 24–25
Moiseyev, Igor, 275
Moiseyev Dance Company, 13, 50, 275
Mohammedans, 239
Moja Diridika, 340, 343
Mon Pere Avait un Petit Bois, 112
Moreau, Yves, 28, 109, 119, 122, 360
Morris dances, 97, 99–100

Musical instruments
  accordion, 60, 112, ill. 113, 252, 293, 337, 345, 355
  agogo bells, 32
  bagpipes, 293, 305, 317
  balalaika, 281, ill. 282
  bayan (button accordion), 281, ill. 283
  biniou (a bagpipe), 112, ill. 113
  bodhran (Irish drum), 181
  bods, 193
  bombarde, 112
  bombos, 43
  bongo drums, 32
  bouzouki, 142, 146, 150
  castanets, 242
  Celtic harp, 112, 181
  charangos, 43
  cimbalom (*cymbalom* or hammered dulcimer), 83, ill. 170, 171, 266
  darabuka, 193, 317
  davoul/tahul, 52, 60, 317
  desert flutes, 193
  domra, 281, ill. 282
  double gongs, 32
  duda, 171
  duduk (a seven-holed whistle), 70
  fiddle, 293, 304
  finger cymbals, 252
  frula, 354
  gâdulka (a bowed fiddle), 70
  gâida (*gajda* or bagpipe), 70, 150, 354, 363
  gamelan, 242, ill. 243
  goat horns, 305
  gourds, 32, 234
  gusla, 354
  herding flutes, 305
  hurdy-gurdy (*vielle*), 112, ill. 113, 171
  Jaw harp (Jew's harp), 214
  kanoons, 193
  kaval, 70, 317, 363
  klarino (clarinet), 150
  koto, 225
  lyra, 150
  marimbas, 234
  marranzana, 214
  metal sticks, 242
  naï, 266
  nyckelharpa, 305
  ocarina, 70, 234
  o-daiko (taiko), 221
  ood, 60
  psaltery, 281, ill. 282
  quârtara, 214
  quenas, 43
  recorders, 32
  reed pipes, 234
  saz, 317
  shakers, 32
  shakuhachi, 225
  shamisen, 225
  sicu (panpipe), 43
  sonagliera, 214
  tambourines, 213–14, 317
  tambura (*tamburo, tamburitza*, a fretted lute), 70, 171, 214, 344, 346, 354, 363
  tâpan (*tupan*), 70, 354, 363
  tárogató, 171
  tulum, 317
  ütögardon, 171
  voice, 70, 234, 265, 317, 346, 355, 363
  wooden pipes, 32
  wooden spoons, 123, ill. 124, 281, 317
  zither, 171
  zourna (*zurna*, oboe), 52, 60, 70, 317
My Love Is But a Lassie Yet, 104

N
Nebesko Kolo, 348–50
Neda Grivne, 349
Neda Voda Nalivala, 7, **64**
Never on Sunday, 142, 152
Nigun, 370
Niguno Shel Yossi, 203
Nizamikos, 141
Noh theater, 220
Nord, Heinrich, 131
Norteño dances, 230, 232, 235
Novak, Jeannette, 79
Novelty dances, 323, 326
Novo Zagorsko Horo, 64

O
Oh, How Lovely, 370–71
O'Keefe Slide/Kerry Slide, 180

Oláhos, 158, 162, 168
Omorean, John, 258, 263
Orchesography (Arbeau), 109–10
Ordan Sedi (*Deninka*), 363
Oriental dance (belly dancing), 313
Orijent, 348–49, 352
Oro, 335
Osmica, 64
Ottoman Empire, 8, 47, 49, 65, 142, 153, 159, 257, 266, 311–12, 314, 333, 344, 351, 357, 360
Özkök, Bora, 312–13

P
Pachpi Kozh, 112
Pagtanim, 240
Paiduşca, 256, **264**
Pajduşko, 70
Palais Glide, 291–92
Palamakia/Koftos, 141
Palóc Táncok, **158**, **162**
Pasadoble, 230
Pasarelska, **64**, **70**
Pas de bas. See Dance figures and movements
Pata Pata I, 370
Pata Pata II, 30, 35–36
Pavlova, Anna, 248
Pennsylvania Polka, The, 150
Pentozalis, 141
Percussive dances
  clog dancing, 11, 119, 121, 180, 202, 225
  flamenco, 180
  gaucho, 180
  hard-shoe types, 179
  kathak, 180
  stamping rhythms, 179
  tap dancing, 180
Pinosavka, 349, 353
Playford, John, 101
Playparty games, 119
Plevensko Dajčovo Horo, **64**, **70**

Pljeskavac Kolo, **349, 350, 353**
Pogonissios, **141**
Polka Alegre, **228, 232–33**
Polkas, 77, 83, 99, 131, 230, 277–78, 301, 328, 339
Polska, 301–2
Pomoleţul, **256, 264**
Popcorn, **370**
Popescu-Judetz, Eugenia and Gheorge, 260, 263
Porunceasca, **64**
Poskočice, 355
Povrateno, **358–61**
Pravo, 70
Pravo Horo, **8, 24, 64**
Preplet, **349, 351**
Presto, Nils, 303
Progressive Circle Dance, **104, 370**
Progressive dances, 104

Q
Quadrilles, 119, 129–31, 135, 301
Quebradito, 230

R
Râčenitsa, **70**
Rampi Rampi, 317
Rav B'rachot, **203**
Rebetic Hasapikos, **141, 152**
Recreational folk dancing, 13, 20
Reed, Jerry, 324
Reel of the 51st Regiment, 295
Reels, 104, 119, 123, 177
Reeves, Nina, 326
Reigen, 129
Religion, 8, 34, 42, 47, 49, 57, 97, 110, 129, 159–62, 177–88, 187–88, 194–96, 219, 221, 239, 273, 289, 299, 311–12, 314, 333, 339
Rhythmically Moving (Weikart), 24
Rhythmic vocalization, 314
Ridée (Laridé), 109–10, 112

Riley, Martha, 104
"Riverdance," 179
Road to the Isles, **288, 290–93**
Roman Empire, 97, 129, 142, 187, 257, 266, 289, 311, 333
Romanian Hora, **19, 198**
Romanian State Folk Ensemble, 264
Ronee Bat Tsion, **203–4**
Roubanis, 143
Round dances, 110, 119, 129, 301
chain, 162
couple, 101, 290
women's, 165
Royal Scottish Country Dance Society, 289
Rumunjsko Kolo, **264, 349, 350**
Russian Dance Sport Association, 275
Rustemul, **256, 258, 264**

S
Sabras, 188
Sally Down the Alley, 323
Saltarello, 209
Samba, 371
Santa Lucia Day, 299
Santa Rita, **8, 228, 232–33**
Sapari, **191**
Sapri Tama, **199**
Sarajevka Kolo, **349, 350, 354**
Sauerländer Quadrille, **128–32, 134–35**
Savila Se Bela Loza, **349, 352–53**
Scandinavia, 89, 299
Schottis. See Schottische
Schottische, 5, 77, 230, 248, 251, 279, 292
Schuhplattler, 134
Schutzenberger, Erna, 132
Seljančica Kolo, **349, 354–55**
Sellenger's Round, **96, 101–4**
Semitic people, 57, 187
Sephardic Jews, 188

Servihasapikos, **152, ill. 153**
Šestorka from Bela Palanka, **349, 351**
Set dances, 177
Šetnja, **348–49, 353, 355**
Seven Jumps, **88–89, 92**
"7s and 3s" pattern, 336
Sham Hareh Golan, **202**
Sharm-el-Sheikh, **202**
Sharp, Cecil, 100–102
Sheikani, **56, 58**
Shibolet Basadeh, **203**
Shiru Hashir, **203**
Shoes
  cârvuli, 72
  geta, 7, 225
  ghillies, 293
  hard-shoes, 179, ill. 181
  opanki (opanci), 72, 347, 355, ill. 356, 364
  sabots, 110, ill. 111, 114
  zori, 225
Shopsko (or Šopsko) Za Pojas, **64**
Shottish. See Schottische
Shtetl, 187, 202
Sicilian Tarantella (or Tarantella Siciliana), **208, 210–11, 213**
Siege of Carrick, 177
Silivrianos (Kykladitikos Syrtos), **141**
Singing, and folk dance, 8, 52, 68, 162, 195, 202, 225, 242, 259, 363
Sîrba, 264, 350
Sitno Zhensko (or Žensko), **64**
Skudrinka, 358
Slavonsko Kolo, **340, 343**
Sliding, **370**
Sneaky Snake, **370**
Sobor, 357
Soldier's Joy Contra, **104, 370**
Somogyi Csárdás, **158, 162–63, 168–69**
Somogyi Karikázó, **158, 162, 164**
Soude Soude, **46, 49, 52**
Soultana, **141, 146**

Soviet Union, 47, 65, 77, 159, 161, 257, 273
Spanish-American War, 239
Spanish Coffee, 370
Spivak, Rayah, 371
Springars, 301
Square dances, 35, 100, 132
Srbijanka, 348–49
State Academic Ensemble of Popular Dance of the Soviet Union, The. *See* Moiseyev Dance Company
Step dances, 177–78
Stivell, Alan, 112
Stockton Folk Dance Camp, 260, 277
Stoker, Bram, 257
Strauss, Johann Jr., 160
Strigaturi, 265
Sukačica, 340
Sukačko Kolo, 7, 340, 343
Sulam Ya'akov, 203
Sweet Girl (Siroon Aghchig), 46, 49–50, 52
Sword dances, 97
Syrtaki #7, 141, 144, 146, 152
Syrtos, 24, 141, 143, 153–54
Szakacsne Tánc, 158, 162, 166, 168

T

Tai Tai, 141, 146
Takirari, 42
Tamburashi, 346
Táncház, 161, 172
Tanko Bushi, 7, 218, 221–22
Tant' Hessie, 30, 35–36
Tarantella, 198
Tarantellas, 7, 209–11
Teaching Folk Dance: Successful Steps (*TFD*, Weikart), 5, 24

Teaching Movement and Dance: Intermediate Folk Dance (*TM&D*, Weikart), 5, 24
Te Ve Orez, 203
TFD, 5, 24
Tino Mori, 358, 361, 363
Tipsy I, 370
Tipsy II, 370
TM&D, 5, 24
Toi Nergis (Hoy Nergiz), 8, 46, 49, 51
Toulama, 58
Tracie, Gordon E., 89, 92, 299, 303
Transylvania, 159, 162, 171, 257
Trata, 141, 146
Trei Păzeşte Bătrinesc, 256, 264
Trei Păzeşte de la Bistret, 256
Tri Godini Kate, 358
Tri Martolod, 112
Troika, 272, 275, 280–81
Trŭgnála (or Trâgnala) Rumjana, 64
Tsakonikos, 141
Tsamikos, 8, 19, 24, 141, 143, 154
Turcotte, Richard, 119, 122
Turdanser, 301
Twelfth Street Rag, 322, 328
Two-part Dance, 370
Tyrolervals, 89
Tzadik Katamar, 194
Tzlil Zugim, 199

U

Ugrós, 158, 161–62, 165–66, 168–69
United Kingdom of Great Britain, 97, 177, 289
Uri Zion, 203
U Šest, 19, 24, 349, 350
U.S.S.R. *See* Soviet Union
U'va'u Ha'ovdim, 203

V

Vari (Varys) Hasapikos, 141, 143, 152–53
Ve David, 198
Verbunk, 161, 163
Vie Se Vie, 363
Vikings, 177, 289, 299
Virginia Reel, 177, 323
Vranjanka (Šano Dušo), 349, 350, 352, 354
Vranjsko Kolo, 349, 350
Vrni Se Vrni, 358, 360–61
Vulpiţa, 256

W

Walls of Limerick, 177
Waltz, 77, 90, 99, 230, 339
Weikart, Phyllis S., 5–6, 24, 49, 371
West, Rebecca, 334
Whirling dervishes, 312
Wixman, Ron, 49
Women's dances, 80, 165, 264. *See also* Gender segregation
Work dances, 131

Y

Ya Abud, 191–93
Yankee Doodle, 370–71
Yemenite Jews, 199
Yibanei Hamigdash, 203

Z

Zagoritikos, 141
Zajko Kokorajko (Arap), 358–60, 363
Žalna Majka, 358–60
Zamfir, Gheorghe, 266
Zanzi di Chavarria, Laura, 42
Zaplanjski Čačak, 349, 351
Za Pojas, 64

Zemer Atik, 194–95
Zervos Karpathos, 141
Zibnšrit, 336–39
Zigeunerpolka, 128, 131–36, 370–71
Žikino Kolo, 348–49, 352, 354–55
Zionism, 187, 189
Zonaradikos, 141
Zorba, 141, 152
Zorba the Greek, 142, 153

About the Authors

Sanna H. Longden is a folk dance teacher and multicultural movement educator. A resident of Evanston, Illinois, she has been teaching in schools and at educator conferences locally, nationally, and internationally since 1980. Her specialty is to focus on the "folk," emphasizing ethnic movement, music, styling, and cultural background.

A well-known clinician at Orff, Kodály, and other music organization events, Sanna teaches in world music seminars and continuing education courses and is a Silver Burdett Ginn author and workshop leader. She has also presented at many physical education conferences and workshops, as well as at in-service events for K–12 classroom teachers.

In the Chicago area, Sanna teaches courses at universities and colleges, choreographs for theater and opera companies, leads family folk dance parties, and participates in integrated arts projects. In addition, she serves as an artist-in-residence around the state through the Illinois Arts Council's Arts-in-Education program.

A long-time recreational folk dance leader, Sanna, together with her husband, Mars, leads a popular weekly international group in Evanston. They have been members of several exhibition folk dance ensembles and performed in international festivals in Macedonia and Hungary, taught workshops in Spain, and led dancing on cruises in the U.S. and abroad. They also teach dances of the classical music repertoire to piano teacher organizations and give private ballroom dance lessons.

Sanna has published articles in many folklore magazines and is editor of the *National Folk Organization News*. Her three instructional videotapes, *Favorite Folk Dances of Kids & Teachers*, *More Favorite Folk Dances of Kids & Teachers*, and *Living Ethnic Dances for Kids & Teachers*, are sold worldwide; she also has three accompanying audio cassettes and a CD. In addition, Sanna's new "ethnic" novelty dance, *The Matzorena*, has been recorded by the Maxwell Street Klezmer Band and is available on cassette with a dance-instruction insert.

Phyllis S. Weikart, Director of the program "Education Through Movement: Building the Foundation," is one of the United States' leading authorities on movement-based active learning and recreational folk dance. She bases her approach to teaching on her ongoing work with students of all ages—from preschoolers to senior citizens. She is the author of numerous movement and dance books, including *Foundations in Elementary Education: Movement* (with Elizabeth B. Carlton as second author); *Teaching Movement & Dance: A Sequential Approach to Rhythmic Movement; Round the Circle: Key Experiences in Movement for Children; Movement Plus Music: Activities for Children Ages 3 to 7; Movement Plus Rhymes, Songs, & Singing Games;* and *Movement in Steady Beat*. Phyllis is the second author of *Foundations in Elementary Education: Music*, written with Elizabeth (Libby) B. Carlton. In addition, Phyllis developed the *Rhythmically Moving 1–9* and *Changing Directions 1–6* musical recording series. Phyllis's videotapes include the *Beginning Folk Dances Illustrated 1–5* demonstration videos and two *Teaching Folk Dance: Successful Steps* teaching videos. Libby and Phyllis also have co-authored guides for the first four of the *Rhythmically Moving 1–9* recordings.

Associate Professor Emeritus in the Division of Kinesiology, University of Michigan, and visiting Associate Professor at Hartt School of Music, Phyllis is also Movement Consultant for the High/Scope Educational Research Foundation. Her formal education includes a B.S. degree from Beaver College in Pennsylvania and an M.A. degree from the University of Michigan. In addition to being a nationally known and highly respected educator-author, Phyllis is a researcher, curriculum developer, workshop leader, choreographer, and promoter of high-quality international folk dance recordings. Through her wide-ranging experiences, she has developed an approach to teaching folk dance that ensures the success of both teachers and students.